Meen

HOW TO TEACH
HIGH SCHOOL ENGLISH

How to Teach High School English

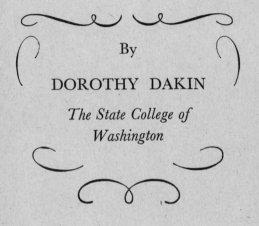

By

DOROTHY DAKIN

*The State College of
Washington*

D. C. HEATH AND COMPANY
Boston

78955

FOREWORD

THIS book had its genesis some years ago, in the early days of my teaching experience. Then, as an instructor of English in a small high school, I struggled to adapt my theory and brief practice to actual teaching conditions, with their demands for classroom instruction, disciplinary problems, extracurricular activities, and personal relations both in and out of school. Slowly I solved these problems for myself, and as I continued in other and larger high schools, I gradually acquired a teaching procedure satisfactory to me. Later, when I had oversight of cadet teachers, I found that they had to face questions and problems similar to my own of earlier years. Still later, I became greatly interested in helping poorly prepared college freshmen gain a mastery of fundamental principles of composition, which, for one reason or another, they had missed in their high school training. At the same time, I worked with college seniors preparing to teach English, with experienced instructors who had returned to college for a bit of "brushing up," with those in other fields who had learned, to their consternation, that next year they were scheduled to "teach English." Recently, as a member of the State of Washington "In Service" staff, I have visited numerous junior and senior high schools and have discussed all sorts of problems with teachers and pupils. Parents, too, have talked to me concerning the instruction given their children in high school, as well as the place and importance of those "activities" so dear to the heart of the high school boy and girl, so time-and-energy-robbing if improperly handled. This book, then, is the result of my own early gropings toward satisfying teaching procedure and of the many questions asked me by members of the groups just mentioned. In effect, though not in form, it is a book of questions and answers, giving, I hope, definite replies to the many queries propounded me. That what I have said is the *only* solution, the *only* method applicable, I make no claim; but I have endeavored to give a practicable solution for the many problems confronting the beginning teacher in particular.

Although the untried will benefit particularly from this book, I trust that experienced teachers will find within its pages something of value. Those of us who have left behind our early days of struggle, can still gain, I believe, from a consideration of the methods of others. Perhaps, just as I am continuously learning from ideas presented by them, my discussion of the problems common to us all will prove suggestive to this group.

Some may consider that I have touched too lightly upon literary writing. Reasons for my apparent slight are three. First, this book is directed to the beginning teacher, on the whole, therefore, to one in the small high school. Ordinarily, little opportunity is given the heavily loaded instructor so to adjust his work that he can allot time to a course in creative writing. Second, I am firmly convinced that much actual harm is done by attempting to force this sort of composition upon an average, unsectioned class. For the one or two who yearn to write short stories, poems, or any other type we call literary, there are many more who look with scorn and actual dislike upon this, to them, unpractical kind of writing. Their attitude they soon carry over to writing of all types, with the result that many pupils distrust composition training of any sort. And, third, teachers may do a positive and far-reaching unkindness by encouraging boys and girls with some facility in writing to look upon themselves as potential creators. I am, of course, using the term *creative* in its limited sense, not in its broad application to include any piece of original writing. Particularly beginning teachers, inexperienced in reading student themes and forgetful of the natural enthusiasm of the adolescent, overrate a certain facility of writing, a flash of imaginative insight. Vivid as are these threads against the dull background of the average theme, they do not, on the whole, indicate genius and must not be construed as such. In my opinion, both the experienced and the inexperienced teacher of unsectioned classes should be alert to recognize and encourage creative ability; but he should not demand it.

I should comment, too, upon the place of grammar in the modern secondary school. Various attitudes toward the teaching of grammar are presented in Chapter IV. All of these are easily recognizable in today's classrooms. My personal feeling is that grammar should be considered as a tool for the expression of thought, along with spelling, punctuation, and accurate sentence forms. At no time should it be considered as an end in itself; rather, it is a means — an important one — by which ideas are transferred from writer to reader, or from speaker to listener. Although the meaning of such sentences as "I have went home" or "Running down the stairs, his arm was broken" is quickly grasped, yet transfer of thought is interfered with, for most of us pause mentally to notice the incorrect usage in "have went" and the amusing picture of an arm running. Hence communication between writer and reader or speaker and listener is disturbed. As a tool, then, grammar requires emphasis because of its relationship to communication of ideas, the basic purpose of the language arts. Ideally, what one should teach should develop from pupil needs. In any circumstances, both teacher and pupil should recognize grammar for what it is and relegate it to its proper place. In the chapters devoted to grammar, I have attempted to include all usages likely to confront secondary school teachers and their pupils, and to present simple, workable methods for teaching them.

On the title page of this book and again and again throughout its pages the word "English" occurs. Yet somehow this is a cold word, one failing to connote the rich and human experience that an understanding of our mother tongue actually is. Custom and convenience demand its use; yet may I suggest an enlargement of the term in your thinking? Actually, in all its facets, it represents the rich heritage of the past and the expression of the present and the future. Basic to understanding personal, national, and world relationships lies communication, and it, in turn, depends upon a mastery of the language arts. When we teach composition and reading, we are helping our pupils to transfer their ideas to the minds and hearts of others and to gain from the printed word both factual information and the stuff men live by. "English," then, is not narrow and constricted, not a "skill" subject; but a full, rich, and free-flowing communication art.

In preparing this second edition of *Talks to Beginning Teachers of English*, I have attempted to retain the approach and procedures of the earlier book but to expand its usefulness. In this volume, suggestions are made to teachers in both the junior and the senior high school fields, and to experienced as well as inexperienced instructors. The relationship of the English teacher to guidance is stressed, and an entirely new chapter on reading has been prepared. All bibliographies have been revised; in fact, in every way possible I have tried to eliminate the outmoded and to include the new.

My thanks are due to many who have aided me, consciously or unconsciously, in the preparation of this book. A number of teachers of the Pullman High School have given me valuable assistance; many of my colleagues on the faculty of the State College of Washington have taken time to consult with me on the relation of the teaching of English to their particular fields.

In my own department I am especially grateful to Dr. Murray W. Bundy, Dr. Paul P. Kies, who, as Director of Freshman Courses, has aided me unstintingly, and Miss Ella E. Clark. Dr. Leslie L. Chisolm of the University of Nebraska, Dr. J. Murray Lee, Dean of the School of Education of the State College of Washington, and Miss Harriett Carmody, of the Reading Clinic of the State College of Washington, also have my thanks. To the many students, both in high school and college, whose problems have resulted in a definite plan of teaching procedure goes my appreciation. Although throughout this book I have attempted to express my indebtedness for the many devices gleaned from sources other than my own experience, I know that my acknowledgments are necessarily incomplete, for I have gathered ideas "as pigeons pease."

DOROTHY DAKIN

ACKNOWLEDGMENTS

Grateful acknowledgment is made to the following publishers for permission to use selections from their copyrighted publications:

D. Appleton-Century Company for a selection from *An Experience Curriculum*, quoted on page 105, and for selections from *A Study of the Types of Literature*, by Mabel Irene Rich, quoted on pages 369–370; the *Atlantic Monthly* for selections from its book reviews, quoted on pages 383–384, and for anonymous verse, quoted on page 126; Ginn and Company for a selection from *Correct English, Second Course*, by William M. Tanner, quoted on pages 19–21, and for a selection from *You and Your English*, by Roy Ivan Johnson and others, quoted on pages 513–515; Houghton Mifflin Company for a selection from *The Teaching of English in the Secondary School*, by Charles Swain Thomas, quoted on pages 277–278; The Macmillan Company for selections from *Writing Craftsmanship*, Revised Edition, by Maurice Garland Fulton, quoted on pages 15–16, and 471; Scott, Foresman and Company for a selection from *A Year's Course in English Literature*, by Robert C. Pooley, quoted on pages 358–359; Seattle Public Schools for "A Sequence of Standards for Oral Work," *Guidebook for the Language*

Arts for Junior and Senior High Schools, quoted on pages 197–200; The State of North Dakota, for selections from "Lessons on Journalism for North Dakota High Schools," by Lawrence W. Murphy, published in *English Syllabus for North Dakota High Schools*, quoted on pages 484–491; *Time Magazine* for a selection from an advertisement for its publication *Letters*, quoted on page 163; The University of North Dakota for a selection from "A Study of Argumentation and Debate," by Mayme Bach, published in *School of Education Record*, quoted on pages 473–484; *The English Journal* and Carol Hovious for "Following Directions," pages 507–509; Edgar Dale for bibliographies taken from *The News Letter*, pages 560–571, and Miss Ella E. Clark for suggestions for an oral review of a book of non-fiction, pages 384–386.

CONTENTS

PART THREE

Extracurricular Activities; Odds and Ends;
Reading

APPENDICES

CONTENTS

PART ONE
THE TEACHING OF COMPOSITION

I. INTRODUCTORY REMARKS

To begin a methods text with the statement that there is no method of teaching English appears contradictory. That, nevertheless, is exactly what I am going to say to you: There is no one established method of teaching English. As he works out of his period of apprenticeship and becomes experienced, the instructor acquires certain techniques, which, if he is wise, he varies to meet the needs of each particular class. The successful teacher is the growing one — the wise man or woman who realizes that times and seasons alter, and that with changing ideals must come changing methods.

However, I am convinced that the beginner is greatly strengthened by having at his command definite suggestions to help him through the opening days of struggle. Most experienced teachers look back with a somewhat rueful smile at their first "job." That first day! Yes, and that first month, and that first year! Loaded down with work and responsibility, the novice needs definite help, and that immediately. There is no time to "work out" a method; thirty or forty high school youngsters cannot wait. The beginning teacher grasps at what he knows, utilizes it gladly. Only after he has gained control of his group and himself can he begin to adjust, discard, and formulate his own plans.

So much of this text is addressed to the beginner. It makes no claim to laying down "methods"; it merely aims to offer practical suggestions that will form a basis for the technique that is a part of the equipment of all good instructors.

A fundamental principle I suggest first is this: Remember that you are teaching individuals, not merely a subject. You come out of college equipped, you think, to teach English. But you frequently find that the subject to which you have given so many hours of loving labor must be set aside while you instruct your boys and girls in such matters as class attitudes, intellectual curiosity, courtesy, the ability to give and take; you wonder, somewhat ruefully, what use your college work has been to you. Never mind. You will find a place for it; your first task is to recognize the needs of the human beings who sit before you.

Because of the exigencies of present-day civilization, we cannot assume that attitudes, manners, personal hygiene, and study habits are the responsibility of the home. These burdens and many more have been shifted to the schools. This the public, no longer satisfied with the three R's, expects and exacts from modern education. If we teachers of English are not to lag behind, we must recognize these demands of our people and adapt our teaching accordingly. Training for better living, for as complete and well-rounded a life as each individual is capable of achieving, should be, it seems to me, our philosophy of teaching English. It is for this purpose that we often place attitudes ahead of subject matter, although, when properly chosen, study content advances these ends.

But, lest I should be misunderstood, let me say here that the best of intentions, of interest in the welfare of growing boys and girls, cannot substitute, on your part, for thorough equipment; nor should formation of attitudes supersede the training in subject matter which your students have a right to expect from you. After all, you are teaching both human beings *and* subject matter, although temporarily you may have to set one aside while you emphasize the other. Without, however, a desire to learn, a mental alertness, a sense of co-operation on the part of your pupils, your efforts to implant knowledge will bear no fruit. If your teaching is to be successful, then, you must always remember the human element.

Now, English has many phases. Consider what is demanded of you! You must teach your students how to write — "written composition"; you must teach them how to talk — "oral composition"; you must teach them to "appreciate literature"; and you must be able and willing to help them in what are termed "extracurricular" activities, such as dramatics, debate, oratory, declamation, the "literary society," the school paper, the annual. You must chaperon their dances and go with them on their hikes. And, by precept and practice, you must help them to be citizens in a democracy. Is it any wonder that the high school teacher, especially in the small community, frequently feels himself to be a "jack of all trades and the master of none"? But youth and enthusiasm will go far to carry you through; so be not discouraged.

But because of this multiplicity of interests, this pressure that our present school system places on teachers, more than ever must the beginning teacher have some notion of his plan of attack, in order that he may not go blindly into this welter of responsibilities. For that reason, I am suggesting a procedure.

The first step consists of taking stock of your class. To teach the individuals composing it, you must learn, as quickly as possible, something of their background, for the method of teaching you employ must be adjusted to the personnel of the group.

How can this be done? How can you learn, quickly, something of the background, the ability, the previous training of each of your boys and girls? It does seem an impossible task, but you will be surprised at how much you can learn within the first week or two.

First, you must observe carefully. As soon as possible, your pupils should become individuals, not a mass of form and color. Utilize every means in your power to get acquainted quickly; learn the names; study the appearance and manner of each member of your classes. Such power of observation can be acquired, and is an important factor in high school teaching. As soon as a student becomes a person to you, study him. You will learn a great deal about him, his interests, his training, his experiences. You need that knowledge, strange as it may seem, before you can teach him English.

Next, consult the records that should be on file in your principal's office. These will tell you something of the interests of the student, and much of his previous accomplishment. But let me warn you here that you should not allow an especially favorable or unfavorable statement to prejudice you. Never forget that you are dealing with a group of adolescents, capable of changing, as it were, overnight. But, intelligently used, these statistics will help you to know your students.

In the third place, you can do some diagnosing yourself. Very probably this process will aid you only in learning the present accomplishment of each member of your classes, but, coupled with careful observation and the sympathetic study of records, it will give you a starting point in your teaching.

In making this analysis, you may use one of the many excellent standardized tests on the market. (See p. 555.) The cost of these may be prohibitive, however, especially if you teach in a community hard pressed for funds. If so, you can compile a simple test of your own. To do this, make a study of the material for mastery in the grade preceding that with which you are concerned. Using that as a basis, work out an objective type test, the results of which will show you something of the proficiency of the group with which you are to deal. But remember that *no test*, standardized or your own, gives *final* judgment; it is simply indicative.

After you have diagnosed, to the best of your ability, the accomplishment of your class, the second step in your teaching procedure is to plan your course. This cannot be done, except in a general way, until you know something of the preparation of your students, for you must build on what they know. Never assume that your pupils have retained all the material that they have studied in previous courses or that they have the background you had at their age. You will probably discover that they have not, and you will then realize that you have wasted precious time. So find out where they stand, and plan your work accordingly. If the class as a whole is deficient in preparation, do not shrug off responsibility; stop where you are and teach them the needed basic material. Only in that way can you build a firm foundation.

Unless you have a conception of your procedure as a whole, you cannot plan your work intelligently. To a certain extent, you have ascertained what your students know. Now ask yourself: What do I want to accomplish? Working from the definite basis that I have discovered, what do I want to accomplish during the semester? During the first six-weeks' period? During each week of that period? During each class meeting? Make a temporary plan, realizing as you do so that you may need to change it for the reason that you are teaching individuals, not a subject only. This will take time and thought. Before you begin teaching at all, jot down a rough outline of what you think may well be achieved by your class. During the first week, observe, consult records, diagnose. Then give the week end to remaking your tentative plan. A few hours of careful, systematic thought at the beginning will be a godsend to you later.

Go about this task of yours, then, with as clear a concept of it as is possible to the untried. Let your teaching have a meaning far deeper than the hourly round, devoted so often to such utilitarian matters as spelling and punctuation, suggests. Toward these boys and girls who meet you daily you have a duty and a responsibility, demanding from you a sense of order, of progress, and an understanding of the relation your teaching has to fitting your pupils for present and future living. Train them not only in composition and literature, but also in the "intangibles," which every conscientious teacher recognizes as part of his responsibility: human relationships, formation of attitudes, intellectual alertness — the thousand and one circumstances that develop from sympathetic association between the high school teacher and his pupils.

ASSIGNMENT

A. Examine the course of study for your state, noting the philosophy toward the teaching of English as expressed by the compilers of the course.

B. Study at least two of the references given below to determine the attitude of their authors toward the teaching problem as a whole.

C. Be prepared to state your philosophy toward teaching English and to uphold your point of view.

D. Prepare a panel discussion based on one or more of the books mentioned in reference 16, "Further Readings," page 11.

FURTHER READINGS

1. *An Experience Curriculum in English.* A Report of the Commission of the National Council of Teachers of English, W. Wilbur Hatfield, Chairman, Chapter I.

This expresses a practical conception of educational theory and should be read and digested by all teachers of English.

2. THOMAS, CHARLES SWAIN, *The Teaching of English in the Secondary School*, revised edition, pp. 1–2.

In this you will find a clear statement of purpose by a teacher whose theories have been tested and approved over a period of years.

3. WARD, C. H., *What Is English?* Chapters I and II.

Here the author gives a definition of the term "English" and establishes a starting point for beginning teachers.

4. COX, SIDNEY, *The Teaching of English*, Chapter I.

The chapter title, "Teaching as Offering Friendship," suggests Mr. Cox's attitude.

5. FISHER, DOROTHY CANFIELD, "Family Problems — New and Old," *Journal of the American Association of University Women*, XXVIII (June, 1935), pp. 199–205.

In this Mrs. Fisher discusses changed family relationships and their bearing upon present-day problems.

6. Mirrielees, Lucia B., *Teaching Composition and Literature in Junior and Senior High School*, revised edition, "Introduction," pp. 3–31.

Experiments, present-day tendencies, and some sample units are presented in these pages.

7. "Basic Aims for English Instruction." Prepared by the Basic Aims Committee of the National Council of Teachers of English, Dora V. Smith, Chairman.

A study of the thirteen aims stated in this pamphlet charts a path for beginning teachers and reviews and adds to objectives for experienced instructors.

8. "Junior High School English." Prepared by Helen J. Hanlon, Miriam B. Booth, and Committee for the National Council of Teachers of English. "Introduction," pp. 5–6.

Attitudes toward junior high school teaching and its purposes are here discussed.

9. Glaser, Emma, *On the Teaching of Junior High School English*, Chapter I, pp. 1–16.

Although written in 1935, this chapter points toward present-day attitudes regarding the teaching of English.

10. Parker, Roscoe Edward, *The Principles and Practice of Teaching English*, "Editor's Introduction," pp. xi–xii.

These brief paragraphs show the relation of the teaching of English to the modern philosophy of education.

11. Webster, Edward Harlan, and Smith, Dora V., *Teaching English in the Junior High School*, "Preface," pp. iii–vi.

You will be interested in noting the forward-looking attitude of the authors of this book written in 1927.

12. Appy, Nellie, "Pupils Are People," National Council of Teachers of English Monograph.

This collection of essays illustrates pupils' individualities.

13. Cross, E. A., and Carney, Elizabeth, *Teaching English in High Schools*, Chapter II, "The Direction English Is Taking."

This chapter looks back on practices of teaching English and forward to those of the present and future.

14. RUCH, FLOYD L., MACKENZIE, GORDON N., and McCLEAN, MARGARET, *People Are Important*. Illustrated by photographs, this book seeks to aid the pupil to understand himself.

15. CERTNER, SIMON, "Adapting the Curriculum to Non-Academics: Idealism, Democracy, and the Common Man," *The English Journal*, XXXIV (March, 1945), pp. 127–132.

This article will help to clarify your thinking on the relation of your teaching to the child.

16. PERRY, BLISS, *And Gladly Teach;* FENNER, M. S., and FISHBURN, E. C., *Pioneer American Educators;* BARZUN, JACQUES, *Teacher in America;* and *Great Teachers*, PETERSON, HOUSTON, editor.

These books about teachers and teaching will add to your professional knowledge.

17. ROBINSON, BRUCE B., "Teaching Should Be Fun," and McCABE, ROSE MAY, "All the Fun I've Had," *Pi Lambda Theta Journal*, XXIII (March, 1945), pp. 79–85.

There is no need to point out the attitude toward teaching in these articles!

II. ENGLISH AND OTHER SUBJECTS

I s it true, as I was told the other day, that we teachers of English are not "on our toes," that we fail to adjust our teaching methods and subject matter to the conditions of the moment, that we are still, in this era of airplanes, in "the horse and buggy age"? Undoubtedly our critic has not studied the recent literature in our field dealing with the necessity of adjusting our teaching to the activities undertaken by secondary school boys and girls. She is judging us by results as she has observed them from her vantage point as instructor in another subject in a large city high school, and her verdict is that we do not study the needs of boys and girls and arrange our courses accordingly; but rather that we cling to the traditional, vainly attempting to force twentieth-century youth into a nineteenth-century mold. And often this criticism of our practice — although not usually of our theory — is justified.

Again and again we are told that our duty as teachers is to prepare our high school students for a full, well-rounded existence. In this book, I shall attempt to show how you beginning teachers of English can plan your activities toward this end, in your teaching of both language arts and literature. But now I want to pause for a few moments to suggest ways in which your teaching can correlate with that of other departments, thus illustrating the necessity of training and accomplishment in English as a prerequisite to success in adult life. First, you must realize that "English" is not an isolated subject, to be confined to the English classroom for one period a day, five days a week; it is a fundamental tool, an essential to the complete understanding of all subjects. Many a student fails in arithmetic. Why? Because he cannot combine numbers properly? No, because he cannot *read* the problem set him. Many another gets nothing from history save a few scattered facts — and for the same reason: the pupil cannot *read*. Too, he has trouble in giving directions, in applying for a position, in mastering his secretarial courses, because he is not able to utilize the English composition he has been taught laboriously in the classroom. You beginning teachers of English should recognize your responsibility toward the work of other departments and plan your procedure accordingly.

Let us consider a field closely allied to our own — that of secretarial training. The stenographer or the typist is not a *creator* but an *interpreter* of ideas. The stenographer takes down in shorthand the thoughts of someone else; it is then his duty to transcribe them into a well-appearing, correctly written letter or other document. In doing this, he needs to know and to apply the fundamentals of English; to train him in these basic elements is your responsibility. You must teach him so to read that he can interpret his shorthand symbol ∿ (from the context itself) as "firm's employees" or "firms' employees." You must drill him so carefully that he will understand the significance of the apostrophe and will place it with exactness. You should teach all the other so-called "mechanics" of composition with equal care; teachers of secretarial courses have a right to expect precision in their use as a result of your pupils' training in English.

Does it seem to you that I am making too great a point of this matter of training for business? Consider for a moment the fact that in one of our large industrial cities fifty-three per cent of the high school pupils are enrolled in the commercial course, and ask yourself what is your responsibility toward these future men and women. I suggest that you and the commercial teachers in your high school early form a friendly alliance, determining upon the essentials for both subjects, and reaching an agreement regarding such matters as the form of business letters. It may be that in this co-operative plan you will have to adjust some of your preconceived and cherished ideas (although good English *is* good English wherever one finds it); but such a concession is infinitely to be preferred to setting one standard for secretarial courses and another for the English classroom. When you say to your group, "Very well, do that for Miss Blank, but in your English work follow *this* plan," you are fixing upon the impressionable mind of the child the idea that "English" belongs only in the classroom. And this impression (not confined, by any means, to those of high school age) is one which you must do your utmost to dispel.

Because of training, culture, and methodology there is usually a close *rapport* between teachers of social studies and of English. What is your responsibility toward this highly significant group? Let me suggest that here, as in the secretarial field, you can co-ordinate your English teaching with that of the history instructor. In a study by Arthur N. Cook, "The High School Student and Freshman History," it was found that pupils fail in history partly because of their inability to understand the printed word. Surely your instruction in the interpretation of literature should be of such a nature that it can carry over to the study of history. If it does not, you have failed in your efforts to teach your students to read. All principles of composition are, of course, applicable to the field of history, as Professor Cook remarks; but your pupils do not realize this connection unless you point it out. For some reason, the boy or girl who (possibly under compulsion) will write for you a paper in which he gives attention to such matters as organization and correct expression will ignore these principles completely in his history test or term paper. You must first build up an *attitude*, a will to learn; and you must next show the importance of these principles to composition of every sort, both within and without the classroom.

Specifically, you can co-operate with the teacher of history and of civics (often the same person) by showing your pupils how to arrange a test paper in good form, how to phrase an answer to a question (for a discussion of this see page 20), how to master the vocabulary in the subject (Professor Cook states that high school graduates are unable to define with the exactness necessary for comprehension such ordinary words as *empire*, *colony*, *race*, *sovereign*, and *nomad*), and how to write a definition. In *Writing Craftsmanship*, compiled by Maurice Garland Fulton, is an excellent discussion of the writing of definitions, part of which I shall quote:

The object or term we are to define is first put under the class of objects to which it belongs. . . . We must next specify in what particulars the object or term under consideration differs from others in the same class. . . .

Logic lays down four rules about definition making. Put briefly, they are: (1) Exclude from the class all that does not belong to the class; (2) Include in the class all that does belong to the class; (3) Express the definition in terms simpler and more familiar than the term defined; (4) Avoid in the definition the name of the thing defined or any derivative of it.

Applying these requirements to the definition: "A noun is a word used as a name," you observe that *noun* is put under the class to which it belongs — a *word;* and next that its particular or distinguishing characteristic is given: "used as a name." Careful adherence to these principles will help your pupils to substitute accurate thinking and phrasing for the incomplete, inchoate expression often passing for definition.

Perhaps the history teacher will turn over to you test papers written by students enrolled in your class. You can then put on the board the answers to some of the questions, showing how the pupils' statements could have been made effective by attention to principles of composition drilled on in their English class. If you and the principal of your school agree, you may well consider the history test as an exercise in composition, grading the student on his expression (not, of course, on the content) of this work done outside the classroom. It seems self-evident that expression is the supreme test of subject matter — that not until one thoroughly understands can he *express* his ideas completely. This truth is of concern both to you and to the teacher of history.

Although courses in sociology and political economy are usually taken by prospective teachers of English, because of their many facets only experts can discuss these subjects adequately. You, as a teacher of English, naturally cannot give your pupils instruction in these technical fields. Perhaps in these — in fact, in any subject demanding special and full preparation — your responsibility is oblique, not direct. If you can teach your pupils to read understandingly, to acquire an unbiased attitude toward the unfamiliar, to question the printed word (too many adults believe wholeheartedly anything appearing in print), to find out something about both author and publisher of books and articles, particularly background or bias, and to write correct English, I believe that teachers of all subjects will call your task well done. As a teacher of English, you should not assume the prerogatives of those trained in a particular field; yet as an intelligent, educated person, you can and should seek to broaden your own knowledge and that of your pupils, and to aim specifically to provide the tools requisite for understanding and expression of thought.

As old as Adam and Eve is the experience of human relationships; yet only rather recently have educators recognized this as part of their formal program. As a result, courses in psychology, the family, the physical aspects of the home, and so forth have become a part of college curricula. In a few universities courses in Home Relations are offered, and at least one state, Washington, requires such a study for all girls enrolled in high school. What share in all this have teachers of English?

Without our conscious knowledge, perhaps, we have been pioneers in this field, for our literature, being the record of the emotions, ideals, and experiences of the human race, has always concerned itself with the attitudes and relationships of human beings to one another.

Much of the reading you will do with your high school boys and girls bears upon these relationships. When you consider *Silas Marner*, direct the thought of your pupils to the sort of home that produced Dunstan and Godfrey — two undisciplined youths, growing up motherless, at one moment pampered, the next punished by their father. In the attitude of Aaron toward his mother Dolly, and in the rehabilitation of Silas through his love for Eppie are displayed verities of human living. Similarly, the courage of the boy Jim Hawkins in *Treasure Island* evidences a quality of manhood belonging to no one race or time. By these suggestions I do not intend to imply that literature is composed of a series of tracts, and that you should turn your classroom into a factory for producing moralists. But, in this day of shifting values, it may be well for your pupils to observe with respect and understanding, forces and qualities of human nature as displayed in much good literature.

Nor is it only through reading that you and the home economics teacher can co-operate. Both boys and girls can interest themselves constructively in studying some of the physical aspects of the home: buying carefully, investigating different heating systems and kinds of refrigeration, and so forth. On page 472 you will find listed some theme topics that bear upon the home and family. No doubt the home economics teacher in your school will aid you gladly in adding to this list.

Possibly your nearest relatives in the teaching field are instructors in foreign languages. Like yours, much of their elementary teaching lies in the field of grammar. Along with the secretarial teachers, foreign language instructors will thank you for your aid in helping their pupils to recognize grammatical forms and constructions.

If you have students who are so familiar with a foreign tongue that they can read it easily, both you and your colleagues will get pleasure in encouraging translation of prose or poetry into idiomatic English. For suggestions, you may like to examine Robert M. Gay's *Writing through Reading* (Atlantic Monthly Press), pages 6–21.

In making these somewhat specific comments, I have not, naturally, mentioned *all* courses taught in high school, but have been content to refer to those with which the need for co-operation is, on the surface, most obvious. Yet even with such technical subjects as mathematics or science, the desire of the teacher of English to connect his work with that of other departments can be achieved. One of the most profitable means lies in the exchange of papers previously mentioned, in which a report or examination written for one department is read and marked for expression by the English instructor. After you have taught long enough in a school system to venture to make suggestions, present a plan for uniformity in examination and term papers. The following directions, taken from William M. Tanner's *Correct English, Second Course,* may not of course be mimeographed or reprinted except by special permission of the publishers. They do indicate, however, a valuable type of student help.

WRITING EXAMINATIONS

In answering a question on an examination we summarize briefly the information asked for in the question. Success in writing an examination requires that we (1) think quickly and accurately, (2) plan our answers carefully, and (3) express them in clear, correct English. In developing greater skill in this important type of composition we shall find the following directions helpful:

1. As soon as all the questions are before you, read them over, and try to estimate the time that you will need to answer each question.
2. Read each question attentively. Think of what it means, and decide what a satisfactory answer will include.
3. Plan your answer carefully. Unless a question can be adequately answered in one or two sentences, take time to collect the necessary facts and ideas and to arrange them in the right order.
4. In beginning your answer repeat the words of the question in the first sentence or in the first part of the sentence.

Question. Enumerate the principal causes of the Hundred Years' War.

First sentence of your answer. The principal causes of the Hundred Years' War were the following:

---

5. If the answer to a question includes several subtopics, you may write it in the form of an enumerative paragraph. If no discussion is required, you may arrange the answer in the form of an outline.
6. Be sure to arrange the parts of each answer in the order demanded by the question.
7. See that you cover each question fully in your answer, but do not include any unnecessary facts or details.
8. Make your sentences brief, clear, and to the point. Long sentences are likely to become involved and vague.
9. Unless you are solving problems in mathematics or are answering a question in the form of an outline, express all your answers in complete sentences.
10. If you do not know the answer to a question, omit it. You can rarely guess correctly, and writing merely to fill up space wastes time and does not deceive the teacher.
11. Every examination paper in every subject is an English composition. Do your best, therefore, to write grammatically, spell correctly, and capitalize and punctuate intelligently. Legibility, proper arrangement of material on the page, and neatness in every detail count strongly in your favor.
12. Try to apportion your time so that you will have a few minutes left in which to read over and revise your examination paper. A carefully revised paper almost always wins a better mark.

Perhaps, too, as you advance in grace, you may be able to persuade the busy members of other departments to consider the form and expression of every paper handed in.   I know that many teachers of other subjects think (and rightly) that such a plan increases their already heavy marking load; but only through some such procedure can a school system hope to send out graduates who speak and write literately.   With the best of training and intentions, teachers of English cannot, alone, produce this desirable result.

I come now to a suggestion for co-operation which is not confined to any school system, nor indeed to any nation, but which must occupy, if countries are to survive, the mind and heart of all.   I refer to the outlawry of war. As a subject for the English classroom, international relations afford far too many complexities for inclusion in your teaching program.   Yet perhaps all teachers can aid in furthering the sympathetic understanding which must be the basis for intelligent living in this world of ours.   You, naturally, are not sufficiently expert in this involved field of international affairs to dabble in it — far less should you encourage your pupils to do so.   Yet a fair, unprejudiced (as far as is humanly possible) attitude toward the many world problems which your classroom activities touch on may do its part in teaching your pupils to think straight and act fairly.   Perhaps some theme topics may seek to point out the *good* in people or customs of other lands.   Reading from the literature of other peoples may help your pupils to become conscious of cultures other than their own.   You do not want your classroom to become a hotbed of propaganda; yet you do, I believe, desire to lead your boys and girls to the acquisition of an ordered, balanced mind.   *Understanding* attitudes of others without *censuring* them is surely needed today.

If we are to succeed in outlawing war, we must encourage democratic principles and practices; for never, in the history of the world, have the common people desired war. It is therefore essential that teachers understand democratic theory themselves, that they seek to put it into practice, and that they guide their pupils along democratic paths. To demonstrate that each individual plays an important part in a democratic society becomes the patriotic duty of all teachers. To aid each student to prepare himself for his obligations to society becomes a sacred trust. Perhaps no subject, not even the social subjects, affords such opportunities as does English. For without ability to read with understanding, to write and speak clearly, to think logically, and to listen attentively and critically, no one can take his proper place in a democratic state. English teachers, responsible for teaching these basic skills in communication, recognize that their work underlies that of all other departments. You need never feel apologetic concerning it, as it affords the foundation for all activities, both in and out of the classroom.

This recognition of the relation of English to the student's complete environment leads naturally to your responsibility for pupil guidance. I am not referring here to the sort of guidance performed by specialists, but to the less formal kind practiced by good teachers in their homerooms and in their classrooms. This type falls naturally into three divisions: guidance through subject matter, through extracurricular activities, and through teacher-student relations. Let us briefly consider each aspect.

If you can teach your students to read, write, speak, think, and listen intelligently, you are *guiding* them toward development as individuals, as members of a democratic society, and as wage earners. In their reading, particularly recreational reading, you can help develop attitudes, ideals, and principles. Books on travel and biographies suggest possible vocations. Through choice of topics for oral and written expression, you can enlarge your pupils' experiences and suggest new worlds of thought and action for them to enter. As you read further in this book you will find many suggestions for teaching both literature and composition that actually offer opportunity for guidance, for teaching and guidance cannot successfully be separated.

Extracurricular activities also present opportunities for personal and vocational guidance. Many a boy or girl has turned to journalism, to acting, or to teaching because of his enjoyment of work on the school paper or in plays. As all extracurricular activities call for "give and take" between pupils and between pupils and teacher, demand self-reliance, and develop responsibility, they may be directed toward aiding pupils to select a vocation or an avocation, and toward developing desirable personal qualities.

Ordinarily a teacher of English has many opportunities for close contact with his students. It is important, therefore, that pupils become aware, not through words, but through actions, of such qualities in the teacher as honesty, sincerity, and a genuine and wholesome concern for the welfare of students. When pupils sense these attitudes, they are likely to turn to the teacher for advice and counsel, not only in choice of vocation, but also in matters of personal relationships. Not until a teacher has developed this feeling of *rapport* between himself and his students can he be really effective as a guide or as a classroom teacher. Working closely with pupils affords an enviable opportunity for helping them to develop as individuals in such a manner that, when the time comes, they may take their proper place in a democratic society. Both in and out of the classroom, then, you may and should become your pupils' guide, philosopher, and friend.

I hope that you do not receive from this chapter the impression that I am advocating the allocation to the English classroom of everything except the teaching and reading of our mother tongue. If any of you has such a notion, the reading of the following chapters, with their plans for full and constructive hours, will dissipate it. My only desire is to demonstrate that your teaching — in one or all of its phases — inevitably bears upon all activities within and without the classroom. A recognition of this relationship, translated into classroom experiences, should produce a fuller and more complete education for your boys and girls.

ASSIGNMENT

A. Read and report on Dora V. Smith's chapter, called "Co-operation and Correlation," in the bulletin *Instruction in English*, United States Department of the Interior, Office of Education, 1932.

B. Distinguish between "integration" and "correlation" as used in educational terminology. Prepare a simple and an extended definition of each.

C. Your instructor will assign sections of *A Correlated Curriculum*, English Monograph No. 5, for study and class discussion.

D. Study carefully Chapter XV "Sharing Experiences in an Integrated Program," pp. 243–257, in *Conducting Experi-*

ences in English, English Monograph No. 8, National Council of Teachers of English.

E. Prepare a brief unit in which you show how some phase of English may be related to some phase of another subject. As a guide, refer to *A Correlated Curriculum*, "The Fusion of English with One Other Subject," pp. 82–128. Follow the plan presented on pages 113–121.

FURTHER READINGS

1. *An Experience Curriculum in English*, Chapter II.

This chapter, "Integration," defines the term and indicates the importance of the act.

2. McCoy, Helen F., "Correlation of English and Science," *The English Journal*, XXIV (October, 1935), pp. 668–669.

Miss McCoy advises showing the average boy that good English *is* of some use to him in the field of his present and future interests.

3. Neville, Mark A., "English as a Positive Factor in Correlation," *The English Journal*, XXXII (January, 1938), pp. 44–49.

The essential aspect of English in correlation is here stressed.

4. Broening, Angela M., Chairman, *Conducting Experiences in English*, English Monograph No. 8, National Council of Teachers of English.

This monograph supplements *An Experience Curriculum in English*.

5. Sattley, Helen R., "Children's Books for Democratic Survival," *The Elementary English Review*, XXII (March, 1945), pp. 77–80; 93.

Titles of books which further democratic thinking are given in this article.

6. Rashkis, Lillian R., and Mittelman, Hazel R., "Teaching Brotherhood at P. S. 37, Manhattan," *The Elementary English Review*, XXI (November, 1944), pp. 251–255.

This is an account of an experience in "The School of Opportunity."

7. SALT, GEORGE, "Thinking Together," Pamphlet Publication No. 6 of the National Council of Teachers of English.

The promotion of democracy through class discussion is explained and illustrated.

8. *Educational Policies Commission* publications, 1201 Sixteenth Street, Northwest, Washington, D.C.

Of special interest are: "How May We Defend Democracy?" "How You Can Strengthen Democracy," "Current Documents on Democracy," and "Our Democracy."

9. JACOBS, IDA T., and DEBOER, JOHN J., "Educating for Peace," prepared for the National Council of Teachers of English.

This monograph presents a specific program for peace education.

10. JACOBS, IDA T., "War and Peace," prepared for the National Council of Teachers of English.

Included in this anthology are plans for assembly programs.

11. HANLON, HELEN J., BOOTH, MIRIAM B., and COMMITTEE, *Junior High School English*, prepared for the National Council of Teachers of English.

This entire pamphlet offers suggestions for understanding the pupils' world.

12. CHISOLM, LESLIE L., *Guiding Youth in the Modern Secondary School*.

This very recent text in guidance has much to offer the teacher of English.

13. HAMRIN, SHIRLEY A., and ERICKSON, CLIFFORD E., *Guidance in the Secondary School*, Chapter IV, "The Teachers Studying Their Pupils."

This chapter stresses the importance of teachers understanding their pupils.

14. LEFEVER, D. WELTY, TURNER, ARCHIE M., and WEITZEL, HENRY I., *Principles and Techniques of Guidance*, Chapter IV, "The Role of the Teacher in Guidance."

The necessity of fine personal qualities in the teacher is stressed.

15. BOWLES, FRANCES, "English As a Guidance Subject," *Platoon Schools*, XIV (June, 1940), pp. 14–21.

You will find many excellent suggestions in this article.

16. DENNY, VELMA, and JOHNSON, MARY, "Predelinquency and Juvenile Guidance," *National Education Association Journal*, XXXV (October, 1946), pp. 386–387.

This account of a study of juvenile delinquency made by the Grade Teachers Section of the Minneapolis Teachers League, offers suggestions for teachers in other communities.

17. MORGAN, JOY ELMER, "The Teacher and World Government," *National Education Association Journal*, XXXV (January, 1946), p. 1.

In this, the editor of the *Journal* presents the challenge offered teachers to see that the United Nations "works."

18. ROLLINS, CHARLEMAE, "New Trends in Books about Negroes for Children and Young People," *The Elementary English Review*, XXIII (November, 1946), pp. 287–289.

A Negro educator points out recent trends in literature toward presenting the Negro as he actually is.

19. CRAWFORD, VERNELIA A., "Vocational Guidance in the English Class," *The English Journal*, XXV (September, 1946), pp. 397–398.

After you have read this plan for a vocational-guidance unit you will want to read W. W. Hatfield's comment that follows it.

III. WRITTEN COMPOSITION

This "English" which you are preparing to teach actually consists of several divisions, the greatest being language arts and literature. For best results, to both teacher and pupil, these should, I think, be separated. I am aware that opinions vary in regard to this and other matters that I shall discuss with you; but for the purpose of discussion, I shall be positive in my statements, giving you freely my permission to alter these suggestions as your experience dictates. But, until they demand changes, I advise that you accept these ideas as a working basis. You should, then, teach composition during one semester and literature throughout another. If this arrangement is impossible, always teach in units of some length, sufficient to round out a phase of composition or to complete the reading of a piece of literature. Never teach composition for, say, two days a week, and literature for the remaining three. I can think of no method better calculated to kill enjoyment of reading than just that. Whichever plan you adopt — division by semester or by shorter units — will no doubt be determined by the requirements of your state or by the advice of your administrative officers.

Since World War I there has been a marked change in the emphasis placed upon these two important divisions of "English." Previous to that event, instruction in high school leaned strongly toward training in literature; accurate writing developed, apparently, through the process of osmosis. Euphemistic references on the part of college entrance readers — noted by C. H. Ward in his *What Is English?* — to "what an examiner ought not to find" indicate, however, that this method did not always result in the desired perfection. Not until the overwhelming ignorance of the great mass of our soldiers shocked us into action did we undertake in our secondary schools formal instruction in composition comparable to that given in literature. Today most courses of study and secondary school textbooks recognize the need of adequate training in the humble mechanics of writing. That the change has been slow, however, is indicated by the apologetic attitude of Alfred Hitchcock in his preface to *Composition and Grammar*, published in 1929:

> It has taken a little courage to let the word *grammar* appear in the title. Yet sentiment has so changed during the last ten years, that I think few teachers will be grieved to find that in this manual prominence has been given to grammar, especially since I have tried to make the study practical and simple.

Today few authors of grammar texts consider that they must apologize for their treatment of the subject; instead they present it as a composition tool. The general tendency, as indicated by the division of the work into semesters of composition and of literature, places the emphasis equally upon both. I suggest that you go a little further, giving the preponderance of attention to composition. This I advise for three reasons.

First, because training in composition has been deficient in the past, you will find your high school boys and girls untutored in the simplest elements of expression, except in particularly efficient school systems, of which you, as a beginner, probably will not be a part. Second, because of the drudgery of marking papers, demands of an over-crowded curriculum, and pressure of extracurricular activities, composition will be neglected unless teachers determine to emphasize it. And, third, composition should be stressed because of its practical value, which, rightly or wrongly, is the standard applied to many of our policies today. Boys and girls can see how a knowledge of correct speech and writing aids them in their struggle toward a "white collar" job, the goal of many. That habits of speech and writing have a dollar-and-cents value, easily demonstrable, constitutes perhaps, in the eyes of our critics, the greatest justification for the teaching of English. For the next few years, then, until our present educational theories bear fruit, determine to give your earnest attention to helping your pupils to speak and write.

Before we can intelligently aid our boys and girls to complete living, we must ourselves know what end we have in mind; for as haphazard as the well-known "cabbage patch" will be our efforts if we know not what we want to do or where we want to go. In this regard, as in others, I do not want to force your thinking; yet, as we must have a starting point, permit me to advance the following end or objective of your composition teaching: *ability of the student to express his ideas with clarity and some degree of effectiveness.*

Now let us examine this statement in some detail. To be efficient, an objective must be expressed simply and concretely and must be possible of attainment. Too often a high school pupil (and his teacher, too) is unnecessarily discouraged by attempting the impossible. The aim stated above I consider expressed in understandable terms and possible of attainment. Furthermore, it has a direct bearing upon the ideal of complete living, the ultimate goal which must never be lost sight of in your teaching.

Next, consider the first phrase: *ability to express ideas*. This implies that the student has ideas, but after reading your first batch of themes you are going to be discouragingly certain that he has none. Perhaps he hasn't, but part of your work as a teacher of English is to give him some. This in itself will keep you pretty busy for the next six years! Now notice the words: *to express*. Your pupils will say to you, "I know that, but I can't say it." With this I disagree. If we know — really understand something, have a vivid picture in mind — we can express our ideas — given sufficient tools: words combined into sentences, sentences into paragraphs, paragraphs into a connected whole. Next, consider the expression: *with clarity*. To accomplish this demands knowledge of "the mechanics": spelling, punctuation, grammatical forms, accurate sentence structure. As I shall point out later, violation of accepted usage in these clouds what is after all the primary need of human beings: communication of thought. Now to note the last phrase of your aim: *with some degree of effectiveness*. This implies a knowledge of rhetoric: the putting together of ideas in a direct and forceful manner by subordinating some and emphasizing others, by varied sentence structure, by a sense of logical development, in which the eye and the mind of the reader are carried from point to point.

Although not easy, all this is possible of attainment, presupposing normal pupils imbued with a desire to learn. As most of your teaching is barren of results without co-operation on the part of your class, awakening of mental curiosity, utilization of the pride of accomplishment inherent in each of us should occupy the mind of the teacher to the same degree as training in abilities. Granted this mental alertness, with this aim as guide, you will equip your high school boys and girls adequately for whatever the future has to offer: college or a "job."

"But," says someone, "where in all this do I find promise of creative work? I have always longed to introduce my students to the joys of literary writing — to help them express themselves in poetry, to write short stories, drama. Don't you expect us to do this?"

My reply to your question is: Remember that your class is not composed of potential litterateurs; no, nor of potential teachers of English. Who sit before you? Why, future shoe clerks and salesmen and housewives and ditch diggers and engineers and farmers; the list is lengthy. How many "creative artists" were in your class in high school? How many teachers of English? And of these latter, how many — I ask it gently — do literary work? No, you should put that idea aside as a part of your general aim, being content with the implication in the words "expression of ideas," and leave such writing to special classes.

So much for your comprehensive aim for written composition. As you note, this aim correlates with an objective of the language arts — communication of ideas. Let us now consider how this basic aim relates to the teaching of junior and senior high school composition.

Perhaps you may accept as your objective for the junior

high school years: *accuracy and simplicity of expression, with the beginning of organization of material.* Because you must lay the foundation in these early years, training in accuracy must be emphasized. Correct spelling, punctuation, grammar, sentence structure — those mechanical essentials to clarity — must concern you here. Expression should be simple. I have had a football hero say to me that he was unable to write themes because he knew no "fancy adjectives." "Fancy adjectives!" That boy did not need them. When he forgot his hateful theme he could write vividly and clearly on the subject that interested him — football. Somewhere in that boy's past a misguided teacher had tried to force upon his practical mind elaborate expression. Don't do it; encourage simplicity in these foundation years.

Upon the matter of organization I feel strongly. Mr. Thomas C. Blaisdell in his *Ways to Teach English* says that training pupils "to think through a subject and to put on paper an outline of what is to be spoken or written is to develop a power that will probably be of more value in life than any other power developed during school years." Without plan, logical development, a sense of progress toward one's goal, writing is pointless — ideas, if there are any, being at such cross-purposes that the reader, especially the teacher-reader, is left wallowing in a slough of despond.

Realize, then, that these junior high school years constitute a great challenge to your ability as a teacher, because of their constructive nature. You must teach accurate writing habits and logical plan. Perhaps you do this best by encouraging your boys and girls to write about what they know or would like to know, showing them how important to the conveying of thought are these two pieces of framework: *accurate expression and logical development*.

For the sophomore year, continue the foregoing aims. Never, after teaching a principle, set it aside to rust from disuse; but bring it up again and again, until its practice becomes habitual. As a preparation for your plans for this tenth year of school, familiarize yourself with the aims of the teacher of the ninth grade, using them as a basis for your tenth-year work. You do your pupils a great injustice if you teach with no reference to what has preceded your own class or to what is to follow it. If you study the aims of your associates in charge of the other classes in English in your high school and adjust yours accordingly, secondary English teaching will have continuity and you may expect good results. In this sophomore year, then, continue stressing accurate expression and organization. With increasing experience and maturity, your pupils are meeting new conditions both in and out of school. Some are applying for and obtaining work; all are enlarging their social life. If you can help them to meet these new responsibilities with confidence, you will be aiding them in their progress toward the ideal of better living. To your previous aims add, then: *effectiveness in meeting daily situations requiring expression of thought*.

During the junior year, the aims of the preceding years must of course be continued; but consideration must be given to the complexity of the demands beginning to be placed upon these fifteen- and sixteen-year-olds. Both in and out of school their experience is widening, through reading, observation, and activities. At home many boys and girls assume a share of its support, have a voice in its management. In school, through the study of social and physical sciences, political economy, an enriched reading program, their activities and interests are enlarged increasingly. More and more are they assuming the responsibilities of adults. As their ability to weigh, analyze, discard, and arrange grows, give them more difficult material with which to deal and more practice in doing it. For this year, add: *skill in collecting and arranging material; enlarging experience.*

In the senior year, continue, of course, the aims of the preceding ones, adding to them: (1) *development in strength of expression,* and (2) *continued broadening of interests.* If the preliminary work has been well done, you should now reap your reward. This is the time to emphasize effectiveness of expression; to encourage special interests; to develop attitudes. Now you are dealing with students who have put away (with occasional lapses) childish things, and if the foundation has been sure and true, you can expect "a certain degree of effective writing."

For the attainment of these, or any aims, careful attention must be given to the material taught, selecting that which will further your purpose, always keeping in mind the fact that you are teaching *human beings,* as well as subject matter. Whatever is chosen should bear upon the aim for the year, for the entire course, and upon the ultimate objective of all teaching — fitting the individual to take his place in the social scheme.

Application of these principles would result in some such selection as the following. Your aim in the preparatory years — *accuracy and simplicity of expression* and the *beginning of organization* — demands drill in correct language usage, in spelling, punctuation, sentence structure, grammar; and practice in writing. In selecting composition topics, consider the broadening interests of the high school student, his new experiences in school, class, and social activities. He is beginning to consider himself a member of a community; in short, he is growing out of childhood into manhood and his writing should reflect this development. Work out a unit called "Know Your School"; another, "Know Your Town." "Resources of Our State" may open his eyes to what is right at his door: mining, clay deposits, forest reserves, shipping. As adolescents are deeply concerned with doing the proper thing, you might compile a "Courtesy Code," listing points in good manners for the school, the street, the home. A unit on health correlates well with other departments, and like that on good manners, can be counted upon to arouse interest. In relation to his other subjects let your pupil write on a project or development of present-day science; interest him in myths and fables of his own country and of other peoples. (Many of these suggestions, and those following, appear in the *English Syllabus for North Dakota High Schools*, 1928.) Remember, too, that the most important person to each of us is "I," and the second is "you." Autobiographical subjects, then, of every sort, often produce excellent results, because of your pupils' vivid interest in whatever concerns them. On page 491 you will find an autobiographical unit prepared by the teachers of Pullman High School, Pullman, Washington. Because of its length, you may decide against using it as it stands, but many of the theme subjects will prove valuable. In every way possible, show that English is not an isolated subject, but one having a direct bearing upon every human activity.

In the sophomore year lies your greatest opportunity to bring English home to your boys and girls, for your aim here is to aid the student to meet in an effective manner daily situations requiring expression of thought. Immediately, that suggests letter writing, the form of written composition most frequently employed by adults. For this reason, textbooks give training in letter writing and so should you; but let me warn you against too much of this kind of composition. You can and should, however, teach the writing of business and friendly letters, notes of invitation, acceptance, regret. Practice in writing advertisements and telegrams also will further your aims, being excellent training in succinctness and clarity.

As the additional aim for the junior year is to acquire skill in collecting and arranging material as well as to enlarge experience, your students may gather information for papers connected with music, sculpture, painting, architecture. Their study of civics suggests articles on city and school administration, and on local, national, and state organizations. They may keep journals or diaries, write minutes, and summarize speeches. Consider and make use of their widening activities.

You want your seniors to develop new interests and strength in expression. In this semester comes your opportunity to smooth out the rough spots and to entice your pupils along the way of effective writing. More attention than heretofore you should accord to the encouragement of an increased and colorful vocabulary, to the practice of strong, virile sentence forms, resulting in picturesque and forceful writing. Throughout the preceding years you have hewn the rough timbers, fitting them together as opportunity allowed; now in this last year comes the period of polishing and decorating. To further new interests, try different types of writing. Most students do well with the informal essay; some few want to write narratives. In expository writing, turn to the fields of geography, travel, vocations, present-day literature, biography, and interviewing. The alert high school pupil has a thousand interests that you can appeal to, which will help you accomplish your purpose.

A little later I shall discuss in detail the writing of themes; at present I merely want to show how *what you teach* has a bearing on *why* you teach. By having in mind some such simple, practical aims as are here presented, and by selecting subject matter that will advance them, chosen with an eye to help fit your boys and girls for present and future responsibilities, you will be doing your part to help the school to do for future citizens what civilization demands. To this end, all your teaching should be done with a purpose; nothing should be attempted haphazardly. No self-respecting carpenter would try to build a house without his blueprints to guide him. Why should you attempt a much more delicate task without having a clear idea of what you are trying to do and how you hope to do it?

ASSIGNMENT

Consult your state course of study and analyze (1) the aims of written composition, (2) its subject matter. See whether it recognizes the relationship of English to the ideal of better living.

FURTHER READINGS

1. *An Experience Curriculum in English*, Chapter XVI.

This offers a number of teaching units, for each of which is stated a "Social Objective" and the "Enabling Objectives" requisite for attainment of the stated aim.

2. THOMAS, CHARLES SWAIN, "Variables and Constants," *The English Journal*, XXV (February, 1936), pp. 101–113.

In this article the author examines constant and variable aims and methods in teaching English.

3. STRATTON, CLARENCE, *The Teaching of English in the High School*, Chapter I.

Are there any aims stated in 1925 (the year in which this book was published) with which you disagree, or can you accept all today?

4. SEELY, HOWARD FRANCIS, *On Teaching English*, p. 17.

Here are summarized Mr. Seely's statements of aims. Criticize these.

5. STERLING, EDNA L. "We All Had a Hand In It," *The Elementary English Review*, XXI (November, 1944), pp. 247–250; 269.

This account of curricular changes in the Seattle Public School System offers many helpful suggestions.

6. SEELY, HOWARD FRANCIS, *On Teaching English*, Chapter XI, "The Meaning, Purposes, Materials, and Forms of Written Composition," pp. 223–239.

This chapter presents objectives in teaching composition.

IV. GRAMMAR: THE VERB

WITH some trepidation I broach the topic of grammar, for no branch of our teaching has afforded more controversy than this. Some educators believe that grammar should not be *taught*, but *acquired* through drill and exposure to correct forms; another group holds that grammar should be mastered, as preparation for college and as mental training; whereas a third, to whose tenets I subscribe, maintains it should be taught, but from a *functional* point of view, developing from pupil needs.

Before commenting on these last two approaches to grammar, let me make clear to you *why* I believe in teaching it, why I oppose the first school of thought noted. Judging from my own experience and my observation of that of others, I know that we all work better if we understand what we are trying to do, if we see a goal for our efforts. To me it seems only reasonable that your boys and girls will apply themselves more purposefully if they comprehend that a sentence is the smallest unit for the expression of ideas, that it is capable of being combined into paragraphs, and thus into a paper of any length, upon any subject. Surely it is essential that they analyze the framework of a sentence, in order to see how words are put together to express thought. Now, this accurate understanding is possible only through the grammatical approach. Those who have heard — at home, at school, on the street — nothing but correct English can no doubt write effectively without a knowledge of grammar; but to how many does this apply? Obviously, only to the favored few, not to the great mass of us. Grammar, then, must be our guide to correct and forceful expression.

Granted that we teach grammar, shall it be *formal* or *functional?* Formal grammar would include all angles of "the science of language": detailed classification of parts of speech, a complete study of mode, and so forth. Much of this has no bearing upon correct writing but holds merely an academic interest. Formal grammar, with its treatment of such distinctions as the cognate accusative: "I dreamed a dream," "he wreaked vengeance"; the absolute use of transitive verbs: "The horses *drank* from the brook," offers ramifications difficult even for the college student. We must never forget that our pupils *dislike what they do not understand.* Can we, then, reasonably expect our high school boys and girls — intelligent, but in whom the sense of logic so necessary in a study of formal grammar yet lies dormant — to grasp this complicated subject? Yet boys, especially, enjoy their study of grammar, I believe, provided its teaching is progressive and adapted to the age and capabilities of the children to whom it is presented.

Having rejected the tenets of the first two groups of educators, we are left with that of the third — functional grammar — today the most generally accepted point of view, the only difficulty being that there is no unanimity among members of the group as to what should be included in the term. The principle, however, you can accept: Teach only forms necessary for correct usage. In my own thinking (and here I follow Ward) I amend this statement to include also frequently used expressions such as the indirect object and the objective complement, both of which appear so often that sentence analysis would be difficult without some knowledge of these forms.

If, then, we believe in *functional* grammar, what may we reasonably expect it to do for our pupils? It will result, I think, in (1) helping to produce accurate expression and (2) forming style. Ungrammatical, involved sentences are not clear, as they almost invariably require a second reading for an understanding of the thought. Unless the idea expressed in the sentence is one that should be pondered carefully, rereading is a waste of time. The thought should be immediately apparent and a knowledge of grammatical relationships leads to this result. Furthermore, grammar aids definitely in producing style. What good will it do for you to say to a student: "Your sentence structure is correct but monotonous. Vary it. Use gerunds and participles. Try the effect of dependent clauses," if your pupil does not know what gerunds and dependent clauses are? Functional grammar, properly taught and applied, should aid definitely in producing style.

When shall grammar be taught? In my opinion, in each year of secondary school. On examining courses of study, however, you will find that many provide for its teaching only in the ninth and tenth grades, with possibly a review in the twelfth. To me it appears advisable to teach grammar slowly and progressively, with constant application to writing, throughout junior and senior high school, rather than to concentrate the dose. If you work out minimum essentials in grammar you can base your teaching upon them, remembering always that they, being minimal, should meet the immediate needs of only the lower quartile of your group.

As to what you should teach, you should concentrate upon functional grammar, with possibly a study of frequently (and correctly) used forms, such as the objective complement. But, if your class is having difficulty, forget such abstractions and emphasize forms important to correct and forceful speech and writing. As I continue this discussion, I shall comment on what appear to me "important" points as opposed to those holding a merely academic interest; at present, suffice it to say that employment of correct verb and pronoun forms, an understanding of the principle of agreement of verb with subject, pronoun with antecedent, a recognition of the various sorts of dangling elements, the rhetorical qualities of verbals, all come under the head of essential grammar.

Never teach peculiar idioms or oddities. Our language is filled with them, many having a long, honorable history, but one too complex for the secondary school student, who naturally is not a philologist, to understand. An example of this is the retained object found in such sentences as: "Mary was given a *medal*," a construction that has come down to us through a thousand years, tracing its ancestry to an old dative case form. Dispose of these by calling them idioms. If one or two members of your class wish to pursue the subject, offer to explain the expression to them after school. To take class time for this would be both wasteful and confusing to the slow members of your group, who are having difficulty enough, anyway. Whenever possible, avoid such pitfalls. Collect illustrative sentences that contain no complexities.

(Every experienced teacher collects examples; I myself have "thrown" more "balls" in teaching the direct object than I ever have in actual life.) Select a text that uses straightforward examples and does not confuse the student unnecessarily. But you will always have pupils with inquiring minds who will bring you complicated sentences, and whom you should treat as I have suggested.

Now, what methods shall you use? If the class is sectioned according to ability, your problem is lessened. Your good pupils will have had training; they will be mentally alert; they will learn easily. But your poor students will have much difficulty, and it will require your best effort to teach them. In a mixed group, the contract method may solve the problem; for by it superior students may progress rapidly, whereas those ill prepared may take the time necessary.

My presentation of methods for teaching grammar assumes that your pupils are beginning the subject. True enough, they may have passed examinations in grammar, but do not infer that they have a mastery of the subject, for the chances are that they have not. Reasons for this failure probably lie in the fact that grammar, as such, has been presented too early and has been considered as a separate subject, without relating it to communication skills. Furthermore, under either the junior high school or the traditional four-year high school plan, you will find your classes composed of students from many grade schools, with varying skills and preparation. Begin with the assumption that pupils know nothing about grammar; if you find yourself mistaken, you will receive a delightful surprise.

In all your teaching never forget to apply the principle

of *one thing at a time*. Unless you put yourself in the place of your students — many of whom are poorly prepared, self-conscious, overwhelmed with the newness of high school life — you will fail to realize how befuddled they are, how complicated to them is this subject of grammar. Present one principle at a time, being certain that it has "soaked in" before going on to something else. "Make haste slowly," and you will be repaid by the progress of your class.

Always, in every year in which you teach grammar, begin at the beginning: the verb. The verb is the pivot of the sentence — the hub from which all constructions radiate like spokes in a wheel — the indispensable element. Start your teaching with it.

You will first be concerned with its recognition — only that and nothing more. You must teach your students to know a verb when they see it; to understand what its work is in the sentence. Put on the board such groups of words as these:

> I   home.
> you   home?
>   home!

Ask if the first group gives any information; if it *tells* anything. Then insert *am going*. The group now gives information: *I am going home*. Consider the second. Because of the interrogation point, we guess that it asks a question, but shall we answer *yes* or *no*? Dangerous business, this; we must be careful. Insert *are going*. Now we are safe; we can answer *yes* or *no*, for the group clearly asks a question: *Are you going home?* Notice the third *home*. The exclamation point shows feeling, but *what* feeling? Does it indicate joy, horror? Put *go* in front and we know; it gives a command, perhaps to our dog.

The words that have made these groups convey information, ask a question, give a command, are *verbs*. That is what verbs do: They force a group of words to make a statement, ask a question, or give a command. This is as much of a definition as you need. Work it out with your class in some such way as this; it will mean far more than will a memorized definition.

Next, call the attention of your students to the fact that a verb may consist of more than one word. In the illustrations above, one of the verbs consists of two words: *are going*. Verbs may have as many as four parts: *will have been forgotten*. Tell your class to train their eyes to notice the sort of word that may be a verb. Give them a list of *helping* or *auxiliary* verbs: *shall, will, may, might, could, would, should, must, can, do*, and forms of *be*. In referring to *be* see that the students understand your terms. Remember that *be* does not appear either in the present or past tense.

Several pitfalls should be noted. In the first place, your pupils are going to call infinitives verbs. (You know that they are verbs, but you also know that an attempt to distinguish between finite and non-finite forms would be very confusing.) Point out to your class that such an expression as *to go* does not do any of the things they know a verb should do. Tell them that a verb form preceded by the word *to* is not a verb in the way in which they use the term, but an infinitive. Later you will discuss its uses; just now you are not concerned with them. Again, in such a sentence as: "The hills are green," you will be told that *are green* is the verb. Tell the class to test *green* to see whether it will make a statement. Does *I green today* give information? Then *green* is not a verb, but something else. Another danger lies in such expressions as: *Running down the hill.* Say that no word ending in *ing* is ever a verb, unless it is preceded by a helping verb: *was* running, *shall be* going, *had been* playing. Again, although you know that the word in the original sentence is a participle, a non-finite verb form, you do not say so. To the occasional precocious youngster who recognizes the construction, say that, although his statement is true, you are at present concerned only with the recognition of the verb and will discuss the participle later. Point out, also, that *not* is never a part of the verb.

In all this, note that the word *action* is not mentioned. Avoid it, for it will get you into trouble. An old definition of a verb is that it is a word expressing action, being, or state of being. For some reason, all your students know that, or, rather, they know the first part. Because, very probably, the last two ideas mean nothing to them, they conveniently omit them. A verb, then, indicates action, and they can see no verb in such a sentence as: "They sat on the fence." Where's action in that? Keep away, in this introductory work, from the idea that action is a quality of a verb, and you will save your class trouble.

Although this is all that you should do with the verb until you are well along in your course, I shall discuss here, for purposes of convenience, the other phases of the verb you will want to present. But remember that your teaching must be progressive. Each day you work on the sentence as a unit, analyzing its make-up. The verb your student must recognize before he can go on, but not for many months — depending upon his ability — will he need to know anything more about it. Be content if you can teach him to recognize verbs; you will find it is no easy task.

As the verb is very important from the rhetorical as well as the grammatical point of view, your class should have some knowledge of the quality called *voice*. *Voice* indicates whether the subject acts or is acted upon and may be illustrated by such sentences as: "Ralph polished the car today" (active voice, as *Ralph*, the subject, is doing the polishing), and "The car is polished after every trip into the country" (passive, because the subject *car* is submitting to being polished). In explaining this, I try to show the *alive* quality of the verb and subject; how the latter does whatever is being done when the verb is in the *active* voice; and that the reverse is true for the *passive*, in which the subject submits passively. An amusing illustration is: "Oh, I lost my purse!" (active); and "Oh, my purse was lost by me!" (passive). Some bright lad always remarks concerning the second sentence that he wouldn't look for it if it were said like that. Its absurdity makes this illustration remembered. One great difficulty lies with such verbs as *seem*, *appear*, and forms of *be*. Obviously, these show no action, yet most grammarians call them *active* when they are used as the principal verb in such sentences as: "The problem *appears* simple." (Some grammarians prefer to consider copulative verbs as a third class.) To help my students with this, I remark that the subject receives nothing, but does whatever the verb indicates. From the rhetorical angle, illustrate the awkwardness of a sentence in which one verb is active, another passive, as in: "We *visited* the Grand Canyon, where many strange sights *were seen*." Not only does this sentence show shift in voice, but it also demonstrates the inadvisability of change of subject within a sentence, both of these being points of writing deserving of emphasis. Probably, though, the most important principle dependent upon knowledge of voice is the avoidance of the passive and the selection of the active, for usually we prefer a verb that gives life, strength, vividness to our expression. Teach your class to avoid writing: "A good time was had by all."

Along with *voice* you must teach *transitive* and *intransitive* verbs, as every verb that we use falls into one of these classes. Tell your students that *trans* means across; that a transitive verb is one in which the action expressed by the verb "goes across" to a receiver of the action. That a transitive verb is one having a receiver is a definition to be preferred to the explanation sometimes heard that a transitive verb is one having a direct object. Although true with *transitive active* verbs, such a statement omits entirely any explanation for *transitive passive* verbs, in which the *subject*, not the *object*, receives the action: "He was acclaimed a hero by the crowd." (As your discussion of voice will come late in your course, you are probably safe in referring to action as a quality of the verb.) Put on the board sentences like this: "John cut the grass daily during the summer." "The grass was cut every day during the summer." Show that in the first sentence the action of the verb "goes across" to *grass*, the direct object; in the second the action again "goes across" to *grass*, the subject. The verb in both sentences is transitive, because there is a receiver of the action: in the first sentence, the direct object; in the second, the subject. The verb in the first sentence is transitive active, for the subject acts; in the second, it is transitive passive, for the subject is acted upon.

Then put on the board a sentence like "Birds fly."

Show that there is no receiver of the action. This verb, then, is *in-* (not) transitive, as the action expressed by the verb does not "go across" to a receiver. Point out that upon the wording of the sentence depends whether or not the verb is transitive active, transitive passive, or intransitive. In "Birds fly," *fly* is intransitive; in "Boys fly kites," *fly* is transitive active; in "Kites are flown in China by men, women, and children," *are flown* is transitive passive.

This knowledge of transitive and intransitive verbs becomes particularly useful in dealing with such trouble-makers as *lie, lay; sit, set; rise, raise.* A student of mine once told me that he found it very helpful to remember that the forms containing the sound *i* are *in-*transitive and therefore have no receiver of the action. Do not attempt to explain the correct use of these words until you have taught voice. It may be that even then you should not attempt all these in one lesson, although their similarity may make permissible this violation of the "one thing at a time" principle. Because of its usefulness with these verbs and its aid in effective expression, *voice*, with the accompanying transitive and intransitive forms, justifies itself as functional grammar.

An explanation of *tense*, as of voice, belongs well along in your course. I believe that your students should learn principal parts of verbs, should learn to conjugate. Possibly you may consider this somewhat academic or pedantic, but after all, there are some parts of any subject that must be memorized and conjugation is one of them. Show your group that the second of the principal parts of a verb (*go, went, gone*) never forms correct compound tenses. It is, of course, incorrect to say "I have went." Point out that the word "played" in such a group as "have played" is not the second or past form of the verb, but is the third or perfect form: *play, played, played*. Explain the "progressive" forms of the verb. No form is much more puzzling than are these: *am playing, are going, will be writing,* and almost invariably they are omitted from sample conjugations given in textbooks. You may want to have a paradigm including these forms mimeographed for your students. See to it, also, that the terms you use actually mean something to your boys and girls. No doubt the pupil who explained the present tense as indicating *now* and the perfect as *right now* had a faint glimmering that *tense* indicates *time*, but how imperfect was the gleam!

You have no doubt noted that in this discussion I have avoided the use of the term "verb phrase." This is another of those matters for you to know but to conceal from your class. Given the inch of the word "phrase," they will soon take the ell of calling any group of words a phrase. You should avoid it.

Last of this trio comes *mode*, at once the most difficult and the least useful, from the point of view of functional grammar, of any of the qualities of the verb. You should concentrate upon a few uses of the subjunctive, the one in which we make the most mistakes. At the present time, although we use the subjunctive with considerable frequency, we make few changes in form to indicate it. These occur, usually, in the past form of the verb. Occasionally we say: "if it *be* true," but frequently we say: "if I were you," "if that were true," "I wish I were you." You should confine your teaching, then, to the simple uses of the subjunctive, such as in wishes: "I wish I were in New York," and in conditions contrary to fact: "If I were an aviator, I would fly to France." Because of the difficulty of this form, you should defer teaching it until late in your course — possibly, if you are dealing with a retarded and poorly prepared group, until the senior year. As a matter of fact, if some of your students escape without knowledge of the subjunctive, that lack will not greatly hinder them in their "struggle with life."

Far more important from the point of view of functional grammar than mode is *number*. See that your group understand the term; drill into them the principle that a verb agrees in number with its subject. Give them sentences of various types for analysis. Let some have a compound subject: "The men of the Kiwanis Club and the women of the Business and Professional Women's Club were united in their drive for a school nurse"; some a simple subject followed by the words "as well as" or "in addition to": "The daughter, as well as her father, was employed by the firm." One of the refinements of this rule, to be given to advanced groups, is that a verb agrees in number with the last member of a compound subject when the parts are connected by *or* or *nor:* "The mother or her children are going to the Fair." Place considerable emphasis upon this point of *number*, for it is an artful wolf preying easily upon simple sheep.

Usually *person* may be taught in connection with *number*. As with conjugations, your pupils will have to memorize the three persons — first, second, and third — and the pronouns referring to them. A simple device, given to me by a skilled teacher, is to point out that the most important person to each of us is *I*; hence pronouns indicating the person speaking are *first* person. The next most important person is the one to whom we speak. Life would be very dull without *you*, the second person. To each of us, the least important is the *third*, the *they* always referred to in gossip. This is so simple, so frivolous a way of remembering that it never fails, even with the dullest who refuse to memorize. As errors, if made at all, are usually with *be*, it is well to call especial attention to this verb. Frequent conjugation drill helps form correct speech and writing habits.

To sum up, then, the teaching of the verb: Be content at first with recognition. Build up, with your class, a definition. Point out the usual pitfalls. Not until your boys and girls confidently recognize verbs — indeed, not until they have acquired a mastery of fundamental sentence structure — should you teach, probably in this order, the qualities of the verb: person, number, voice, tense, mode. Always keep in mind the *functional* nature of the grammar taught, eliminating without qualms any matters purely *formal*.

Some time ago I mentioned the fact that verbals, although they are actually non-finite forms of the verb, should not be included in your early discussion. Although convinced of the wisdom of this, for the sake of convenience I am including verbals under the head of verbs, without meaning that the two should be taught together.

Because of their difficulty, any discussion of verbals should be postponed until late in the course, after you have taught simple, compound, and complex sentences. You should begin with *participles*, as offering the least difficulty. In introducing them, I usually bracket together on the board the three kinds of verbals:

$$\text{Verbals} \begin{cases} \text{Participle} \\ \text{Gerund} \\ \text{Infinitive} \end{cases}$$

Then I comment upon their *hybrid* nature, stating that the participle is a verb form used as an adjective; the gerund, one used as a noun; and the infinitive, most versatile of all, one used as a noun, adjective, or adverb. After this introduction, I put on the ever-useful board such expressions as "*running* horse," ". . . the horse, *running* down the street . . .," "*running* down the street, the horse . . . ." (Early in your teaching, explain the significance of the three dots. This will prevent the necessity of writing complete sentences on the board.) Then I show that, as *running*, in each instance, modifies the noun *horse*, it is a participle. As my explanation advances and my illustrations become clear, I include some examples of the subjective complement use of the participle, as in "She sat sewing" and "We remained standing." For an assignment after this explanation, you might ask your pupils to memorize the forms of the participle given in their text. (Some think this too cut-and-dried and opposed to the principle of functional grammar. But it may be very helpful as an aid to *recognition*, always your first concern.) In addition, you should assign a number of sentences, most but not all of which contain participles, with instructions to list each participle and the noun or pronoun it modifies. In class the following day, you may send your group to the board, having them write participial forms of the verbs dictated. In these ways *recognition* of this form is taught.

Next your concern lies with *analysis* of sentences containing participles. As preparation, explain their dual nature that permits them to be modified by any adverbial expression, "Shifting *quickly*, he avoided an accident"; and to be completed by a subjective complement, "Being a *boy* . . ."; or by a direct object, "Having shot a *duck* . . . ." If you use simple diagraming as an aid to sentence analysis, it will serve you in good stead here.

After your group can recognize participles and explain

their use, turn to their rhetorical values. Most elementary
is the fact that a participle is never used to assert or to
make a group of words into a statement, a question, a
command. A group of words, then, containing a participle and not a finite form of the verb, is a "sentence
fragment," not a sentence. If you have been zealous
from the first in emphasizing the fact that "no word
ending in *ing* is ever a verb, unless preceded by a helping
word," your class should long ago have conquered any
tendency they might have had to call such a group of
words a sentence. Give considerable time, too, to the
"dangling participle," pointing out that a participle, to
be one, must have a noun to modify and that this relation
must be logical. In "Hurrying up the street, my hat was
lost," although *hurrying* may, by some quirk, be assumed
to modify *hat*, logically such a relationship is impossible.
Often the advertising columns of the newspaper afford
amusing examples, which your class will enjoy collecting.
In this, do not neglect the dangler at the end of the sentence as in "He has left school, *caused* by the death of his
father," in which *caused* dangles for the reason that it can
modify logically neither *he* nor *school*. And last, give
frequent practice in the use of participles as a device for
economical and forceful sentence structure. For three
reasons the participle justifies the time and trouble you
will give to it. In the first place, all verbals are important
from the point of view of style. The effective use of
participles will aid your students in subordinating ideas
and will add life and vividness to their writing; next, it
will prevent them from perpetrating "sentence frag-
ments"; and it will keep them from the inaccuracy of
such statements as: "I fell on the ice yesterday, caused
by the slippery pavement."

Some pupils will be disturbed in an attempt to distinguish between a verb in the *passive* voice and a participle used as a subjective complement. As this distinction lies in the field of formal grammar, you should not introduce the point yourself; but if brought up by your class, it must be considered. If the question occurs before you have presented participles, you should instruct your interrogators to call all related verb forms the *verb* until they study participles. When the question comes up later, try to show the difference in *meaning* in such sentences as: "The windows were barred nightly by the watchman," and "The windows were barred with heavy iron." In the first, the verb is passive, because the verb refers to the *act of barring;* in the second, *barred* is a past participle used as a subjective complement, for it indicates a quality of the subject.

Not until your class recognizes participles easily should you go on to gerunds. To the usual verbal difficulties is added the fact that the gerund forms are exactly like those of the participle, with the exception of the past passive participial forms: Participles: *going, having gone, being gone, gone, having been gone;* gerunds: *going, having gone, being gone, having been gone.* This means that gerunds and participles can be distinguished only by their *use* in the sentence and not by their *form.* Put on the board illustrations of the ordinary uses of the gerund: subject, direct object, subjective complement, appositive, object of a preposition: "*Dancing* is my favorite amusement" (subject); "We began *moving* today" (direct object); "His childish pleasure was *gathering* shells on the beach" (subjective complement); "His pastime, *golfing*, took much of his time" (appositive); "He was arrested for *forging* the check" (object of a preposition). By means of such examples as these, you show that the gerund is used as a noun. Be content first with the recognition and uses of the gerund. Later, introduce the use of the possessive form of a noun or a pronoun with a gerund: "*Our* going was a great surprise"; "*John's* singing is much improved." Warn your students against the dangling gerund phrase. Although an introductory gerund phrase grammatically modifies the verb, it should refer logically to the subject; therefore such sentences as "Upon entering the room, a burst of laughter was heard" are incorrect, for "Upon entering" does not logically refer to the subject. Again, collect amusing examples of the dangling gerund. Point out that its dual nature permits it to be modified by an adverb, and an adverbial phrase or clause, and to be completed by a subjective complement or a direct object. Show the economy of using gerunds: how they enable one to express an idea in a few words and at the same time add to the vividness of the sentence.

As by far the most complicated of the verbals is the infinitive, it should be taught last of the group. Recognition is not one of its complexities, for usually it carries its sign *to* before it. Furthermore, the students are accustomed to looking for infinitives, as you have pointed them out early in your discussion of the verb. But their use *is* difficult. You should begin first with the infinitive used as a noun. Illustrate on the board infinitives as subjects: "*To be given* an allowance was his desire"; direct objects: "John offered *to explain* the game"; appositives: "My idea *to pick* blackberries met with immediate approval"; and objects of prepositions. This last offers especial problems, for usually the red flag *to* is omitted in this construction, as in such sentences as: "He was willing to do anything *except resign.*" Familiarize your students with the infinitive forms, both active and passive, and let them have experience in formulating sentences illustrating the infinitive in any of its noun uses.

After the infinitive as a noun has been successfully dealt with, go on to its adjective use. Show that an infinitive may modify a noun, as in "Room to Rent." Give numerous examples of this use. As this construction very likely will not afford much concern, you can probably teach the infinitive used as an adverb at the same time. Again, have in mind a number of illustrative sentences. Show the infinitive used to modify a predicate adjective: "The hill was too steep *to climb*"; as an adverb modifying a verb: "He stayed *to watch* the practice." And point out that an infinitive, too, may be modified by an adverb: "If you want to excel, you must agree to practice *daily*"; by an adverbial phrase: "I want to stop *at the bank*"; or by an adverbial clause: "To resign *because you can't have your own way* seems childish"; and completed by a direct object: "You must have a license to hunt *deer*"; or a subjective complement: "Oh, to be a *boy* again!"

One special infinitive construction that must be pointed out is that of the "objective-infinitive." After verbs of commanding, wishing, advising, perceiving, believing, making, etc., the infinitive used objectively is preceded by a noun or a pronoun (called the subject of the infinitive) in the objective case: "We wanted *him to go*"; "We heard the *baby cry*." Both the infinitive and its subject are considered to be the object of the verb. If the infinitive is *to be* the noun or pronoun following it is in the objective case: "We expected it to be *him*."

It is this use that makes inaccurate the statement, "No

form of the verb *to be* is ever followed by the objective case." Nevertheless, you will find this rule helpful to students who are struggling with the subjective complement construction.

After you have given your group some grammatical foundation, certain points in usage should be taught. An adverbial infinitive may "dangle." Like the introductory gerund phrase, the infinitive, although it modifies the verb, should logically refer to the subject. In this sentence the infinitive dangles: "To do good work, good tools are required." Another point in usage is the "split infinitive" construction. This consists of inserting a modifying word or phrase between *to* and the infinitive proper: "To barely see." As the split infinitive is justified under certain conditions, you should postpone discussion of this point until late in the course. Possibly you will not want to refer to it until you teach senior composition, although this of course depends upon the preparation of your class.

In teaching these infinitive uses (and, indeed, in dealing with any construction that offers similarities and differences), provide a number of "distinguishing" exercises. See that the students know the difference between the participle and the gerund. Give them exercises in which the noun, adjective, and adverbial uses of the infinitive are illustrated.

After having taught a grammatical form, always try to tie it up with actual use. Only by doing this can you justify a study of grammar to your practical students. Verbals offer a good opportunity. Send your class to the board; dictate to each student a sentence containing two or more clauses. Have them rewrite the sentence, substituting one of the verbals for a clause or a part of a clause. With your group criticize the sentences thus formed from the points of view of economy and of effectiveness. As it belongs in the field of rhetoric, not grammar, this sort of work should be given in the senior year, or whenever the construction is taught.

Before concluding our discussion of the verb, let me emphasize again the importance of building slowly, one step at a time. If you attempt to force too much upon a beginning or a retarded class, you will close their minds to the learning process and will establish an antagonistic attitude difficult to break down. Make your explanations simple, clear, and forceful; and confine yourself strictly to teaching *one thing at a time.* For months (I cannot be definite about the time as I do not know how much or how long you will teach grammar) all your group will need for sentence analysis is verb *recognition.* To force upon a class a study of the aspects of a verb — voice, tense, number, person, mode — while they are yet struggling with simple sentence analysis would defeat your purpose. Similarly would a study of verbals be disastrous before a firm foundation in sentence structure has been laid. I strongly believe that one of our great errors in teaching procedure has been our attempt to force upon the child, *before he is ready,* complexities incomprehensible to him. So my plea to you is to teach only essential aspects of the verb — *but to teach them thoroughly.*

ASSIGNMENT

Using one or more of the topics discussed in this chapter, write a lesson plan in which you present the topic to the class; build up, by means of illustrations, a satisfactory definition; make clear any especially troublesome points; and suggest a suitable assignment. Remember that your method of presentation is somewhat determined by the class for which it is designed.

FURTHER READINGS

1. *An Experience Curriculum in English*, Chapter XVII, pp. 228–238.

This entire chapter, "Instrumental Grammar," you will want to read carefully. It may interest you to contrast my statement that the teaching of functional grammar should help to produce accurate expression (p. 42) with that made in *An Experience Curriculum in English*, p. 228. Note especially the emphasis placed upon the difference in *meaning* conveyed by the subjunctive and the indicative modes.

2. MIRRIELEES, LUCIA B., *Teaching Composition and Literature*, revised edition, Chapter III, pp. 76–86.

Here are presented some especially pertinent comments on the importance of the verb as a sentence element.

3. THOMAS, CHARLES SWAIN, *The Teaching of English in the Secondary School*, pp. 84–93.

Here is presented in a résumé the time-honored controversy between *formal* and *applied* grammar.

4. WARD, C. H., *What Is English?* Chapter V.

Mr. Ward answers his question, "Why study grammar?" by showing the relation of grammar to an understanding of sentence structure.

5. WARD, C. H., *Grammar for Composition*, Parts II, III, IV.

At this point in your progress, read carefully these sections. They will provide a course in practical grammar for those of you who are beginning to realize that your own grammatical foundation is "shaky."

6. WARD, C. H., *What Is English?* Chapter VII, pp. 183–187, 198–204.

In the first reference Mr. Ward comments on teaching the verb, and in the second he comments on the verbals, including a suggestion that infinitives always be taught as nouns.

7. SHANKLE, GEORGE H., "Aims and Methods of Teaching English Grammar in American Schools," *Education*, LI (September, 1930), pp. 41–43.

Here you will find a brief historical summary of aims and practices in the teaching of English grammar in American high schools from the colonial period to the present time. Although merely a survey, this article will give you a sense of perspective.

8. LEONARD, S. A., *Current English Usage*.

You will want to familiarize yourself with the survey begun under the direction of the late S. A. Leonard, and completed after his death. Although in a sense merely a collection of personal opinions, this survey is bound to be suggestive.

9. MARCKWARDT, ALBERT H., and WALCOTT, FRED, *Facts about Current English Usage*.

This study provides factual evidence concerning the findings of the Leonard report.

10. KENNEDY, ARTHUR G., *English Usage*.

This continues the studies begun in the Leonard and Marckwardt monographs.

11. FRENCH, FRANKLIN J., "A Note on the English Subjunctive," *English Journal* (college edition), XXIII (June, 1934), pp. 504–506.

In this the author contends that the subjunctive still holds its own.

V. GRAMMAR: THE NOUN AND PRONOUN

Although the verb acts as the pivot of the sentence, the hub from which all constructions radiate, it can accomplish little for expression of thought without the stalwart aid of noun and pronoun. Look first at the noun, as usual being concerned with recognition. On the board put illustrative sentences containing examples of different classes of nouns, avoiding, however, any mention of this phase of formal grammar. These might be: "The *girl* is standing near the *window*," "*Mary* is going to *Canada*," "*Happiness* is important to us all," "The *crew* rowed strongly." Underline each noun. Next demonstrate that every underlined word is a name: *girl*, a name given to a young woman; *window*, an opening to let in light and air; *Mary*, the name of a particular girl and *Canada*, of a particular country; *happiness*, of an emotion or feeling; *crew*, of a group of men manning a boat. All these words, used as names, are nouns. A noun, then, is a word used as a name. In some such way, you and your students build up your definition, which, I venture to say, will then mean much more than an arbitrary pronouncement by you of a definition of a noun.

Because it is more easily recognizable than is a verb, do not assume that your class will from this point on know a noun when they see it. For those having trouble, suggest the use of this device, given me by a college professor (not, however, of English): A noun is a word that *may* have *a*, *an*, or *the* in front of it. Although not often applicable to proper nouns (not troublemakers, anyway, because of their capital letter sign), this bit of help may be more suggestive than a definition, no matter how carefully you build one.

After laying this foundation, start your discussion of noun uses, beginning with the *subject*. To introduce this, put on the board several short sentences, each containing a noun used as a subject. With your class, pick out and mark the verb in the first example; then put the word *who* or *what* before it. The answer to the question thus formed is the subject of the verb. Your procedure might be: "The game resulted in a tie." *Resulted* is the verb. *What* resulted? *Game*. *Game*, then, is the subject of *resulted*. This device is, I believe, infallible, and will prove very helpful, especially in dealing with complicated structures. Our unfortunate practice, however, of inserting a prepositional phrase between the subject and the verb will at first cause some confusion, but as you will want to teach the recognition of prepositional phrases very early in your discussion of the sentence — possibly even before you do the subject — it need not disturb you long. From this starting point, you can show that the subject is that part of the sentence about which something is said. In this, as in any sort of analysis, insist that the verb be the starting point, even though, in the simple illustrative sentences you have placed before the class, the subject is obvious. By so doing, you will build up the habit of careful study of the sentence before an attempt is made to analyze it. As your explanation advances, provide sentences containing compound subjects, as: "Our *team* and the *boys* from Crosby play their final game tomorrow." If you have taught the recognition of personal pronouns, you may also include examples of these. Certainly let several sentences contain prepositional phrases, in order to help overcome this troublesome point.

After the subject, you should teach the *subjective complement*. This term I prefer to *predicate noun* or *predicate nominative*, inasmuch as it is more suggestive to the average pupil — but more of that later. As usual, put on the board sentences with nouns (or pronouns, if you have presented them) as subjective complements, for example: "Edison was a great *inventor*"; "Was your brother appointed *delegate* to the Boy Scout conclave?"; "The only boy there was *I*." With the class, find the verb in the first sentence, then its subject. Next, place the word *who* or *what* after the verb, thus forming a question. If this question can be answered, and if the answer explains or describes the subject, the word fulfilling these requirements is a subjective complement. In the sentences given, *inventor*, *delegate*, and *I* mean the same as, or explain, the subject of the sentence in which each occurs. Point out that *complement* means aid or help (incidentally, teach its spelling, concentrating on that first *e*); and that the term suggests that the expression aids or helps the subject. Then formulate your definition: A subjective complement completes the verb (in this you are anticipating your presentation of the appositive), answers the question *who* or *what* placed after the verb, and explains or describes the subject (in this, you are looking toward your discussion of the direct object, which does not explain the subject, and of the adjective as a subjective complement, which describes the subject).   Although the illustrations given above show nouns or pronouns as subjective complements, I have never found that the thinking of my pupils is disturbed by the inclusion of the word *describe* in the definition.   Looking forward to the constructions you expect to teach, and planning your presentation accordingly, constitute good teaching strategy on your part.   As you proceed with your discussion of subjective complements, include sentences without them — "The young woman played beautifully" — but be very careful not to include a direct object, as you do not want to confuse your class by introducing another use of the noun at this point.

After your group has the subjective complement well in mind, proceed to the *direct object*.   This you should not do immediately.   You could have an assignment on pronouns as subjective complements, or a "distinguishing" exercise, in which you review the noun constructions previously taught, or a theme, or all three before you teach the direct object.   In other words, let your pupils conquer the subjective complement before attacking a form difficult to distinguish from its sister construction.

As usual, follow the procedure of putting on the board illustrative sentences, taking care to include only nouns or pronouns as direct objects.   Show that this word, ordinarily coming after the verb, answers the question *whom* or *what* placed after the verb, but does *not* explain or describe the subject.   This last point, the important difference between the direct object and the subjective complement, I find most helpful to my pupils.   After you have had an exercise in selecting direct objects, give your boys and girls a "distinguishing" assignment, in which you include some sentences containing neither a direct object nor a subjective complement. Always take great care to exclude constructions not previously taught (for example, an adjective as a subjective complement or a noun clause as a direct object); but be equally certain to review in these exercises whatever has been discussed.

The teaching of the *indirect object* should always follow that of the direct. Your illustrative sentences should show four points concerning the indirect object: first, each sentence should include a *direct* object; second, it should contain a word telling *to* or *for whom* the action is done; third, this word should answer the question *to* or *for whom;* and fourth, the words *to* and *for* should not be expressed. Upon the first three points base your definition: The indirect object is a noun or pronoun, always used in connection with a direct object, telling *to* or *for whom* something is done. To the field of formal grammar belongs the distinction between the objective of service ("Mother baked *me* a cake") and the indirect object ("He handed *me* the evening paper"), never to be commented upon in high school teaching, permissible only in advanced college classes. As a matter of fact, if it were not for mistakes in case with pronouns as indirect objects, this construction hardly justifies the time given it. Be careful to avoid teaching that the indirect object is the object of an "understood" preposition; this has never been true, the construction being a survival of an old dative case form. It is helpful to notice that this use often follows such words as *give, ask, bring, buy, lend,* and *teach*.

Probably you will present the noun as object of a

preposition before you do the direct object. In this the
principal point to remember is that a noun or pronoun
in the objective case, answering the question *whom?*
or *what?* invariably follows the preposition. (The prepositional phrase is discussed on page 80.) Other ordinary
noun uses, which, however, cannot be taught until you
have discussed modifiers, are adjective nouns ("the
church steeple") and adverbial nouns. Understanding
of the latter will be aided if you ask constantly, as you
do about all adverbial constructions: "What does th
word tell?" Thus your class will be able to see that a
noun telling *where* ("We hurried *home*"), or *how much*
("This weighs a *pound*") actually expresses an adverbial
relationship.

In teaching a noun in apposition, point out that the
term comes from a Latin word meaning "set next to";
say that an appositive is a noun "set next to" — placed
after — another to explain it. It has some similarities
to the subjective complement, in that it explains another
noun, but it does not complete the verb, is not connected
with the subject by means of the verb, and may explain
any noun in the sentence. In your illustrations, have
some that show appositives with nouns used as subjective complements: "He was a plainsman, a lean, silent
chap"; as direct objects: "I bought a paper, the morning
edition"; as objects of prepositions: "We gave it to the
guard, a stern-looking *man*." Because we frequently
employ appositives to explain the subject, your pupils,
unless you take care in selecting examples, will connect
the appositive, as they do the subjective complement,
with the subject only. If you wish, in presenting this
construction, you may include the personal pronoun,
although we seldom use it in this way. When we do,

usage demands that the case of the pronoun be the same as that of the word with which it is in apposition: "I refer to Queen Elizabeth, *her* whose policies have so profoundly affected our history."

In dealing with nouns of address, you will find they cause very little trouble, except as they are confused with the subject of the verb. To forestall this, have your class first find the verb and then its subject. Usually they will see that the noun of address is not the subject of the verb, but is the word naming the person spoken to. Place this sentence on the board: "Mary, please open the door for the cat." Then move *Mary* to the last of the sentence or strike it out altogether, and with your class again determine the subject of the verb. As imperative sentences in which the subject is not expressed produce the most difficulty, emphasis upon the fact that the omitted subject is invariably *you* helps to straighten out the trouble.

Whether or not you want to teach the objective complement depends largely upon the background and ability of your class. As I have said, we use it correctly and frequently; but you may want to explain its construction. In doing this, point out that it aids the direct object very much as the subjective complement does the subject. It is always used in connection, therefore, with the direct object, often after verbs of *calling, choosing, naming, electing, making;* and it shows the effect of the verb upon the direct object. A useful test for this construction is: If *to be* can be inserted between the direct object and the word following it without materially changing the meaning, the word after *to be* is the objective complement: "The team chose Albert *to be* captain." As answer to the inevitable "But why isn't it an appositive?" explain that the objective complement shows what the direct object, by means of the verb (particularly those listed above), is *made to become:* "We elected John *captain*" ("John is *made to become* captain"); "The class appointed Mary *secretary*" ("Mary is *made to become* secretary"); whereas the appositive merely explains: "We enjoyed the *dessert*, a delicious cherry *pie*." After you have wrestled with this subtlety for a while, you will be convinced that you have trespassed upon the preserves of formal grammar.

Although there are other properties of the noun aside from those here discussed, in your beginning work I suggest that you do little more than strive for recognition of nouns and their constructions noted here. Because of the importance of *case* in the use of pronouns, however, you are justified in teaching it in nouns. Have your class decline a number of nouns (stereotyped, but necessary); have them determine upon the case of the noun by its use in the sentence. Familiarize them with possessive case forms, and — if possible — teach them to spell these correctly. When they learn the declension of nouns, they become acquainted with the term *number* and its meaning. Later, as I have remarked, when you teach this property of the verb, you can point out the necessity of a verb and its subject agreeing in number. A discussion of *class*, if indeed it comes at all, should be held rather late in the course, except for three important types: *common*, *proper*, and *collective*. Of these, collective nouns are particularly important because of their bearing upon *number:* "The jury *are disagreeing* on their verdict"; "the jury *agrees* on a verdict." Senior students may be interested in classifying nouns as *abstract*, *concrete*, and *compound* in addition to the classifications given above; but as this

comes dangerously close to being formal grammar —
beware!

Much of what has been suggested for the teaching of
the noun applies to the personal pronoun. Following
the usual procedure, first aid your pupils to recognize
these pronouns. To do this, I list them on the board,
commenting as I do so that they live up to their name in
that they show the person or persons speaking: *I* or *we;*
those being spoken to: *you;* and the persons or things
spoken about: *he, she, it, they.* As a part of the assignment, I require the memorization of the declension.
. other aid to recognition, as well as a necessary piece
of information, is a comment on the antecedent of a
pronoun. I explain that the word means *going before,*
the prefix *ante* meaning *before.* On the board I write
some such sentence as: "John hurt Mary's head when
John threw a ball and struck Mary with it." For the
second *John* and *Mary* I substitute the proper pronoun
form, explaining that the first *John* and *Mary* are the
words for which the pronouns stand — their antecedents.

After an assignment on recognition of the pronoun and
its antecedent, you will begin to discuss their *use,* best
taught, as I have remarked, in connection with noun
constructions. Responsible for many errors in usage,
the personal pronoun may never be put aside for any
length of time, but should be reviewed again and again.
Because most mistakes are those of *case,* you should try
in every way possible to fix *right habits in speech and writing.*
An explanation of the *reason* for the use of *I* in such sentences as "Yes, this is *I*"; or *she* in "This is *she*"; or
of *her* in "They invited George and *her,*" will be very
helpful to the boy or girl who wants to know *why.* But
with the other type of person, *drill* may prove more

useful. Some teachers spend a few moments of each class period for recitation in unison of sentences containing personal pronouns used correctly. Although this serves to fix correct usage in the combinations you select for practice, it cannot possibly provide for every contingency, whereas grammatical knowledge of the structure is always applicable. Furthermore, I believe you should sufficiently respect the intelligence of your pupils to give them an adequate explanation of everything you teach, omitting what is beyond their comprehension. In your classwork, then, use both drill and explanation. Particular attention should be given to object forms, inasmuch as few errors are made in the use of the nominative case, except in subjective constructions. There is such division of opinion regarding "It is *I*" and "It is *me*" that I often wonder whether insistence upon this does not set us apart from common men, as pedants whose suggestions belong to the classroom and not to the street, home, or office. But because the former has not yet been discarded, it should be taught, if not emphasized. In their sentence analysis, your pupils will be helped to understanding if you ask them to state the *case* — and their reason for so identifying it — of every personal pronoun. Furthermore, you may frequently require from your class original sentences in which they use a noun and a pronoun or two pronouns as a compound subject, direct object, subjective complement, object of a preposition. As you will discover, in much of your teaching your most arduous task is to instill in your pupils a *desire* to speak and write correctly. Just how you can accomplish this, I don't know — possibly through your own practice and that of others; certainly not through preaching. Be alert to any opportunity for

showing the importance of correctness in these forms
(to me nothing, except inaccurate verb usage, so indicates illiteracy as incorrect pronoun forms); but remember
that a captious attitude on your part may easily be interpreted as criticism of the speech habits of the parents of
your boys and girls, and will arouse resentment.

In comparison with the personal pronoun, the other
types of pronoun — relative, adjective, and interrogative — afford few problems. The relative pronoun is
best taught in connection with the adjective clause;
and the interrogative with the noun clause or with
direct and indirect discourse. In this, the main problem
in usage is that of case; in, for example, "I asked *whom*
I should give it to." As with the personal pronoun,
require the memorization of the declension (a simple
matter, as there are only three changes: *who*, *whose*, and
whom). No new principle is needed, as whatever you
have taught regarding the uses of the nominative and
objective case of nouns and personal pronouns is applicable here. That *which* (affording no complexities, as
its form does not change to indicate case) refers to
things and *who* to persons is a matter of usage to be
presented at some point in your course. The adjective
pronoun — *one*, *another*, *that*, *everyone*, *all*, and so forth —
will come bobbing up at almost every stage. When your
beginners encounter it, merely give its name, saving
comments until you teach agreement of verb and subject. With the spelling of the possessive forms, this
matter of agreement constitutes your most important
responsibility. Such frequent errors as "Everyone must
have *their* own golf clubs," even on the part of educated
people, leave us wondering whether this point should
concern us greatly. My own practice is to admit frankly,

when the question arises — as it does — that this may be in the process of change, but until educated people *generally* use this form, it behooves high school pupils, not yet ready to act as arbiters of good taste, to follow established custom. Whenever this conflict between precedent and practice appears, readily admit the fact, advising adherence to rule until usage becomes fixed.

So much, then, for the basic elements of the sentence, the noun (and its substitute, the pronoun), and the verb. Upon them rests the responsibility for expression of thought. Next we shall consider modifiers, our means of elaborating an elementary idea.

ASSIGNMENT

Prepare a lesson plan for teaching one or more of the topics discussed in this chapter. Give (1) the topic, (2) the class for which it is designed, (3) your approach to the topic, (4) your plan for class procedure, (5) your assignment.

FURTHER READINGS

1. WARD, C. H., *What Is English?* Chapter VII, pp. 187–192.
Here Mr. Ward gives vivid directions concerning the teaching of nouns and pronouns.

2. WARD, C. H., *Grammar for Composition*, Chapter VI, pp. 57–65; Chapters XVII, XVIII, pp. 163–231; Part IV, pp. 393–404.
The first reference discusses the noun and pronoun as subjects; the second gives other noun and pronoun constructions; and the third presents information concerning these parts of speech which you as a teacher will need.

3. KITTREDGE, GEORGE LYMAN, and FARLEY, FRANK EDGAR, *Advanced English Grammar*, Chapters II and III.
In these are given simple, scientific explanations of noun and pronoun uses.

4. CURME, GEORGE O., *Syntax*.

This is an excellent reference book if you desire to enlarge your acquaintance with your mother tongue.

5. FRIES, CHARLES CARPENTER, *American English Grammar*.

This book discusses the inflections and syntax of American English, especially as they exist in various social strata.

VI. MODIFIERS

WITH your discussion of the *recognition* of the verb and the *ordinary* uses of noun and pronoun (subjects, subjective complements, direct objects, and objects of prepositions), you have articulated the skeleton of the sentence; now, by means of modifiers (adjectives, adverbs, phrases, and clauses) begin to put some flesh upon its bones. The first — and easiest — form of adornment should be the adjective.

As an introduction, you will want to make meaningful the word *modify*, explaining that it indicates *change*. When we speak, then, of a *small* boy, we *modify* or *change* the somewhat indefinite picture produced by the word *boy* to a more accurate concept — at least from the point of view of size. If we should add the word *ragged*, we should make still more vivid the appearance of the child. By doing this, you not only explain the meaning of a term, an understanding of which you must not take for granted, but you also indirectly call attention to the fact that words produce an image more or less striking in the mind of the reader.

After making this explanation, turn your attention to the recognition of the adjective. On the board put such groups of words as these: "yellow house"; "two girls"; "that house." With your class, note that *yellow* tells *kind* or *sort* of house; *two*, how many girls; and *that* points out the house almost as if one were indicating it with his finger. In teaching all modifiers, make frequent use of the "tell" test; in these sentences, the italicized words tell something about a noun by describing (*"yellow house"*); by indicating number (*"two girls"*); by pointing out (*"that house"*). From this determine your definition: Any word that modifies a noun (or its substitute, a pronoun) by describing, pointing out, or telling number is an *adjective*. Lay stress upon the fact that this part of speech never modifies any word except a noun or pronoun.

Next, place on the board a sentence containing an adjective used as a subjective complement: "The river is *wide*," noting that *wide* tells something about the noun *river*. By means of the *who* or *what* test, show that *wide* is an adjective used as a subjective complement. Class procedure may be: "The river is *what?*" *"Wide."* *Wide* answers the question *what?* placed after the verb and describes the subject; it is, therefore, a subjective complement. Your group now understands the reason for the inclusion of the term *describe* in their definition of this construction.

Continue your presentation by saying that *a, an,* or *the,* although referred to as *articles,* are adjectives. You will want to show, too, that several adjectives may modify the same noun: *"a little brown bird."* Above all impress upon your class the fact that adjectives that describe answer the question *what kind* or *sort?* (*"yellow house"*); those telling number, the question *how many?* (*"ten dollars"*); and those pointing out, *which one?* (*"that*

girl"). This I indicate graphically by a diagram on the
board:

> *brown* bird — what sort? — describes
> *two* ships — how many? — tells number
> *this* toy   — which one? — points out

As you go over in class the exercise you have assigned, have
your pupils state in which of these ways each adjective modifies. Thus you fix the requirements for this part of speech.

Following your principle of "one thing at a time,"
you will not want to combine your teaching of the adverb
with that of the adjective. When you do present the
former, you will find that with some groups you may
discuss adverbs modifying verbs, adjectives, and other
adverbs in one lesson, whereas with others you will have
to proceed more slowly. In the latter event, I suggest
you first discuss adverbs modifying verbs and adjectives,
following this with those modifying adverbs. Of course
your first concern lies with the recognition of this part
of speech. On the board place such sentences as:

1. The paper comes *daily*. (When?)
2. A great crowd had gathered *there*. (Where?)
3. *Why* do you look like that? (Why?)
4. Their fingers were *too* stiff to open the door. (To
what extent?)
5. They advanced *slowly* and *painfully*. (How?)
6. They were *not* sorry it had happened. (To what
extent? *Not at all*.)
7. The children shouted *very* noisily in their play. (To
what extent?)

In examining these sentences with your class, you will
note that each of the italicized words modifies a verb,
an adjective, or another adverb, and that each tells

when, where, why, how, to what extent, or *in what manner.*
From this study, build up the definition that an adverb
is a word that modifies a verb, an adjective, or an adverb.
(I prefer the definition that an adverb is a word that
modifies any part of speech except a noun or pronoun.
For this "elimination" definition I am indebted, I believe, to C. H. Ward. In "It is *just* after six o'clock,"
just modifies a preposition *(after)*; and in "I stayed *only*
because I wanted to talk to you," *only* modifies a conjunction *(because)* — possibilities not taken into consideration in the old definition. Whichever you choose
will depend on your personal preference and upon usage
in the text from which you teach.) You will want to
illustrate the relationships of *time, place, cause, manner,*
and *degree,* as expressed by an adverb, yet you will not, I
think, be so technical as to name them, contenting yourself with having your boys and girls understand that an
adverb tells *when* or *why* or *where* and so forth, and leaving
classification for advanced students.

Although, on the whole, the recognition of the adverb
does not present many troublesome points, yet it, too,
has its minor Waterloos. That the frequently used word
not is an adverb modifying the verb and answering the
question "to what extent?" will have to be explained.
Confusing, too, are words like *down* or *up*, which, depending upon their use, may be either adverbs or prepositions. As you should have taught the recognition of
the prepositional phrase before presenting the adverb,
a reminder here that, in order to be a preposition, a
word must have an object, should dispel this cloud.
Constant recourse to the "tell" test and insistence upon
careful consideration of the work of each word will
ordinarily straighten out any confusion.

Complete your unit on the adjective and adverb by a "distinguishing" exercise before going on to new matter.

In connection with adverbs and adjectives you will want to teach their use after verbs referring to the senses: taste, smell, sound, sight, touch. Point out that an adjective used as a subjective complement gives a quality of the subject; therefore, in such a sentence as "I feel different about the whole affair," *different*, an adjective, refers to the subject *I*. But in this sentence: "Each evening, I feel my way *carefully* through the dark hall," *carefully* is an adverb, answering the question *how?*, and telling my manner of feeling. Because of the delicate nature of this distinction, you may wish to omit it until dealing with advanced classes.

As soon as you have taught adjectives and adverbs, you can go on to the use of prepositional phrases. Again following Ward, you should limit the word *phrase* to *prepositional* phrase. The term *noun* or *verb* phrase, although undoubtedly correct, frequently confuses beginning students. You should also limit your discussion to the use of phrases as adjectives or adverbs, rather than complicate the presentation by mention of "noun phrases," even though for yourself you prefer this third category.

Because of the frequency with which they occur, you should very early — possibly immediately after your class has learned to identify nouns and pronouns — teach the recognition of prepositional phrases. In doing this, I always use a device suggested to me by an instructor under whom I did some of my practice teaching. The name of this person has long since escaped me, but I employ her device and thereby keep green her memory. I draw upon the board figures that I call a cat and a house, although I admit that some imagination is necessary to recognize them. Then I write in certain words, thus: "The cat went *over* the house, *under* the house, *by*, *beyond*, *into*, *behind*, *on*, *around*, *against* the house." I draw another house and list *between*. With the help of the class, I obtain a surprisingly long list of words. I point out that unfortunately *at*, *for*, and *of*, all frequently used, do not fit into the device. When no more words can be suggested, I remark that the words we have listed are *prepositions* and that the noun *house* is the object, commenting that a word, to be a preposition, must have an object. Of course I employ other examples of prepositional phrases aside from these, including compounds such as *on account of* and *because of*, and personal pronouns and dates as objects: "to *me*," "in *1933*." Again the *whom?* or *what?* device proves its value as a test for the object: "In what?" "In 1933"; "To whom?" "To my father." And this is all that I do with the phrase until I have taught the use of adjectives and adverbs.

When my class recognizes adjectives and adverbs, and can determine their use, I turn to the construction of phrases. I begin with the adjective phrase, as usual putting on the board illustrations: "the man on the horse." I show that *on the horse* modifies the noun *man* by answering the question "which one?" It therefore modifies by *pointing out;* it distinguishes the man *on the horse* from the man *in the field*. Because it modifies a noun by pointing out, it is an adjective phrase.

To explain the adverb phrase I follow the same procedure: "I hurried *into the house*." As the phrase tells *where*, it is adverbial. In presenting both types of phrase, I select for illustrative purposes examples indicating numerous relationships: "weakens *at a woman's tears*" (why) or "are fascinated *by the hope*" (how).

At first, your class will have trouble in considering these phrases as a unit, because heretofore their experience has been with single words. Now they must deal with a group of words as if it were one word — no easy task. Try to make them picture the words as a whole by drawing lines about them, underlining them. Then, thinking of the phrase as a unit, get your boys and girls to determine what it *tells*. In doing this, do not quarrel over classification, but be content with a reasonable explanation. In such a sentence as: "His hair stood on end when he saw the cougar on the trail," admit the possibility that the cougar *on the trail* rather than one in the tree is responsible for the phenomenon mentioned. To most of the class (and to you) the phrase is adverbial, but much time can be wasted by quibbling over such matters. More frequent troublemakers are phrases at the first of the sentence: "At my call, he hurried to my aid." Many examples of this sort and recourse to the "tell" test will help solve this problem.

After your group has a good grasp of the somewhat simple modifiers — adjectives, adverbs, and phrases — proceed with caution to the clause. To a certain extent, study of the phrase has accustomed your class to dealing with words as a unit, but as the clause is much more complicated than the phrase, you can expect it to be correspondingly more difficult.

Of course your first step will be to teach the definition of a clause: a group of words containing a subject and a verb. Previous to this, as you have used only simple or compound sentences for class analysis, you have not, probably, mentioned the term *clause*. Now, however, a knowledge of the term is necessary and the definition should be memorized. State that there are two kinds of clause: main and subordinate, also called principal or independent and dependent. On the board place the word "subordinate" and bracket with it adjective, adverb, and noun. Explain that a subordinate clause is one that is used like a *word* in the sentence: noun, adjective, or adverb; and that a *main* clause is one that makes a statement, asks a question, or gives a command. Carefully avoid saying that a main clause can stand alone. This statement is true only from the grammatical point of view, not from that of meaning, and is provocative, later on, of much trouble. For example, in the sentence: "All that I can do is to conform," the main clause, "all is to conform," although independent grammatically, is far from being so logically. In a complex sentence containing a noun clause, the main clause need not "stand alone" even grammatically, as in "That he has wasted his time *appears probable*." Because of the frequent occurrence of such sentences as these, I believe you will have success if you emphasize the subordinate clause — especially the fact that it is used as a word in the sentence — and touch very lightly on the main clause. Usually your remark, "The other clause is called the *main* (or principal or independent) clause," is accepted without question by your class.

In first presenting dependent clauses, you should limit your discussion to the adjective clause. Place on the board such groups as:

> A treeless plain
> A plain without trees } is a very barren waste.
> A plain that has no trees

Show that in the first sentence *treeless* is an adjective modifying *plain;* in the second, *without trees* is an adjective phrase; and in the third *that has no trees* is a clause used to modify *plain:* an *adjective* clause, as *plain* is a noun.

Next, put on the board two or three complex sentences containing adjective clauses. With your class, determine upon the clauses, marking in some way, perhaps by underlining, the subordinate and the main clauses. In each instance, show what the adjective clause modifies. Let some of your illustrations contain adjective clauses modifying nouns in various constructions: "The house *which is on the corner* is my home" (modifying the subject); "I handed George his hat, *which he put on at once*" (modifying the direct object); "That is my brother *to whom you spoke*" (modifying the subjective complement); "I went through the door *that stood open*" (modifying the object of a preposition). Still other sentences should contain illustrations of adjective clauses introduced by a relative adverb: "The house *where I was born* is still standing"; "The hour *when I was to meet him* came and went."

Do not try to teach any more than this in your first discussion of clauses. Give an assignment on the recognition of adjective clauses. In class see that the students know the substantive that the clause modifies.

On the second day, call the attention of your group to the word connecting the clause to the substantive it modifies. Begin with an illustrative sentence containing a relative pronoun. Show the three requirements of a relative pronoun: That it relates or connects, that it has an antecedent, and that it has a use within its clause. This last point will cause the greatest concern. To determine the use, it is sometimes helpful to divide the sentence into two, substituting the antecedent for the pronoun. For example, this sentence: "Mr. Thompson,

whom you may remember, has decided to open a store"
may be rewritten thus: "Mr. Thompson has decided
to open a store. You may remember Mr. Thompson."
That *Mr. Thompson* is the direct object of *may remember*
is thus easily seen. Then substitute the pronoun *whom*
for *Mr. Thompson* and you help your group to grasp the
construction.

Previous to this you should have taught *case* in nouns
and personal pronouns. Point out that relative pronouns,
too, have *case* but that *who* is the only one to change its
form: *who, whose, whom.* By the way, you should limit
your discussion of relative pronouns to *who, which,* and
that. *What* has a number of complications, principally
its lack of an expressed antecedent and its use as an interrogative pronoun — "I wonder *what* he meant" — and
as is too seldom used as a relative pronoun to warrant
its inclusion here. With your class, diagram several
sentences to show the construction within its clause of
each relative pronoun.

Next, consider the clause introduced by a relative
adverb, showing its adverbial and connective aspects.
Again, diagraming will aid in presenting this. For an
assignment, require the diagraming of a number of sentences containing both types of connective, if you use this
method. If not, have each connective labeled as relative pronoun or relative adverb, and the construction of
each pronoun marked. In class, see that the group know
the substantive that the clause modifies and have them
test each word they select as a relative pronoun, emphasizing its three requirements.

After you think that your boys and girls understand
adjective clauses, go on to adverbial ones. Follow the
same procedure: "The man walked *quickly*"; "The

man walked *with haste*"; "The man walked *as if he were in a hurry*." Put on the board complex sentences containing adverbial clauses to show several of the ordinary adverbial relationships: time, place, manner, and cause; but, except with advanced students, carefully avoid these terms: "My friend went to the theater, *after I had gone home*" (time); "I followed *where the children led*" (place); "The old man walked *as if he were lame*" (manner); "I could not go *because I had hurt my foot*" (reason). Underline the clauses and see that the class understands what each adverbial clause *tells: how, when, where, why, to what extent*, and *in what manner*. Perhaps you may want to explain the *degree-result* clause by such a sentence as "It is *so* hot that I fell asleep," in which you point out that the *degree* of heat expressed by *so* had the unfortunate *result* of causing you to fall asleep. For a sentence illustrating pure degree, you might select "He is as tall as I am," showing that "as tall as I am" answers the question "to what extent?" and, provided you are dealing with an advanced class, state that it indicates degree. As an assignment, ask your group to list adverbial clauses, in class being very careful to see that they understand what each clause *tells*.

Your discussion of the adverbial clause demands attention to another part of speech, hitherto not commented upon: *subordinating conjunctions*. Perhaps an understanding of the prefix *sub* as meaning *under* or *below* may serve to fix the term. A list of the ordinary ones — *if, as, as if, so that, although, unless* — may be useful. It may be that you will not want to differentiate between relative adverbs, which your group already understand through their study of adjective clauses, and subordinating conjunctions; but as this distinction has to be made with one sort of clause, it may as well be done with the other. However, your principal concern is not with pedantic classification, but rather with laying a foundation for discriminating use of these small but important connectives.

Let the adverbial clause "soak in" before discussing the noun clause. Probably you will want to assign a "distinguishing" exercise on adjective and adverb clauses before attacking this last, but not least, subordinate clause.

Let your procedure in this be as usual. List the ordinary noun uses: *subject, direct object, object of a preposition, subjective complement*. Then put on the board some such sentence as "His *interest* in basketball is evident." Show that *interest* is the subject of *is*. For *interest*, substitute: *That he is interested in basketball*. Point out that this group of words — a clause — expresses the same idea as does the word *interest* and has the same construction: the subject of *is*. Similarly, illustrate a direct object: "He asked *permission* from his father"; "He asked *that he might go*." Again: "He ran *to the fire*"; "He ran to *where the fire was burning*" (object of a preposition). "His idea was a good one"; "His idea was *that each should contribute equally*" (subjective complement). Point out that, as the clause in each example does the work of a *noun*, it is a *noun* clause. (Another somewhat usual use of the noun is that of the appositive: "My idea *that we should buy the car* met with enthusiastic response." Should you desire to teach this also, approach it in the same manner; but with beginning students, it may be well to omit it.) In your assignment, have your class mark each noun clause, giving its construction. And as usual, you will want to review by means of an exercise containing examples of all types of clauses before you leave your direct teaching of the subject.

In your presentation of the other clauses, you have given much attention to the words used to introduce the clause: relative pronouns and relative adverbs and subordinating conjunctions. Are you to do the same with the noun clause? My advice is to omit this from your discussion, unless someone questions you concerning it, for the reason that we use so many kinds of connectives that their display would prove most confusing. If you will glance at those in the illustrative sentences suggested, you will find in sentence one a subordinating conjunction (*that*); in two, the same; in three, an adverb (*where*); and in four, a subordinating conjunction again. In addition, you might have had an interrogative pronoun ("I wonder *who* he is"); an interrogative adverb ("Tell me *when* you will be ready"); the conjunction *whether;* several others; or none at all. ("I thought he was going tomorrow.") In fact, we use so many different sorts of words in this way that an attempt to include all of them in the beginning work is fruitless.

This comment leads me to remark particularly on one of these frequently used words — *that*. Like *what*, a troublemaker, *that* may be a demonstrative adjective ("*that* man"); a demonstrative pronoun ("*That* is mine"); a relative pronoun ("I shall outline the points *that* concern you"); a subordinating conjunction in a noun clause ("My reply was *that* I would consider the matter"). The versatility of this little word makes it very difficult to pigeonhole, and I suggest care in presentation.

One of your difficulties in teaching this type of complex sentence lies in the fact that frequently the main clause will be incomplete. This must be true when the noun clause is used in any way except as object of the preposition or in apposition. It is for this reason that I advised against the statement that an independent clause may "stand alone" or that it "makes a complete thought." In the sentence, "He said he will go," the clause "he will go" is definitely more complete in meaning than is the main clause, "He said." Concentrate, then, upon the subordinate clause, particularly in dealing with sentences containing noun clauses.

This matter of clauses is of fundamental importance, for the clause constitutes the backbone of every sentence. Because of its difficulty it must be taught relatively late in the course. To me it is a waste of time to demand "sentence sense" before you have taught the clause; and how can you teach it until you have presented the fundamental elements of a sentence? Let it wait, then, until you have laid the foundation of the make-up of a simple sentence. Remember that, like the phrase, it is a *group* of words used as a *unit*. Be patient and painstaking; work slowly; and your reward *may* be that your students will be graduated from high school knowing what a sentence is. And that, we are often told, is a bit of equipment that the high school senior has lamentably lacked.

So much for the grammar one should teach. Now let me make some general suggestions concerning method. Contrary to pedagogical principles, I shall begin with a few *don'ts*. In the first place, do no parsing with beginning students. With advanced groups (provided they are really advanced and not merely seniors) parsing is often good fun as well as excellent review. But it is *formal*, not *functional*, and as such does not really belong in your course. I have pointed out certain essential bits of knowledge connected with each part of speech discussed, to which you should limit your parsing. (Parsing consists of giving a word its grammatical classification and construction. To parse a noun it is necessary to give (1) its class, (2) its gender, (3) its case, (4) its construction or use. The first two points are really formal, not functional grammar.)

Next, avoid "understood" words. Perhaps I am over-emphasizing this point, but much trouble, I am convinced, can be prevented if this is kept in mind. I am inclined to say that one should limit "understood" words to the omitted subject of an imperative sentence, in which the understood subject is always *you*. I am aware that, in doing this, I am neglecting ellipsis, which has a very useful place in our speech; but it should be taught late in the course (possibly in the senior year) to students who can analyze the structure of an ordinary sentence.

And my last *don't* again is repetition; be very careful to avoid teaching two or more elements simultaneously. *One principle at a time* should be your unfailing method.

Now for some *do's:* I suggest you use diagraming. I find this interesting and valuable to all students, good, bad, and indifferent, for it presents a graphic method of showing relationships of words or groups of words. The accurate, painstaking pupil will often find a real pleasure in this work, for it gives him something to do with his hands. When you see your "problem boy" busily working on diagrams, you will exclaim in your heart, "Blessed be diagraming!" And when you see your good student turning to it to make clear certain relationships, you will also praise the system. I should select a simple, expressive method, such as the old Reed-Kellogg plan.

This system, with some adaptions, you will find in *A Brief Review of English Grammar*, by Ethel B. Magee, Chairman (Schwabacher-Frey, Los Angeles); *A Writers' Manual*, by Paul P. Kies, *et al.* (F. S. Crofts); and *The Daily Life English Series* (Ginn and Company). But be careful that diagraming does not become an end in itself. It is a very useful device, but it *is* a device, a mechanical means. I suggest that you do not begin its use until you have taught the constructions found ordinarily in a simple sentence. Then teach diagraming to show word relationships quickly and graphically. You will find it a valuable visual aid to understanding.

Very important to your teaching is the use of a wealth of illustrations, for these are far more valuable than theory. Form the habit of collecting them, particularly from current literature, books, or magazines read by the class. Suspicion is usually attached to "literary examples," for, after all, what high school student wants to "talk like a book"? Be very careful, in selecting these sentences, to see that they do not contain unfamiliar constructions or idiomatic oddities.

Always require a full explanation. You will get tired of hearing, "This is the direct object because . . .," but unless you do insist upon each pupil's telling *why*, you will be amazed to discover, probably on a test, that too many of your class are guessing, not reasoning, encouraged or discouraged, as the case may be, by the expression on your face. Remember, and see that your group remembers, that *no* word is anything of itself. Its *use* determines its part of speech; therefore use is of paramount importance. In this connection, let me say that it is unfair to ask students to name the parts of speech in a sentence until you have given them careful training in the requirements of each. Sometimes even experts disagree over a part of speech; so do not expect your beginning students to know a noun until you have taught its requirements. For, I ask you, is *rose* a noun or a verb? You cannot tell, can you, until you know its place in a given sentence? *Use*, then, cannot be over-emphasized.

In your teaching, begin with the single word and build up from it. I suggest the following order of topics: recognition of verbs, recognition of nouns, recognition of prepositional phrases, recognition of personal pronouns; ordinary noun and personal pronoun uses (subject, object, subjective complement, and object of the preposition); recognition of adjectives and of adverbs; use of prepositional phrases; main clauses; simple sentences; compound sentences; subordinate clauses; complex sentences; verbals. This appears to me to be an orderly and progressive arrangement of topics. Just where you should present the various aspects of the verb, other noun and pronoun uses, and so forth, depends largely upon your class. What I suggest here serves only as a basis for your teaching procedure.

You must encourage questions. Every query, no matter how foolish it seems to you (provided, of course, it pertains to the subject) must be given serious consideration. Do not be irritated; above all, do not be evidently *patient*. Assume a serious attitude on the part of the student; and remember that a misstep on your part will shut him up like a clam, not only in this particular class, but also, if he is sensitive, in other classes as well. Questions are necessary; they are not evils, but are evidences of a desire to understand. Whether or not you are tired, whether or not you have explained this point a dozen times — if the question is sincere, give it the consideration that is its due.

An unnecessary difficulty connected with the teaching of grammar lies in terminology. Unfortunately, there is no uniformity in the terms used. Some years ago, a committee on nomenclature attempted to clarify this point, but little progress was made, as a study of a half dozen texts will determine. Why, when a subjective complement is sufficiently difficult in itself, should the poor student be further harassed by having to recognize it under one of many names: predicate noun, predicate nominative, predicate attribute? Nor is this construction the only one to masquerade under various disguises. I prefer terminology that suggests the attributes of the construction, and I prefer English to Latin terms. At present, most texts use *possessive* rather than *genitive* (yes, I grant you that there is a distinction, but is it worth while?) and *objective* rather than *accusative*. And I applaud the change. But why not *subjective*, rather than *nominative?* Search secondary school texts, and you will find: nominative, possessive, and objective. Confusing, is it not?

But whatever your personal opinion, you must use the terminology of your text. It is far easier for you, familiar as you should be with the construction itself, to change your term than it is for the student to learn the construction and also a term not in the book. And always, to the pupil, what "it says in the book" is right; another jolt to one's ego, you observe. But notice terminology in selecting a text, and other things being equal, choose the text with suggestive nomenclature.

Another much-discussed point is that of definitions. Shall we require our students to learn them? A few years ago I should have told you that the memorizing of a definition is pedantic and useless procedure. *Today* my teaching experience leads me to tell you that your group should memorize the definitions that you give them. *But* memorization comes last, not first, in your approach. Build up each definition *with your class*. See that it is simply and clearly worded and that it includes, as much as possible, the attributes of the construction. Indeed, if you choose, do not use the term definition: say *requirements* or *characteristics*. The following are some that I prefer. Remember that these are to be arrived at through the joint efforts of you and your class.

A *noun* is a word used as a name. A *verb* is a word that causes a group of words to make a statement, ask a question, or give a command. An *adjective* is a word that modifies (changes the meaning of) a noun or pronoun by describing, pointing out, or telling number. An *adverb* is a word that modifies any part of speech except a noun or pronoun by telling how, when, where, why, to what extent, in what manner. A *relative pronoun* is a word having an antecedent, a use within its clause, and a connective use. A *clause* is a group of related words containing a subject and verb. A *subordinate clause* is one used like a noun, an adjective, or an adverb. A *main clause* is one that makes a statement, asks a question, or gives a command. A *phrase* is a group of words consisting of a preposition and its object.

And last, always teach grammar — and indeed all the attributes of composition — in connection with writing. Grammar is not an isolated subject, taught primarily for the purpose of exercising the brains of your boys and girls. We teach it because we believe that a knowledge of the grammatical structure of a sentence is a valuable tool for the transfer of thought. If this is not true, it cannot be justified under our present aims for teaching. After you have taught a point in grammar, see that your students apply it in their speech and writing. This I shall discuss further in future chapters.

Let me sum up, now, what I have said concerning the teaching of grammar. (1) It should be taught each year, if possible or necessary. (2) It should be taught from the functional point of view, avoiding hair-splitting or the inclusion of rare constructions. (3) It should be taught positively and definitely. (4) It must be taught in connection with expression, for if it is functional it must be usable.

ASSIGNMENT

Select any topic under the teaching of grammar that you desire, and present a plan for teaching it. In this plan give (1) the topic, (2) the class for which it is designed, (3) your approach to the topic, (4) five questions that you would ask, (5) your assignment.

FURTHER READINGS

1. BLAISDELL, THOMAS C., *Ways to Teach English*, Chapters XIX and XX.

Although these contain much which pertains particularly to elementary school teaching, they also give many practical suggestions applicable to high school teaching.

2. Throughout this and preceding chapters I have frequently referred you to C. H. Ward's two books, *What Is English?* and *Grammar for Composition*. By this time you undoubtedly know whether or not you accept the teaching principles of this master. If you find his suggestions positive and provocative, I refer you again to the chapters on grammar in both books.

3. HATFIELD, W. WILBUR, "What Grammar? How?" *The English Journal*, XVIII (May, 1929), pp. 425–426.

This editorial is a sane comment on the teaching of grammar for daily use.

4. SYMONDS, PERCIVAL M., "Practice vs. Grammar in the Learning of Correct English Usage," *Journal of Educational Psychology*, XXII (February, 1931), pp. 81–95.

Here is presented an authoritative account of experiments stressing *practice* of correct forms vs. *learning* of rules, definitions, etc. You may be surprised at some of the findings.

5. MOFFETT, H. Y., "Grammar and Power," *The English Journal*, XVII (December, 1928), pp. 800–810.

This pleasant, informal address, given before the National Council of Teachers of English, will please you.

6. SMITH, DORA V., "English Grammar Again!" and SMITH, REED, "Grammar: The Swing of the Pendulum," *The English Journal*, XXVII (October, 1938), pp. 637–643; 643–649.

In these articles the two Smiths present opposing points of view on this controversial topic.

7. PERRY, PORTER G., "Teaching Realistic Grammar," *The Elementary English Review*, XXII (February, 1945), pp. 41–45.

Much good advice is contained in this article.

8. POOLEY, ROBERT C., "Communication and Usage," *The English Journal*, XXXIV (January, 1945), pp. 16–19.

Three significant principles for teaching usage are here presented.

9. ROBERTSON, STUART, "Grammarians," *Atlantic Monthly*, CL (August, 1932), pp. 254–255.

If you find that you are taking the subject of grammar too seriously, this essay will prove a pleasant and effective antidote.

VII. SPELLING

OCCASIONALLY I am told that spelling is the least important of the mechanical phases of composition; in fact, that it does not justify the time and red ink that we teachers of English expend upon it. From one point of view I agree with the first statement of the contention, for poor spelling does not necessarily interfere with the understanding of thought, whereas errors in grammar, sentence structure, and punctuation may easily produce an interpretation far from that of the author. But really poor spelling may cause great mental confusion, as witness the following sentences, culled from student work. Note that both sentence structure and the expressed idea are correct, but can you understand these sentences upon the first, casual reading? I doubt it, forearmed though you now are. These are the sentences:

"The results was that he found favorer in her I by puting his hole hart and sole into his juggling." And, "She was going to try and save his sole, not let it go to waist" — a consummation devoutly to be desired, no doubt.

Now, I submit to you, *is* the teaching of spelling worth while? Is there any excuse for the uneconomical waste of time made necessary by the rereading of these simple thoughts? Furthermore, rightly or wrongly, literacy is judged by spelling. Today, one of the frequent criticisms made of our high school graduates is "Why, they can't even spell!" No doubt one reason for its importance is that practically everyone can recognize errors in spelling, whereas errors in grammar and in sentence structure go undetected. We expect educated persons to spell correctly; and as long as this is true, I think you are justified in giving attention to spelling.

Theoretically, spelling as a subject belongs to the elementary, not the secondary school, but probably your pupils will need further drill in forming spelling habits, and aid in overcoming spelling faults. Do not, then, take for granted that your class knows how to spell. Test their spelling proficiency, and, if necessary, plan to help them form correct spelling habits.

Spelling should be taught, I believe, in each year of secondary school — directly in the junior high school and in the tenth grade, indirectly in the eleventh and twelfth. That most educators agree with this point of view you can determine by examining texts and courses of study.

What do I mean by teaching spelling directly? I mean that in the seventh, eighth, ninth, and tenth years a certain amount of time should be given to teaching definite words. Some schools have lists prepared by the members of their staff; others use such a list as that of Horn. Most texts contain lessons in spelling.

The indirect method, followed throughout the upper years of high school and in the college or university, consists in pointing out errors in spelling and having pupils correct them. There is no general class drill; the student is given credit for sufficient interest and energy to correct his mistakes, once they are pointed out to him.

In your teaching, concentrate upon a few general errors. Sometimes these are listed in the minimum essentials requirements of your school or state. In any event, you can soon compile the words misspelled by a majority of your class and use these as a basis for your spelling lessons; or you can depend upon the words listed in the text that you use.

In teaching, you should depend quite largely upon the visual appeal. Put the words on the board, divide them into syllables, pointing out the troublesome letter or letters. Sometimes it is helpful to contrast the correct spelling of a word with the incorrect, but *never* leave an incorrect form on the board. The final picture of the word in the mind of the student must be a correct one. In that connection, let me suggest that you watch your own spelling carefully, taking great care to spell correctly every word you write for your students; for, strangely and sadly, our pupils seem always to remember our occasional lapses far more vividly than they do our ordinary exactness.

Oral appeal has, I think, less force than has visual, for the reason that our language contains many "silent" letters. You should, however, appeal to the ear; correct pronunciation frequently results in correct spelling, and vice versa. Our slipshod speech habits probably have considerable to do with our poor spelling. To some persons, also, the muscular appeal helps in their learning process. Such persons like to "write it down," perhaps many times, in that way fixing correct forms. All three of these methods — the visual, the oral, and the muscular — should be utilized.

In upper grade teaching, you are trying to break down poor spelling habits rather than to teach spelling as such. This must not be forgotten; your assault must be upon habits formed through years of incorrect use. What you want to do, then, is to attract the attention of the erring pupil to the word in such a way that he forms a vivid mental picture of it. Lend your energies to that end.

One method of doing this consists of teaching similar forms at the same time. For example, *paid* and *laid* are frequently misspelled, but never *said*. Put the three together, then, pointing out the same *ai* combination in them. Underline the *ai*, make it stand out, so that *layed* and *payed* will ever after look wrong to the student. Similarly group *all right* and *all wrong*. No one, I think, writes *all wrong* as one word; many write *all right* in that way. Grammatical knowledge will lend a hand, too. For example *there* the adverb and *their* the pronoun can be distinguished by means of their function; and *to* the preposition, *two* the numeral, *too* the adverb (despite its brevity the most difficult word in our language) straighten themselves out in the mind of the pupil who knows his grammar.

Gather up any devices that have proved useful to you or to any of your acquaintances. For example, in *separate*, the trouble almost invariably lies in the first *a*. Put the word on the board; underline the *a*; write it as a capital letter; put it in with red chalk. Pronounce the word carefully, giving the *a* and not the *e* sound to the letter. Point out the family relationship in *separate* and *grammar* — the *pa* and *ma* in the words; thereby killing two birds with one stone, for the *a* in grammar is a point of trouble also. Say that *till* is a little word and needs

the help of two *l's;* that *until* is a longer word and is
therefore more independent. Amuse your class with
this: "Merry Mary married me" (incidentally an
exercise in pronunciation also). Give the homely word
lice as a key to the spelling of *li* and *ce* words; recall the
old rhyme for the exceptions: "*I* before *e* except after *c.*
But *leisure* and *seize,* they do as they please." The sentence "Neither did the weird man seize his leisure"
includes a number of demons which may be exorcised
by concentration on this sentence. Devices like these
frequently are of more value than rules.

A group of words that you can help your pupils to spell
correctly are the *ly* words and those having the prefix
mis or *dis.* Always there is the question: Shall I, or
shall I not, double that *l* or that *s?* Put the root of the
word on the board: *final, former.* Then add *ly: final + ly;*
former + ly. Point out that *ly* is a syllable added to the
word proper (use "suffix" if the students know the term;
otherwise, don't confuse them with it). If the word
itself ends in *l,* naturally there will be two *l's* if *ly* is added;
otherwise not. Similarly, put on the board *satisfy* and
appoint. Place the prefix *dis* before each: *dissatisfy, dis-*
appoint, again showing that there are two *s's* only if the
word proper begins with *s.*

A few minutes ago, I referred to rules. Shall we or
shall we not teach them? Sometimes we concentrate
so much upon rules that our students can't see the forest
for the trees; that we certainly do not want to do. But
I believe that a few are useful; in particular, the following:

First, words ending in silent *e* usually drop the *e* on
adding *ed* or *ing.* Two ordinary exceptions are *dye* and
singe. The first is necessary to distinguish between

dyeing, meaning *to color*, and *dying*, *to expire;* and as for
the second, by observing it we are freed from the absurdity of "singing a chicken." Also exceptions are the
oe words, such as *hoeing, shoeing, canoeing*.

A very useful rule is that words of one syllable ending
in a single consonant preceded by a single vowel double
the consonant upon adding *ed* or *ing*. Put several examples on the board to illustrate this, such as *drag, din,
moan*. Note with your students that *moan* does not follow
the rule for a single consonant preceded by a single
vowel; therefore the *n* is not doubled. (Probably you
should list the vowels on the board before you begin this
discussion; your class *may* know them, but again, they
may not.)

Another similar, equally helpful rule is: Words of
more than one syllable ending in a single consonant
preceded by a single vowel, with the accent on the last
syllable, double the final consonant upon adding *ed* or
ing. You notice that I am avoiding the terms "mono-
syllabic" and "polysyllabic." If you know that your class
understands these terms, use them, by all means; but
if your group does not, you are not making your meaning
clear. Follow the same procedure of putting on the
board words to which this rule applies, such as *occur* and
begin. You will have to indicate syllables; do this by
marking each in some way. Accent will have to be
explained. Pronounce your illustrative words carefully
to show what you mean by accent.

Many errors in spelling are made in the formation of
plurals and possessives. These, then, need your careful
attention. Plurals are trying, for the reason that there
are numerous ways to form them. You should have the
students memorize the more ordinary rules: the usual

addition of *s* to the singular, except in words ending in *s* or *x* or a similar sound; then *es* is added. Words like *valley*, ending in *ey*, add *s*. (If you discuss this about Thanksgiving time, your students may enjoy a game of finding *turkeys* spelled correctly or incorrectly on signs, in advertisements, and in news stories.) Other words ending in *y* change the *y* to *i* and add *es*. As there are so many ways to form the plural, you should concentrate on these, with considerable drill, and urge the class to consult the dictionary in case of doubt.

Fortunately, rules for spelling the possessive forms are fixed and can and should be taught. The possessive singular may always be formed by the addition of an apostrophe and *s*. Beyond this you should not go. You know, and your brighter students will soon discover, that the possessive singular of words ending in *s* may be formed by adding the apostrophe only. But *Burns's* is preferable to *Burns'*; even *Dickens's* has respectable backing; hence you should teach this positively and boldly, without confusing your pupils with exceptions. For, strange as it may seem to you, correct spelling of possessive forms is far from easy.

The spelling of the possessive plural, although more difficult, is fortunately as definite as is the spelling of the possessive singular. The process consists of three steps. First form the plural. (It is obvious that this must be taught *after* you have taught plural formations. It should also be obvious that you do not teach the formation of the possessive singular and the possessive plural in one assignment. Far from it; be certain that your students can spell the singular forms before you go on to the plural.) Then, notice the ending of the plural form. If the plural ends in *s*, add an apostrophe; if it does not, add an apostrophe and *s*. As a review, dictate a number of sentences in which ownership is expressed by an *of* phrase — "The hats of the men"; "The courage of the boy"; "The fragrance of the lily" — and require your pupils to substitute the proper possessive form. In this way you teach both spelling and meaning. Many of your pupils will have a very hazy notion indeed of the idea conveyed by the possessive case. In part, this failure accounts for their inability to distinguish between possessive and plural forms.

Unfortunately for both teacher and pupil, the pronoun is not so amenable as is the noun. True, indefinite pronouns follow noun usage, but the relative pronoun *who* has a distinct form *whose;* and as for the personal pronoun, it discards entirely the carefully taught apostrophe. So the poor student has to learn to spell *its* and *hers* and *theirs* without an apostrophe; and I know of no royal road to this learning. I am convinced that sometime there will be uniformity in spelling the possessive forms of nouns and pronouns — I am also convinced that the uniformity will consist in dropping the apostrophe in the noun forms, for the amateur writing public is determined to ignore the apostrophe, as your first batch of themes will tell you — but this will not come in our time; so nothing remains except to teach the spelling as it is today. You should teach the spelling of pronoun forms when you teach *case* in pronouns. Certainly it must not be taught at the same time as the spelling of possessive forms of nouns.

Perhaps in the first two years of high school you will want to teach spelling directly twice a week. Seldom will you wish to use an entire period for this. Assign the spelling a day or two before the class period in which you discuss it, and select one group or class of words and only one. Make your assignment with care, pointing out troublesome spots, similarities, differences, meanings, pronunciation. Then expect the class to learn to spell the words assigned. Let me quote from *An Experience Curriculum*, page 259, directions for learning to spell a word:

> In studying a word, a good procedure for a learner is, (1) to say each syllable distinctly and look at the syllable as he says it, (2) with eyes closed to think how the word looks, (3) to look at the word again to check his impression, (4) to write the word and check with the book, and (5) to repeat twice the writing and checking. If on any one of these five trials he misspells the word, he should copy it in his spelling notebook for review. Finally he should write the group of words studied as a parent, brother, sister, or friend pronounces them for him.

At the next meeting, dictate some sentences containing the assigned words, including words used in previous lessons. Only those taught should be considered in your marking, but you should hold your group responsible for words studied previously. Never dictate *lists* of words; always use sentences. Make those planned for dictation interesting. I suggest the following procedure: First read each sentence aloud. Your students must do no writing during this first reading. Read naturally, as vividly as possible. Then reread the sentence in groups of words. This time your class writes as you dictate. When the group has finished writing, reread the sentence in an easy, natural manner, so that your pupils can check their work. As you dictate, watch the rate of writing and gauge your reading accordingly. As dictation is not easy, you will probably need some practice in it. Be careful to pronounce each word clearly and distinctly.

Errors made by your class should not be due to your faulty pronunciation or enunciation.

The most important bit of advice that I can give you in regard to the teaching of spelling is that you must remember that you are dealing with a habit established over a period of eight, ten, or twelve years. Such a habit is not easy to break. Be patient with your group but be strict. You should hold them responsible for words that they misspell *after you have taught these words*. You may be justified in marking a paper *F* that contains repeated, careless errors. Before going to this length, however, you should consult your principal. After all, he may, some day, have to placate an irate parent who wants to know why James should receive an *F* merely for misspelling *too*. You want to be assured that your principal is on your side, not against you. In fact, this whole matter of spelling is one that should have the co-operation, not only of your principal, but also of every teacher in the school. You, seeing James for fifty minutes for five days a week, cannot possibly overcome the habits of a lifetime. You need the help of the other teachers, and you need the help of James. If you can make him ashamed of poor spelling, if you can show him that good spelling is definitely an asset, and if he is willing to *try* — then and only then can you accomplish what you should.

Students frequently write what they fondly think is "simplified spelling." You should discourage this. In the first place, simplified spelling is not so simple as the pupil imagines; in the second place, his use of it is frequently dictated by mental laziness, not by an interest in language; and in the third place, simplified spelling is not yet generally accepted by writers that set the standards. When the student finds examples of simplified spelling in such magazines as the *Atlantic Monthly* and *Harper's Magazine*, then he may use it with freedom — but not until then.

Some years ago a survey was made in the state of North Dakota regarding the achievement of the high school students of the state in the mechanics of writing. You may be interested in this study, called *Achievement of North Dakota High School Pupils in the Minimum Essentials of English with Suggested Remedial Measures*, a report of a survey conducted under the direction of the Department of Public Instruction (Bismarck, 1928), by Helen J. Sullivan. In spelling, it was found that contractions, such as *you're*, caused the most difficulty. Next in order of frequency of error were: *immediately*, *niece*, *seize*, *disappoint*. Failure to capitalize a proper adjective, such as *Latin*, also caused considerable trouble. These, and other findings, may be suggestive.

Finally, help your boys and girls to understand that a word, far from being a group of letters put together for no apparent reason, actually symbolizes an *idea*. Behind the word stands a thought. Until you examine their reading habits, you will have no conception of how meaningless to many children are the words they pronounce, so that they see nothing absurd in writing about a "dinning room" or a "shinning sun." In this, as in all your teaching, seek to arouse your pupils to the significance and potentialities of the groups of letters we call words.

ASSIGNMENT

Plan a lesson for teaching the spelling of plurals of nouns, possessive singular forms of nouns, or possessive plural forms of nouns. Include sentences for dictation.

FURTHER READINGS

1. *An Experience Curriculum in English*, Chapter XIX.

This chapter will acquaint you with the titles of several investigations made in the field of spelling, and offers a list of words which should be spelled correctly by all high school graduates.

2. *The Elementary English Review*, IV (April and June, 1927).

In this special spelling number you will find many valuable suggestions and devices.

3. WARD, C. H., *What Is English?* Chapters III and IV.

Here Mr. Ward presents what are possibly the fullest and most positive suggestions available.

4. THOMAS, CHARLES SWAIN, *The Teaching of English in the Secondary School*, Chapter XV.

Here are comments on changing material in spelling, inquiries into reasons for poor spelling, and suggestions for definite teaching procedure.

5. MIRRIELEES, LUCIA B., *Teaching Composition and Literature*, revised edition, Chapter IV, "Four Years' Growth," pp. 113–126.

The author comments on changing fashions in spelling instruction and the present indecision regarding the efficacy of rules, and makes some definite suggestions for procedure. Let me also call your attention to the "Suggested Exercises," pp. 124–126.

6. HARRISON, JUANITA, "My Great, Wide, Beautiful World," *Atlantic Monthly*, CLVII (October, 1935), pp. 434–443.

For an entertaining example of phonetic spelling, read this article.

7. PARKINSON, ETHEL, "Another Asp — Misspelling," *The English Journal*, XXXIII (April, 1944), pp. 190–195.

Correct spelling as socially desirable is here discussed.

8. HORN, ERNEST, and PETERSON, THELMA, *Spelling You Need*.

A recent text, this book attacks the spelling problem on the high school level.

9. Cross, E. A., and Carney, Elizabeth, *Teaching English in High Schools*, Chapter X, pp. 189–203.

These pages offer suggestions for teaching and testing.

10. Lee, Dorris May, and Lee, J. Murray, "Spelling Needs a Teacher," *The Elementary English Review*, XXIII (May, 1946), pp. 203–206.

Directions for a spelling program based on teacher-pupil discussion are given in this article.

VIII. PUNCTUATION: MINIMUM ESSENTIALS

I F Y O U consider that the teaching of spelling presents almost unsurmountable difficulties, I wonder what you are going to think about punctuation. For after all, a word usually is or is not correctly spelled, offering at the most two variants. But such cannot be said for punctuation. We teach our students, for example, to separate by commas the elements of an *a*, *b*, *c* series. The next day our contrary or our curiously minded pupil brings in an example, from a reputable book or magazine, in which the usage we have so carefully taught is not followed. What are we to do? Perhaps this particular violation of rule is not serious, but most of us consider that "comma-splice" sentences constitute a grave error; yet examples of these may be found in current literature. We are indeed in serious straits, as we must convince our doubting students that what we teach is preferable usage — always difficult, for the average pupil views with distrust the opinion of a teacher, particularly if it comes in conflict with something expressed on the printed page. Probably your best procedure is to admit variations in usage, but to insist that the student follow the standard rules until such time as he is an authority in his own right, when he may claim the privileges of talent. In that connection, the following paragraph written by Sam Gordon and published in the *Spokesman-Review* for October 2, 1935, although pertaining to contract bridge, offers the argument I have suggested.

> A player should first know all the standard rules. Then if he wants to dabble in the experiments of experts, he is capable of knowing what not to do. Until then, he is a chump for taking on unproven rules which are not standard; rules which are not so easy to apply in the majority of situations; rules which he and his partner cannot recognize without hesitation.

Realize, then, that you are facing a difficult problem in the teaching of punctuation. Teach definitely, concentrating on a few important points.

Punctuation is best presented, I believe, as a means of *communication*. As English is a language art, one of its main purposes lies in the sharing of ideas. If your pupils can be shown that the insertion or omission of punctuation points actually has a bearing upon the *meaning* of sentences and aids or hinders the transfer of thought from writer to reader which constitutes the main purpose of composition, they will approach the problem with an open mind. Relating punctuation to grammatical knowledge aids materially in teaching established procedures (for example, in presenting appositives, nouns of address, and subordinate clauses, teach their punctuation also); but your main emphasis should be placed on demonstrating that punctuation bears upon communication of thought. Thus punctuation is lifted from a level of memorization to an important role in expression of ideas.

As in every other phase of your composition teaching, the principle upon which punctuation is based rests upon meaning, the desire of the writer to clarify or to make impressive his thought. In oral expression, this interpretation occurs through the pause that separates one idea from its fellows; through the emphatic nod of the head, the vigorous stamp of the foot, or the shake of the finger; through play of facial expression; through the voice, capable of running the gamut of emotion. In writing, these physical means of indicating ideas are denied us; and as a result, through a number of centuries, a system of punctuation has developed — a code understandable to all readers — the careful adherence to which produces clarity and power. I believe emphasis upon the purpose of punctuation to be of more lasting value than is the memorization of rules. If you can make your pupils conscious of the fact that each punctuation point conveys to the brain, by means of the eye, a definite message; if they understand that each comma says to the reader, "Stop a second! Here's something you don't want to confuse with what's to come"; that each semicolon and each end punctuation point indicate the completion of a large unit of thought, to be separated in the mind of the reader from that following it — if you can do this, you will have an intelligent approach to this problem of punctuation. For, of course, its purposes are to clarify and to emphasize thought. Try to make the subject as reasonable as possible. Gather examples. Put several on the board and have each student write his interpretation of the meaning of the sentence. Here, for instance, is one clipped a few days ago from a daily paper: "A guardsman on duty along the San Francisco waterfront challenged a trespasser who attempted to seize his rifle." What, exactly, is the situation here? If one were to dramatize this little bit of action, when would he have the trespasser attempt to seize the guardsman's rifle? Do this sort of thing often, so that the pupil uses or omits punctuation points advisedly. In this way you will do more for him than you will by taking the time of the class in a fruitless argument of what is "right" or "wrong."

You should, then, emphasize that the purpose of punctuation is to clarify thought or to make it forceful by the separation of elements in the sentence; you should avoid too many rules, but you should insist upon accuracy in the use of those emphasized. You cannot, for instance, condone the failure to punctuate correctly compound sentences; nor can you permit a pupil to neglect an end punctuation point. If you concentrate upon those matters that develop in connection with your teaching of grammar, you will give the students an excellent working basis.

By far the most difficult, although possibly not the most important point to teach is the punctuation of restrictive and nonrestrictive clauses. I call this the most difficult, for the reason that correct punctuation of these expressions depends entirely upon interpretation; and interpretation demands both ability and willingness to think. It is possible to learn, provided one knows his grammar, the rule for the correct punctuation of an appositive, a noun of address, an introductory adverbial clause. But restrictive and nonrestrictive expressions cannot be disposed of so summarily.

I am, I believe, following Ward when I say that a restrictive clause indicates "that particular" and a nonrestrictive one indicates "in addition to." Some prefer the terms "essential" and "nonessential," pointing out that restrictive elements are essential to the meaning of the word they modify, whereas "nonessential" elements are not.   Perhaps you can help your class by saying that restrictive clauses are very closely related to the word they modify, whereas nonrestrictive clauses show less intimacy.   This, of course, accounts for the omission of commas to set off a restrictive, an essential, a closely connected clause; and the insertion of commas to separate from the rest of the sentence an additional, a nonessential, a loosely connected clause.

Whatever you say, I believe that you will gain the best results by the use of many examples of sentences containing restrictive and nonrestrictive clauses.   Emphasize clauses, rather than words or phrases; for although these latter are used restrictively and nonrestrictively, we make so few errors in them that you should not confuse the student by referring to them.   Similarly, you should limit your discussion to the punctuation of adjective and adverbial clauses, for practically all noun clauses are used restrictively.   Collect, then, sentences similar to the one I referred to a few minutes ago.   Here is another: "The Italian who had a flower in his coat smiled at me." Experiment with this sentence by inserting commas. How is the meaning changed?   Emphasize, you see, the importance of the *meaning* indicated by punctuation points.

A few years ago I read, I believe, in that very useful little publication of the **G.** and **C.** Merriam Company, *Word Study*, this device.   The incident deals with the attempted assassination of Theodore Roosevelt.   (You can show your pupils how necessary it is to distinguish, by some qualifying expression, between our two President

Roosevelts.) This device is concerned with the first one. The instructor who described it gives his class a little historical background; then he puts on the board this sentence: "At the President's New Year's reception the tenth man who had a revolver was stopped at the door." After the students have had time to study the sentence, the instructor announces, with all the dramatic force of which he is capable, "I shall now save the life of the President!" and forthwith places a comma after "man" and "revolver." Such devices as this direct the attention of the class to the change in thought caused by the insertion or omission of commas.

Probably your heaviest emphasis should be laid upon the punctuation of the compound sentence. Fortunately, most high school boys and girls place an end punctuation point of some sort after each sentence. They do not, however, always choose the correct point, sometimes putting a period after an interrogative sentence, and frequently neglecting entirely the exclamation point. This is all due, I believe, to failure to consider the *meaning* of each punctuation mark. But, at least, they usually terminate each sentence in some way or other. Such responsibility toward clauses they do not always admit. Because faulty punctuation of the compound sentence usually indicates inaccurate thought processes, you must insist upon careful punctuation of this type of sentence. The simplest and most helpful rule that I know is this: If the two parts of a compound sentence are connected by *and, but, for, or, nor,* the conjunction is preceded by a comma; if the two parts are not connected by one of these five conjunctions, the clauses are separated by a semicolon. (I am aware that there are other co-ordinating conjunctions besides those listed. However, these make an excellent working basis.) This rule *must be memorized*. If the pupil once *learns* those five conjunctions, he will have no problem in punctuating compound sentences the second part of which is introduced by *then*, *moreover*, *nevertheless*, or similar terms. He needs only to concentrate upon these five words; no others should disturb him. I am using the term *should* advisedly, for among these transitional words is that villain of the piece — the little word *so*. When placed at the beginning of an independent clause, *so*, like *then* or *nevertheless*, should be preceded by a semicolon. But as your pupils will see no necessity for doing this, you should advise them to let *so* strictly alone, unless it is followed by *that* (when it becomes a subordinating conjunction).

As you recognize, the punctuation of a compound sentence cannot be taught until you have discussed this type of sentence. Until that time you may close your eyes to "run-on" or "comma-splice" sentences, but after you have taught the compound sentence, be very strict in enforcing its correct use. By a "run-on" sentence I mean one in which the two independent clauses are not separated by any sort of mark; by a "comma-splice" sentence, one in which the two clauses are separated by a comma and not by a semicolon. Demonstrate that a semicolon indicates the end of a complete idea and promises another complete idea.

Let me interpolate here a plea that you teach your pupils the names, as well as the uses, of punctuation points. To many, a semicolon is "a comma with a dot over it," and quotation marks frequently masquerade as "parentheses." And do you suppose you can teach their spelling also?

As your purpose is to induce the student to consider

the *effect* upon the mind of the reader made by each punctuation point, you should collect examples of all sorts of sentences. Here are a few that I use: "Woman, without her man, is a failure." By a change in punctuation this may read: "Woman! Without her, man is a failure." The story goes that a superintendent, arguing one day with a teacher in regard to punctuation, used the following sentence to prove his point that punctuation is overemphasized. "Now," said he triumphantly, "here is a sentence that needs no punctuation. It is perfectly clear as it stands." The teacher looked at the words that the superintendent had written on her blackboard: "The superintendent thinks the teacher is a fool." Without comment, she added a few points of punctuation, making the sentence read: "'The superintendent,' thinks the teacher, 'is a fool.'" And further, deponent sayeth not.

Then there's the tale of the Congressman who was forced to apologize to a colleague. He did it in writing, unpunctuated, in some such way as this: "I called Mr. Jones a liar it is true I am sorry."

Tell your students that lawsuits may be won or lost because of a comma. Tell them the sad tale of the United States government, which had drafted a tariff bill designed to admit all "foreign fruit-plants," duty-free, into our country. But the bill was copied to read: "all foreign fruit, plants," etc., and for a year, until it could be amended, all foreign fruits — lemons, oranges, grapes, bananas, pineapples — were admitted duty-free, to the great indignation of our local planters.

In your teaching, then, emphasize *meaning*. Concentrate upon a few important points. Until you have taught each principle, you cannot hold your students responsible for its use; but after you have, be strict in your requirements. In theme revision, the rule violated may be copied and a number of sentences illustrating the principle may be written. A valuable exercise consists in asking students to draft a number of original sentences illustrating the principle under discussion.

As I said, the teaching of punctuation is not easy, probably because of the variations in usage that may be found in the books and magazines read by the students. It is important, then, to build up a right attitude. Do not permit yourself to be dragged into discussion. After all, you and the text must be the final court of appeal. If a student says to you, as he may, "Yes, but in such and such a class we do so and so," answer with care lest inadvertently you criticize the methods of another teacher; but consult with him, and if possible reach some point of agreement. Above all, do not reply, "Very well, do so for him, but in your English class do as I direct," for by so saying you are strengthening the unfortunate impression of many people that two standards of usage exist: one belonging to the English teacher, the other to the common man. Emphasize the principle upon which the rule is based and endeavor to show that the accepted form of punctuation best interprets the thought of the sentence, and that properly employed, it furthers communication of ideas, a basic purpose of composition.

Frequently I have suggested that you determine upon certain minimum essentials to be used as a basis for your teaching of the tools of composition. It may be well to consider, for a moment, what these are.

This principle recognizes the fact that certain rudimentary pieces of knowledge must be learned by every student before he is permitted to continue with advanced work. Now, every unsectioned class comprises three groups: those with poor background, or limited ability, or both; those with average background and ability; and those with superior background and ability. Minimum requirements are those considered desirable for all three groups. The first will probably learn no more factual knowledge than is listed in the minimum requirements; the second will acquire the minimum with comparative ease and will add to it further information; the third will learn the minimum requirements very easily and will have time and energy for much additional work.

The plan consists in establishing certain essentials that are considered to be the least that a student needs to know in order to do advanced work. A teacher should determine upon minimum requirements for each year of composition teaching. (Minimum requirements are also sometimes determined upon for the teaching of literature.) The success of this plan depends upon strict adherence to these requirements, and severe penalties for failure on the part of the student to learn and apply them. You should not be satisfied, in these, with a passing mark of seventy or seventy-five per cent. Because of the elementary nature of the requirements, you must insist upon almost perfect attainment. A few years ago I heard Mr. C. W. Washburn, then superintendent of schools at Winnetka, Illinois, tell a story that well illustrates my point. The tale goes like this. A man who was unfortunate enough to break his right shoulder consulted a physician. "What about your left shoulder? Is it all right?" asked the doctor. "Yes, there's nothing wrong with that. It's my *right* shoulder." "Anything wrong with your right elbow?" "No."

"Your left?"   "No."   "With your left knee?"   "No."
"With your right knee?"   "No."   "With your left ankle?"
"No."   "Then what have you to complain about?
You're eighty per cent perfect, aren't you?"   We can well
imagine that the patient replied, as the teacher of English
should, that only one hundred per cent perfection would
satisfy him.   As this strict accounting may cause an
administrative problem, you should consult your principal before putting such a plan into effect.

In preparing these requirements, be very careful to see
that they really are minimal and reasonable.   As you
are insisting upon perfect attainment, you must see to it
that your demands are reasonable and possible.   Furthermore, you must recognize that these represent the minimum not the maximum of attainment.   Only in the
low group should you be satisfied with a grasp of these
minimum requirements.   Both the middle and the upper
levels should accomplish far more than this.   Because
there has been a tendency to permit the minima to become
the maxima, there is today a certain amount of criticism
against this plan.   Nevertheless, properly used, you may
find the scheme desirable, and should experiment with
it.   Minimum essentials for the whole school have justified themselves, but do not sacrifice the welfare of the
child to minimum requirements.

ASSIGNMENT

A. From your reading, list ten sentences that illustrate five
of the internal punctuation points that you will teach.

B. Construct a presentation to a freshman class of one
sort of punctuation usage you will teach.

C. Report to the class on one of the references given below
that deal with minima.

FURTHER READINGS

1. WARD, C. H., *What Is English?* Chapters VIII and IX.
According to T. C. Blaisdell, these contain "probably the best discussion of punctuation in the literature of English teaching."

2. MIRRIELEES, LUCIA B., *Teaching Composition and Literature*, revised edition, Chapter IV, "Four Years' Growth," pp. 126–142.

Here are listed twenty-seven punctuation symbols essential in high school teaching, with methods for teaching them, and devices found effective. In Chapter II, pp. 59–75, the author urges the establishment of minima and presents plans for compiling them.

3. DUNSANY, LORD, "Building a Sentence," *Atlantic Monthly*, CLII (December, 1933), pp. 705–707.

Here the author discusses charmingly punctuation usage as determined by thought.

4. BLAISDELL, THOMAS C., *Ways to Teach English*, pp. 175–179; 254.

Note particularly comments on the use of the semicolon.

5. BLOORE, STEPHEN, "Motivating Grammar and Punctuation," *The English Journal*, XXIV (March, 1935), pp. 220–222.

The purpose of punctuation is here well expressed.

6. *A Manual of Style*, 10th edition (1937), University of Chicago Press, and *Style Manual of the United States Government Printing Office*, revised edition (1934), Washington, D.C.

Two standard treatises on punctuation.

7. *Stops*, with an introduction by Robert M. Gay.

Published by the Middlebury College Press, this gay little handbook is designed "for those who know their punctuation and for those who aren't quite sure."

8. SALISBURY, RACHEL, "New Roads to Punctuation," *The Elementary English Review*, XXII (April, 1945), pp. 117–123; 138.

The writer advocates teaching punctuation through reading.

9. THOMAS, CHARLES SWAIN, *The Teaching of English in the Secondary School*, pp. 73–79.

Mr. Thomas comments on the importance and growth of the minimum essentials plan, and ends with a pertinent warning: "The more important phases of English work, — interpretation, appreciation, harmonious development, regard for individual differences, — though unlisted in the inventory, are nevertheless of constant importance and must not be slighted in the endeavor to bring pupils temporarily up to a standard which will enable them to pass a superimposed objective test."

10. *An Experience Curriculum in English*, p. viii; Chapter XVIII.

This section, headed "Grade Placement," states the thought of the committee concerning attainment before a student is permitted to move on to another unit of work.

All of Chapter XVIII, "Usage," should be read with care, for this discussion of remedial work is actually a statement of minima.

11. SHOVER, ESTHER FAY, "How Much English Grammar Can High School Pupils Learn?" *The English Journal*, XXIII (September, 1934), pp. 568–575.

Here is a valuable explanation of an "intermittent, functional English grammar experiment" carried on for twelve years at the Arsenal Technical Schools, Indianapolis.

12. NEWSOME, VERNA L., "Making English Grammar Function," *The English Journal*, XXIII (January, 1934), pp. 48–58.

Here you will find formal and functional grammar contrasted and a useful "Sliding Scale of Grammar Values" presented.

IX. SENTENCES, PARAGRAPHS, WORDS

IN MY previous discussion of grammar, spelling, and punctuation I have had frequent occasion to refer to the importance of the sentence. I want to take time now for further comment.

The sentence, our smallest unit for expressing thought, is of fundamental importance, for sloppy sentence structure almost invariably indicates sloppy mental processes. Not for purely academic reasons do we object to the dangling participle. A dangling participle indicates that the user does not understand relation of ideas; his mental picture is so vague that he sees nothing absurd in saying: "Falling down the stairs, his arm was broken." Nor is it an idea of the classroom only that sentences and independent clauses must be set apart from each other. Behind every group of words is an idea, which is indicated by their relationship. Some years ago I listened to a Dean of a College of Liberal Arts in one of our well-known universities address a group of high school teachers. He urged upon us one thing. What? That we teach our students to conduct a newspaper, to write short stories, to "express themselves" by means of the familiar essay? No indeed; he asked, begged, pleaded with us that we teach them to write a sentence. To the inexperienced instructor this seems absurd, for surely *anyone* can write a sentence, but the experienced teacher shakes his head and says, "I'll try." He knows the importance of this request, and he also knows how difficult it is to comply with.

Personally, I think the sentence is best taught from the grammatical approach. I believe that any intelligent student, with the will to learn, can be taught to write a correct sentence. I believe that he can learn this best through a knowledge of the grammatical structure of a sentence. I grant you that there are writers who, as they proudly tell you, don't know a noun from a verb. But they are the exceptions, not the rank and file. And it is with the latter group that we must deal.

In your first presentation, then, attack the sentence from the grammatical point of view. Start with the simple sentence. Show your class how a sentence is built, following the suggestions made previously in this book. After they know the structure of a simple sentence, go on to the compound. Point out that this type is nothing more nor less than simple sentences combined. Give particular heed to the punctuation of the compound sentence. Then approach the well-named complex sentence. Work it out, as suggested, from the point of view of the clause. Show that the main clause is the common denominator of every type of sentence: there is one, and only one, in the simple sentence; there are at least two in the compound; and there is at least one, plus at least one subordinate clause, in a complex. (You should not teach the compound-complex sentence to all groups. Advanced groups will have no difficulty with it, but slower students will find it most confusing. Be satisfied if you can get your students invariably to recognize a complex sentence.) Now, war against the so-called "sentence fragment." If your boys and girls recognize a main clause, and if they understand that such a one is the essential element of every sentence, they should be able to overcome this very distressing habit. Consider the vague mental processes that result in the habitual use of the illiterate "sentence fragment." Consider the childlike faith that expects it to convey a thought!

During the beginning composition semesters this is all that you should do with the sentence if you have an average class. And quite enough you will find it. But in the succeeding semesters, granted this foundation, you can begin to teach the rhetorical principles of a sentence, and there the fun comes in. (Of course, if you find that your juniors or seniors lack this foundation, you must discard your plans and begin at the beginning. *Effective* sentence structure is desirable, but *correct* sentence structure is essential.)

Three rhetorical principles named in their order of importance deserve your attention. First I place the principle of *compression*. Surprisingly enough, we are accused of teaching wordiness; of encouraging, nay, requiring it. And if a teacher sets a certain number of words as a goal for theme writing, these criticisms are not far wrong. But I hope you will not do that; I hope you will discourage wordiness with all the strength that is in you. Show your students how much more effective is an idea expressed in a few well-chosen words than is the same thought clothed in verbiage. Give sentences to be reworded more directly; consider this principle always in theme marking, and have your group revise wordy sentences. "Boil it down" is excellent advice.

Some time ago I clipped from the "Contributors' Column" of the July, 1934, issue of the *Atlantic Monthly* a bit of anonymous verse sent to the editor by C. C. Hubbard.

> If you've got a thought that's happy —
> > Boil it down.
> Make it short and crisp and snappy —
> > Boil it down.
> When your brain its coin has minted,
> Down the page your pen has sprinted,
> If you want your effort printed,
> > Boil it down.
>
> Take out every surplus letter —
> > Boil it down.
> Fewer syllables the better —
> > Boil it down.
> Make your meaning plain — express it,
> So we'll know — not merely guess it.
> Then, my friend, ere you address it,
> > Boil it down.
>
> Cut out all the extra trimmings —
> > Boil it down.
> Skim it well — then skim the skimmings —
> > Boil it down.
> When you're sure 'twould be a sin to
> Cut another sentence in two
> Send it on, and we'll begin to —
> > Boil it down.

Despite the facetious tone of this bit of verse, it contains some excellent advice, which your group may profit by.

You may like to employ précis writing as a device to produce succinctness. A précis is nothing more than a summary. The plan consists of reducing the content of a somewhat long passage to a few sentences or perhaps to one sentence. The writer of a précis must include in his summary every important idea of the original, and he must use correct and effective sentence structure. This process gives excellent training in careful reading and in sentence structure, particularly if one emphasizes the one-sentence précis. The efficiency of verbals, phrases, and dependent clauses is easily demonstrable. Like all such devices, précis writing is effective only if practiced frequently. During the junior or senior composition semester, plan to use it two or three times a week. For material to be summarized, select a passage from the text you are using or from a magazine. As your class becomes proficient, have them summarize the introduction, conclusion, or discussion of a speech heard in assembly. The steps in a written précis are: (1) read with care the passage to be summarized; (2) reread, taking notes of the main ideas expressed; (3) write the précis; (4) criticize it for content and form; make any necessary changes. Many texts today include a chapter on this, or you may wish to own Mr. Samuel Thurber's *Précis Writing for American Schools*, published by the Atlantic Monthly Press, or *Reading through Précis*, by Mabel A. Bessey and Isabelle P. Coffin, published by D. Appleton-Century Company.

Next in importance to *compression* as a principle of writing, I place *relationship* of ideas as expressed in simple, compound, and complex sentences. The simple sentence contains, of course, only one principal idea. Related thoughts, however, are often expressed by means of phrases and verbals, until the simple sentence is sometimes far from being such except in its grammatical framework. You will wish to show your class the connec-

-tion in thought between the modifier and the word to which it belongs. Generally, a modifier is placed close to the word it qualifies; and always the connection must be immediately clear. Show how the meaning of a sentence may be changed by moving a modifier; emphasize the importance of compact sentence structure. As always, collect examples, such as: "The papers he then placed in her hand without a tremor." "The man possessed an income large enough to support a wife and two children of moderate means." "She planned to be married two days before her death." "I have seen slacks, one pair in one hundred, on beaches that hung perfectly and looked well." In this way, you show how the meaning of a sentence may be changed by careless placing of modifying elements, thus defeating one purpose of writing — clear expression of thought.

All that you say pertaining to the simple sentence applies to the compound, but in addition you will want to comment on the implication of the connectives used between the clauses of this type. To do this, point out the meaning indicated by each co-ordinating conjunction: *and* shows addition; *but*, contrast; *for*, reason; *or* and *nor*, alternative. Try to make your pupils choose these connectives advisedly. Perhaps an understanding of the force of the word *and* would prevent such incoherent expressions as this: "The physique of the speaker was quite impressive, and the reference he made to the Cascadian Hotel was appealing to the audience." Do the same sort of thing with relative adverbs and transitional words, such as *moreover*, *nevertheless*, *then*. Ask your students to collect from newspapers examples of such expressions and to criticize the author's choice of connective.

In dealing with the complex sentence, you have to

consider the meaning of the connective used to introduce each dependent clause. Two types introduce an adjective clause: relative pronouns and relative adverbs. Your students should know that *who* refers to persons, *which* to things, and *that* to either. They may be interested in the impersonal *that;* they may like to see the difference in effect in the use of *who* or *that.* For example, the person who likes a dog "in its place," would probably say, "I like a dog that is of some use in the world"; whereas the dog lover would seldom, if ever, so put his pet apart as to refer to him by the impersonal "that." You are teaching here the *feel* of words, not the grammar; for sometimes *who* or *that* may be used interchangeably. Relative adverbs introducing adjective clauses are likely to be either *when* or *where* and afford little difficulty; nor, indeed, do the relative pronouns in common use. Always demand exact pronoun reference.

Connectives introducing noun clauses need more attention. Be particularly concerned with the choice of word to introduce a subjective complement construction, especially in definitions: "Geography is *where* one learns of the contour of the earth." Show that *where* indicates place. Likewise, *whether* is usually preferable to *if* in a noun clause, for *if* indicates concession or condition. Collect sentences containing noun clauses and with your students study the meaning of each connective.

Particular attention will have to be given to the connectives introducing adverbial clauses, for these show the relationship of the clause to the word it modifies. *When*, of course, indicates *time; where*, *place. As* may suggest passage of time: "*as* I walked along the bridge"; or it may indicate cause: "*as* you are determined to go." *While* usually shows duration of action: "*while* you learn this conjugation." The study of the relationship conveyed by each subordinating conjunction or conjunctive adverb aids materially in *exact* expression of ideas. Such critical examination as this is both fascinating and useful.

The third rhetorical principle to emphasize is *sentence variety*. Study of the principle of compression and practice in précis writing have already given your pupils training in sentence variety. So has your discussion of relationship of ideas. But you will probably want to do something more specific than this. In current literature study sentences that are forceful or weak, and try the effect of rearranging them, of substituting a dependent for an independent clause. Ward, in his book *Grammar for Composition*, gives an excellent discussion of this. Devices that you can use are these: Make a list of sentences containing modifiers, such as: "The leaves rustle when the wind blows in the forest." Have your class arrange such a sentence in three different ways, then discuss the effectiveness of each. Dictate words or phrases and ask your pupils to use each in a sentence as an adverb or an adjective; for example, they are to use *in the night* and *with my help* first as adjective phrases, then as adverbial. After you have discussed sentence variety and the group has worked on some of these exercises, have them write a brief class theme, giving no instructions except suggested titles. When they have finished writing, have each make a list of the methods he has used to secure variety. In such ways as these you can help boys and girls to become conscious of their writing; and that, I repeat, is all that we can hope to accomplish.

One warning I should give you concerning sentence variety: It is a means toward effective expression, not an end in itself. Overattention to this produces forced, unnatural, pedantic sentence structure and should of course be avoided, for good English is usually simple English. But this is a risk you can well take, if you yourself have as your ideal the writing of correct, pleasant, and idiomatic sentences.

And what of your old friends — unity, coherence, and emphasis? Are they to be discarded? By no means, for they serve a purpose today as definitely as they did fifty years ago. But perhaps you will be wise to avoid these terms, substituting for them a constant emphasis upon logical and effective presentation of thought. For example this sentence: "The speaker was not impressive physically and made no reference to his audience" violates unity; but I doubt that you will aid your pupil to avoid this weakness in future writing by noting "unity violated" on the margin of his theme. Instead, call his attention to the meaning indicated by the conjunction *and*, showing how illogical is the juxtaposition of two such unrelated ideas as appearance and audience recognition. Again, perhaps your pupil writes: "He was a child pianist, which instrument he began to play at the age of six." Is it more constructive, do you think, for you to place the abbreviation "coh." in the margin of his paper with instructions to correct the error, or for you to question him concerning the loose grammatical structure of the sentence, with a view to indicating the practical relationship of grammar to composition? So, too, with the principle of emphasis. A recognition that the beginning and close of a sentence constitute strategic positions for important ideas (a principle I illustrate by reference to the debate coach who places his strongest debaters as first and third speakers) may be induced by such questions as: "Have you left your reader with a strong impression?'' or "Why sacrifice the most significant position in the sentence to an unimaginative word like *however?*'' Indeed, the CUE to good writing must not be neglected, but I am convinced that emphasis on the *idea* intended to be conveyed will prove of much more lasting value to the average boy or girl than will the employment of the frequently meaningless terms (to the pupil) of unity, coherence, and emphasis. Perhaps by conscious pressure you can train your pupils to avoid uttering such sentences as this, made not long since by a radio announcer: "The new dresses are causing admiring cries from all eyes at every angle." Words, words, words, indeed — and little more.

Our second unit of expression is the *paragraph.* We begin to speak in words, unconnected ideas; next we put words into sentences; then sentences into paragraphs; and finally paragraphs into a unified whole. When this last is accomplished we have "put away childish things" and are thinking as adults.

From the beginning of your teaching of composition, it is most important to stress division of thought. Your class should see that every expression of ideas — no matter how simple — falls into three parts: a beginning, a middle, and an end. As a phase of organization of material, which I shall discuss more completely in Chapter X, you must teach three types of paragraph: the introductory paragraph, the paragraph developing the thought of the writer, and the concluding paragraph.

The introductory paragraph should limit or define the subject — that is, it should state what one wants to write about and why; and it should interest the reader. By this I do not mean to suggest that an introduction is as inelastic as the formal term implies. It may be long or short, state a problem, present a setting, or suggest a mood; but every piece of writing, irrespective of type, must have a beginning by means of which the reader is introduced to the topic at hand. The paragraphs of discussion, the second division of a composition, develop the idea of the writer. Each should represent a stage in the progress of the thought; there should be at least one separate paragraph for each idea. The concluding paragraph sums up what has been said, makes a comparison, looks forward to some result, rounds out, or "clinches" the idea of the writer.

I am aware that much more can be said in regard to the paragraph; that I could suggest that you train your pupils to write different types: those developed by comparison, or contrast, or definition, or detail, or analogy. But I am not going to make such suggestions, for I doubt that we accomplish very much by this. Indeed, I think we overemphasize the paragraph as a separate unit, rather than as a step in the orderly arrangement of thought. Furthermore, I am doubtful that people write in this way. I think it highly improbable that an author says to himself "I must develop my next paragraph by detail. I used comparison in the two preceding paragraphs. I must get some variety in my writing." A writer is concerned, rather, with an expression of an *idea;* with making a thought clear and forceful. In your high school teaching you should emphasize, I believe, that each paragraph is a step leading the reader on toward a goal, and let the *method* of development take care of itself. It may be that your seniors, if they are well prepared, will enjoy working with different types of paragraphs, but you should leave such matters until late in the course.

One other type, aside from the three mentioned, you may like to use. This is the paragraph of *transition*. Somewhere in your composition teaching, probably in the junior year, you are going to need to teach devices for transitions: words, phrases, and paragraphs. The paragraph of transition should be taught last, for it is used only in compositions of considerable length, and those will be written by your junior or senior students. As a part of planning a long paper, point out the use of transitional paragraphs, examples of which may be found in current literature. Show that in this type of paragraph a writer sums up what he has said and points out its connection with what he is going to say. Such a paragraph is needed in a long, complicated discussion, but has little place elsewhere.

I should forget, then, if I were you, the academic approach to the paragraph and concentrate upon its importance as a unit of thought. "One idea to each paragraph" is excellent advice to the young writer. Insistence upon this will go far toward bringing about orderly and progressive arrangement of ideas.

A fundamental tool for the expression of thought is the *word*. It is important, therefore, that we give to our students as many as possible of these useful implements.

Vocabulary, as such, is difficult to *teach*. Like the paragraph, it is best approached indirectly, I believe, not taught as a separate subject. As you work with the sentence, as you illustrate the importance of exact expression of thought, you teach vocabulary. Try to develop in your pupils an interest in and a consciousness of words. Much of your success in this will depend upon your own knowledge and appreciation of words. You should attempt to enlarge your own vocabulary, and to choose vigorous and effective words. You must never forget, however, that simple English is always to be preferred to elaborate English. Students are inclined to laugh at pretentious speech, but they recognize the effectiveness of exact and forceful expression.

Your first responsibility, then, is to awaken the interest of your group in words, both by precept and example. But you may want to do something more definite than this. A study of Greek and Latin prefixes and suffixes is very helpful. If the text you are using does not give a list of these prefixes and suffixes, your dictionary will. You might take five a day until you have completed the list of the ordinary ones. Then list some common Greek and Latin roots and teach them as you have the prefixes and suffixes. Following this, select a number of words for analysis. If you have the necessary background, encourage your students to bring you words for analysis. At all events, develop the dictionary habit. A dictionary should be a part of your classroom equipment, so that your pupils can consult it both for meanings and pronunciations. You will have to take the time to explain to your class the significance of the diacritical markings used in their dictionary, for you must not take for granted that they understand how to interpret dictionary markings; they probably do not.

In addition to using the dictionary freely in the classroom, you can plan devices that will teach your boys and girls what information there is in the dictionary and how to find it. The G. and C. Merriam Company, publishers of *Webster's Dictionary*, will send you, on request, several valuable pamphlets that will help you to teach the use of the dictionary. Failing those, you can do such things as giving to your pupils a list of words, such as *Red Cross*, *propaganda*, *Civil Service*, *Theodore Roosevelt*, *Mesopotamia*, *metric system*, *carpe diem*. Consult the dictionary used in your institution and compile a list that will force your students to examine its different sections. Have them make reports, either written or oral, on their findings. And as a part of your avowed intent to co-operate with other departments, include words pertaining to subjects outside the English curriculum. A short chat with the science teacher will perhaps result in your adding to your list *pisces*, *primates*, *reptilia;* the history teacher may suggest *Boer*, *Bolshevik*, *Celtic*, *dynasty*, and the distinction between *Plato* and *Pluto*. These words, and others, have interesting histories.

The following little tests may prove suggestive. A copy of the first should be given to each pupil, with instructions to consult his dictionary and bring to class the following day the answer to each question. During the next class period fifteen minutes should be allotted to the second form, a speed test. Before adopting these, consult the dictionary used by your pupils to ascertain that every word included actually is in their dictionary. For example, *vers libre* may be found in the third edition of *Webster's Collegiate Dictionary* but not in the fourth, the English term "free verse" having supplanted the French — an interesting evidence of how rapidly the dictionary adjusts itself to speech habits.

Test I

In the blank spaces at the left, write the numbers of the pages in the dictionary adopted by your school on which the following questions are answered.

—— 1. What does Mar. stand for?

—— 2. What does the Scottish word *beuk* mean?

—— 3. Between what countries lies the Gulf of Bothnia?

—— 4. What does I.O.O.F. stand for?

—— 5. What temperature is used in the pasteurization of liquids?

—— 6. Who was Fatima?

—— 7. When is *f* or *fe* changed to *ve* when a plural is being formed?

—— 8. Is Mary Roberts Rinehart married?

—— 9. How many people had the state of Washington in 1920?

—— 10. What does *cherchez la femme* mean?

—— 11. How many masts has a brig?

—— 12. How long is a fathom?

—— 13. How is *ll* pronounced in Spanish?

—— 14. How long is the Bzura River?

—— 15. How many English words rhyme with *camp*?

—— 16. What does the name Hiram mean?

—— 17. What was the hegira?

—— 18. Who invented Ro?

—— 19. Who was Simon Bolivar?

—— 20. How many presidents of the United States were there before Lincoln?

TEST II

(Fifteen minutes of class time allotted for this)

In the blank spaces at the left, write the numbers of the pages on which the following questions are answered.

—— 1. What were the Moabites?

—— 2. How is *ch* pronounced in Spanish?

—— 3. What is philately?

—— 4. What is coral?

—— 5. What is the meaning of "wanderlust"?

—— 6. What does the name "daisy" mean?

—— 7. What is the meaning of Litt.D.?

—— 8. At what temperature does pure water boil?

—— 9. Who wrote the famous song *Dixie?*

—— 10. Who was Joseph Smith?

—— 11. What words rhyme with *dunce?*

—— 12. Is the copperhead a poisonous snake?

—— 13. When did John Donne die?

—— 14. In what country is Mandalay?

—— 15. How much did the United States pay for Alaska?

—— 16. Where was the original home of the Seminole Indians?

—— 17. What three knights achieved the quest of the Holy Grail?

—— 18. What city was built on seven hills?

—— 19. After whom is the month of July named?

—— 20. In what constellation is the Dipper?

Among devices finding favor with teachers are student-prepared tests. The authors of the textbook, *Working with Words and Ideas*, suggest that a class committee select words beginning with each letter in the alphabet and prepare a multiple-choice definition test; for example: *abdicate:* dictate, give up, dedicate, go away. In *Scholastic* for September 25, 1939, you will find a vocabulary test prepared by Gretta Baker, in which this question is asked: Are you a Mrs. Malaprop? (In connection with this, read to your students from Sheridan's play *The Rivals*.) The student is asked to correct sentences in which words are amusingly misused, as in: "The inn is built on a high promissory overlooking the river." Your boys and girls could compile similar sentences, utilizing words recently added to their vocabulary.

Perhaps your pupils might enjoy preparing a glossary of words peculiar to a certain field, possibly the one of their major interest. Some amusing contrasts may develop, for your girls, interested in home economics, may explain "seam" in an entirely different way from the definition presented by boys concerned with geology. To illustrate the definition, the word should be used in an original sentence and in sentences taken from newspapers and magazines. Following professional procedure, the amateur lexicographers may include cartoons or diagrams. Such a glossary may well develop into an important class project.

A particularly interesting device, in my opinion, consists of translating passages into Basic English. The experience of putting ideas, often figuratively expressed, into a vocabulary of 850 words serves to emphasize the breadth and vigor of our native tongue.

Games of various sorts are frequently recommended. One teacher, Mr. G. B. Feldman, prepared a vocabulary "Bingo," using words-to-be-learned instead of numbers. Other teachers suggest experimenting with rebus, or picture writing; with making and solving crossword puzzles; with anagrams; with a variation of anagrams, in which new words are formed by adding a specified letter, such as *grade* $+ r = regard$. Use your ingenuity and that of your students to adapt old "parlor games" and new ones to the procedure of the English classroom.

Because of the close relationship of vocabulary to reading of all sorts — developmental, remedial, and recreational — you will want to try to develop an interest on the part of your pupils in their own vocabularies. A little study of the size of their active and passive vocabulary may be made by following these suggestions given in *Working with Words and Ideas*. Ask your pupils to select at random one page from each one hundred in their dictionary. On each page selected, ask them to read quickly down the list of main words and count those they actually use in speech or writing. Then tell them to add the numbers of words on the various pages they have chosen and multiply the sum by 100. The product will be a rough estimate of the number of words in their active vocabulary. To find the extent of their passive vocabulary, they should count the words that they recognize but do not use, and multiply the sum by 100.

Somewhat to our chagrin, we teachers frequently discover that discarded methods actually have some merit after all. A procedure recently released from limbo is the teaching of phonics. Today high school instructors are teaching the sounds of individual letters and diphthongs, ordinary initial sounds and word endings; accent; and syllabication. Boys and girls — and older students, too — often skip over a word in reading or refuse to employ it in speaking because they cannot pronounce it. Some attention to phonics in your classroom will afford pupils a key to pronunciation and will enable them to increase their vocabulary. Incidentally, I am convinced that an understanding of phonics will also help to overcome poor spelling habits. If you wish advice and help, consult an elementary school teacher. Many methods employed by elementary teachers have a place on the high school level, and you will do well to recognize this fact and glean from the experience of others.

To be effective, as we have stressed, teaching must be related to need. In addition, any type of learning which is somewhat mechanical requires a considerable amount of drill. Applying these principles to training in an effective vocabulary, you will readily understand that games, formal drills, and any other methods will be futile unless they deal with words required for the everyday needs of your boys and girls within and without the classroom, and unless they are frequently and regularly reviewed. No one can make a word really *his* simply by looking it up in a dictionary. He must understand it, practice using it, and savor it before it becomes a part of himself.

In Chapter X, "Theme Writing," and in Chapter XXI, "Reading: Your Problem," you will find further suggestions for enlarging the vocabulary. But better than all the devices is the development of a critical attitude on the part of your boys and girls. This you must build up gradually by attention to your own speech, by the comments you make on papers written by your students, by bringing to their attention examples of effective or ineffective diction. Be ever on the alert. Ask constantly: Does this word express your idea? Is this accurate? Why overuse this? Is this definite, specific? Why select such a meaningless word as *thing* to indicate your idea? Teach your group to avoid trite, overworked words or phrases. Show them how the overuse of words clouds the meaning intended by the writer. Above all, teach them that a word is merely a symbol for an *idea*. Back of every word should stand a thought. The more definite and clear the idea, the more definite and clear will be its expression.

ASSIGNMENT

A. Prepare a plan for teaching some phase of compression, relationship of ideas, or sentence variety. State for what class this lesson is designed, your approach to the topic, and the explanation you would make to your group.

B. Your instructor will select a paragraph for which you will prepare a one-sentence précis.

C. Prepare a synopsis of Chapter VII, "The Paragraph," in *On Teaching English* (American Book Company), by Howard F. Seely.

FURTHER READINGS

1. Mirrielees, Lucia B., *Teaching Composition and Literature*, revised edition, Chapter III, pp. 90–105.

Here is explained how grammar functions in securing sentence variety. Why not develop (mentally, at least) a number of the "Suggested Exercises" at the end of this chapter? Also on pages 86–90 you will find devices for vocabulary drill. And will you please note her comment on thinking of high school pupils as "children"?

2. Ward, C. H., *Grammar for Composition*, Part I.

Here you will find much helpful strategy for teaching sentence structure. Consider particularly the plan for warring against *so*.

3. Parker, Roscoe Edward, *The Principles and Practice in Teaching English*, Chapter X, "Teaching Sentence Patterns," pp. 140–153.

The relation of psychological principles to the teaching of English is here discussed.

4. Mirrielees, Lucia B., *Teaching Composition and Literature in Junior and Senior High School*, revised edition, "Teach Logical Sequence," p. 190.

On this page you will find listed four steps in paragraph analysis.

5. Cross, E. A., and Carney, Elizabeth, *Teaching English in High Schools*, Chapter XIII, "Developing the Longer Composition," pp. 290–296.

Examples of paragraph types and a comment on transitions are given here.

6. Strong, Ruth, "Levels of English," *The English Journal*, XXIV (September, 1935), pp. 577–579.

This provides suggestions for discussion of formal speech, ordinary English, slang, and bad grammar, as well as giving a plan for an assembly program.

7. Richardson, C. B., "Elegy for a Dying Tongue," *Scribner's Magazine*, XCVIII (August, 1935), pp. 120–122.

This will delight your older pupils who long to follow the sea.

8. HITCHCOCK, ALFRED, *Bread Loaf Talks on Teaching Composition*, pp. 60–90.

"Lords of the Word" is as ringing a challenge as the title indicates.

9. DUNSANY, LORD, "Decay in Language," *Atlantic Monthly*, CLVII (March, 1936), pp. 360–362.

Writing with his usual charm, the author sounds a warning that teachers should heed.

10. *Words*, "a monthly publication devoted to the origin, history, and etymology of English words," published at 808 South Vermont Avenue, Los Angeles, California, contains material of interest to you and your class.

11. CLARKE, MARY VIRGINIA, "The Making of a Dictionary." *A Pageant*.

This may be obtained free by writing the G. and C. Merriam Company, Springfield, Massachusetts.

12. Write to the G. and C. Merriam Company, Springfield, Massachusetts, asking that your name be placed on their mailing list in order that you may receive that invaluable monthly leaflet called "Word Study," edited by Max J. Herzberg.

13. GRISMER, FRANK A., "Good Set Phrases," *The English Journal* (college edition), XXIII (1934), p. 329.

Here are noted many trite phrases in general use.

14. CROSS, E. A., and CARNEY, ELIZABETH, *Teaching English in High Schools*, Chapter VI, "Basic English," pp. 94–108.

Here you will find a discussion of Basic English, the vocabulary of 850 words, and examples.

15. FELDMAN, G. B., "Vocabulary Bingo for Remedial Reading Classes," *High Points*, XXIII (May, 1941), pp. 75–76.

Directions for playing the game and an account of its value are given.

16. JENKINS, M., "Vocabulary Development: A Reading Experiment in the Seventh Grade," *Peabody Journal of Education*, XIX (May, 1942), pp. 347–351.

This gives practical suggestions.

X. THEME WRITING

Not long ago a writer of several successful books said to me that nothing he had studied in his composition classes, either in high school or in college, had aided him in the least in the writing which has played such an important part in his adult life. A theme, to him, he said, was merely something to be done to satisfy the demands of his teacher and had no bearing upon the activities in which he, as a student, was engaged or upon his occupation as an adult.

Now, if this is true (and I hasten to say that I believe he learned more than he is cognizant of), we cannot justify our composition courses; for whatever we teach should have a bearing upon human needs. Perhaps the fault lies, not so much in what he was taught (for I insist he learned *something*), as that he, and possibly his teachers too, had no clear conception of what a theme is, had made no attempt to connect "theme writing" with everyday use.

Now, what is a theme? Is it a piece of writing, so many words in length, ground out at the behest of a tyrant enthroned in the teacher's chair? Or is it a piece of writing in which is set down, for the author's own pleasure and for that of others, his ideas, opinions, information, and, possibly, his emotions? Or is it an exercise, pure and simple, in which he puts into practice the principles of composition learned from his text and workbook? That there exists no unanimity of opinion regarding this, articles published in our professional magazines and comments made by a group of teachers "talking shop" bear witness. Yet, manifestly, before we can tell others how to write, we — and they — must know what is being attempted.

In my own thinking, I first use the "elimination" method: to me a theme is not a "literary composition." Perhaps I feel too strongly about this, but my teaching experience has shown me that many boys and girls have been falsely encouraged by a teacher, misled possibly by a certain fluency passing for originality, to think themselves geniuses; whereas their ideas are mediocre and their expression trite, insincere, and even faulty. Such people are fair game for promoters promising to produce short story writers in five lessons. Our place is to encourage talent in the rare souls in whom we find it, but to discourage literary ambitions impossible of realization. Consideration of a theme as an attempt at a literary masterpiece leads to this false, even dangerous, point of view. Furthermore, as our purpose is to prepare our pupils for future living, we are not justified in insisting upon literary writing, as a very small per cent undertake this type in later life.

Nor do I subscribe to the opposite pole: that a theme is merely an exercise, designed for the practice of grammatical and rhetorical principles. Although this may produce mechanically perfect papers, it is deadening to initiative and smothering to expression of thought.

Indeed, I have been somewhat perturbed lately at a tendency observable in some teachers to consider training in grammar as synonymous with instruction in composition and therefore to be taught by means of a workbook. Desirable as is a knowledge of grammar, it should no more be considered as the whole of composition than should the nose, important as that appendage is, be thought of as the face.

In almost everything, except walking down a busy street, the middle way is probably best. To me, then, a theme is a piece of writing arising from the need of self-expression and communication. Under the first come all sorts of writing involving personal elements: narratives, descriptions, arguments, some kinds of exposition, friendly letters. Belonging to the second are the utilitarian types of writing: business letters, reports, minutes of a meeting. Both have a place in our everyday needs, deserving, therefore, equal emphasis. To be successful in self-expression and in communication, a writer must give heed to his arrangement of material and to his diction, from the point of view of both clarity and effectiveness. This conception of a theme ties up with your aim for written composition: to express ideas with clarity and some degree of effectiveness. Through wise and sympathetic direction you can lead your pupils to the knowledge that within the experience of each exists much that is interesting, significant, and helpful to others. That these experiences fail in effectiveness if they are not planned with care and expressed with correctness should be easily demonstrable. And that practice enhances proficiency can surely be understood by the runner who spends months in preparation for a single event, by the girl who makes biscuits again and again before achieving perfection, by the 4H Club member who breeds his cows for increased milk production.

If, as a high school student, the iconoclast mentioned in the first paragraph had been shown that his writing was for the purpose of communicating his ideas, or for giving him training in "everyday writing"; if he had understood that the principles of organization, grammatical correctness, accurate and effective sentence structure, living punctuation, blameless spelling — all constituted his tools for expression in other courses and for his present and future needs outside the classroom; if this connection had been made for him, surely he would not look back upon "composition courses" as a waste of time. To justify our existence, we teachers of composition must ourselves understand the purpose of training in the expression of ideas and the transfer of them from writer to reader.

Before continuing our discussion, let me pause for a moment to comment on the word heading this chapter: "theme." In these remarks, I am using it merely as a matter of convenience. But it is a dull, drab word, an inexact one, with, I fear, a disagreeable connotation to your pupils. Avoid it, then, in your teaching, substituting for it a more definite term, such as discussion, reaction, criticism, narration, comment, description, paper, report, argument, letter, exposition. In this way, you not only indirectly teach precision in words, but you also connect composition with everyday experience; for who ever sat down to write a "theme" to a friend or to order a bathing suit or a catcher's mitt?

Perhaps your first responsibility in this matter of theme writing is to develop a co-operative attitude toward it. You might begin by having your class make an inventory, informal, of course, of their writing needs at present and their possible requirements in the future. Some will use this form of expression more than will others, but all will do *some* writing. The usefulness of composition having been established, you have done much to develop a responsive mood. Your next step is to show (and this may be done similarly) that only a few of us write for ourselves alone; that almost always there is someone who reads what we have written: the salesman who fills our order, the teacher who reads our paper, the friend who receives our letter. Looking to the future, we observe the same: a newspaper reporter writes for the reading public; so does the editor, the sports writer; the poet for the poetry lovers; the novelist for fiction readers. The engineer makes his report for his superior or for publication in his professional magazine; the salesman contributes to his trade journal; the grange leader puts into print his opinion concerning the policies of the Department of Agriculture. Almost all writing, either for our pupils' present or future use, unless it be a diary, is written for someone else.

In your teaching of a theme you should build on these motivating elements: self-expression and communication. Let us consider now the more subjective element — self-expression. If you should use this term in your class, you would immediately antagonize them. They would jump to the conclusion that you intend to make them literary artists and would close their minds to your suggestions. Keep this term to yourself, then, but let it color your class procedure. Encourage your boys and girls to write of themselves, for, at its best, writing puts into words something of importance to the author: an experience (perhaps of no greater moment than a picnic), a careful analysis of opinion, a poignant expression of emotion, a vivid bit of description. In reply to a commendatory comment of mine, a student once wrote, in reddest ink, "Of course, I felt it myself." This inner glow will not alone produce good writing, but, guided and controlled, it is the basis of effective utterance. Thus you seek to draw out and strengthen the "inner man" and develop attitudes, for nothing so clarifies thinking as the setting down of ideas in writing. In this way you stimulate mental curiosity and imagination, without which Jack is a very dull boy indeed. Here lies your opportunity to arouse (not dictate) a critical yet sympathetic attitude in your boys and girls toward opinions and ideas of others. Truly creative, subjective writing deserves your encouragement, for from it your pupils grow into fuller and more complete manhood and womanhood. It differs from literary or professional writing in that it accords with the interests and activities of the pupil himself and that it lies within the capabilities of every boy and girl.

But, unless you want to produce a whole nation of people "talking to themselves," you must show the importance of the tools for the transfer of thoughts previously discussed; how attention to established usage in grammar, punctuation, spelling, and sentence structure is for one purpose: to make clear, without a shadow of a doubt, what we are trying to say. How necessary is the orderly arrangement of ideas, not perhaps for ourselves but for others, is also easily proved. This possible reader must be visualized and his attention aroused and retained. If these aspects of a theme are kept in mind by pupil and teacher, theme writing should have sufficient practical value to commend it to the advocates of the utilitarian philosophy, as well as to satisfy those who seek to awaken their pupils to the possibilities within them.

It is not enough to know what a theme is; the conscientious teacher will understand that each paper written constitutes a step toward the goal of good writing. Add to your general purpose, then, of helping your boys and girls to increase in wisdom and understanding a particular problem for each theme assignment — perhaps the logical arrangement of ideas, or effective sentence patterns, or descriptive writing. Whatever this objective is, let it be clear to your pupils, for nothing is more confusing than working without a sense of direction. And a second principle grows out of the first: always tie up theme writing with the elements of composition you have taught. Having discussed, let us say, verbals, encourage their use. To assign a paper in which a certain number of verbals must be included may be overly pedantic procedure; but you can comment upon their value and suggest their use. Furthermore, you can point out in your criticisms on each theme certain sentences which would be improved by this device. Nothing, I believe, results so unfortunately for our boys and girls as to receive the impression that the skills taught them have no bearing upon writing. Once taught, a principle should be applied, and that your class should understand.

The foundation of all successful writing is careful planning. Because logical organization demands careful thought, you must help your students to see that the first step in writing is thinking. After a writer decides upon a subject, he must determine upon his point of view: whether he is going to approve or disapprove, whether he is going to explain, narrate, or describe. Next, he must determine upon a few points pertinent to his subject; then he must bring his remarks to a logical conclusion. This matter of *thinking before writing* leads directly to what may be called the composition process. You may wish to give the steps in this process to your advanced classes very much as I am giving them to you. For younger pupils, emphasize the limitation of subject, the organization of material, the writing of the theme, and the revision of it. The composition process, then, as I see it, is as follows:

First, it is necessary to select a subject about which to write, one of interest to the writer and therefore presumably to the reader. After the subject has been selected, it must be limited, reduced in such a way that it can be discussed in a few paragraphs. This point can hardly be overemphasized. Too many students think that "Music," "Mining," "Literature," or even "Anglo-Saxon Literature" are satisfactory subjects for a paper. The fact that music has been known among all peoples and in all ages, that it is a highly technical subject, does not occur to the pupil unless you point it out. Ask him to limit this subject to "Why I Enjoy . . ." or "Why I Am Studying Music," and he will have something about which he can write. The subject, then, must be limited and defined.

The next step is to gather material, which may come from several sources: (1) from one's own experience, (2) from that of others, (3) from conversation with others, (4) from thought, and (5) from reading. Any, or all, of these methods may be used. Of them, the last is the least valuable for high school students. Please do not think, because I say this, that I consider reading of little good to high school boys and girls — far from it; but it is very difficult for a secondary school pupil to consider his reading as a *basis* for his writing. He is inclined to utilize what he has read as his own without due regard to sources or their proper documentation. Until he is sufficiently mature to be able to adopt the written words of others and use them to strengthen his own ideas, not as a substitute for them, he should be discouraged from deliberately gathering material for themes from his reading.

You will want to point out to your class that, with the exception of the last method, much of this gathering of material is done informally. As one walks back and forth to school, as he dresses in the morning, he can be thinking of experiences of his own or of others; at the dinner table he can induce his family to discuss the topic about which he is to write; and when he is entirely alone, he can formulate and weigh his own ideas. Composition begins long before a person sits at his desk with paper and ink before him, a truth which your pupils should learn.

Next comes the organization of the material. The preliminary planning and arranging is very important and should not be hurried. As a part of this process, the possible readers should always be kept in mind — their interests, background, age, experiences, education being determinative factors in selection or rejection of material.

The organized theme consists of three divisions: introduction, body (or discussion), and conclusion. As has been pointed out previously, the introduction of any piece of composition arranges the stage, so to speak, and seeks to interest the reader in what the writer has to say. The body of the paper discusses the subject under a few important heads. The conclusion summarizes, suggests action, points to a future policy, clinches a narrative, or completes a description. Always it comes as the logical result of what has been brought out in the body of the paper. In order to emphasize these three divisions of a composition, you should require an outline to be handed in with each theme. (I am aware, of course, that certain students will write the paper first and the outline second. At first glance, this practice seems to defeat one's purpose. But, although it is not desirable and should be strongly discouraged, this plan is not entirely devoid of worth; that is, if the pupil checks the outline with the paper. There remains some value to him in making the outline conform to the material in the composition, so that his effort is not entirely wasted. If you are greatly disturbed by this possible abuse of the outline, you can require that it be submitted before the paper is written. Except for a long and formal paper, however, I think you should not do this. It doubles the work for you and detracts from the spontaneity of the writer.) Outlines vary, of course, in form. Some authors take slips of paper and on each write the point to be discussed. Then these slips are shifted about until the points are arranged in the best climactic order. Others prefer to use a rough outline, crossing out and writing in the points. Some method must be used so that the writer has before him in outline form the material to be used in his introduction, body, and conclusion. Such a preview is analogous to a railway trip across the continent. Even before one starts, he knows his destination and the routes he must traverse to reach his goal.

During your teaching of composition, you will probably want to give your students practice in the four kinds of discourse: narration, description, exposition, and argument. Each of these requires an outline, somewhat like the following samples:

Outline for Narration

1. How it began.
2. Important happenings leading to the main happening.
3. The most important happening.
4. The result of the most important happening.

In this outline for a narrative (for which I am, I believe, indebted to Ward) you will note the absence of technical terms; yet you will see that the necessary exposition is provided for in the first point, that rising action in the second is indicated, that the third is actually the climax, and that the fourth is the conclusion. You will also observe that although the words *introduction*, *body*, and *conclusion* are not used, the outline falls into these divisions. If you insist that your class write a paragraph for point one; a paragraph for each happening listed in point two; and one each for points three and four, the result will be a well-planned narrative. As narration is often the principal type of beginning writing, you will find a simple, nontechnical outline such as this very desirable.

Another outline for a narrative (the plan of which comes from *Writing Craftsmanship*, revised edition, by Maurice Garland Fulton, and the development from a student theme) is the following:

An Automobile Mishap

(*Preliminaries*)

Johnny and I arrive at Lewiston, Idaho, and are met by our grandfather.

(*Incident Proper*)

I. We begin the trip, progress five miles, and have an accident.

II. My personal feelings and grandfather's concern.
III. Helpful motorists drive Johnny and me up the hill and
     we find our injuries to be scratches and bruises.
IV. We arrive home, and grandfather tells of the damage
     to the car, while we look to the damages to ourselves and
     clothing.

(*Results*)

   I dread the thought of an accident, and grandfather ceases
to drive a car.

   Two types of outline for description will prove valuable.
This form of discourse, by the way, often affords an
escape from the "thin writing" so distressing to teachers.
The first may be used to describe the emotional effect
produced by an activity, a place, or a thing; the second
applies best to the description of the characteristics of
a person.

OUTLINES FOR DESCRIPTION

I.

Subject	Moment	Impression	Concrete Details
Haying	Before the storm	Intense heat	Sweat running into eyes; hay scratching blistered necks; dog's tongue hanging out; air shimmering in distance; blue sky with thunderclouds.

II.

1. The first I knew of him.
2. Finding out what sort he is.
3. The way he treats people.
4. An anecdote to show why I admire him.

To whom I am indebted for the first outline I cannot say. I have used it for years, with good effect, not only as a framework for the writing of descriptions, but also as a guide in analyzing descriptions found in the works of skilled writers. For the second, Ward is, I believe, again responsible.

For expositions — the type of writing most useful to all of us and therefore to be stressed — an outline similar to the following may be used. You note the statement of theme and the careful analysis of material.

Patriotism Names the Baby

Theme: During the pre-Revolutionary and Revolutionary periods in our country, personal names of babies were frequently chosen from patriotic motives.

Introduction: Personal names in early America reflected patriotic attitudes.

I. In the pre-Revolutionary period, parents named babies for British or European patriots.
   A. John Wilkes and Oliver Cromwell
   B. Pascal Paoli

II. As feeling against Britain intensified, babies were named for Revolutionary patriots.
   A. For the statesman, John Hancock
   B. For military leaders
      1. George Washington
      2. John Warren and others

Conclusion: This practice of the pre-Revolutionary and Revolutionary periods indicated patriotic attitudes of parents.

The outline for a simple argument is similar to that used in exposition, except that the conclusion may be an appeal, instead of a summary. In formal debate, a *brief* is used. Forms for this specialized type may be found in any textbook that discusses debate. The following is an outline for a simple argument:

CELERY VS. SAGEBRUSH

Purpose: To convince the reader that no more arid land in the West should be put under irrigation at the present time.

I. *Introduction:* Much land has been put under irrigation in the last few years.
II. *Development:*
    A. Irrigated land in the West produces only a few crops.
    B. A limited amount of the produce can be consumed.
    C. The demand increases slowly.
III. *Conclusion:* No more land should be put under irrigation until there is a market for the produce.

It will help your pupils in clear thinking if you point out how a "key word" is carried throughout in a good outline. It or a derivative usually appears in the title, statement of purpose or theme, the introduction, the main points in the discussion, and the conclusion. For example, in "Patriotism Names the Baby," note that the words "patriotism," "patriot," and "patriotic" are used throughout.

As a part of organization stress with your pupils the necessity of affording "thought guides" to the reader (technically known as "transitions"). Accurate pronoun reference, agreement of subject and verb, indications of change in place and time, employment of such expressions as "therefore," "hence," and "in addition," all offer clues to the reader. You can hardly overemphasize the fact that because your pupils write, almost invariably, for someone else to read, they have a responsibility to the reader to lead him unobtrusively but firmly from point to point. When the pupil accepts this concept, he will see the *purpose* in such abstractions as pronoun reference and transitional expressions.

The fourth step is the actual writing of the theme and this, I think, should be done quickly, while the person is eager to express what he has to say. Encourage your pupils to write rapidly, putting off for some future time any consideration of mechanical matters or form.

After this comes the fifth step — the revision of the paper — and next to the actual writing, the most important. Preferably, it should be done a day or two after the paper is written. This means that you should make your assignments far enough ahead so that the student can think out his topic, gather his material, write his paper, and lay it away for a considerable length of time. When he gets it out, he will be far enough away from the actual writing to consider it somewhat as he might the work of a stranger to whom he had no great responsibility. As impersonally as possible, he should go over each sentence with care, applying the principles of writing *that you have taught* and making the necessary corrections. Reading aloud is an invaluable aid to revision.

After revision comes the sixth and last step — the careful copying of the paper according to the directions you have given.

Such is the composition process. For younger pupils it should be simplified, although no part of it should be eliminated. Older students can put into practice each phase discussed.

The emphasis placed upon revision has probably suggested to you the matter of the *length* of themes. When your students ask you concerning length, as they will, say to them, "How do I know? How can I tell how much information you have on your subject? That is for you to decide; only be certain to analyze your subject carefully and to *finish* it." Personally, I think suggestions such as these are of far more value than is the setting of a certain number of *words* as a goal for a theme. Emphasis upon words is false; it causes the pupil to be more concerned with number of words than with ideas. Despite this, I do not condemn entirely the assignment of a paper of an approximate number of words. Especially with advanced classes, this gives training in compression. It is particularly valuable in news writing. But in general, tell your students to "finish the subject."

All papers should be short enough so that the pupils have time to revise carefully before handing in their work. This applies to class themes, as well as to assigned papers. Furthermore, the class that you are teaching must be considered. Usually beginners or poorly prepared upperclassmen may well be limited to a three- or a five-paragraph theme: one paragraph of introduction; one, two, or three paragraphs of discussion (a paragraph for each point made); and a paragraph of conclusion.

The *number* of themes to be required depends upon several factors. In the first place, your school may have a set number of themes to be written during each semester. If so, you must adhere to the regulations of your school. In the second place, your requirements must depend, to a certain extent, upon the time at your disposal for paper correction. Every theme written by a student deserves and should have the careful reading of the teacher, for it is worse than useless to require the writing of themes unless you correct them with care. In the third place, the *preparation* of the class for writing may dictate the number of themes to be written. Bad habits of speech may be perpetuated by writing; in my opinion, then, it is useless — in fact, it may be actually detrimental — to require writing before you have taught principles. This may mean that you will not start theme writing with beginning students until you have taught the fundamental requirements of a sentence — the verb and its subject. This may also mean that you will have to put off theme writing with a senior class until you have reviewed the elements of sentence structure. Whenever possible, the mastery of principles should precede writing. But, as old Squeers of Dotheboys Hall used to say, "The way to learn a thing is to do it." The way to learn to write *is* to write; there is no way to teach composition without requiring the writing of themes and without the correcting of papers. Demand, then, as much writing as is permitted by the preparation of the students and by your strength to correct.

A very important part of theme writing is the assignment, for in this you define your objectives for the theme and you seek to interest your class in writing it. To plan your assignment with great care and to explain it carefully constitute major responsibilities. As a rule, it should be given at the beginning of the period, so that you will have time to outline it clearly and will not be forced to shout, as your class rushes to the door, "Oh, yes! Write a theme for Monday!"

Always the assignment should arouse interest. Your own personality and enthusiasm will go far toward exciting enthusiasm on the part of your students, but I have a few definite suggestions to make.

1. Read to your class an article that is controversial, and discuss it with them. When interest is aroused, say:

"Very well. Write your ideas on this subject. Have your paper ready by Tuesday." In discussing a controversial subject, use care in selecting the article to be read, avoid any subject that might be offensive to your particular group, and use tact in commenting upon it. Consider the point of view of the community in which you are teaching. As a teacher, you may have the *right* to be an individual; but you should use good sense in expressing your opinions. In fact, this type of approach to an assignment may be used more safely with older than with younger pupils, who often lack sufficient judgment to interpret what is said.

2. Tell the class an incident that interested you. Ask each member to write a similar one. This is a good type of assignment for junior high school students. Much of its success depends upon your ability to tell a story effectively. Among the many qualifications of the good teacher of English is undoubtedly that of being a raconteur. We sometimes think that such are born, not made; nevertheless, you may be surprised at your storytelling powers!

3. Discuss the nationality of the persons in your class. Ask each member to write an account of a favorite family custom or tradition. Although this often results in very interesting papers, it may, unless handled very tactfully, be provocative of trouble. There are certain racial or national groups to which, for various reasons, persons feel ashamed to belong. This is particularly true of the sensitive adolescent. If this condition exists in your class, make your discussion general and not particular.

4. Read a good student theme and ask for a paper on a similar subject. Like all the other suggestions made,

this one also carries with it a warning. Your pupils will write more freely for you if they believe that they are writing confidentially. You will be surprised how frankly they will discuss their ideals, aspirations, hopes, and failures, *if they know they can trust you*. But, if their paper is to be public property, if it is read to the group without their consent, you will dam that stream of free expression and will get only stale and stagnant results. Select with care a paper to be read in class and *always ask the consent of the writer*.

5. Call attention to exhibits in local shop windows and ask for a description of a particularly pleasing exhibit. Often a community is celebrating a certain period in its history. Exhibits then offer excellent material for writing. An old breechloader will suggest to some boy the history of the rifle; an Indian headdress will produce a description of its elaborate construction or an account of the Indians living in the community at present or of the Indian history of the past. Exposition, narration, description, argument — any or all of these forms of writing may result from a study of local exhibits. Furthermore, this sort of thing tends to connect the school with the community.

6. Read a description and analyze it according to the first outline given on page 155. Write a similar description.

7. Both radio and moving pictures afford theme material that should not be neglected. Those showing life in pioneer days may lead to the retelling of pioneer tales, experiences of local "old timers," or biographies. Some advertisers hint at the romance of the tea industry — a topic capable of division into many fascinating theme subjects. Accounts of experiences abroad may lead to a

desire for foreign travel — on paper. The many excellent musical programs heard over the air afford valuable suggestions. Equally productive are the better moving pictures, with their portrayals of historical events and their dramatizations of literary masterpieces. Class comment on radio and movies will often lead to lively theme writing.

8. Particularly fertile is the field of periodicals. Let me quote from an advertisement appearing in *Time Magazine* for August 26, 1935, for the pamphlet *Letters*. Note the arresting title, the provocative opening. Read to a class, this should produce the kind of "personal letter that makes you sit up."

Did You Ever Spend a Night in the Post Office?

Imagine yourself, overcome with curiosity, slipping into the New York Post Office at night with a lantern and a paper knife.

Dodging the guards and night shift you rip open a mail sack, slit the first envelope, and begin a night's reading.

You begin to doze with dozens of drab business notes, scores of personal letters of the "having fine time, wish you were here" school. Then you strike a personal letter that makes you sit up. It's absorbing; intensely absorbing. It is personal and real. It is worth the hours you spent among the dullards.

To this list of suggestions your own experience and observation will add many. Keep your eyes and your ears open and utilize what you see and hear. With such additions from your own experiences you can hardly fail to arouse the interest of most of your students.

Several times during the semester you are going to want your group to write themes in class. Such a plan is an exercise in rapid thinking and expression; it often serves to hold the interest of a class on a particularly restless day, such as that of the great game; and it gives you an opportunity to judge the student's ability to do his own writing. I do not go so far as to say, as do some, that *all* themes should be written in class in order to prevent cheating. I have more faith in human nature than this practice indicates. Nevertheless, idealism should be coupled with common sense. Some students *do* cheat, and you can protect yourself and your honest pupils by having them write an occasional theme in class. Furthermore, the writing of this type of theme may be fun, which also is desirable.

As an inspiration for a class theme, you might give a germ plot:

A businessman is seated at his desk. Suddenly the door opens. He whirls about and sees — what?

You will be amused at the results. Such a theme should be read aloud in class, for your clever students will want their friends to enjoy with them the fruits of their efforts. Use care in selecting the papers to be read, for the pupil who lacks imagination will receive scant applause. Yet you can't neglect him entirely; so call on one or two of this group in addition to the brilliant ones. Teaching presents all sorts of problems not learned in college courses, does it not? After several papers have been read, you can discuss with the class the effect of methods of opening and of closing, the value of using specific rather than general terms, the importance of compression. You will be surprised at how much composition you can teach by this device.

Another device useful for arousing interest in words is this: Ask each student to suggest a word and write it on the board. Then tell the class to write a narrative in which each word is used, although not necessarily in the order given. Before the list is completed, you might suggest the inclusion of a few proper names.

Read to your class the first paragraph of Lamb's "Poor Relations." Ask for similar definitions of: *maiden aunt, girl, boy, football hero,* and so forth.

Put on the board a list of proverbs: "A stitch in time saves nine," "A rolling stone gathers no moss." Ask each pupil to select a proverb and tell an incident illustrating its truth or untruth.

To these suggestions for class themes, add your own. An excellent idea for you is that you begin to acquire material from every possible source. Clip suggestions from books or magazines; ask experienced teachers what they do; jot down ideas that come from conversations or lectures. Place all these in an easily accessible file. You will turn to them with relief on days when, for some reason, you have not planned sufficient work to fill the period; or on days when even your most amenable students seem filled with the evil spirit. At such times, occupy their hands and their minds, and your own nerves will be saved much torture.

Throughout this discussion I have made a number of suggestions for theme subjects, but I shall add to those already noted. Your best source is local — something pertaining to the school or the town. A football game can offer inspiration for any type of discourse that you may want — a narrative, to begin with the kick-off and to end with the closing gun; a description of the crowd at the game; an explanation of the most complicated play; an argument for or against football as a sport. (The last is the least usable, for it is possible to get material on it from magazines or books; moreover, your pupils will see little to argue about.) The activities of the community always afford excellent material, as do the occupations and new experiences of your group. For example, junior high school pupils are concerned with the new world into which they are entering. As a means of utilizing this interest, work out a project called "Know Your Own School," in which your pupils find out what they can of its history, the men and women responsible for its founding; have some of the boys with an engineering turn interview the janitor, finding out something about the heating system and other matters under his care; do the same with the library, the athletic department, and any other special divisions of the school. (For a more complete unit, suitable for mature pupils, consult the *Journal of the National Education Association*, October, 1933, page 189.)

As your students are interested in correct form and manners, you might compile a "Courtesy Code," in which they enumerate situations about the home, the street, the classroom, assembly, the corridors, and at parties in which application of the principles of good form is desirable, and then determine on the correct social usage to fit the occasion. Many subjects of the curriculum offer similar sources for theme topics. Ancient history gives suggestions for the retelling of myths, fables, legends; science classes offer fascinating material for papers based on the life of famous scientists, or on present-day contributions of science. Health links up with athletics and community and school projects for health betterment. (Although planned for the younger pupils, any of these ideas may be adapted for upperclassmen.) Any wide-awake teacher can list numerous interesting and valuable theme subjects by considering the activities of his students.

Similarly one may select subjects for sophomore theme writing. As letters, both business and social, are often listed in the course of study for the sophomore year, the teacher can base many of his theme assignments upon letter writing. Whenever possible, use an actual situation. Through friends, you may arrange an exchange of letters with pupils in other parts of the United States, England, Canada, Australia, South America, Europe, and Asia. "English" will be learned by all concerned, for your pupils must write simple, correct language, without slang! A sick student will enjoy letters from his classmates. Be alert to every such opportunity. For training in succinctness, experiment with the composition of telegrams, particularly night letters. Work out several situations, and have your class write a fifty-word message to include all the important points. For example, you have looked at an apartment for a friend. In fifty words, you want to describe it adequately, give the rental price and terms of the lease, and state that the owner insists on an immediate decision. The fields of home economics and manual arts; inventions, new or old; topics connected with biology; industries of your town or community — all lend themselves to interesting and valuable themes.

Juniors and seniors may do more ambitious work. The school newspaper (discussed on page 333) may be in charge of one of these groups. Interviews afford useful experiences for your students. Have each select a business or professional man or woman of the community. The membership list of such organizations as the Chamber of Commerce, the Rotary, Kiwanis, or Lions Club, the Business and Professional Women's Club, the American Association of University Women includes the names of most of the outstanding people of your community. Send to each a letter, in your name, but composed by the class, asking permission for the interview. Replies may be posted on the bulletin board. Then let each student arrange for his interview. Instruct him in the etiquette of such meetings and see that he has in mind several questions to ask. Impress upon him the importance of not wasting the time of the person interviewed. After he has had his interview, have him write an account of it. The members of the class will enjoy an oral report of the interview. This is an excellent project, for it combines several types of written and oral expression, gives some business experience, familiarizes the student with a certain business or profession, and serves to interest the members of the community in the school.

Essays written by high school seniors, for which prizes are offered by local, state, or national organizations, are good material. So, too, is a study of your town: its history, industries, professions, outlook. This makes a good class project. The class may be divided into small groups, each working on the aspect in which its members are most interested, and the parts may then be combined into a whole history of the community. A round table discussion of findings may well complete such a unit.

Because high school juniors and seniors are thinking of their future, a study of vocations is valuable. Let each student gather material concerning an occupation in which he is interested. He should try to find out something about the qualifications needed for a person entering it; its present status; its future possibilities. The lives of men and women who have made enviable records in their occupations prove interesting subject matter. Travel, geography in its various phases, music, painting, architecture, literature — every activity affords material for writing.

If, however, none of these suggestions serves, consult *The Teaching of English in the Secondary Schools* by Charles Swain Thomas, for a list of 1049 subjects, all passing the tests prescribed by this skilled teacher. Appendix A of *Ways to Teach English* by Thomas C. Blaisdell also gives a number of suggestions.

You are wondering, I know, whether you should arbitrarily decide upon a subject for a theme or whether you should permit a student to make his own choice. You should compromise by suggesting several subjects, for there will always be those who "can't think of anything to write about." But you should permit students who wish to, to select their own topics, with this proviso — they must consult you before making a change in the topics suggested. This will enable you to insist upon original subjects, if you so desire, and it will also prevent a student from writing a so-called poem or description when you want an exposition. But if the student writes the type of discourse that you require, I see no reason why he may not choose his own subject.

Train yourself and your students to look for subjects about which to write. Remember that original topics are better, especially for younger pupils, than are those based upon library readings. Before you use one of the latter type, explain to your students what plagiarism is and how it must be avoided. Above all, make your theme writing interesting, valuable, and alive.

What are you to do with the type of theme entitled

"A Picnic," beginning in some such way as this: "We got up at six o'clock that morning and in an hour had everything packed into the car, then we drove for ten miles to the picnic place, and there we . . ." did this and that and the other? Often the abandoned author of such a theme further complicates the situation by writing a mechanically perfect paper. This sort of "composition" constitutes one of the reasons why teachers (as well as mothers) "turn gray."

To prevent this distressing result, anticipate such bald narration and plan a campaign calculated to produce a slightly more vivid picture of an enjoyable experience — for, as a fitting close, your pupil will assure you that "all had a perfect day." In talking with your class, say to them that, although personal experience comprises the best of all sources of writing, only something important and interesting to ourselves can be important and interesting to the reader. What does the girl tell her mother when she returns after her exciting day? A long, dull catalogue of events, logically enough arranged, but lacking any picture of self? Indeed no; her chatter concerns itself with *happenings* — perhaps the swim, or the games, or a near-accident, or an intimate glimpse of deer or bear. This, then, is the incident about which to center her theme, an experience sufficiently vivid to justify writing about it. With older pupils, although personal experience still remains the best choice, you will, I hope, help them to distinguish the merely trivial from the significant episode. Couple with selection of incident some sort of outline (or *plan* if you prefer that term) similar to that suggested, strive constantly to produce effective expression, and eventually you will receive narratives that will delight you. A "gripping opening sentence," a "clinching close," although somewhat suggestive of a wrestling bout, nevertheless provide advice productive of effective technique.

Like narratives, descriptions lacking your guiding touch may be dull and monotonous. Insist upon a clearly understood point of view: from the top of the hill, a walk down Main Street, near the weighing machine in the corner drugstore; a positive general impression: intense cold, a dust storm, kindliness overshadowed by surface gruffness; specific details to depict the impression desired; ruthless elimination of all that does not pertain; and a definite close. Call into play the evidence submitted through the senses, especially sound, sight, and most provocative of all, smell. Close and accurate observation should have a strong appeal to farm boys and girls, accustomed to careful study of various forces of nature; to the budding scientist; to those with the eye and the heart of the poet.

Effective and forceful exposition and argument demand a clear conception of *purpose* or *theme*, that goal toward which the thought of the writer advances steadily. Careful selection, logical arrangement, employment of incident, example, illustration, will result in systematically arranged and interestingly written papers. Each type of writing serves its own purposes, offers its own problems. Daily in our speech, although not always in our writing, we narrate, describe, argue, and explain. By helping your pupils to understand the underlying principles of these types (although you may not name them) and the technique requisite for each, you will give them the skills demanded of educated adults.

Sometime during their six semesters of composition experience, your pupils should be taught to use the resources of the library as a basis for writing. I know you are thinking: "'Sometime!' Why can't she be definite?" And indeed I wish I could, but by now you understand that all plans must be adapted to your pupils' needs and capabilities. Some junior high school boys and girls can easily learn to utilize library facilities; other seniors will require almost individual guidance.

Although I have remarked that the so-called "library or investigative" theme in many ways affords less training in writing than other types, inasmuch as subject selection and limitation, point of view, purpose, organization of material, expression (only too often) have all been, to a certain extent, already determined, nevertheless, this sort of writing has its place in both adult and school life. Instructors in subjects other than English frequently call for reports demanding the use of library facilities. Many adults find themselves required to prepare papers based upon reading sources. You are, then, justified in offering this training.

You can't, of course, turn your pupils loose with instructions to write a theme based on library reading. First, they must become acquainted with the information found in books: title, author, publisher, date of printing, copyright, table of contents, index. Then they must learn the arrangement of the library, the interpretation of the Dewey decimal system, general and particular reference works, and the main classification of books. How to use the card catalogue and the *Readers' Guide to Periodical Literature* must be explained. After your pupils know what to look for in the library and in the books themselves, explain to them the form for preparing bibliography cards (3 x 5 inches):

Books

Lewisohn, Ludwig
  Expression in America.
  Harper and Brothers: New York and London, 1932.

Magazines

Sokolsky, George E.
  "Huey Long."
  Atlantic Monthly, CLVI (1935), 523–33.

Next, instruct them in taking notes. The information should be either in *exact* quotation or in the pupil's own words. You must discourage as forcibly as possible the taking of notes in the words of the author without benefit of quotation marks. Otherwise the resulting paper will consist largely of ideas and phrases gleaned from several sources and put together with varying degrees of skill. Insist that the heading of each note be that of one of the major divisions of the pupil's outline and require careful indication of source. For example, let us assume that a pupil is writing on the life of John Galsworthy, one of the subject divisions being "Travels." At the top of the card or paper (not at the moment of taking the note, but later), he writes "Travels." Then all these notes may be assembled, all those bearing upon other points put together, and the whole arranged in order before writing begins.

Travels

   Traveled widely in America, Canada, Australia, other countries.

Kaye-Smith. John Galsworthy, pp. 14–16.

Another point in this connection is the arrangement of titles of references in a bibliography. The form is usually as follows:

Kaye-Smith, Sheila. *John Galsworthy*. New York, 1926.
Lewisohn, Ludwig. *Expression in America*. New York, 1932.
Sokolsky, George E. "Huey Long." *Atlantic Monthly*, CLVI (1935), 523–33.

Whether or not you will teach the use of footnotes depends greatly upon the class. If you decide to require them, provide a form such as this:

George E. Sokolsky. "Huey Long," *Atlantic Monthly*, CLVI (November, 1935), pp. 530–32.

All that I am suggesting here should not be attempted at once. Becoming acquainted with the library comes first and may well occupy a considerable length of time. I suggest that you read on this subject *Junior English in Action*, Book Three, fourth edition, pp. 128–141, or *English in Action*, Book One, fourth edition, pp. 122–146, by J. C. Tressler and others. You can see that these plans constitute a unit of some length. Take up slowly the teaching of the other steps preparatory to the assignment of a "library" theme, perhaps requiring first bibliography cards and a list of the works consulted; later adding to this the filling in of note cards; and still later requiring the addition of footnotes. You would hopelessly bewilder your pupils should you demand from them without slow and careful procedure this sort of preparation and writing.

As you read this, no doubt many of you are recalling high schools which contain *no* library, no card catalogue, no *Readers' Guide*. Should you teach in such a school as this, are you to shrug your shoulders and say to yourself, "What's the use? I've nothing to work with." You are mistaken, for every school, no matter how struggling, owns an encyclopedia; always there are textbooks, magazines (perhaps your own), and newspapers. With these resources you can give your pupils training, limited, naturally, but reliable as far as it goes. Never let circumstances discourage you, for usually there is some way out of the difficulty if you look for it. The small high school, also, affords an excellent opportunity for teaching composition as a group activity. Ideally, you and your pupils should sit down together, discuss composition problems, write, read, and criticize. You who teach small classes can provide this desirable setting much more easily than can teachers of large groups. To teach composition in this way, they must divide their classes — a problem in planning. But the teacher in a small school often has no such problem. There is compensation in everything, you see.

ASSIGNMENT

A. Make a list of ten theme subjects for each high school year. For each set, have at least two topics that pertain to the widening interests of the students, and two that are developed from a subject, other than English, that he may be studying.

B. Suggest a plan for a theme assignment to a group of freshmen; to a group of seniors. Be definite and suggestive.

C. Examine theme topics listed in Appendix A and indicate their suitability for use in the six high school grades. Be prepared to uphold your ratings.

FURTHER READINGS

1. THOMAS, CHARLES SWAIN, *The Teaching of English in the Secondary Schools*, Chapter IV, p. 107.

Here are presented five imperatives in composition teaching. You will do wisely to acquaint yourself with these and to read with care the subsequent discussion.

2. BLAISDELL, THOMAS C., *Ways to Teach English*, Chapter XXI.

As Mr. Blaisdell remarks, "The ninety-and-nine will write letters throughout life, and they will write nothing else." Therefore it behooves you to teach your pupils *how* to write this form. This chapter, "Teaching the Letter Form," gives several helpful suggestions.

3. THOMPSON, JAMES M., *Write for the Job and Get It*, Southwestern Publishing Company, Cincinnati, Ohio, 1940.

Directions for writing application letters of all sorts, correct and incorrect examples, and good advice are simply presented in this very useful little book.

4. *An Experience Curriculum in English*, pp. 208–216.

"Writing Experiences, Grades 7–12" in its statements concerning "social objectives" and its "enabling objectives" lists types of letters to be taught and techniques desirable for effective writing.

5. PEDIGO, LOUISE, "A Letter Writing Unit in the Seventh Grade," *The English Journal*, XXXIII (September, 1944), pp. 377–380.

This is an account of a letter writing unit based on "collecting postmarks."

6. CLARK, THOMAS ARCKLE, *When You Write a Letter*.

You will gain pleasure and profit from this little book.

7. WARD, C. H., *What Is English?* Chapter XI, pp. 318–326.

In this is stated the author's conception of what a theme actually is.

8. HITCHCOCK, ALFRED H., *Bread Loaf Talks on Teaching Composition*. "A First Essential in Composition," pp. 3–21; "A Second Essential in Composition," pp. 22–43; "A Third Essential in Composition," pp. 44–59.

Don't expect these essentials to be as prosaic as they sound. Also, in the same volume, read "Digging Up Ideas," pp. 91–120.

9. LINDAHL, HANNAH M., "Vitalizing the Language Program," *The Elementary English Review*, XXI (January, February, 1944), pp. 286–291; 300.

Suggestions for composition — oral and written — based upon children's language needs are here presented.

10. SCRIPTURE, ELIZABETH, and GREEN, MARGARET, *Find It Yourself: A Brief Course in the Use of Books and Libraries under the Contract System*.

This is recommended for textbook or reference.

11. FISHER, DOROTHY CANFIELD, "Theme Writing," *Familiar Essays of Today*, Benjamin H. Heydrick, editor, pp. 137–142.

This offers palatable advice on writing themes.

12. KIES, PAUL P., and OTHERS. *A Writer's Manual and Workbook*, enlarged edition, pp. 137–147; 229–233.

Here you will find detailed instructions for preparing an investigative paper.

13. RUTAN, EDWARD J., and NEUMAYER, ENGELBERT J., "Composition with Meaning," *The English Journal*, XXXIII (December, 1944), pp. 547–551.

Meaning as an approach to writing compositions is stressed in this article.

XI. THEME CORRECTION

PERHAPS one of the greatest compensations of theme correction — drudgery, it is often called — lies in the opportunity thus afforded you to come very close to your pupils, to learn something of their hopes, aspirations, ideals, and disappointments. Lest you spoil their confidence, you must exercise care, tact, and good judgment in the remarks with which you decorate each paper handed in for your perusal. For, as I have mentioned previously, every theme, to be of value to your boys and girls, must have a careful and sympathetic reading from the teacher. Not only is this necessary as a means of detecting errors in expression, but also in clarifying their ideas and aiding them with their problems.

After the teacher's corrections are made, the pupil has the duty of revising his paper, which aids him as materially as does writing the theme and, therefore, must not be neglected. As a teacher, then, you have a triple responsibility toward this matter of theme writing: to see that your class has a provocative assignment, to read each paper with care, and to insist upon careful revision of every paper handed in.

Your first consideration is the marking of the themes.

Upon what basis shall you judge: accuracy, content, or both? You must determine what you expect from theme writing, for upon that decision depends your scale of marking. That instructors vary greatly in their estimates is indicated by the fact that the same theme, marked by several readers, may vary in rating from *A* to an *F*. Such deviations indicate that teachers, even in the same school system, do not agree as to what a theme is or what should be expected from the writer.

Before formulating an opinion, think back upon the two aspects of a theme previously discussed: self-expression and communication. As communication demands accuracy and clarity, your marking scheme must include attention to these matters. But as self-expression is of equal importance, content must be included in your estimate of a theme. An *A* theme, then, would be one accurate in the elements of usage stressed, arranged in a logical manner, and containing ideas suited to the level of the group in each junior or senior high school year. It is quite possible that an *A* theme, written by a freshman, may contain errors in matters of usage that you have not yet discussed. Close your eyes to these, and concentrate upon the principles you have stressed. But at the end of the senior year, no *A* theme should contain errors in the principles taught; in fact, such a theme, written by a senior, is an *F* theme, unless the subject matter shows evidences of real originality. On the whole, I believe you will find that worth-while content and satisfactory expression usually go together, for the type of mind that thinks an idea through carefully also desires to express thought accurately. You may, then, wish to give a double mark to themes — one for content and one for form. Whether or not you do this, you should always keep in mind these two phases of writing and gauge your marking scheme accordingly.

What have your pupils the right to expect from you, the judge of their efforts? Undoubtedly, they have the right to expect for each theme a careful, sympathetic reading, reinforced by constructive criticism. As each paper written should show improvement over that preceding, your comment should include definite suggestions for the next paper. Perhaps you find the ideas good but the expression of them monotonous. In your comments, then, suggest several ways to secure variety (always keeping in mind the preparation and experience of your pupils) and ask the writer to experiment with what you suggest. Perhaps your criticism deals not so much with effective rhetorical phases as with the ideas presented. If you have encouraged free expression, you may find yourself in the role of father-confessor, confronted with the problem of helping your boy or girl to think straight on a personal problem. Often you will be called upon to point out errors in logic, to deprecate an intolerant attitude not only toward individuals but also toward racial groups or toward standards of morality. In doing this, you must set aside your own predilections, endeavoring to help your pupils to think straight. On your part this demands the widest sort of experience, coupled with a sympathetic and understanding attitude. In saying this, I do not mean that you should seek to dominate the thought of your impressionable high school youngsters, but only that you have here an excellent opportunity to aid your pupils to that clear, logical, and tolerant attitude so important in private and public relations.

You can see, then, that theme marking demands far more than the checking of mechanical errors or even a consideration of thought content.   Your comments, whether they deal with attitude, expression, or subject matter, must always be *helpful*.   Writing *Good* or *Very poor* on the bottom of the theme will never urge a student to better effort.   Even worse is sarcastic comment.   Sarcasm, the most scathing weapon known, is inexcusable in the correction of themes; at all times your attitude must be sympathetic, fair, and courteous.   Constructive criticism — dealing as it may with ideas and logical reasoning — affords one of the most difficult tasks that we teachers are called upon to perform, demanding a clear mind and a rested body.   I realize that I am urging the impossible when I ask you to put your themes aside until you are relaxed and at peace with the world, for well I know the multiplicity of duties thrust upon you. But I offer this advice.   Have your papers come in at a time in the week when you may expect some free hours — perhaps on Friday.   Do not mark them at the end of a long day, and do not stay at it for too long a time. If necessary, let other work slide but themes *never*.   And remember that, to be of value to the writer, each theme must be corrected and returned before the next is due.

As for the mechanical aspects of theme marking, they are comparatively simple.   *Mark only errors that you have taught,* but hold your pupils responsible always for the application of any principle already discussed.   At first, this will be difficult, for you will be forced to close your eyes to certain flagrant errors in grammar and sentence structure.   In high school, you may expect correct spelling, as this is primarily a grade school subject.   Your marking of papers containing misspelled words, however, should depend somewhat upon what you have taught. You should always mark every misspelled word, although occasionally you may simply note on the margin "three misspelled words," leaving to your pupils the task of finding and correcting them. But as you gain experience in teaching, you will recognize that your work is *progressive* — that you teach certain principles each year and thus lay your foundation. The senior year should show the results of the work of preceding years. After the first six weeks of the twelfth year, you should teach no new grammatical principles, but should concentrate upon the rhetorical aspects of writing. The senior student, then, may and should be held responsible for accurate writing; junior high school, sophomore, and junior students should be held responsible only for what has been taught. Be strict in your accounting of errors in expression, and be just.

After you have corrected a theme, see that the writer revises it. As important as the writing itself, this revision — pertaining usually to the correction of the tools of expression — must not be neglected.

Several methods of theme revision are in use. In extreme cases, when the organization of the paper is utterly hopeless, you may have each theme rewritten and corrections made. (If, however, you have taken great pains in your assignment to show your students *how* to organize a theme, they probably will not have this difficulty. If they do, rewriting is the only remedy.) I advise against this method for the reason that it doubles the work for you, as you have to check every word of the second version with the first in order to see that the corrections have been made.

A second, fairly satisfactory plan is to have the pupil make his corrections in red ink on the original paper. If you use pencil for your corrections and the student uses black or blue ink for his theme, the red ink corrections will

be easily seen and checked.   Or, if you prefer, the error
may be corrected on the back of the preceding page.   This
means that there must be an extra sheet to take care of
corrections on page one.

Or you may like to use a "correction notebook."   The
plan I am giving you is taken from the one suggested by
Stith Thompson in the *English Journal* for January, 1917,
in an article entitled "A Notebook System of Theme Correction."   Have each member of your class buy a loose-
leaf notebook and divide it into three parts.   Section 1 may
be used for class notes; section 2 as a file for themes; and
section 3 for corrections.   After each theme is returned
it is filed in order in Section 2.   Section 3 is arranged
in the following manner.   There should be a division for
each of the mechanical points discussed: grammar, spelling, sentence structure, punctuation, diction.   If desired,
add a sixth section for "New Words."   Each page in the
first five parts should be arranged in this way:

SPELLING

Error	Correction

January 6

occured	occurred

The sixth section for "New Words" has three columns:

NEW WORDS

Word	Meaning	Example
itinerary	a traveler's guide or route book	The station agent prepared a detailed *itinerary* of our trip.

As you see, the error is entered in its proper section, under the date on which it occurred, and the correction is made. You can check the corrections and errors very easily if the themes are filed properly and the corrections made neatly. The great advantage that this plan has over the others mentioned is that it enables the student, and you, to note the number and type of errors and their repetition.

A comment as to the "New Words" section. Theoretically, this is highly desirable; actually, it affords some problems. The theory behind this is that pupils are sufficiently interested in their own improvement to desire to enlarge their vocabulary. With a few boys and girls, but only a few, is this true. If, then, you require a certain number of "new words" a week, many of your group will go to the dictionary and list them, taking no further interest other than to record them. I believe your best plan is to make this voluntary, giving praise to those who are sufficiently interested in their own improvement to list and use new words.

To return now to correction of mechanical errors. The notebook plan that I have outlined is too detailed for use with young students; you should use it only with seniors. You can, however, require every pupil to have a small notebook in which he lists his mistakes in grammar and spelling and in which he records his assignments. He should check every theme before he hands it in to see that he is not repeating an error that has been pointed out to him. Occasionally you can glance at these books to see what each pupil is doing, but you need not mark them.

In addition to correcting the error, you can, if you wish, have the pupil state the rule or principle violated. Misspelled words may be spelled correctly ten times. (I am not convinced of the value of this. You know the story of the little boy who wrote "I have gone" one hundred times, then left his teacher a note, "Dear Teacher: I have went home.")

You must see that corrections are satisfactorily made before the final mark is recorded. To simplify your own bookkeeping, record the theme mark in your class book in pencil. Then, when the paper is returned corrected to your satisfaction, change the pencil mark to ink. A glance at your record will show whether or not each theme has been revised. You should require that the corrected theme be returned before the next is written, for the purpose of revision is to call to the attention of the pupil his mistake so that he will not repeat his error. Some instructors raise the mark of a student after he has corrected his theme. This you should not do, for two reasons: (1) this plan doubles the work for you, as you must reread and regrade his paper; (2) it permits careless pupils to hand in hastily written work, knowing that they can raise their mark by careful revision. You should encourage in every way possible the careful preparation of themes, but once done and handed in, they must stand or fall without your giving the pupil an opportunity to rewrite his paper.

The best method for obtaining improvement in theme writing and careful revision of themes is by means of the conference. I wish that every teacher had time to confer with each student after the writing of each theme. In schools operating under the supervised study plan, something of the sort is done. It is, I think, highly desirable, except that the teacher must guard against "spoon-feeding" the pupils. But in schools operating under the old system, conferences, for the overloaded teacher, are well-nigh impossible. If you can work out some plan for frequent interviews, do so by all means. An occasional conference possibly is better than none, as it at least gives an opportunity for you to become better acquainted with your group. To be effective, consultations should be private. No doubt the school of the future will allow for conference periods, but at present the overloaded teacher, particularly in the small high school, must do the best he can.

From my own experience I know how full are the days and nights of the beginning teacher in the small high school. It seems unnecessarily cruel to force the inexperienced teacher, to whom everything is new and hard, to conduct more classes and to do more extracurricular work than the experienced teacher; yet this is usually true. Only youth and enthusiasm carry the beginning teacher through those years of apprenticeship, in which he may teach six separate subjects, supervise a study hall, and have charge of a half dozen extracurricular activities. Impossible as it may seem, this is often the load of a beginner. In every way, then, one must conserve his strength. Attention to details will often save hours of time. Be efficient in planning and conducting every phase of your work. I shall give you several suggestions for saving energy; others you can add to the list.

In the first place, insist upon uniformity of all papers handed in to you. Before you assign your first theme, take time to explain the form in which the paper is to be written. If the school in which you teach has a uniform method of endorsement, use it; if not, supply your own. A good form is the following:

> John Jones
> English I, Section 2
> January 12, 1945
> Theme Number 6

Explain to your class how the paper should be folded — lengthwise, with the fold to the left; require the use of ink, black or blue-black; see that only one side of the paper is written upon. Put on the board a plan for the form of the theme, showing the placing of the title, the leaving of an adequate margin. (You should require the use of ruled and margined regulation-sized paper; otherwise you will have trouble.) All this will take a good deal of time and talking, but uniform arrangement and careful form are valuable both to you and to your students — to you, because of the saving in time that they will effect; to your pupils, because of the good habits they will form. Experiment with a pile of papers that are not uniform, and note the time you waste in handling them.

In the second place, arrange the papers in alphabetical order before marking them. Some persons disapprove of this because they say the name of the writer of a paper should be unknown to the reader. But as you soon learn to distinguish George Jones's writing from that of Emil Kline anyway, you should not let that worry you.

Next, you should put the grade on the outside of the paper, toward the top, for ease in recording. I know there are some kindly souls who say that this offends the sensibilities of pupils; that a mark is a private matter and should not be on the outside of the paper for all the class to see. After you have watched your group exchanging papers and after you have heard the whispered "Say! What did you get?" a few times, you won't think your class so very sensitive in this respect. I do agree, however, that a mark *is* private. Distribute corrected papers yourself, giving each person his own, and you will not be responsible for making public the mark. If you are doubtful that this plan saves time, try recording the grades on a hundred papers with the marks on the outside and a hundred with them on the inside, and time the results.

Next, turn your papers endorsed side down, as you enter each grade in your class book. If you are careful to do this, the pile of papers will be in alphabetical order when you pick it up. A small matter, yes, but sixty seconds make a minute and sixty minutes make an hour. You can do a good deal of constructive theme marking and recording in an hour.

Probably the school in which you teach has a set of symbols for use in correcting errors in expression. If not, compile your own and give a list to each student: *sp.* for spelling; *gr.* for grammar; *d.* for diction; *s. s.* for sentence structure. Place the proper symbol in the margin of the paper, by the line containing the error. Some textbooks have a correction guide on the inside of the covers of the book. If so, use it. You will save a great deal of time employing a set of symbols to indicate mistakes. (Perhaps I should have said previously that except with beginners you should not mark the error itself, but should indicate, by the placing of the proper symbol, the type of mistake and the line in which it occurs. At no time should you actually make the correction, for this method defeats the purpose of theme revision — to help the pupil to overcome his mistakes.)

Furthermore, require that all work be handed in on time. This means, for themes, at the beginning of the class period at which they are due. Never accept a paper during or after the class period unless you count it as late. See that your pupils are giving their attention to the work at hand and are not surreptitiously completing the theme due at the beginning of the period. Exercises which you discuss in class cannot be handed in until the period or

the discussion is over. But themes should be ready —
endorsed and folded — at the beginning of the period.
You should not accept assignments prepared outside of
class — except themes — that are handed in late, unless,
of course, the boy or girl has a legitimate reason for not
doing his work on time. Absence from school the preceding
day is not a legitimate excuse, as a pupil is responsible for
obtaining and doing the assignment. Themes must always be accepted, no matter how late they are, for each
student must write and revise a certain number a semester.
But late themes should be severely penalized. Reducing
the mark a grade point is often effective: an *A* theme
receives a *B*; a *B* a *C*, and so forth. Indicate this reduc-
tion on the paper, so that the student will see what his
tardiness has cost him. Early in the year make all this
clear to your classes. Do not give the impression that you
are doing this to be vindictive, but point out that promptness is a requirement in any activity in which a person
engages successfully. Do not deviate from your rule, once
it is made. Be fair about accepting excuses, and take
pains to be just. Your group will not resent this rule,
provided you are unbiased in enforcing it; but if you are
not, they will. In these ways you build character.

Although I have said many times that all themes
written should be corrected, I am going to step back a bit
and suggest a substitute that may be used occasionally.
Sometimes you are justified in correcting only part of a
paper — say, for instance, the opening or closing paragraph. If you were to do this, have these paragraphs
placed on the board. Then you can compare them,
pointing out those that best exemplify the requirements
of such a paragraph. In this way, the members of the
class have an opportunity to compare their work with

that of others, and you are spared the necessity of marking the entire paper. This plan should be followed only when you are emphasizing paragraphs or transitions or some point that lends itself to comparison.

Another timesaver is to jot down several errors made by the majority of the class and discuss these with the entire group instead of with the individual.

Some teachers try to save time by having papers corrected by members of the class. If used at all, this can be done only for mechanical points. As I have remarked, your principal duty in theme correction is to give constructive criticism, which a student seldom can do effectively. Furthermore, only a trained reader can detect mechanical errors. To a person skilled in reading themes, mistakes seem to jump from the page, but the eye of the inexperienced person cannot detect them. Therefore, do not depend upon students, even good ones, to mark the mechanical errors in a theme. As you will have to go over the paper, anyway, you may as well do it once and for all. The only papers, then, that can be corrected in class are exercises. These should be distributed at random, and too much dependence should not be placed on the marks. There is, I fear, no royal road; theme marking must be done by you. But you are justified in checking exercises, rather than in marking them carefully. Far too often exercises done outside the classroom are not the unaided work of the student. For that reason marks on these papers are not a reliable index of the knowledge of the pupil. I should prefer simply to record these exercises (but do not take your class into this secret) and give my time and energy to frequent class tests over the daily assignment. Occasionally mark an exercise and return the papers, but do this because of its moral effect and not because you place great dependence on the grade.

Reluctantly I turn from these remarks on teaching composition. All the accusing looks and words of high school graduates come back to me, and from these ghosts arise criticisms, I fear too often justified. They cry out against our lack of plan and purpose, so that one teacher knows not what another does; against our neglect of composition, resulting sometimes in theme requirements so few as to be negligible; against our shortsightedness that permits mechanical work on the school paper to substitute for writing; against our gullibility that allows a pupil to boast "I got by on my 'rep'"; against our failure to show beginners *what* to write, *how* to write, and *why* one writes. Such accusations are good for the soul if they help us to approach this problem of composition teaching with resolution, energy, common sense, and — above all — a recognition of responsibility toward our boys and girls.

ASSIGNMENT

Your instructor will give you a theme written by a high school student. After taking into consideration the year and probable preparation of the pupil, mark the paper for mechanical errors. Write on it — inside, not outside — a piece of constructive criticism. Give it the grade you think it deserves: *A*, *B*, *C*, *D*, or *F*.

FURTHER READINGS

1. BERKLEMAN, R. G., "A Letter to My Theme Reader," *English Journal* (College Edition), XXII (January, 1933), p. 62. You can obtain no better advice concerning theme correction than by reading this.

2. WARD, C. H., *What Is English?* Chapter XI.

Section *D*, "Penalizing Lack of Literary Skill," and *F*, "One Way of Grading," will help you to determine your own standards for theme correction.

3. Mirrielees, Lucia B., *Teaching Composition and Literature*, revised edition, Chapter I, pp. 46–54.

This upholds and explains the author's "double marking" plan for themes.

4. Bishop, Ernest G., "To Improve the Student's Technique in Theme Correction," *The English Journal*, XXIV (December, 1935), pp. 835–836.

Here is suggested a plan by which students are forced to make careful theme revision.

5. Lloyd, Charles Allen, "Mistaken Teaching about Certain Points in English," *The English Journal* (college edition), XXII (May, 1933), pp. 404–410.

XII. ORAL COMPOSITION

Because I am devoting only one chapter of this text to oral composition, let no one suppose that this indicates its relative importance. Far from it. Perhaps no other branch of teaching has such lasting bearing upon the present and future needs of your pupils. For every thought conveyed by means of writing, your boys and girls will speak a hundred times. And this communication may be conversation, which includes explanations of various sorts; argument, often heated; bits of description; narration, more or less vivid; or it may be formal presentation of these same forms. Ask for a direction or for some information; listen to someone read aloud from the daily paper; demand proof for some controversial remark; request an explanation of a plan or process — observance of any or all of these ordinary activities will convince you of the widespread share speech holds in everyday life. If you desire documentary proof, read a report prepared a few years ago for the National Council of Teachers of English under the chairmanship of John Mantle Clapp, called "The Place of English in Everyday Life," which not only studies our frequent recourse to speech, but also summarizes responsibilities of the classroom toward this aspect of adult needs. By no means do I consider oral English unimportant; I am devoting one chapter to it merely because almost all I have said concerning written expression applies to oral. Both enable us to communicate with our fellows, both afford means of self-expression. Having something to say of import to our hearers, consideration of our audience, logical arrangement, effective detail — all these concern us deeply in the presence of a hearer who can and does indicate indifference, anger, disagreement, amusement, concurrence. So with the mechanical aspects of composition — correct grammar, accurate sentence structure, punctuation (pause, gesture, change of position)— all are as necessary in speech as in writing. Indeed, spelling alone of the elements of composition belongs strictly to the field of writing; all else pertains to both. In teaching the principles of written composition you also instruct in oral address.

Perhaps I should define what I mean by "oral composition." To me, it is accurate, and, if possible, effective oral expression arising from the demands of everyday life. Orders, given directly or over the telephone, instructions, expression of opinion concerning daily events, a résumé of the plot of a movie, depiction of a sunset — any of our speech activities is, to my understanding of the term, "oral composition." My stress falls upon *composition*, as you see, and not upon *delivery*. I believe you should train students to speak lucidly, accurately, and forcefully, and to read clearly and naturally, with due regard to meaning; but I do not expect you to give instruction in dramatic reading, for this belongs to the department of speech and should not be exacted of the teacher of English. Your emphasis and your aims, then, for oral composition are very much like those for written composition. Everything that has been said concerning the composition process, organization of material, accurate and forceful portrayal of thought, applies here. For expression by means of the written word, merely substitute that of the spoken. Your general aim remains the same: To aid the pupil to express his ideas with clarity and with some degree of effectiveness. The word *effectiveness* must be enlarged here to include *delivery:* correct posture and clear, accurate, forceful speech. To your junior high school aim — accuracy and simplicity of expression and the beginning of organization — add the ability to stand before a group and to speak with ease. Your sophomore aim may remain as in written composition — effectiveness in meeting ordinary situations requiring expression of thought. Material for practice will vary here, for you will want to afford your group experience in such activities as telephone conversations, giving directions, joining in conversations; but your *objective* does not differ. To the aim for the junior year — skill in collecting and arranging material; broadening of interests — add: increased power in delivery. The fourth-year objective — development in strength of expression and continued broadening of interests — may be taken exactly as it stands, except that "strength of expression" be understood to include the effective command of voice and body. Oral composition, then, is not a separate subject, but has in general the same aims and principles as has written composition.

Subject matter for oral address, as for written, should seek to further the aim set. In the beginning years, simple narratives and expositions will give training in appearing before a group and aid in producing ease in speaking, as well as affording practice in accurate expression and in organization. So, too, in the sophomore year: a telephone conversation, the introduction of two or more persons, a direction for playing a game or making some object, instructions to a stranger as to how to find his way to the schoolhouse, will all offer practice in meeting ordinary situations. In the junior and senior years, the interests of the class may be appealed to in the choice of oral English topics. Talks in these years should be longer than in the others. Sentence and paragraph divisions should be marked occasionally by pause or change of position or both. Style in composition should be stressed. These are the years in which to use debate and parliamentary law. Broaden the information of members of your group by choosing subjects of general interest. Any worth-while topic will give practice in management of material and in forceful delivery.

Perhaps the following requirements for oral work from *Guidebook for the Language Arts*, prepared by the teachers of the Seattle Public Schools may provide a progressive plan upon which to base your teaching of oral composition:

A Sequence of Standards for Oral Work

Seventh Grade

The pupil keeps in mind the directions for speaking given him in preceding grades and tries to follow them

1. He gives talks on how to do something, keeping each step of the process in proper order
2. He uses new words in such a way that their meaning will be clear; otherwise, he explains their meaning
3. He follows an outline when giving a report
4. Before giving a talk he reads the sections in a handbook on standards in speech and voice
5. He takes part in club meetings as a good listener and a helpful speaker, following the proper forms in speaking and in gaining permission to speak

Eighth Grade

The pupil observes the standards set in previous grades

1. In group discussions he waits his turn to speak, listens courteously to other speakers, and speaks to the point in a restrained voice when his turn comes
2. He speaks when he is called on or is acknowledged by the teacher or the group chairman
3. He prepares his reports on reading and his reports for other classes carefully so that he will cover the subject of each report without waste of words
4. He plans his talks as carefully as he prepares his written compositions
5. He rereads those sections of a handbook on oral work that apply to the kind of speaking he is to do and follows the directions

Ninth Grade

The student observes the standards already established

1. He chooses his subjects for oral reports to interest his audience as well as himself
2. He is careful to understand clearly what he talks about
3. He prepares strong opening and closing sentences
4. He completes each part of a talk as outlined so that he will not have to go back to any part later in his talk
5. He finds out how to pronounce all the words he intends to use
6. He uses exact terms when giving a book report
(Not *this boy* or *this girl*; not *it was when* or *it was where*)
7. He listens attentively to teacher and fellow students
8. He makes helpful comments on the work of his classmates
9. He refers to those sections of a handbook that will help him in his speaking
10. He takes his part in social conversation without interrupting others

11. He follows proper form as to manners and time in telephone conversations

Tenth Grade

The student observes the standards that have been set in previous grades for speaking and for organizing material and strives to improve in his use of them

1. He reads more than one source to secure information for giving a talk and takes accurate notes on his reading
2. He prepares his outline for a talk so that each main point will produce a paragraph and each paragraph will further his thought or develop his subject
3. He speaks on a variety of subjects
4. He uses a variety of words, avoiding overworked expressions
5. He strives to use exact words to express his meaning, avoiding unacceptable expressions
6. He uses examples and illustrations that all in his audience will understand
7. He does his share in group discussions
8. He may explain his plans for writing a composition and invite comments and criticisms
9. He listens attentively and courteously to others who may explain their plans and he makes helpful comments

Eleventh Grade

At this point the student establishes himself as an independent and effective speaker

1. He selects subjects appropriate to the occasions and follows a suitable style in the development of each
2. He prepares his talks by careful reading of a number of sources of information and by taking sufficient and usable notes
3. He prepares topical outlines which show logical division and development of each subject

4. He works out interesting and effective introductions and conclusions
5. He holds in mind the purpose of each talk and strives to make everything he says aid in carrying out that purpose
6. He uses a variety of vivid illustrations and figures of speech in making his points clear and his talks interesting
7. He does his full share in planning and carrying on group discussions
8. He listens critically for facts and opinions and checks what he hears against what he has previously learned
9. He follows correct form at all times in activities calling for parliamentary procedure
10. He follows the suggestions and directions given him for improving his voice, speech, and posture

Twelfth Grade

The student maintains the power he has developed previously as a speaker

1. He speaks with dignity on all serious subjects
2. He makes comments thoughtfully and explicitly when given occasion to do so
3. He does his full share in planning and carrying on group discussions
4. He applies to his prepared talks all applicable standards set down for the preparation of written work

In addition to the subjects listed for written composition, most of which are applicable to oral composition, I make a few suggestions: A type of early speech, helpful in overcoming timidity, is one which occupies the *hands*. Demonstrations of first aid treatment, which can be made by any Boy or Girl Scout, afford a familiar starting point. Similar talks may explain how to make a campfire, how to cook a camp meal. Scout lore will do you yeoman's service. Talks on health not only act as "ice-breakers" but also correlate with instruction given in the home economics and physical education departments. A device I picked up a few years ago from a newspaper provides a springboard for your beginning work. Have each of your freshman students select a person, preferably not a teacher, to ask this question: "How useful to you is good English?" Each day, until you have completed the roll of the class, have one or two persons report their findings. The results will be interesting; also, the procedure is so informal that even very diffident pupils are willing to make such reports.

Sophomore students may dramatize correct social customs, telephone conversations, sales talks, the housewife buying her groceries from the neighborhood store. Students are often clever with this sort of thing, and usually enjoy doing it. Explanations of such activities as the life of a forester, bee-keeping, how to ski — all these further your aims for the sophomore year.

In the junior and senior years, pupils should have practice in parliamentary law and in informal debate, possibly in formal. The class may resolve itself into any organization that it chooses to be — the town council, the faculty, the school board, the Chamber of Commerce. This group conducts its meetings according to parliamentary law, adopts resolutions, appoints committees, holds elections. Also, conversation is an excellent form of oral composition in these years, possibly also in the sophomore year. Select a subject about which to converse and ask a pupil to act as host or hostess, whose duty is to introduce the topic for discussion. Each member of the class should have read and thought about the matter and be able to contribute to the general comments. Be prepared yourself and join in if need be. I hope you have movable chairs in your classroom, so that they may be grouped in a way similar to those in any living room. If your class is large, possibly you should divide it into two or three groups, allotting to each a part of the period. To be successful, this must be an informal, courteous, yet purposeful discussion. (An extension of this idea is the "Panel Discussion" so popular today.) Or your class may have an "eatless banquet," at which after-dinner speeches are made. (With the consent of the principal and the instructor in home economics this may be a banquet with food — a dessert course. But do not attempt this without the permission of the two persons mentioned.) Whatever the subject, the speeches should be from five to ten minutes in length and should show increasing maturity of thought and effectiveness of expression. Let the talks center about the following purposes: to explain, to convince, to entertain.

Always keep your eyes and ears open for new ideas and suggestions. Some time ago, in listening over the radio to the "Better Speech Institute of America" program, I received a suggestion which I shall pass on to you, as it illustrates what may be gained simply through listening. Let your class consider themselves as part of the personnel of a store, we shall say a grocery. One group works in the candy department, another in the green groceries, a third with the canned goods, a fourth in staples, a fifth with meats — for this, as you see, is an up-to-date concern. Each group will bring to class a list of ten words, let us say, pertaining to its department: *marron*, *pistachio*, *broccoli*, *endive*, *sauerkraut*, *artichokes*, *spaghetti*, *flour*, *fillets*, *turkeys*. Then the words may be placed on the board, pronounced, defined, and commented upon. In the end, there may be a spelling and pronunciation bee, in which all members of groups take part.

Another time you might prepare ten or twenty poorly planned sentences pertaining to the workings of the store and have them rearranged into effective sentences. For example, "The boss okeyed the project" might become "The manager approved the project"; "Respectively yours" would be rewritten "Respectfully yours" (or better, "Very truly yours"); "Yours of the 19th instant" may be changed to "I have your letter of June 19." Be on the alert for ideas such as these which you can adapt to the pleasure and profit of your class. ·

For one series of talks, divide your class into several groups. Let each consider itself an oral magazine. One pupil — the most clever — acts as editor. He gives the name of the magazine, its purpose, and makes an editorial on whatever subject he likes — perhaps the issue appears about the time of a holiday, such as Washington's or Lincoln's birthday; perhaps it comes at a time significant to local or state history. If so, these events afford material for an editorial. He then introduces the editor of the "National Affairs" section of the magazine, who gives a digest of significant national events. The editor-in-chief then comments briefly on this and introduces the editor of the next division, possibly "Foreign Affairs." As many departments as you like can be reported on, but you should not fail to include the fields of science and religion, for much of value is occurring in these aspects of modern life. At the close, the editor makes a few summarizing remarks and the pages of this issue of the magazine are shut.

Although I have said several times that the subjects suggested for written composition may be adapted for oral, I do not mean that the same may be used for both. Some instructors, I know, follow the plan of having each theme presented in oral and then in written form. Possibly this constitutes good training, but I do not see how anyone can retain great enthusiasm for his topic when he is forced to deliver it twice. Only occasionally should you follow this plan, and preferably with interviews which will bear repetition. Again, if you have your seniors write a long paper, you may ask each pupil to give a résumé of it to the class. If the themes are worth while, the group enjoys sharing them and the author gains pleasure from the approval of his classmates.

In your teaching of oral composition, whatever the year, you have three responsibilities: to plan the assignment, to see that the talk is made, and to criticize the performance. As in written composition, the assignment acts as a lever to successful talks. It should be both provocative and definite, bearing upon the objective you have for this particular class. Perhaps, as a part of your concern with organization, you plan practice on introductions and conclusions. Let your group, then, prepare an introduction to a speech, trying to make it arresting to their hearers, so that they will clamor for the entire account. A forceful opening sentence, a careful setting of the stage, an intimation of what is to follow (in exposition or argument), consideration of the audience — these and other qualities of the introduction afford objectives. So, too, with the conclusion. Let your group experiment with various types, such as a "clinching" close to a narrative, a well-weighed summary to an exposition, an appeal to an argument. Or you may be concerned with giving practice in effective sentence structure. Very well; assign a talk in which must occur examples of participles, dependent clauses, and phrases as sentence openings. Somewhat cut and dried, but affording good fun as well as training, is a talk giving practice in the correct forms of the troublesome verbs: *lie, lay; sit, set; rise, raise.* If this seems too stereotyped (although younger pupils really enjoy the mental agility necessary in this), you might, having in mind the same objective, assign a subject which makes necessary the use of these troublesome verbs: "How to Plan a Garden," "How to Cut Out a Dress." To assist your boys and girls to be "audience conscious" assign a talk, perhaps on the forthcoming game, to be delivered to the children in the grade school, to the members of the Chamber of Commerce, to a group of women. Whatever your objective, see that both you and your pupils have it clearly in mind. Furthermore, you desire to fire your group with enthusiastic interest in each speech. Much of your success here depends upon your own personality, your ability to stimulate response. Any or all of the devices suggested for written composition offer a starting point, but be ever on the alert to add to them. Never forget that logical development underlies every successful speech and to that end require an outline. If the pupil wishes to use notes, tell him to arrange them upon cards — the outline belongs to you.

Your next responsibility is the performance itself — the delivery of the speech. What may you expect? Obviously, not so much from beginning pupils as from experienced ones. Your requirements in oral composition, as in written, should be progressive. As for the delivery itself, you can at first ask no more than that the pupil stand before the class (and he may object to doing that). As time goes on, you can require more, until, at the end of the freshman year, you can expect each student to appear before the class, to stand firmly on both feet, and to look at his mates. As for subject matter, it will compare with that of written compositions. The talks will be immature in their point of view, but should be carefully planned and have some intrinsic merit.

In the sophomore year, you build on the foundation laid in the ninth grade, aiming to increase ease and power. Enunciation and pronunciation may be stressed, and a friendly, informal, easy manner may be cultivated. If you follow the suggestions made for dramatizing certain situations, you will help your group to feel free before an audience. The talks should, in general, be somewhat longer than those made by freshmen. Actually, you may have more trouble in persuading your group to condense their talks than to lengthen them. From about the middle of the freshman year, after your pupils have overcome their natural timidity in appearing before a group, limit the speech to, say, five minutes — and have the speaker stop at the end of that period. If a talk is carefully planned and sufficiently practiced, a person can confine his remarks to any given period. At first you may allow a little leeway, but as soon as you think it advisable, put this rule into effect and continue until the bitter end. Who of us has not listened to a speaker who has failed to learn how and when to stop?

Junior and senior pupils should grow in ease of manner and power of speech, feeling so at home that they can move about the stage, and can use diagrams or other illustrative material. Facial expression, audience contact, gestures can be developed with these students, provided they have had training in the freshman and sophomore years. Otherwise, as in written expression, you must start at the beginning and expect very little more from them than you can from first-year pupils. Be satisfied, if, at the end of the senior year, each pupil in your class can deliver a ten-minute talk with ease and clearness. Perhaps he has not a voice that will melt a heart of stone, or power that can move mountains — these he probably will not need. But most of us today have occasion to express our ideas to a group of some sort — in our living rooms, in class, in the business office, over the radio, in the organizations to which we belong. For these purposes, we need to know how to plan a speech, how to deliver it clearly and effectively, how to stop it promptly. This you can teach your boys and girls to do.

Your next responsibility is that of *criticism*. As in written expression, this constitutes one of your most important responsibilities. Several methods are frequently used, any or all of which you may wish to employ. The first is criticism by the teacher. This may be oral or written or both. The beginning talk or two should receive no adverse comments. The teacher may make a few suggestions, preferably upon the content of the speech — ideas of interest to the class, a comparison of what has been said with points made previously, the relation of a similar experience — anything that will make the pupil feel at ease. With the third speech you can ordinarily begin with critical comment, both of the ideas presented and the manner of delivery. I say *ordinarily*, for oral composition presents problems foreign to written, the chief being the self-conscious attitude of the pupil. Usually the boy or girl has so conquered his stage fright that you can begin to make both favorable and unfavorable comments. Expand the remarks of the speaker, as you have previously. In addition, on small slips of paper write some suggestions, commendatory and otherwise, and hand these to the speaker, retaining a carbon copy for yourself to file as a help in determining the improvement made by the pupil and as a basis for private discussion, if you are so fortunate as to be able to arrange for conferences with your boys and girls. As in written composition, your comments should be limited by what you have a right to expect from the class, for you should not judge a beginner as you do an experienced speaker.

A second method of criticism, to be combined with the first, is to have the class select a member to act as student critic, which has the advantage of pupil participation in classroom activities, but also has its disadvantages. Often you are dealing with a group of youngsters who have spent eight, nine, ten, eleven, or twelve years together. During this period they have built up friendships and enmities, which predilections color their criticisms. If you can make pupil criticism impersonal, fair, and significant, I say employ it by all means. But it should never substitute for *your* comment. If your group is as competent to judge as you, you may as well retire, for clearly your place is not in the classroom. Personally, I doubt that student criticism ever has the value of teacher comment, but it may well be employed in connection with your own.

Much of what has been said applies to the third method: criticism from the class as a whole. To a much greater extent than the second, this plan affords student participation, thus encouraging the speaker to regard the audience as a group of individuals with varying tastes (an important advantage). But it, too, admits opportunity for the exercise of personal favoritism or prejudice. Like the former plan, it should be combined with your written and oral remarks.

As a guide for your criticism, but particularly for that of your pupils, I suggest consideration of the following points. That some target is needed to prevent such remarks as "Oh, it was all right, I guess"; or "I didn't like it much; maybe it was all right" a little experience will convince you. These targets may be placed on the board as a basis both for preparation and for criticism: (1) subject matter — is it worth while or valueless? (2) interest — is the subject of intrinsic interest and is the speaker able to gain and hold the attention of the class? (3) is the talk well thought out, so arranged that it moves forward steadily to the set goal? (4) delivery — is it simple, natural, and sincere? (5) posture — has the speaker selected the best place to stand? is his weight placed firmly on both feet? is he free to move about? (6) pronunciation and enunciation — are any words mispronounced or poorly enunciated? (7) grammar — is his speech free from ordinary grammatical errors? You understand, of course, that these points are taken up one at a time and that the beginner is not expected to put them all into effect. During the period in which you are stressing subject matter, for example, class criticism should center about this; when you go on to the next phase, comments should be concerned with subject matter plus interest; and so on, until your experienced speakers consider themselves responsible for every aspect noted.

Characteristic of all good public address is the sense of give and take between speaker and auditors, a feeling of communication. At its best, speech is really conversation, in which one person expounds his ideas by means of the spoken word, while his auditors indicate their share of the experience by change of facial expression, by posture, by bodily movement. A skilled speaker learns to become very conscious of the attitude of his audience, watching them closely for indications of their response to him and his ideas. Not an individual but a group activity, speech should ever be taught from the angle of the hearers. Because of this, choice of material must first concern each speaker, for it must be of such a nature as to appeal to the audience. To this end, pupils must be taught to visualize their probable listeners, and to select the material suited to their age, ability, and experience. How to choose and develop a subject so as to gain and retain the interest of a group constitutes one of the primary duties of a speaker. In this connection, let me quote the words of James Truslow Adams concerning the preparation of President Franklin D. Roosevelt for his talk to a stricken nation concerning the banking situation, given on March 12, 1933. Says Mr. Adams in his *History of the United States*:

> It explained the position in the simplest terms, as well as what he was trying to do, and made a tremendous popular hit. It has been said that the permanent officials of the Treasury sent him a draft of a speech, which was full of involved statistics, and which no one but a banker could understand. Roosevelt at once said it would not do, and then sitting a few minutes before a blank wall, he visualized the ordinary Americans who would be listening to him — tradesmen, farmers, mechanics, clerks, professional men, and others with no technical knowledge of banking, and decided what he would say to them.

Logical and orderly development, clear and, if possible, effective presentation — all considered from the angle of the auditors — take on new importance in the presence of a group. Teach your pupils, then, that oral composition, whatever its nature, is actually conversation, in which the speaker holds the major responsibility. But as classroom address, no matter how well motivated, must always smack of the artificial, see that your pupils understand their share in its success. A class of mine once voted one of their number a medal because he had been the most responsive and inspirational listener of any of the group. Well deserved is such a tribute, as anyone who has faced the indifferent eyes of an unwilling audience knows. In an even more marked sense than in written composition does oral composition represent communication of thought.

As I have hinted previously, the successful teaching of oral composition demands a good deal of tact as well as some of the other social graces on the part of the teacher. Perhaps you do not know — but perhaps you do — how very difficult it is for some students to appear before a group. I remember one who came to me three times, with tears rolling down her face, to tell me that she simply could *not* talk before the class. Eventually this girl conquered her fear and learned to make a well-planned, clearly delivered talk. I also recall another, who later became an excellent speaker, whirling around from view of the class, with her hands before her face, and exclaiming, "Oh, Miss Dakin! I can't! I can't!" These people had stage fright, pure and simple, and had to be dealt with gently but firmly. Sometimes you can persuade such a one to make a talk if you give him the opportunity to do something with his hands, as I have suggested previously. I have in mind a senior who day after day took a zero rather than make a speech. I urged him, in private of course, to conquer this fear, and he agreed to make a talk on the front-page make-up of the local newspaper. Armed with the sheet, he actually appeared before the class; and although the paper rattled so that we could barely hear his words, and although he eventually hid himself behind it, he had overcome his fear and afterward talked whenever called upon. Sometimes, too, you can encourage the timid student to express an opinion while seated at his desk. After he has talked a minute, you can say, "Albert, if you will come up here to the front, the class can hear you better. That is very interesting information you are giving us." Often he will do it, and once met, his fear is gone, or at least mastered. Sometimes a frank statement that you yourself have experienced this same nervousness will help. So may the remark that even trained speakers know that "gone" feeling in the pit of the stomach, yet are able to forget it, once they have begun. For your oral English work, you see, you need all the tact and charm with which you are endowed.

Nor should you make the oral talk an issue to show your authority. In fact, the longer you teach the less often will you feel the need to exercise your power, anyhow. But never, in oral composition, be constrained to *force* a pupil to speak. Probably you will fail, thus weakening your disciplinary power; moreover, almost every time, refusal to speak is not the result of stubbornness, but of fear. Accept the negative response, call on the next person, and have a private conference with the pupil, in which you try to find out *why* he will not speak and to aid him to overcome his shyness. Those physically handicapped call for special treatment, also. If the pupil is at all self-conscious (some are not), you might accept a written paper in lieu of the speech, and include this boy or girl in as much class discussion as possible. In no way should such a pupil be made to appear conspicuous, even by marked kindness on your part. By all this I do not, of course, mean that you should be more lax in your oral composition requirements than in your requirements for written composition. Not at all. A student who fails to prepare an assigned speech should receive a zero unless he has a legitimate excuse. My remarks pertain to the abnormal, not the normal situation.

Very important to the teaching of speech is a pleasant class atmosphere. Of course, this is desirable at all times — the English classroom should be one to which the pupils like to come — but it is essential in this work. Be cheerful and pleasant yourself; offer your comments in a kindly manner; never, under any circumstances, resort to sarcasm; make your group at home with you and with one another. In other words, assume some of the responsibility of a host or hostess. The atmosphere of the classroom, then, will be conducive to an exchange of ideas, and you will rejoice in the development of your class.

Both friend and foe to the speech class is the radio. Within the last few years its influence has been more extensive than is generally realized. Many of your pupils have the radio "on" during most of their waking hours, reading, studying, playing, talking to its accompaniment. That the radio constitutes a powerful formative influence appears obvious. An important activity of daily living, it serves as an aid or detriment to what you are trying to teach.

Because the radio is comparatively new, very few suggestions for its place in the classroom have been formally presented. For that reason, you can experience the thrill of the pioneer, blazing a new trail into uncharted territory. In *An Experience Curriculum in the Teaching of English*, to which you have been referred, you will find on page 40 a plan for utilizing the interest of your pupils in radio programs. To the suggestions made there, add your own.

As radio listening consumes so much of the attention of both the adult and the child, one of your clear duties lies in fostering such a critical attitude on your pupils' part that they will demand programs which, no matter what their nature, conform to standards of good taste and have an appeal for the person of education. As in all phases of your teaching, you will get nowhere by arbitrary condemnation of certain programs and praise of others. Instead, seek to lead your pupils to censure and approve of their own accord. To that end, have each member of your group select a program that satisfies him, and either in written or oral form, present his views to the group for their discussion. With the class, comment upon the material presented in the broadcast; upon the quality of the voices of those taking part in it; upon the command of subject evidenced by the speaker; upon the good taste and manners shown both by speakers and by announcers.

Your group may enjoy preparing radio programs similar to those presented over the great national hook-ups. Debates, the popular question-and-answer method, dramatizations, explanations of operas, are only a few of the types of program heard daily. Often, broadcasting companies present "Better English" programs in which good and bad usage are very cleverly contrasted by means of dramatizations. Your alert pupils will get much enjoyment from a similar activity.

Informative talks of any nature, political or otherwise, may be criticized from the points of view of delivery and content, particularly the latter. If we are to have an intelligent electorate, we must have a thinking public, and you can do no greater service to your country than to train your pupils to weigh the information they receive. By co-operating particularly with teachers of science, sociology, history, political economy, you can train your students to verify what they hear, thus helping them to separate the wheat from the chaff, to be conscious of false propaganda, to question rather than to receive passively. But of course they must realize that no criticism is valid unless based upon knowledge. Part of your responsibility, then, consists in aiding them in accurate and unbiased judgment.

But I know you are wondering how you can put to service the radio, when, despite the tremendous interest shown in it today, very few schools have yet recognized its place in the school program. You must do the best you can with what the gods provide; in almost every home there is a radio. Your pupils can select a program, all listen to it, and discuss it at the next class meeting. No doubt the school of the future will provide a radio in every room, perhaps earphones for every child; until then you must adjust yourself to the exigencies of the moment.

In a somewhat lesser degree the cinema serves the oral English teacher. Particularly to the fields of dramatics and literature belongs a systematic study of movie productions; but consideration of the very popular travelogue and other special features, and comments concerning posture, voice, manner, enunciation, pronunciation, have a bearing upon the problems of speech.

Oral composition has a few special uses to which I now want to call your attention. The first of these is in class recitations. Try to induce your group to speak clearly and to formulate effective sentences. It is a moot question as to whether you should interrupt a pupil to correct his speech. Perhaps this may best be decided by circumstances, for with some you can do this easily; with others you cannot. The degree of friendliness that exists between you and your class constitutes another factor. Often you can make indirect suggestions, such as saying, "John, I am afraid you aren't being heard by the people in the back row. Won't you please speak a little louder?" or you can remark that the idea of the pupil is not clear to the class and ask him to repeat it. Like all teaching, such corrections demand tact. Keeping this in mind, you should try to encourage good enunciation and sentence structure.

Certain specialized class activities also lend themselves to oral composition. I have spoken of the précis as an aid to written expression. Equally helpful is the oral one, the steps given for the composition of a précis applying to both. Book reviews may also be presented orally with good results. Practice in making announcements and introducing speakers — ordinary activities — should be given frequently. After your group has heard a speaker, perhaps in assembly, let them analyze the means taken to make the speech enjoyable, marking particularly the choice of material, how attention was aroused and retained, how activities of high school boys and girls were considered. Frequently members of the class must appear before assembly: the football captain may tell of a recent trip, the business manager of the annual may outline his plans, the president of the dramatic club may announce a play. Here is oral composition at its best. Encourage it by welcoming every such opportunity for your pupils.

As a teacher of oral expression, you have additional responsibilities besides conducting your class, for you must "practice what you preach." At all times, consider your own voice and manner. Unless you watch yourself closely, you are likely to fall into a dictatorial, over-emphasized manner of speaking. Your voice may become loud, strained, and harsh, and you will annoy the nerves of your pupils merely by your tone. Many of these faults come because the teacher does not know how to manage his voice. Every day he must talk for hours, and he cannot do this without vocal strain. I advise that every teacher (and I do not limit this to teachers of English) take courses in speech, especially those that will effect voice control. And the fact that you are in a position of authority may tend to make you overemphatic. The result of a pleasing or a displeasing voice is immediately noticeable in the classroom.

And you, as a teacher of oral composition, have another responsibility: you must be willing to speak when called upon. You may know in your heart that you are not made to be a public speaker, you may suffer the tortures of your pupils — nevertheless, you cannot teach oral composition and refuse to appear in public yourself. So no matter how great the struggle, speak when requested. It will be good for you — and for your students, too.

It goes without saying that *speaking* implies *listening*. Yet, as has been hinted previously, your pupils require help to become intelligent listeners. Various composition devices can be utilized to form good listening habits, such as the précis, the outline, the summary. After an assembly speech, ask your pupils to summarize its content or to make an outline of the main points. As the chairman summarizes after a panel discussion, suggest that the class check the summary to see that all important points are included. Read a paragraph, have the class take notes and write a reproduction. Utilize the radio by requesting the group to listen to a certain program and state the gist of the discussion. After hearing a newscast, your boys and girls may be asked to locate on a map places mentioned. Require one pupil to give directions for doing or making something and have another follow his directions. In these and other ways develop skill in listening.

A few last words, now, regarding oral English. You will want to teach it throughout the six years of the course, giving it more emphasis, very likely, in the lower years than in the upper. Probably you will not require a separate text for it, for most modern high school books lay considerable stress upon oral composition. If you need a separate text I suggest Painter's *Ease in Speech*, revised edition, published by D. C. Heath and Company, and Craig's *The Junior Speech Arts*, revised edition, published by the Macmillan Company. I hope you will find your teaching of oral composition as pleasant as it ought to be.

ASSIGNMENT

A. List five subjects for speeches with each of the following purposes: to explain, to convince, to entertain.

B. Prepare an assignment to be made to a particular class.

C. Write the sort of critical comment you would make after listening to a talk given by a high school senior.

D. Prepare a statement concerning present-day trends in oral composition.

FURTHER READINGS

1. *An Experience Curriculum in English*, Chapters XIII and XIV.

Although the latter, "Speech Experiences, Grades 7–12," will interest you particularly, you will want to preface this reading by examining the former, "Speech Experiences,

Kindergarten–Grade 6." Every section — Social Conversation, Telephone Conversation, Interviews and Conferences, and so forth — affords subjects for your oral English projects, and the "Enabling Objectives" suggest procedure.

2. THOMAS, CHARLES SWAIN, *The Teaching of English in the Secondary School*, Chapter V.

This chapter includes, among its other valuable features, sample outlines, a plan for criticism, and suggestions for vocabulary improvement.

3. WARD, C. H., *What Is English?* Chapter XII.

Here is a common-sense discussion of the teaching of oral English, showing reasons for faith, reasons for doubt, practical difficulties, undoubted benefits, and a list of four — only four — "rudiments."

4. DAKIN, DOROTHY, "Courtesy and Composition through Pantomime," *The English Journal*, XVIII (January, 1929), pp. 51–52.

This little device will both entertain and instruct your pupils.

5. STOOPS, EMERY, "Oral English in Life Situations," *The English Journal*, XXIV (September, 1935), pp. 555–561.

This summarizes a course constructed by the author and adopted and published for teachers in Los Angeles County and in the state of California. Here you will find epitomized a plan for oral English as everyday experience. Particularly suggestive are sections on motion picture and radio appreciation.

6. BOLENIUS, EMMA M., *The Teaching of Oral English* (revised edition).

This book gives practical suggestions by a skilled teacher.

7. SARETT, LEW, and FOSTER, WILLIAM TRUFANT, *Basic Principles of Speech*.

Two excellent chapters are Chapter VII, "Principles of Bodily Action," and Chapter XXI, "Radio Speaking."

8. ROBERTSON, STUART, *The Development of Modern English*.

Here is a readable account of the historical background of our language, with particularly good chapters on "The

Making of Words," "The Changing Meanings and Values of Words," and "Syntax and Usage."

9. PARRISH, W. M., *The Teacher's Speech*.

This will help you to practice what you preach.

10. STERNER, ALICE, SAUNDERS, KATHARINE, and KAPLAN, MILTON A., "Skill in Listening," National Council of Teachers of English.

This pamphlet is full of good suggestions.

PART TWO

THE TEACHING OF LITERATURE

XIII. GENERAL COMMENTS

W<small>E NOW</small> come to our discussion of the second great division of the teaching of English — that of literature. And most of you breathe a sigh of relief and say to yourselves "At last! Now I can really teach! No doubt composition is necessary, but literature I love!" Perhaps you do, but I wonder whether you have considered for a moment the problems connected with its teaching? Have you any idea of the number of students who "hate literature," who see in it nothing but a waste of time? Have you considered that many of your classmates in college, despite the fact that they have "had" literature for six years in high school, read very few magazines and fewer books? Indeed I have known college seniors, preparing to teach English in high school, who admitted that they had read no books during their college days aside from those required in freshman courses. And a college instructor once said to me that he wished the teaching of literature in high school could be abolished, so poor is the preparation of college students. These facts — for such they are — constitute a challenge to teachers of high school literature. Of what use is it to teach literature in high school if your instruction does not give background for further study on the part of college students, and — of far greater importance — if it does not instill a desire to read? Without going into the reasons for our failure to teach literature as it should be taught, I submit to you that your task here is no easier than it is in the field of composition, except that your college preparation for teaching it may be more adequate than for teaching composition.

As in composition, your first consideration must be to decide upon your reason for teaching literature. What do you want to do in secondary school literature? In other words, what shall your aim be? One of our errors in the past has been, I believe, our failure to have in mind an aim that is definite and possible of attainment by high school pupils. At best, we have used the general aim of "appreciation of literature." I have no quarrel with this; we *do* want our students to "appreciate literature," but in order to do this, I believe they must learn to do something else: I believe they must learn to read, and that this should be your purpose in teaching literature. (I am, of course, not the first person to express this idea. Alfred Hitchcock, in his *Bread Loaf Talks on Teaching Literature* and Lou L. LaBrant, in *The Teaching of Literature in the Secondary Schools* — to mention only two — have analyzed it fully.) When I say that, I do not, naturally, mean that you should teach your students to read as they are taught in the first grade. Not at all; they come to you with that equipment. What I mean is that you must teach them the actual meaning of whatever passage they are reading plus its implications and significance. When I think of how little the average reader gets from the printed word, I do not wonder that he dislikes reading. To him words, often meaningless, are grouped together in a fashion too complicated for him to understand. Why should he bother to dig out the meaning, with Amos and Andy on the radio and the moving picture at the corner?

Now, how can you teach your students to read? I believe you can do it by keeping in mind three steps: your boys and girls must learn to *think* with the author, to *see* with the author, and to *feel* with the author. Let us consider each of these.

First, to *think* with the author, that is, to understand what he is trying to say, means that your pupils must understand his point of view. This may be referred to as the *purpose* of the author and may be approached (at the close of the reading, of course) by the question "What does the author mean to show? Why did he write this story, this play, or this essay?" In this way you show your group that an author has a reason for writing, just as we have for reading. To be of value, this statement of purpose must, of course, be upheld by definite references to incidents, speeches, or comments. To think with the author does not necessarily mean that the reader should agree with him — far from it.

Next, in order to *see* with the author, your students must learn to pick out words and phrases that indicate what they would see with their eyes if they were face to face with the persons in the book or if they were actually in the surroundings described. The author employs words to indicate the appearance of each character — not only the physical nature, but also mannerisms and expressions that depict personality. In real life, we see two sides of every person we meet: his physical aspects and what we interpret these to mean. An author wishes his readers to do the same with his imaginary people, and to this end he must select words that suggest what he wants them to see. These characters he places somewhere — in a room, in a woods, outdoors or indoors at will, and this setting he also pictures by means of words. To see with the author, the reader must interpret these descriptive words and phrases of the writer so that he has a conception of the inner and outer man and a picture of the place or places in which these people live and move and have their being. A good assignment is to ask your class to list a certain number of details to show appearance, character, and place.

Finally, a reader must *feel* with the author. A writer always has a certain point of view regarding his characters. Sinclair Lewis is scornful of his Babbitt and takes no pains to conceal his contempt. George Eliot is sympathetic but stern with her Godfrey; she understands but does not condone the forces that make him what he becomes. This attitude, this point of view, should be understood. Again have your group list details that show the attitude of the author toward his characters — an opinion that may, of course, vary with circumstances, as it does in real life.

Emphasis upon these three steps in teaching your pupils to read will, I think, aid them to see the characters as the author sees them, to understand the writer's attitude, and to comprehend the meaning or purpose in what the author has to say.

Your primary aim in the teaching of literature, then, should be instruction in reading, enlarging this term as has been noted. But I believe there are at least two other objectives in high school teaching of literature that deserve consideration. One of these is to give students a knowledge of a few of the works of our greatest authors. I believe this is a legitimate aim, although I consider it secondary to the first, particularly for pupils who do not go to college. And the third is closely related to the second: to teach students to recognize the distinctive features of the structure of the main literary types. That a person should know whether he is reading a short story, a drama, or an editorial goes without saying. Otherwise he may confuse the bursts of fancy of Lord Dunsany's Jorkens with a travelogue. I think you are justified in having in mind these three aims, remembering always that the first far exceeds the others in importance.

The time divisions in literature I have commented upon before. Literature should always be taught in large units; in my opinion a semester in length, but certainly sufficiently long to complete the piece at hand. Again I say that there is nothing so calculated to destroy enjoyment in reading as to plan your work so as to give two days to composition, two to literature, and one to review. No, a piece of reading should always be completed before going on to something else. As to the placing of the literature semester, I prefer it during the second half, with composition in the first. I know I am going contrary to generally accepted opinion in advising this. Many persons would put literature first, because they fondly think that it is better liked by students than is composition. My experience leads me to believe the contrary; furthermore, boys and girls who are beginning the study of foreign languages are very glad to have the drill in grammar afforded them in the first semester of the ninth grade. To balance your own program, you can arrange your work so that the pupils in one grade are taking up composition while those in another are studying literature.

A glance at your state course of study or a look into one of the anthologies on the market will show you that you cannot, in one semester a year, teach every piece listed in the course or included in the text. That means that you must decide upon certain pieces for class use. Responsibility for this selection quite probably will be yours, and a real one it is. How are you going to choose? I hope you base your choice, not on *your* interests, but upon those of your students. One of the greatest mistakes of teachers of English, responsible for many of the bad results just referred to, is failure to take into consideration pupils' likes and dislikes. You come out of college enthusiastic over certain pieces of literature. (May I say in passing that I hope this ardor is genuine? Pupils will respect, though they may not understand, an honest point of view, but they have for insincerity exactly what it deserves.) In college you have rejoiced over the irony of *Don Quixote*, you have chuckled gleefully at the bitter sarcasm of Dryden's "Absalom and Achitophel," you have dropped into a mood of contemplative calm upon reading Wordsworth's "Ode to Duty." But because you have enjoyed them, is that any reason your pupils should? Although between you and your high school seniors there lies a matter of four or five years only, in reality there is "a great gulf fixed." *For we enjoy what we understand; and we understand what we have experienced, actually or vicariously*. Always consider this in choosing reading for your class. Remember that their interests lie largely in the field of action, as indeed is true of the majority of adults. Contemplative literature of any type belongs to the upper years and then should be weighed in the balance.

In addition to considering the interests of your students, you should also take thought of their background and ability. Many of you will teach in a school with pupils of different cultural or national backgrounds. Possibly the parents of these boys and girls speak at home a foreign language. With such a group you must choose literature that is relatively simple and that affords no national antagonisms. Indeed, you may have to teach these students to read in the limited sense of the word.

Ability of your pupils affords another factor bearing upon choice of selections. In the average ungraded class you will find boys and girls of varying aptitude, and for class reading you will have to select pieces that can be comprehended by all your group. Your bright pupils can be taken care of by additional work of some sort, perhaps by means of an enlarged reading program. Keep in mind the interests, background, and ability of your class, and above all, remember that you are not teaching a class of potential instructors in English. As I have said, the students who sit before you will be clerks, accountants, housewives, lawyers, doctors, bricklayers. Very few will be teachers and of them not one in a hundred will teach English. Test, therefore, whatever you select for class reading by some guide other than that you yourself like it. Strange as it may seem, that may mean you should discard it!

As an illustration of my contention, let me discuss with you briefly a few of the selections often listed for use in high school. Take for example "Enoch Arden," a ninth-grade choice. This poem has certain qualities to commend it: it is a narrative, sufficiently sentimental to appeal to the romantic adolescent. On the other hand, it is rather long for freshman use — I should prefer it for the sophomore year. Although the situation is hardly one with which the average freshman has had direct experience, he may be familiar with it, for today's comic strips and movies and even news stories occasionally reproduce the circumstances of "Enoch Arden" in one form or another. You may select it, but if you do, it will not be because of personal preference, for I greatly doubt that it ranks high among your favorite poems of Tennyson. Similarly, consider "Sohrab and Rustum," noting its length, its medium of blank verse, its great amount of description. Despite the fact that it is a narrative, is it likely to appeal to all freshman groups? "Tam O'Shanter" illustrates another point you must consider. Do not select this poem for reading by students who are struggling with the English language, for they must not be confused by the introduction of Scotch dialect.

The sophomore year is often given over to a study of American literature. Well and good. But how much appeal have Washington's "Farewell Address," Webster's "First Bunker Hill Oration," or Lincoln's "Address at Cooper's Union" for sophomore pupils? Consider their age — thirteen, fourteen, fifteen, possibly sixteen; their lack of background — the only history they know is the highly anecdotal account of the usual grade-school text. Are you likely to teach your students to enjoy reading by such a choice as this?

What do you say to "Andrea del Sarto" or "Rabbi Ben Ezra" for juniors? Have they the experience, are they sufficiently introspective — provided they can read well enough to interpret Browning — to gain very much from these poems? It seems to me that these are included in a high school course for two reasons: first, the compilers enjoy the poems themselves; and second, they are poems the names of which, at least, are generally known. Neither affords legitimate excuse, *unless* there is also sufficient interest for the students in the piece itself.

And "Mac Flecknoe" for seniors — justified or not?

Is the "Rape of the Lock"? Is the "Faerie Queene"?
Or "Prothalamion"? Consider for one moment the
amount of literary, historical, and social knowledge required to understand any one of these poems. And lest
you think I am condemning too much of poetry and too
little of prose, think a bit of *Pilgrim's Progress*, or "Speech
on Conciliation with America," or *Romola*. We expect a
good deal of our sixteen-, seventeen-, or eighteen-year-old
seniors, do we not? Let me make clear, however, that I
am not advocating the selection of the cheap, the tawdry,
or the ephemeral for your pupils' reading. Much of that
written in the past and in the present combines high
standards of style and ideas with content understandable
to adolescents.

But this I want to say: The exceptional teacher can
take almost any of these with almost any class and make
his students enjoy them. But most of us are just ordinary
folk, you know, not exceptions at all. Until you have
tested your own power as a teacher, give great consideration to students' probable interests, to the background,
and to the ability of your class. Remember that the
personnel of no two groups is just the same — that what
is satisfactory in one may not be at all usable in another.
This is again proof that teaching procedure cannot be
determined by fixed rule but must be revised to meet every
new situation.

I have already made the statement that you will be
faced with the problem of trying to teach literature to
pupils who "hate" it, who can't see any use in it. Not long
ago a teacher in a small community said to me, "What
can I reply when my students say, 'I'm going to be a
farmer. What good is Shakespeare to me?'" How will
you answer this question when your turn comes? It's

hard to say, isn't it? But perhaps you can forestall it by trying to show your boys and girls, early in the course, that literature has a definite value for them. Perhaps you can say to them something of this sort: "No matter in what way we earn our living, we can always be sure of one thing — we must deal with people. Some of us, such as teachers, ministers, lawyers, doctors, salesmen, deal primarily with human beings. Others of us, such as farmers, mechanics, laboratory workers, deal primarily with things. But we all must buy; we all must sell; most of us marry; most of us entertain our friends. It is obvious that those of us who best understand our fellow men are the ones who get along most easily in life. Upon what is salesmanship based? A knowledge of human nature, is it not? Upon what do successful home relationships depend? Knowledge and sympathy and understanding, do they not? Now literature depicts life — it tells what people of today are thinking and doing and saying, it describes the people of the past and the people of the future. Because it deals with people, it helps us to understand them. We cannot know every type of person in the world, nor can we have actually every experience possible — indeed do we want to? — but through reading we can gain a wide knowledge of the thoughts and ideals and acts of men. The more experienced we are, the more understanding we are, and the better we can adjust ourselves to living together to our common good." Then when you teach Shakespeare, reveal his understanding of men. Show that his Brutus and his Caesar are more than historical characters; that his Macbeth and his Hamlet may be found in any era. Perhaps, if you try to prove how *true* is great literature, you can convince your students that Shakespeare can be of use to anyone — be he farmer or be he priest. But this your pupils will have to come to for themselves; no amount of telling them to admire Shakespeare will produce the required result. They are iconoclasts by instinct; if you want idols to stand, you must give your class reason to respect them.

Perhaps, too, you should pause to ponder a moment upon what constitutes this literature which you want your pupils to learn to read. Is it an emotion, an incident, a record of human experience? Possibly what it *is* need not so concern you as what it *does:* its power to create mood, to arouse emotions, to re-create a glorious experience; in a word, to reveal man as not entirely futile, useless, hopeless, but rather, capable of rising to great heights. Today, when scientific invention makes man appear of less and less importance, perhaps literature can serve best if it portrays the potentialities of the soul. Its teaching is a challenge. Bring to it knowledge, understanding, sympathy, and enthusiasm, remembering always that you are teaching human beings, not masterpieces of literature.

ASSIGNMENT

A. Examine the statement of aims in your state course of study. Comment upon them, taking into consideration (1) their definiteness, (2) their possibility of attainment.

B. Criticize five titles listed in your state course of study for use in each year.

FURTHER READINGS

1. HITCHCOCK, ALFRED H., *Bread Loaf Talks on Teaching Literature.*

You will want to read all of this book.

2. LABRANT, LOU L., *The Teaching of Literature in the Secondary School*, Chapter I.

Here the author comments upon the uncertainty underlying much of our teaching and the necessity of establishing principles.

3. THOMAS, CHARLES SWAIN, *The Teaching of English in the Secondary School*, Chapter VII.

Here is presented a strong case for selection of good material for class use. Says the author, "The trend of choice should generally be toward the classics." Perhaps you will disagree, but certainly you should know his point of view.

4. LABRANT, LOU L., *The Teaching of Literature in the Secondary School*, Chapters III and IV.

Here Miss LaBrant answers her question and outlines fundamental problems in teaching pupils to read.

5. *An Experience Curriculum in English*, Chapter III.

Here is shown how experiences may be gained both through and with literature.

6. COOK, LUELLA B., "Reading for Experience," *The English Journal*, XXV (April, 1936), pp. 274–281.

This is a spirited attack upon the "easy road" to reading advocated strongly today by many teachers. After all, why should the pleasure theory constitute the only standard for choice?

7. KIGER, KARL WOOD, "Students' Evaluation of High School Literature," *The English Journal*, XXIV (December, 1935), pp. 838–840.

Although based upon the opinion of less than a hundred pupils, the findings stated in this article are nevertheless suggestive. Note that Mr. Kiger does not advocate dropping the least enjoyed selections but suggests that teachers seek the reasons for dislike and try to remove them.

8. FRIES, C. C., *The Teaching of Literature*, Chapter III.

"Enjoyment," says the author, "is secondary to reliving the experience." How does your aim of "teaching students to read" relate to Mr. Fries's objectives?

9. BRADFORD, ARTHUR L., "On the Frustrations of the Literature Teacher," *The English Journal*, XXV (May, 1936), pp. 392–396.

This is a statement of a realistic philosophy concerning the teaching of English.

10. ROSENBLATT, LOUISE M., *Literature as Exploration.*

This book discusses the psychological and social aspects of teaching literature.

11. SMITH, REED, *The Teaching of Literature*, Chapter I, "The Course in Literature: Scope and Problems," pp. 3–11.

This chapter discusses the teacher's most difficult problem, the teaching of literature.

12. TREZEVANT, BLANCHE, "The Function of Literature in the Elementary School," *The Elementary English Review*, XXII (March, 1945), pp. 100–105.

This article discusses the function of literature as a developer of imagination.

13. CROSS, E. A., "Appreciating Literature as an Art," *The English Journal*, XXXIII (November, 1944), pp. 465–474.

This discussion of the emotional appeal in literature will help the teacher to bring this aspect to his class.

14. STRONG, L. A. G., and REDLICH, MONICA, *Life in English Literature.*

This is a well illustrated introduction to literature for beginners.

15. HALLECK, REUBEN POST, *The Romance of American Literature.*

This high school text is arranged in units with helpful questions concluding each division.

16. COLLETTE, ELIZABETH, *Highroad to English Literature.*

You will find this book readable and the topics for reports listed at the end of each chapter particularly helpful. If you have no place in your class work for histories of literature, this book, like the two given above, deserves a place in the school library.

17. SMITH, C. ALPHONSO, *What Can Literature Do For Me?* revised edition, 1929. As a "defense" of literature, this little book is excellent.

XIV. POETRY

Let me now discuss with you the various experiences shared with your pupils by means of reading, which we prosaically refer to as "teaching literature." For convenience, we shall consider each type read in high school, beginning with the most subtle of them all — poetry. As always, we shall first be concerned with our aim, asking ourselves what we want our students to gain from their reading.

I believe that we want to teach our boys and girls so to enjoy poetry that they will take with them after they leave high school an understanding of what poetry is and a liking for it that will remain with them always, whether or not they go on to college. And I believe they will attain this end only if we teach them to read poetry. Coupled with this is the secondary aim of giving the pupils a knowledge of some of the great poems of the world and of the authors who produced them. Beyond that you should not go with most classes. Certain groups will enjoy learning something about such technical points as versification and stanzaic forms, but plainly these matters do not pertain to your aim of teaching students to read, and, if used at all, should be limited to advanced or special groups. You want, then, to help your group to enjoy poetry, and your method for attaining this aim is to teach them to read it.

Now how are you going to accomplish this end? In the first place, you should try to dispose of some of the stumbling blocks with which students are confronted when they read poetry — difficulties that do not pertain to prose. The first of these is concerned with the form of a poem. Unless he is warned, the pupil will think that the thought ends with each line. His eye and his brain will stop, and if, as often happens, the thought is incomplete at the end of the line, the reader becomes confused, and can't understand what the idea is anyway. To prevent this, comment on the importance of punctuation in reading poetry. Tell the pupil that the end of the line does not necessarily constitute a complete thought; that large units are indicated in poetry, as they are in prose, by the semicolon or end punctuation point; and that smaller units are indicated by means of the comma or dash.

Another element of form which clouds understanding is the frequent occurrence of inverted sentence structure. Tell your pupil that his knowledge of grammar will help him here. When he comes across a sentence in a poem that he fails to understand, he should analyze it grammatically: find the verb, its subject and complements; determine upon the modifiers. Frequently the meaning of the sentence becomes clear when he understands its structure.

Closely connected with involved sentence forms as a troublemaker is the complicated grammatical structure frequently found in poetry. Very often there is a marked separation of verb and subject and of verb and object.

Again, grammatical analysis offers the only path out of this morass. I hope you do not understand from this that I am suggesting that poetry be used for grammatical analysis. Indeed I am not, for poetry, by its very nature, does not lend itself to such utilitarian ends; I am merely advising this as a way to clear up complications of thought.

A fourth difficulty lies in the frequent recourse of the poet to figures of speech. Our boys and girls are often very literal-minded, bringing to the reading of poetry a practical attitude. Figures of speech, then, are likely to be taken at their face value, with amazing results. Lead your pupils to expect such symbolism; familiarize them with the metaphor, simile, and personification; beyond these you should not go unless it be with an advanced, specialized group.

Compactness of expression also blurs the meaning of poetry. Lead your class to see that one word frequently suggests an entire idea. Try to get them to determine upon the thought in the mind of the poet when he wrote this brief word or phrase. And see that your group knows the *actual* meaning of the word. (For many of these "trouble points," I am indebted to *An Introduction to the Study of Poetry*, by Richard Ray Kirk and Roger Philip McCutcheon.)

These are the principal means of expression that may confuse your group in their reading of verse. The first three may be explained in your introductory presentation, using a poem in your text as an illustration. Figures of speech and compactness of expression may be commented upon as the class reading dictates.

Now, how may these principles be applied? Consider this well-known, simple poem:

To a Waterfowl

Whither, 'midst falling dew,
While glow the heavens with the last steps of day,
Far, through their rosy depths, dost thou pursue
Thy solitary way?

Vainly the fowler's eye
Might mark thy distant flight to do thee wrong,
As, darkly painted on the crimson sky,
Thy figure floats along.

Seek'st thou the plashy brink
Of weedy lake, or marge of river wide,
Or where the rocking billows rise and sink
On the chafed ocean-side?

There is a Power whose care
Teaches thy way along that pathless coast —
The desert and illimitable air —
Lone wandering, but not lost.

. . . .

Turned into prose, with the modifiers placed next the
words they qualify, the first stanza reads: "Whither dost
thou pursue, 'midst falling dew, while glow the heavens
with the last steps of day, far, through their rosy depths,
thy solitary way?" Even in this form, the structure is
involved, because of the numerous modifiers of the verb.
Added to this are such poetic words as *whither, 'midst,* and
doth; the inversion of verb and subject: *glow the heavens;*
the figurative language in "the last steps of day." In the
other quoted stanzas we find such obsolescent words as
fowler and *marge.* In these degenerate days, the significance of the capitalization of *Power* must be explained.
Desert and *illimitable,* especially the latter, illustrate com-

pression — the big idea, to quote a student of mine, behind the little word. Stanza four contains an appositive, "The desert and illimitable air," the connection of which with *coast* must be explained. "Lone wandering, but not lost" is placed so far from "way" that their relation is not immediately perceived.

In teaching your pupils to read poetry you should of course keep in mind the points in reading any sort of literature: those of thinking, seeing, and feeling with the author. In addition you should consider the following: First, the student should decide upon the speaker, the person spoken to, and the occasion of the poem. He should determine upon the *mood* of the author. Is he gay, playful, bitter, sad? And he should be prepared to quote words or phrases that indicate the author's mood. Furthermore, he should note the rhythm of the poem. In this you should not be technical — it makes no difference, to most people, whether the rhythmic effect is produced by the use of iambic or dactylic feet, or by means of hexameters or pentameters — but enjoyment of any poem is greatly enhanced by a feeling for its rhythm. Certain poems that you will study with your class give excellent opportunity for noting rhythmic effects. For example, in "How They Brought the Good News from Ghent to Aix," the rhythm suggests the galloping of the horses: "I galloped, Dirck galloped, we galloped all three." And in "Agincourt," "Fair stood the wind for France," we can feel the movement of the waves. Rhythm is instinctive in us all. We watch a great machine in operation, and are fascinated by the rhythm of sound and movement. We travel on a train, and are lulled to sleep by the rhythmic "clickety-click" as the train crosses the rails. So, because rhythm is born in us and because it is a characteristic of good verse, you should emphasize it in teaching boys and girls to read poetry.

Closely connected with rhythm is the poet's choice of words. Your class will enjoy poetry more if you point out to them the melodic quality of words. Show that they are smooth and flowing or sharp and staccato. This, perhaps, approaches the technical and may not appeal to your football players. If so, touch lightly on it, for you do not want your pupils to be faintly amused by poetry or to feel that appreciation of it belongs only to a picked group, composed, very likely, of teachers of English. But in any event you must give considerable attention to words; first, because upon them depends an understanding of the meaning of the poem; and second, because consideration of words often adds to one's appreciation. For example, in Coleridge's *The Rime of the Ancient Mariner*, which you will very likely use, observation of the skillful use of archaic words adds greatly to one's enjoyment. Never take for granted that pupils understand even ordinary ones. You probably know the explanation given of "The stag at eve had drunk his fill." To at least one student this line meant that a bachelor by nightfall had imbibed as heavily as he was capable of doing. Emphasize first the meaning of words; second, if possible, show their melodic qualities.

To illustrate the application of a few of these principles I have selected the following poem:

Epitaph

O mortal folk, you may behold and see
How I lie here, sometime a mighty knight.
The end of joy and all prosperity
Is death at last — thorough his course and might.

> After the day there cometh the dark night:
> For though the day be never so long,
> At last the bell ringeth to even-song.
>
> — STEPHEN HAWES

To this, let us first apply the points to be considered in reading any piece of literature.

1. To think with the author, we must understand that a once powerful knight has reached death, the inevitable end of all mankind.
2. To see with the author, we visualize a knight lying in his tomb, his sword and shield — emblematic of his "might" — probably beside him.
3. To feel with the author, we experience a sense of gloom and resignation: there is an end to joy and prosperity, the dark night comes, the bell rings for the close of day — or life.

To continue with the second group of points to be noted:

1. The speaker is the dead knight.
2. He is speaking to all living people, who, like him, must sometime die.
3. The situation is that a powerful knight has met his death and now lies in his tomb.

Brief and simple as this poem is, it presents a few difficulties, particularly a figure of speech.   In

> After the day there cometh the dark night

and

> — though the day be never so long,
> At last the bell ringeth to even-song

we have the experience of life and death expressed by means of metaphor.   Another difficulty lies in the use of the words *epitaph*, *sometime*, *thorough*, and *even-song*, the meaning of which will have to be explained. If your pupils have read Shakespeare's "Fear No More," they might compare it with Stephen Hawes's poem for meaning and mood.

Your choice of poems to be discussed must be determined by the principles already laid down, particularly by the interests of your group. In the first three years, the poems selected should be largely narrative, with an increase in length and difficulty. Simple lyrics, if they are carefully chosen, may be read in any year; but difficult lyric poems, if studied at all, belong only in the upper levels if the class is average in background and attainments; and probably not at all if the group is, in any sense, a "problem class." In the senior year, largely as a matter of convenience, poetry may be taught according to types. To some people, a knowledge of the characteristics of each of these affords interest; but you should bear in mind that the fact that a poem is an elegy or a simple lyric rarely aids in teaching anyone to read.

Now let me discuss with you several methods of presenting poetry to your class. You should experiment with any or all of these methods, discarding and adjusting as occasion demands. An excellent one, especially for introducing a poem to a class, is for the teacher to read it aloud. Part of the equipment of a teacher of English is ability to read, by which I do not mean declamatory or dramatic expression, but simple interpretation of thought. If you do not read aloud well, take a course in interpretative reading and practice as much as possible, for this plan of approach has much to commend it. I have spoken of the rhythm of poetry, of its instinctive appeal. Perhaps of all the "mechanics" of poetry sound ranks first, whether it be the barbaric measures in Lindsay's "The Congo" —

> Boomlay, boomlay, boomlay, BOOM;

the gallant

> Boot, saddle, to horse and away!

of Browning's "Cavalier Tunes"; or the subdued melody of Keats's

> My heart aches, and a drowsy numbness pains
> My sense, . . .

Nor is the effect produced merely by the rhythm, fundamental as that is. Words, their sounds, their length; verse patterns; pause — all contribute to the experience we call poetry. In no other way than reading aloud can this be better presented to your boys and girls. But oral reading should not be carried to the extreme. After all, you want class participation. Although a group may sit quietly listening to the teacher and may thoroughly enjoy the reading, this plan does not allow sufficiently for class discussion and observation. It is a very effective device, one that should be resorted to frequently, but not to the exclusion of every other method.

A second means is discussion by the class regarding the meaning of the poem and its application to everyday situations or emotions. Try to connect it with the experiences of those about you, without, however, being personal. Link it up to life, to ordinary experiences, with a view to giving the student an increased understanding of human emotions.

Memorization constitutes a third plan. As you think back upon your secondary school days, can you recall your attitude toward memorizing poetry? And what is your opinion now, after your high school days are past? Have you or have you not benefited by the verse that you were required to learn? Or, better yet, ask a group of your friends, not English majors, their opinion of memorization of poetry. I am asking you these questions because there is considerable division of opinion concerning the desirability of requiring such memorization. I agree in the importance of a well-stocked mind, but I think strongly that you should avoid any method that causes pupils to look askance at poetry. Probably you are working against dislike on the part of your group, anyhow; you should try not to add to it. Of course you will not require memorization as a means of punishment. Just how responsible for the distaste of poetry held by many may be the committing of a certain number of lines as punishment for tardiness, it is hard to say. My personal opinion is that you should require very little memory work, but that you include memorization as part of a contract, if you use that system. If you do require it, you should permit the student to choose his own passages. Tell him that he must always finish the portion he selects, for if you ask him to memorize twenty lines, he may stop in the middle of a sentence. And how are you going to determine whether or not he has learned his lines? By recitation? Ideally, yes, but after you have listened to several students murder some of the sublimest lines in all literature and after you have observed your bored and listless class, you will wonder whether you are justified in so punishing the individual and the group — whether you are "teaching students to read" poetry. I prefer to have memorization passages written, pointing out that the proper form must be followed.

A fourth method, which has a bearing on memorization, is for the teacher to list famous passages in the poem studied and have the student place and interpret them. Usually, after a pupil has considered a passage with care, he has memorized it. You have accomplished a desired result — and painlessly to all concerned.

Class reports on some subject connected with the poem at hand often add to the interest of discussion and give valuable background material. For example, in connection with the study of *The Idylls of the King*, one may make a report on medieval social customs; another may give an illustrated talk on the plan of the medieval castle. Almost all the poems you read that are of any length afford material for a number of worth-while talks.

What is your opinion of dramatization as a means for teaching students to read poetry? Because it visualizes the scene, and thus trains them to see beyond the printed word, I consider it desirable. Ballads often lend themselves to this type of thing. Try, for example, the humorous "Get Up and Bar the Door." Each student may be required to write his dramatization of this. You will point out the necessity for describing the setting and for suggesting costume. You will also show the class the form in which a drama is written. Then select two or three, give them to a committee from the class who will choose the best, and let the students act the dramatization in your classroom. I have had good results with this. Dramatization involves such matters as a consideration of manners, customs, and dress belonging to the period pictured. The "gude-man" in "Get Up and Bar the Door," for example, could not be portrayed reading the daily paper, as a wide-awake pupil of mine once pointed out. Yes, you should employ dramatization, but you should not overdo it. It is great fun and your group will enjoy it; but it should be resorted to only upon occasion, not as a substitute for the reading and interpretation of verse.

Certain teachers like to have their boys and girls select favorite lines of poetry and illustrate them either by drawings or by pictures clipped from magazines. As a means for developing the imagination and for linking poetry with the other arts, I commend it, but it is, after all, "hand work" and must not be considered as a substitute for reading. I doubt that you are justified in taking any of the class time for this. Furthermore, as a student of mine who had not forgotten the point of view of a boy once remarked, most of the boys in your class will look upon it as a childish device. But as it may be very desirable with some groups, I am mentioning it.

Because enjoyment depends upon understanding — for we like what we understand, be it pictures, people, music, or poetry — you can hardly overemphasize the *meaning* of the poem. The student must, first of all, grasp its *content;* then he must master its significance. A brief synopsis of the poem or a short class quiz at the beginning of the period should frequently be asked for. For the class quiz, I prefer the completion type of objective test. Have your pupils number their papers according to the questions you intend to dictate. Then read each incomplete sentence and in the proper space have them write the words necessary to complete the statement. After you leave a sentence, do not go back to it. Collect the papers at once or have them marked quickly in class. Such a test on "The Ballad of East and West" might be:

1. The two nationalities represented are —— and ——.
2. Kamal is ——.
3. His pursuer is ——.

4. The cause of the pursuit is ——.
5. The "dun" is ——.
6. The one successful in the pursuit is ——.
7. The result is ——.
8. The Guides are ——.
9. The gift of Kamal is ——.

This whole procedure, if well planned, will take only a few minutes and will leave the class period for other purposes. Discussion, then, can bear upon interpretation, significance, and application of the idea expressed to everyday problems. In every way possible help the class to "see the picture" back of the word.

One of the most useful methods for aiding the student to understand a poem is that of paraphrasing. To do this, the pupil studies the passage and rewrites it in his own words. Select a short but significant portion and give the class the following advice: Use your dictionary; put inverted passages into normal word order; study difficult passages from the grammatical point of view; watch out for figures of speech; expand when necessary; keep the mood or tone of the original. (For these directions, I am indebted to Richard Ray Kirk and Roger Philip McCutcheon, authors of *An Introduction to the Study of Poetry*, p. 35.) Here is an example of what I mean:

> It little profits that an idle king,
> By this still hearth, among these barren crags,
> Match'd with an aged wife, I meet and dole
> Unequal laws unto a savage race,
> That hoard, and sleep, and feed, and know not me.
>
> — From TENNYSON's "Ulysses."

There is little satisfaction in being an idle king, living in a quiet house set among unproductive hills, mated with

an ancient wife, acting as judge and jury to a rude race
that work for gain, and sleep and eat and have no understanding of what I have been.

Although an understanding of the meaning of the poem
is of first importance, poetic elements, which make poetry
poetry, should not be neglected. Without being technical,
you can direct the attention of your group to these
elements that arouse the emotions and give pure joy to the
sympathetic reader of poetry. The first of these phases
is a knowledge of figures of speech. As I have said, you
should limit these to simile, metaphor, and personification. Then you will want to point out imagery — that
vigorous use of words to produce in the mind of the reader
vivid sense impressions, such as "poplars, wind-flickering
on a hill crest like *black candle flame*." Rhythm and diction
have already been discussed. Onomatopoeia, that adaptation of sound to sense, may aid in the sensory appreciation of such lines as "The silver snarling trumpets 'gan to
chide." Movement, rhythm, color — look for them, for
they will be there. A device for calling attention to the
hues on the writer's canvas, given me by a former student
of mine, consists in having each pupil copy a short poem,
and, with suitably colored pencils, underline each word
suggestive of color:

> Blue, green, and black
> And every track was a flash of golden fire.

Although simple, this emphasizes, as mere talking cannot do, the need for the "inner eye" in reading poetry.

The effect of such passages as "Soon he soothed his soul
to pleasures" may well justify some attention to alliteration. That these are devices to produce the *effect*, the
emotional appeal desired by the poet, may well be pointed

out. None of these should be approached pedantically or sentimentally, for too many boys and men consider a love of poetry a feminine prerogative. Try first to show that it is a record of the thoughts, ideals, hopes, and fears of mankind. But an understanding of the effect of these poetic elements on the reader should be indicated whenever possible. To this end skillful reading aloud best contributes.

In your own thinking, never forget that the poet, especially the writer of lyric verse, has been created to show us what our eyes are too dim to see, our ears too dull to hear, our spirits too warped to understand. Through the carefully attuned soul of the poet we lesser mortals can re-create our own "vague murmurings," can experience the uplift of spirit that expresses itself in such lines as "Hail to thee, blithe spirit! Bird thou never wert!" In his ability to see the beauty in the commonplace, the motive behind the act, and, perhaps particularly, in his power to express in words that which we vaguely feel, lies the poet's great gift to humankind. This you should understand, and you should therefore seek gently to lead your pupils along familiar paths that branch out farther with experience. Some will travel with you gladly; others will need careful guidance before they see the pot of gold. Upon you rests the responsibility of unhurried direction. Poetry expresses such universal experience that it has meaning for all.

ASSIGNMENT

A. Prepare a brief completion test for five poems listed in your state course of study.

B. Your instructor will give you a passage from a poem listed for high school use, which you will paraphrase.

C. Prepare an introduction to a poem you will teach.

FURTHER READINGS

1. LaBrant, Lou L., *The Teaching of Literature in the Secondary School*, Chapter VIII.

Here Miss LaBrant comments upon difficulties in reading poetry.

2. Blaisdell, Thomas C., *Ways to Teach English*, Chapters XXV and XXVI.

Here you will find excellent suggestions for presenting poetry. Note particularly what Mr. Blaisdell has to say concerning the teacher's preparation for presenting any poem.

3. *An Experience Curriculum in English*.

Because the plan of this monograph does not permit the segregation of pieces of literature according to type (I use the plan merely as a matter of convenience), you will not find a section devoted to poetry alone. Yet the section "Sharing Lyric Emotion" (pp. 52–59) provides suggestions for choice of material and elements for emphasis (for example, the recall of personal experiences, vivid imagery of sights, sounds, odors). Say the compilers, "There are more units here than most schools can use. It is assumed each faculty — not each teacher — will decide which ones to omit." Why this assumption?

4. Untermeyer, Louis, *Yesterday and Today*, pp. 358 ff.

Here you will find a section headed "Suggestions for Study." Questions pertaining to the various phases of a poet — as an observer, a musician, a storyteller, and so forth — and five outlines on poets and their works will prove very useful to you.

5. Cooper, Alice C., *Poems of Today*, "The Enjoyment of Poetry," pp. 273–276.

These pages present a general plan for the study of a poem, which you may like to adapt to your own purpose.

6. Mones, Leon, "Bad Psychology in the Teaching of Poetry," *English Journal*, XXIV (October, 1935), pp. 639–644.

In this are made some pertinent comments concerning pupil slants toward studying poetry.

7. CLARK, E. E., *Poetry: An Interpretation of Life*, pp. 3–16.

Poetry as an interpretation of life is discussed in the introductory essay, "What Is Poetry?"

8. BROOKS, CLEANTH, and WARREN, ROBERT PENN, *Understanding Poetry*.

This anthology with exercises will aid the teacher.

9. GILLIS, ADOLPH, and BENÉT, WILLIAM ROSE, *Poems for Modern Youth*.

The introductory material of this anthology, pp. xx–lix, attempts to answer the question "Why read poetry?" and gives suggestions for adapting the unit method to the reading of poetry.

XV. NARRATIVE AND LYRIC POETRY

Of the three great divisions of poetry — narrative, lyric, dramatic — the first will probably, because of its story nature, engage most of your attention, especially during the first three years of the high school course. In order to convince your doubting Thomases that poetry is not an experience apart, establish its connection with types already read by your group, particularly the short story, possibly the novel and drama. Make clear that a narrative poem, like any story, has three elements: There must be people, they must be somewhere, and they must do something; in other words, characters, setting, and plot. (You may want to avoid technical terms with beginning pupils.)

First, lead your class to visualize where the characters are placed: the setting. Have them list words or phrases that suggest it, including both time and place. In some poems these points are stated definitely: "On the sea and at the Hogue, sixteen hundred ninety-two"; or they may be only suggested, as in:

> You know, we French stormed Ratisbon;
> A mile or so away
> On a little mound, Napoleon
> Stood on our storming day.

Here, since the town, but not the time, is mentioned, the student will have to know the period of Napoleon in order to place this poem as to time. He will have to determine from the context that the ancient city of Troy is referred to in:

> Hector left in haste
> The mansion, and retraced his way between
> The rows of stately dwellings, traversing
> The mighty city.

In addition to time and place, the pupil must learn to look for "antecedent action" or "background circumstances" that give information necessary for an understanding of the poem. As an assignment, you can ask him to state the approximate time and place, *with reasons for his decision;* and to make a one-sentence statement of the events occurring prior to the beginning of the story.

After the student has "placed" the poem for setting, he should consider the characters. Have him observe — make this a part of the assignment, if you like — the persons, their appearance, their manners, their motives, their ideals, virtues, failings. To a short poem you need give only one period of discussion; any discussion of ideals, motives, and so forth in a long one must be left until the student has read the entire work and is capable of judging the characters. In an extended narrative, all that one can do at first with characters is to place them in the order of their probable importance and to form a first impression — as we do in life. Ask the pupil to list details that indicate the physical, the mental, and the moral characteristics of the persons. You may not want to do all this at once, but in any discussion of characters these three aspects must be considered, for it is these that we observe concerning people in actual life.

The third feature of any narrative is the plot, or the acts of the characters. Have your group determine upon the struggle depicted in the poem — for strife of some sort there will be. You may ask them to write a statement of the conflict and its result.

Very important in any piece of literature read is an understanding of the *purpose* of the author. I prefer this word to *theme*, for I think the term means more to students. *Theme* they connect with composition (unless you have been careful to avoid using it, as I suggest); or strangely, to them it means *moral*. Why pupils think that every poem has to have a plainly tagged moral, I don't know; perhaps they can see no other reason for reading poetry! But discourage this tendency, and discuss the *purpose*, not the *theme*, of an author. Approach it by having the student complete the statement: The author means to show ——. But do not be content with that; ask *how* the pupil knows "what the author means to show." This will help the student to see that the sort of characters selected, the setting, and the plot all exemplify the purpose that the author had in writing his poem; all are his means of making clear his idea. For example, in "Enoch Arden," Tennyson wanted to demonstrate the glory of self-sacrifice. For his characters, he selected ordinary fisher folk, a class of society among whom literature has led us to expect sacrifice. Had he chosen society leaders to portray his theme, he would have had more difficulty in convincing us than he has in dealing with these fishermen. The incidents that he uses bear out the impression already made by the characters themselves that these simple, honest, hardy people are capable of enduring bravely any amount of adversity. So when Enoch returns and sees his wife and his children, happy in the home of another, we expect him to do exactly what he does. In this way characters, setting, and action show the purpose in the mind of the author.

Everything that has already been said in this chapter applies to all types of narrative poetry, but I want to make a few suggestions for teaching the types that you will use in your high school classes. Let us consider the ballad — an excellent introduction to poetry, provided the dialect is simplified. In teaching any sort of poetry or indeed any particular poem the first problem is always how to introduce it effectively. In beginning a study of the ballad, you may well tell your pupils something of its origin, how it grew up among ordinary people like ourselves. In class you may have boys and girls who know something of the ballad firsthand, for today in America there are a number of sections in which the ballad is still sung, very much as it was hundreds of years ago. If you can, make use of this information on the part of your class; if not, tell your group of our mountaineers who today sing the ballads of long ago. Show them how they themselves, when they play such "singing games" as "The Farmer in the Dell," are doing much as did their ancestors in England, Scotland, or Ireland. Then read a ballad with your class, acting as narrator yourself and having the group join in the refrain. If you are fortunate enough to have a phonograph, play a record of this same ballad, so that your students can sense its rhythm and its "feel." Perhaps you can use a piano and with your pupils play and sing one of the early ballad airs. Whatever you do, try to get your students to sense the fact that a ballad was a group activity, originating in the folk, and expressing their emotions.

But some of you prefer to enliven your approach by

presenting the ballad in modern dress. If so, the cowboy ballads, familiar through the radio and the phonograph, lend themselves excellently. Perhaps a plan described by Miss Helen Schapner, teacher in the Union (Oregon) High School, will prove suggestive, although all of you may not have the opportunity so ideally at hand as did this teacher. She writes:

> Our freshman course requires the teaching of the ballad. As the form and idea are not in reality new to our pupils, I started my discussion last year with some of the modern ballads. I am teaching in a section of the country where the cowboy ballad is very popular. There is a cowboy orchestra at a dude ranch not far away. I asked these boys to visit my class one afternoon. I gave them an idea of what I wanted. They told of the origin of their type of ballad, its uses and values, and recited and played some of the most familiar. Needless to say, the hour was a very entertaining one, but it accomplished the purpose I intended. The following day I gave some of the background of the ancient ballad, and we read one in class. The work continued in an interesting manner, and I considered the value of linking the old ballad with present-day experiences very helpful. Unfamiliar words and expressions caused no difficulty, as the approach had created interest in the type.

Such an approach, possible in a certain degree to anyone within the range of a radio, surely destroys the impression that ballads — and, hence, we hope, by inference, all poetry — are old and dry.

After you have introduced your group to the ballad, you will want to emphasize some of its characteristics. Because of its paucity of explanation, the ballad is excellent for showing how to read more than the actual word; and for compactness of expression the ballad has few rivals. It also gives excellent training in finding the "story back of the story." In "Sir Patrick Spence," for example, explain the importance of the position at the "king's right knee." Have your class notice that the man who sits there is an "elder knight," and that it is he who suggests that Sir Patrick Spence be sent upon this dangerous voyage. Why? A few such suggestions from you will enable the students to understand the jealousy of the elder for the younger, and to realize that the fear of supremacy caused the elder knight to dispose of his young rival. Similarly, in "Edward, Edward," your group will have to be led to see the signficance of

> The curse from Hell from me shall ye bear
> Such counsels ye gave to me, O.

Why the mother desired the murder of her husband remains a matter for speculation. Again, help your students to see the story back of the words in "The Twa Corbies":

> And nobody knows that he lies there,
> But his hawk, his hound, and his lady fair.

Even unimaginative youngsters will thrill to the drama behind such words as these.

Be careful that the pupils know who is speaking, to whom he is speaking, and the situation described. Because the incident about which the ballad centers was too familiar to the ballad singers to require explanation, it is frequently merely suggested, not described. Be particularly careful, then, that your group has clearly in mind these points. Incidentally, the ballads show the importance of quotation marks, for without these guides we might well have difficulty in following the speeches.

A comment upon a few ballad conventions, although somewhat academic, nevertheless holds a certain interest.

The use of the lucky numbers three and seven (but not eleven); such epithets as *lily-white, cherry cheeks, yellow hair;* fairy-tale superstitions of the wicked elder sister, the cruel stepmother (all appearing, faintly disguised, in modern comic strips and motion pictures); other superstitions, such as the dead returning to life and fear of the forest; the frequent use of the bequest and the curse — all these are of interest in that they show the customs and beliefs of our ancestors, many of which are current today.

More academic still is a study of ballad form. With older students you may wish to comment on the rhyme scheme and the stanzaic pattern. With younger ones I doubt that you will. Both groups, however, should note the use of repetition and refrain, for it is these elements that made the ballad a group and not an individual activity.

To older pupils, ballad themes may be of interest. Such students may like to group ballads they have read according to the elemental emotions displayed: love, hate, jealousy, revenge, superstitious fear, heroism, tragedy — all held in common by us today. Little or no conscious humor is shown in these old ballads, although your students will probably burst into laughter over tragic occurrences, such as "eels fried in a pan" as a means of removing one's cast-off suitor.

In discussing certain of the ballads you may wish to do something with the historical period portrayed. For example "Chevy Chase" needs a little explanation of border warfare between the Scotch and English before it can be understood by your class. But do not make the reading of ballads a serious study. They are of interest particularly because of the picture they give of the folk attitude toward the nobility.

A second type of narrative poetry that you may well teach is the epic. In the ninth year, you may read the *Odyssey* in whole or in parts; in the senior, a translation of parts of *Beowulf* or of *Paradise Lost* may be required by your state course. Personally, I hope you do not teach *Paradise Lost*, for it seems to me far beyond the comprehension of high school students. After all, Milton's most sublime epic was never intended for reading by fifteen- or sixteen-year-old boys and girls.

Although you will do more intensive work with a senior class than with freshman students, I believe that you will emphasize largely the same phases. In any epic that your class may study — the *Iliad*, the *Odyssey*, *Paradise Lost*, *Beowulf*, *Drake* — it will be necessary to do a good deal with its historical period. As *Paradise Lost* is a great epic of religious faith, you will have to lay a very careful foundation concerning the religious ideals expressed in the Old Testament, for pupils of today have a very scanty foundation in Bible literature. Of course, this lack is one of the difficulties that confront one in trying to teach *Paradise Lost*.

As you probably will teach parts of *Beowulf* or the *Odyssey* or both, I shall make my comments particularly applicable to these epics. The *Odyssey* needs a brief but vivid picture of the events leading to the Trojan War, of its outstanding episodes, particularly the success of the Greeks, up to the moment when Odysseus heads his black ships toward Ithaca. If you read only one portion from the *Odyssey*, you will have to supply the narrative up to the episode selected and to round out the whole story to the end of the epic. *Beowulf* requires less background, but the class should know something of the period portrayed and enough of the narrative to bring it down to the sections studied. Your aim in teaching these epics should be to have your pupils share the world's most glorious adventures. In addition, there is much of interest concerning the life, loves, and deaths of the ancient Greeks or our Scandinavian ancestors. To this end, look for incidents or comments bearing on such things as the manners, customs, religious ideas, sports, attitude toward women, and methods of warfare. In this way you will try to show your pupils that these people, legendary though they be, were human beings with a culture different from our own, but in many respects with an amazingly high-minded attitude toward life (although today Odysseus might engage the attention of the G-men!).

As an epic is a very long poem, you will have to budget your time carefully. Planning a course is always necessary in order not to give too much time to one unit of work and too little to another. Because of the length of this type of poem it may be best to read extracts. If you study the whole poem, select certain parts for class discussion. For this purpose, "Ulysses among the Phaeacians" is excellent, as it gives a résumé of many of his adventures. The other episodes in the poem may be covered by class reports, or you can depend upon class quizzes to test the reading of your group. It may be that you will think the entire *Odyssey* too long for your pupils to read. If so, its content may be handled by assigning certain portions to each student for use as a basis for class reports. I do not recommend this plan, but it is one whereby a long piece of literature may be handled in a minimum number of class periods. Young persons, in particular, tire quickly and should not be subjected to any one poem or prose piece for too long a time.

If you use an anthology, the problem of the translation
will be settled for you by the editors. But if you read
from separate classics, you are forced to make your own
decision. The *Odyssey* may be had both in prose and
poetry translations. I suggest that you study several of
these, particularly those by Palmer, Bryant, and Bates,
before making a decision. No doubt a prose translation
is more easily understood by the student than is a poetic
version. On the other hand, if pupils read a prose translation they are likely to forget that the original is a great
epic poem. But perhaps that does not matter. What
do you think?

Another very long type of poem — so extended that it
is seldom used in its entirety in high school — is the
metrical romance. However, one example — *The Lady
of the Lake* — does appear in many courses of study.
Occasionally, too, *Marmion* is called for, as are parts,
never all, of *The Faerie Queene*.

In reading this type of poem, be especially careful
to make clear the setting and the historical background.
But in doing this for *The Lady of the Lake*, do not, I beg
of you, betray the secret of the identity of James Fitz-
James, which Scott took such pains to conceal. The
class must, however, know something of the period depicted, particularly the struggles among the Lowlanders,
the Borderers, and the Highlanders, so called because
of the section of Scotland in which each group lived.
Pictures of the Trossachs, an explanation of such syllables
as *ben* (mountain), Fitz (son), Dhu (black), a map of the
section, on which the route of the stag and the Fiery Cross
may be followed, and a chart of the characters such as
the following all help your boys and girls to understand
this poem.

CHARACTER CHART

HIGHLANDERS	LOWLANDERS
The Douglas (outlawed by his king)	Knight of Snowdoun (James Fitz-James)
Ellen (his daughter)	
Dame Margaret (aunt and foster-mother of Ellen)	Malcolm Graeme (ward of Scotland's king and lover of Ellen)
Roderick Dhu (her son, lover and cousin of Ellen)	Blanche of Devan (half-crazed victim of Roderick Dhu)
Allan-bane (minstrel and retainer of Douglas)	
Malise (henchman of Roderick Dhu)	
Brian (a hermit monk and brewer of sorceries)	
Murdock (guide to James Fitz-James)	

During the reading of the poem by the class, you might make more vivid the ceremonies for preparation of the Fiery Cross by reading the witch scene from *Macbeth;* and for that highly dramatic scene where Roderick Dhu leads James Fitz-James through his territory (Canto V), Kipling's "Ballad of the East and West" provides a similar situation. *The Lady of the Lake,* although a popular poem, is not particularly easy for freshman pupils of today; therefore lay a careful foundation before you begin the class reading, and as that progresses, take pains to keep clear the strands of plot and character relationships. Until your group has completed its first reading, it may be well to omit the introductory stanzas preceding each canto, and lend your energies to unraveling the tale itself. If you teach in a community in which hunting is a favorite sport, you will get off to a flying start with this poem; if not, call into play your creative and dramatic ability in order to arouse the interest and the imagination of your class. *Be* each character, if necessary.

Thereafter, Scott may be depended upon to carry his fair share of the load.

Marmion and *The Faerie Queene*, like *The Lady of the Lake*, also require a careful foundation before beginning the class reading. Particularly *The Faerie Queene* requires a solid approach, for it contains both historical and spiritual allegories. But, as I said about *Paradise Lost*, Spenser's great poem is not fit food for sixteen-year-olds. After all, William Lyon Phelps's "*Faerie Queene* Club" has very few members!

The metrical tale, perhaps because of its brevity as well as its swift action, belongs in each of the secondary school years. Youngsters and seniors, all will thrill to the romantic adventure of "The Highwayman." (Some classify "The Highwayman" as a literary ballad. So be it; what we call a piece never aids anyone to read.) Older pupils will appreciate the quiet pathos of Wilfrid Gibson's "The Brothers," and the cheerful irony of Chaucer's "Pardoner's Tale" (provided it is put into modern English). In teaching this type, apply to it the points enumerated for consideration of all narratives: setting, antecedent action, characters, the struggle, and its results. Note the emotional effect on the reader, strong both in "The Highwayman" and "The Brothers," although different in key. And the author's purpose — romantic, realistic, or satirical — must never be lost sight of. Occasionally some sort of preparation for the study of this type may be required, but ordinarily the metrical tale is so simple in content that it needs no elaborate background for teaching. Link it with the short story, for it is comparable in many respects to this prose form.

Now let us look at "The Brothers," the story, as the title implies, of two brothers. The place is in a mine, the time is modern, the characters English. As one reads, he learns that these two men, Dick, the older, a father almost to the younger Bob, love the same girl. And all day long, as they work, this love, unspoken, comes between them until they almost fight. Suddenly comes the terror of all miners — a cave-in, followed by the "deadly after-damp," a sign of certain death. And in the interval before sleep comes to them, the two forget their strife, the elder murmuring, "And when we're out, lad, you and she shall wed." As Bob sinks, Dick

> Whispered with failing breath
> Into the ear of death:
> "Come, Robert, cuddle closer, lad, it's cold."

This simple tale, simply told, expresses one of the truths of human nature: that in a crisis old affections triumph over new. The men stand out, separate, yet together. You can see how this poem illustrates singleness of purpose, one emotional level, a single struggle, very much as does the prose tale.

To turn from a discussion of the teaching of narrative poetry to that of lyric poetry is like turning from the brilliance of the outdoors, in which all is clear, distinct, and bright, to the shadows of the interior, in which the images are subdued and quiet. Yet the materials are much the same in each; only the lighting, the perspective, differ. So lyric poetry compares to narrative: whereas the one is definite, objective, the other is shaded, subjective. Yet in both lie those qualities that give poetry its meaning to mankind. In both we have experience — one often of the body, brilliant and significant; the other of the spirit. And both are required for a full expression of mankind: its joys, pains, struggles, hopes, fears, ideas.

But truth has it that the first appeals most strongly to youth and the second to maturity. Thus, understanding of lyric poetry, exalted in its form and savor, must perforce be a matter of growth and development. Touch lightly upon it, then, presenting to your group only that which their experience and maturity permit.

Let me now discuss with you, somewhat briefly, the teaching of this elusive lyric poetry. I shall not consider its various divisions — the sonnet, ode, simple lyric, song, elegy — for unless you are concerned with structure, these forms demand the same, not different, teaching procedure. As a lyric represents the ideals, thoughts, fears, hopes, beliefs of the writer, as it is definitely a bit of personal experience, you should be particularly concerned, in teaching it, with understanding the thought in the mind of the writer and with recognizing and responding to the emotion influencing him when he wrote the poem. Now, in an average high school class, any discussion of emotion must be handled with great care. The adolescent, because, I suppose, he recognizes the awakening of emotion in himself, is very self-conscious in discussing it and is likely to affect amusement or scorn. Make your comments, then, as impersonal as possible. Do not ask blunt, matter-of-fact John how a poem exalting the sensation of love makes *him* feel; ask him how he thinks the author was feeling when he wrote the poem and what makes him think this. If you find that you have difficulty in discussing emotional effect, omit it, trusting in the response no doubt experienced by the sensitive among your pupils. Give your class time to an interpretation of the thought expressed by the poem.

Because the lyric is subjective in type, the author is likely to clothe his thought in figurative language. To understand him, we must understand his language. So you may well give time to a consideration of the poetic elements already discussed. But please use care in this. Poetic elements are not ends in themselves but means to an end and should be so considered. College students may well be set to counting the number of examples of alliteration in Browning's *Ring and the Book*, but such emphasis upon poetic device is out of place in high school.

And last a warning in teaching lyrics — touch them lightly, I beg of you, especially the shorter ones. Sometimes you do not need to discuss a poem at all — sympathetic reading by the teacher may say better than words what the author has expressed.

Has it seemed to you in this discussion that I have tied Pegasus too firmly to earth? I am far from thinking that your teaching — especially of that emotional experience called poetry — should be formal or dull. But observation leads me to believe that one of the great reasons why students do not like poetry lies in the fact that no one has taken the trouble to help them to read it — to show them what difficulties they may expect and how to overcome them. Poetry, the earliest expression of the human race, should be enjoyed, not disliked. But I say again — *we can enjoy only if we understand:* your task consists in guiding your pupils to realize the significance of poetry as a universal experience, in which the poet pictures for us duller folk something of the beauty or significance or interest of the world about us, observed through keen yet sympathetic eyes, and expressed in terms beyond the power of ordinary man.

Let me now present for your consideration two lesson plans: one for a narrative, the other for a lyric poem.

A Plan for Teaching "Agincourt"

Approach: Say to the class that heroism in war has long been a subject for poetry. Tell them that the little poem they are about to read is an account of a battle famous in history.

Assignment: In one complete sentence answer each of the following questions:

1. What is the setting (time and place) of the poem?
2. State your reasons for placing the setting as you do.
3. Between what groups is the struggle?
4. What is the result of the struggle?
5. What is the meaning of the following words as used in the poem? *Main* (stanza 1); *rest* (stanza 5); *henchman* (stanza 7); *bilboes* (stanza 11); *maiden knight* (stanza 13); *Crispin's Day* (stanza 14).

Class: Collect the papers prepared by the students. Begin your discussion by deciding upon the setting of the poem, following with such questions as these:

1. What was the cause of the battle?
2. What was the attitude of Henry's men as they entered into the fight? Were they discouraged, dogged, gay?
3. With what weapons was the battle fought?
4. With what previous battles is this one compared? What is meant by "lopped the French lilies"?
5. What is the principal characteristic of King Henry? What lines show this?
6. What does the author intend to show in the poem?
7. In what ways does the character of King Henry show the purpose of the author?
8. How do the incidents exemplify the purpose?
9. In what sort of mood is the author?

10. What movement does the rhythm of the poem suggest to you? (Read aloud a few stanzas, deliberately emphasizing the rhythm, to illustrate this point.)
11. Would such a poem as this depiction of battle be possible today? Why?

If your students have read Shakespeare's *King Henry the Fifth* or if they intend to read it, you should connect the poem with the play, using it as an example of the patriotic fervor of the Elizabethans. See that your pupils know that Michael Drayton lived much later than the period of which he is writing. Select passages that pertain to each question, so that you can easily direct your boys and girls to the details that bear upon each question.

A Plan for Teaching "The Spires of Oxford"

Approach: Talk with your class of the great responsibility toward their country, both in time of peace and in time of war, acknowledged by men of gentle birth in England. During the first World War, universities — then schools — gave their finest. To these young men, trained to accept the responsibility with which their birth endowed them, there was only one path — to fight for their country, to act as leaders. The great universities thus very early were emptied of their finest and best. And in the trenches death met them, almost to a man. Say that "The Spires of Oxford" was inspired by the sight of the tall towers as the author passed by one day during the first World War and thought of the young men who had dwelt therein.

Assignment: Read the poem and write on these points:

1. Where is Oxford?
2. What is the situation upon which this poem is based?

3. Write a one-sentence précis of the content of the poem.
4. Of what old carol is the last stanza reminiscent?
5. Explain (1) cricket field; (2) quad; (3) "cap and gown."

Class: Read the poem aloud. Then base your class discussion upon such questions as these: In what sort of mood is the author? What details indicate this? Point out several contrasts and note their effect (stanzas 2 and 3 contain examples). Ask whether anyone knows of other examples of the situation here described: (Our own country at the time of the War Between the States and in World War II affords a good parallel. Your class will know many tales of youthful heroes.) Discuss what this experience may mean to a young man and to a nation that loses the flower of its young manhood. Have the carol "God rest you, merry gentlemen" read aloud by a good pupil reader. Comment upon Miss Letts's use of "happy gentlemen" as a substitute for "merry gentlemen." Why are these young men happy that have "laid their young lives down"? To be happy in self-sacrifice, in the acceptance of responsibility, can be an experience of noble minds; to be "merry" cannot. Some high school pupils, too, can understand (of course but dimly) that death often affords more of happiness than does life. The tragedy for "the ancient mariner" lay in the fact that "Life-in-Death," not "Death," won at their game of dice. Some, perhaps many, upperclassmen would appreciate Sherriff's great play *Journey's End*, in which two gallant boys meet death.

ASSIGNMENT

Select one narrative and one lyric poem listed in your state course of study. For each write a lesson plan to include: (1) a statement of aim; (2) your approach to the poem; (3) five questions on the poem; and (4) your assignment.

FURTHER READINGS

1. THOMAS, CHARLES SWAIN, *The Teaching of English in the Secondary School*, Chapter VIII.

For both its advice and warnings, you will want to read this chapter with care.

2. HILL, FRANK E. and AUSLANDER, JOSEPH, *The Winged Horse*.

This should be on your desk for all to read.

3. BOLENIUS, EMMA M., *Teaching Literature in the Grammar Grades and High School*, Chapters I to VI.

These offer practical suggestions for teaching different types of poetry.

4. CROSS, E. A., and CARNEY, ELIZABETH, *Teaching English in High Schools*, Chapter XX.

In this chapter you will find discussions of the teacher's preparation, helps for teaching poetry, and lesson plans.

5. DANIELS, EARL, *The Art of Reading Poetry*.

This book defends the reading of poetry, points out "lions in the path," and discusses poems as stories, ideas, and organization.

6. In any of the anthologies listed in Appendix K of this text, you will find specific directions for teaching poetry.

XVI. DRAMA

R EAL, living human beings, who, by their acts and
words, portray a mood, reveal a crisis, re-create
a period, vivify history, expound a thesis — that is drama,
close, indeed, as its history bears witness, to the life experiences of our race. Particularly significant should
it be to your pupils in their quest for new experience and
understanding; lead them gladly toward this interpretation of human emotion. All high school courses advise
the reading of a number of plays, usually several written
by Shakespeare, occasionally non-Shakespearean and
modern dramas. Through the works of the greatest of
all dramatists, then, you introduce your class to what is
possibly their first reading of dramatic literature. Fortunately for you and for them, all have scraped acquaintance with this type in the movies, some in amateur
performances, and a few lucky people in "real plays."

Shakespeare is usually represented in high school
courses by *Julius Caesar*, *As You Like It*, *The Merchant of
Venice*, *Macbeth*, *Hamlet*, and *A Midsummer Night's Dream*.
Of these, the only one you need question from the angle
of content is *The Merchant of Venice*. As this represents
the medieval attitude toward the Jewish race, you can

readily see that it is not the best choice for reading with certain groups.

Any play that you select should always be taught from the *acting* point of view; that is, your students should visualize it, trying to think of it as if it were before them on the stage, rather than regarding it as a piece of literature, to be read or, worse, to be studied. Because visualizing the written word requires imagination on the part of the reader, drama presents certain difficulties. But because it is so alive, it may become favorite reading with your group. Moreover, drama, in the form of the film, has become the popular pastime of our people. By acquainting your group with the best of literary drama, you may help to elevate their taste, and thus to produce better films than many we see at present.

Your first duty, then, is to arouse the imagination of your group. You should introduce the study of any Shakespearean play by reading with your students the first scene or two or by a bit of dramatization. A few days before you plan to begin the reading of *Macbeth*, for example, call aside three girls with dramatic ability, and with your help, let them plan and present before the class the witches' scene, in which Shakespeare strikes the keynote of the play. After this introduction, your group will *want* to read the play. With your class, visualize the setting. Because of the exigencies of the Elizabethan stage, Shakespeare himself was not concerned with elaborate settings, but you must sharpen the inner eye of your pupils: make them see the heath, or the market place, or the castle at Elsinore. Decide upon the time of day; discuss the lighting that a director might want to use. So, too, for the characters, as each enters. What manner of man is he? How dressed? How does he bear himself?

As you read on, picture with the class the action: Does the character stand or sit? Is his bearing haughty or subservient? Make the characters real people.

With a class about to read its first play, you must do more than this. Its divisions into acts and scenes; the way of indicating each speaker; the lack of explanation; the list and meaning of the *dramatis personae* — all must be explained. As Shakespeare always arranges his characters in the order of their rank, the lengthy list need not frighten the reader, for his experience in seeing plays should assure him that the important personages are very few. By the end of the first act, he will have made their acquaintance.

I have suggested that you introduce each play by reading with your students, and I believe you will have to do a good deal of this as you continue the play. Vivid oral reading by you lessens the complications caused by blank verse and Shakespearean diction. As a guide for study and understanding, you should prepare questions as a part of each assignment. Think these out carefully, being sure that they pertain to the plot or characters or both and are guideposts to important points in the scene or act. This plan, plus intelligent reading aloud, should produce both understanding and appreciation. For Act One, Scene Two, of *Macbeth* such questions may be:

1. Who are the king's enemies at the time the play begins?
2. What do the characters in this scene say about Macbeth?
3. What impression of Banquo is given?
4. What sort of man is Duncan? Is he a man of action? Give reasons for your answer.
5. What are the events of the battle reported in this scene?

For Act One, Scene Three, you might ask:

1. Why does Shakespeare devote nearly forty lines to the witches, although their dialogue does not contribute toward the advancement of the play until the entrance of Macbeth and Banquo?
2. What is the difference in the way Macbeth receives the witches' news and the way Banquo receives it?
3. How does each man reward the witches?
4. What is the dramatic effect of having Ross call Macbeth *Cawdor* almost immediately after the witches' prophecy? What is its effect upon Macbeth? Upon Banquo?
5. Is there any indication in this scene that Macbeth has already contemplated the murder of Duncan to gain the crown?

Intelligent presentation of the first scene, either through dramatization or reading, serves another purpose aside from arousing interest, for in the first few lines of his plays, Shakespeare always strikes the keynote, suggests the atmosphere. The eerie chanting of the witches suggests the supernatural nature of the play and the secret depths in the soul of Macbeth. Excitement and fear are indicated in *Hamlet* by the opening lines, in which the relief officer, Bernardo, so far forgets military procedure as to challenge the sentinel at his post. In the milling crowd presented at the opening of *Julius Caesar*, we receive an impression both of the fickle nature of the "vulgar" and the conflict between those who venerate the memory of great Pompey and those who follow Caesar. Antonio's first words in *The Merchant of Venice:* "In sooth, I know not why I am so sad" and the subsequent conversation between the young bloods prepare the audience for Antonio's harrowing experience. Especially in the tragedies (in my experience, the type best liked by students) this strongly struck opening note, if understood, appeals deeply.

Because visualization is so important in reading plays, class dramatizations have a definite place in your teaching procedure. Frequently, perhaps after each act, select a significant scene or scenes and assign parts in them to your pupils. These need not be memorized — probably should not — but they must be read aloud until the student can read his part easily. By an arrangement of chairs, some suggestion of stage setting may be made. Action should be introduced, exits and entrances properly planned. A scarf, a handkerchief, an apron may suggest the grace of an Ophelia or the ague of a Casca. This will be fun, but it should be more than that. In other words, you should try, by some means or other, to get your group to give it adequate preparation; otherwise, you will obtain a halting, stumbling performance far from being an aid to visualizing the scene. As in other aspects of your teaching, class dramatizations require your oversight.

Another means of visualizing the scene, which some of your pupils may prefer to dramatization, consists of asking them to write a paper describing the setting or the costumes for a certain act or scene. This may be called "If I Were Directing the Play." Fortunately their friend and ally, the motion picture, will aid them — for example, *A Midsummer Night's Dream* or *Romeo and Juliet*. Non-Shakespearean pictures, such as *The Crusades*, afford examples of knights, armor, castles, houses, methods of warfare. Illustrations in motion-picture magazines (the pupils can supply these), handsomely illustrated copies of the plays, all do their share in providing suggestions for the amateur director.

Most of the methods we have discussed under the teaching of literature and particularly under the teaching of narrative poetry are applicable here, for Shakespearean drama is dramatic poetry. Familiar quotations may be typed, sufficient space being allowed beneath each for the student to write answers to the following: when, where, and by whom said. More formal memorization may be required if you desire. Charles Swain Thomas, in *The Teaching of English in the Secondary School* (page 308), presents the following plan as a means of review, amusement, and painless memorization. Says Mr. Thomas:

Pupils enjoy making nonsense riddles that are answerable from the plays studied; in so doing they become much more familiar with the lines of the play, so that the results are well worth the time spent on such apparent frivolity. Some examples of riddles composed by pupils during the study of *As You Like It*, *Twelfth Night*, and *Hamlet* are as follows:

What does the music supervisor say to the orchestra before assembly? "'Tis no matter how it be in tune, so it make noise enough."

How might one describe a Ford car? "Compact of jars."

What is a good definition of this high school? "Where none will sweat save for promotion."

What comment are old folks likely to make on the younger generation? "They are of desperate shame and character."

What does our school chorus sound like? "Like an Egyptian thief on point of death."

What does an unsympathetic friend say to a man who has just fallen in love? "Talkest thou of nothing but ladies!"

How might a vigilant father express his feelings when

his daughter receives a caller of whom he disapproves? "What! Has this thing appeared again tonight?"

What is the constant prayer of the fat woman struggling through her "daily dozen"? "O that this too, too solid flesh would melt, Thaw, and resolve itself into a dew!"

Reports on the historical period concerned, projects such as building a model of a Shakespearean theater or garden, dressing dolls in Elizabethan costume, papers comparing or contrasting two characters — any or all of these may provide atmosphere.

As in any narrative, we are concerned with setting, characters, and plot. Of these, setting deserves the least consideration. It should of course be clear. The student should know where and when the action of the play was supposed to take place. You must also explain that the time of the play is not necessarily that of the author; for instance, Shakespeare lived and wrote in the sixteenth and seventeenth centuries, but his Julius Caesar and his Brutus came into conflict about fifty years before the birth of Christ.

Characterization deserves a great deal of your attention, particularly with somewhat mature students. With junior high school pupils you should be content if they have a definite impression of the principal attributes of the main characters and can support their claims by exact references. Sometimes a bit of diagram suggests relationships. For example, in *A Midsummer Night's Dream*, after the antic Puck has done his worst, the situation may thus be explained:

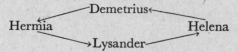

Older students should see character change, should be alert to notice the effect of one character upon another, and of the influence of circumstance. *Hamlet* and *Macbeth*, both plays frequently studied in high school, afford an excellent opportunity for tracing character development. This sort of thing should be confined to a study of one or two persons, for even seniors are not capable of a long study of any one piece of literature.

Plot should be considered in all six years. In the early grades, it may well be handled by having students make a brief statement of what is accomplished in each scene. Be certain that these statements *are* brief; a one-sentence or a three-sentence précis (incidental training in composition) may be required. By these synopses the student is made conscious of the forward movement of the drama. After he has read the entire play, he can formulate a statement of the struggle and its results.

Older students can do this, and, if well prepared, they can do even more with plot. Have them work out a simple plan of the plot structure:

Introduction: A statement of setting, antecedent action, introduction of characters, the first incident of the struggle.

Rising Action: A statement of several (not necessarily all) of the steps in the struggle.

Turning Point: A statement of the incident that marks the point at which the action turns for or against the leading characters.

Conclusion: A statement of the result of the struggle.

This plan may be used either as a method of summing up the action of the play, or as an assignment: for instance, after reading the introduction (in a five-act play, this is usually Act One) the points suggested may be written out. You will have to divide the drama into these parts and see that your assignments include just those desired. I prefer this plan to the more formal plot diagram and suggest that you try it as a substitute. But let me warn you solemnly to avoid the curse placed upon reading by overanalysis. Enough makes for increased understanding, but too much makes for deadly dullness.

An application of this plan to *Hamlet* would be as follows:

Introduction: The setting is in Elsinore, the ancient capital of Denmark and adjoining country, about the ninth century. The young prince, Hamlet, who has been studying at Wittenberg, has been called home to attend the funeral of his father. Two months later occurs the marriage of his mother to Claudius, the brother of the late King Hamlet. The old King of Norway has lost to the late King Hamlet a considerable parcel of land. All important characters, except Fortinbras, are introduced. The action begins with information from the lips of the ghost of Hamlet's father that he was murdered by Hamlet's uncle Claudius, the present king. Hamlet vows to avenge the death of his father.

Rising Action: Hamlet feigns madness. He plans to determine the guilt of the king by having a scene depicting a murder similar to that of his father given in the presence of Claudius. With bitter words he spurns Ophelia, thus convincing the king that he is not mad from love. The king determines to send Hamlet to England. At the play, the king shows deep emotion, thus convincing Hamlet of his guilt.

Turning Point: Hamlet has an opportunity to kill the king while Claudius is praying but does not take it. Later, he kills Polonius by mistake.

Falling Action: The king is determined to have Hamlet killed on his arrival in England. Ophelia, mad, meets her death by drowning. Hamlet, discovering the plot against him, escapes from the ship and returns to Denmark. The king, with Laertes, brother of Ophelia, plots further for the murder of Hamlet.

Conclusion: The queen drinks poisoned wine prepared for Hamlet and dies; both Laertes and Hamlet are wounded by a poisoned sword and die. Before dying, Hamlet wounds the king with the poisoned sword. The king dies. Young Fortinbras, of Norway, will become ruler of Denmark.

After you have read the drama, you and your pupils should determine upon the *purpose* of the author: What does the writer mean to show? And then have the students indicate how the characters and the situations exemplify the theme. From the point of view of the student Shakespeare wishes to exhibit in *Macbeth* the tragic results of inordinate ambition. To show this, he selects a valorous general, Macbeth, a man who is already accustomed to success. He has him married to a woman whose ruthless ambition exceeds his own. He makes him capable of being played upon by circumstance and involves him in incidents that intensify his ambition: the victorious battle, the treachery of the thane of Cawdor, Macbeth's elevation to the title, the king's decision to visit at the castle of Macbeth. Occurrence after occurrence gives power to Macbeth, until, in grasping for all, he falls victim himself. In some such way as this, you can show your students how the purpose of the author is consummated. (High school teaching must be definite. In dealing with Shakespeare, then, it is probably advisable to adopt a simple, direct point of view, rather than to complicate the discussion with comments on the diverse and fascinating aspects of Shakespeare's genius.)

To share, through imagination, the plays of Shakespeare, one should appreciate his principal medium, poetry. A sympathetic and understanding reading of the lines, as well as a visualization of the play, depends upon recognition of the meter, figures of speech, and other characteristics of poetry. You might tell your class something of the pride and exultation experienced by the Elizabethans in their language, emotions which made them delight in great bursts of rhetoric as well as in clever juggling with words: "And here am I, and, wood within this wood." (*A Midsummer Night's Dream*, Act Two, Scene One, line 192.) Verse had long been a requirement of drama, so that the Elizabethan was merely following tradition in his insistence that noble thoughts be expressed in poetic form. Picture with your class the Shakespearean audience, the lettered and the unlearned, alike in their patriotic fervor for their mother tongue and in their ability to listen well, a skill fostered by lack of reading knowledge among the masses and paucity of reading material among the literate. To such an audience, then, soliloquies like Hamlet's "O what a rogue and peasant slave am I!" gave pure delight. If, then, your group desire to re-create Shakespeare, they must concern themselves with his poetry.

With young pupils, perhaps, you will do no more than trust to reading aloud for an appreciation of the rhythm of the poetic form of the plays. Skillful reading to your freshmen of Antony's famous lines:

> Friends, Romans, countrymen, lend me your ears!
> I come to bury Caesar, not to praise him

suggests the poetic qualities of the verse, as well as the mood of the speaker. In the same play (to quote only two of many passages) the closing lines evince the poetic form:

> This was the noblest Roman of them all.
> All the conspirators save only he
> Did that they did in envy of great Caesar;
> He only, in a general honest thought
> And common good to all, made one of them.
> His life was gentle, and the elements
> So mixed in him that Nature might stand up
> And say to all the world "This was a man!"

Skilled reading of the fairies' lines in *A Midsummer Night's Dream* shows how the meter indicates the delicacy of the fairy nature:

> The King doth keep his revels here tonight;
> Take heed the Queen come not within his sight;
> For Oberon is passing fell and wrath
> Because that she as her attendant hath
> A lovely boy stolen from an Indian king.
> . . . .
> And now they never meet in grove or green,
> By fountains clear, or spangled starlight sheen,
> But they do square, that all their elves for fear
> Creep into acorn-cups and hide them there.

Older pupils may like to know somewhat of the structure of Shakespeare's poetry, particularly its greatest form, blank verse. Turn with them to *As You Like It*, Act Four, Scene One, to the conversation between Rosalind and that misanthrope, the "melancholy Jaques." Their talk (in prose, by the way) is interrupted by Orlando, who exclaims

> Good day and happiness, dear Rosalind!

The disgusted Jaques remarks

Nay, then, God be wi' you, an you talk in blank verse

and forthwith quits their company. This passage affords a natural transition to a discussion of blank verse. Very simply, you could say that it is verse without rhyme, consisting of five accented syllables to each line:

Good day | and hap | piness, | dear Ros | alind!

Perhaps you may say further that in poetry groups of accented and unaccented syllables are called *feet*, and that each kind of grouping has a name. In the line quoted, each poetic foot consists of an unaccented syllable followed by an accented one, the name of this combination being *iamb* or *iambus*. To show the unrhymed nature of the verse, turn to another passage, possibly,

O good | old man, | how well | in thee | appears

The con | stant serv | ice of | the an | tique world,

When serv | ice sweat | for du | ty, not | for meed!

No doubt you note my qualifying "perhaps" and "possibly." They are used advisedly, intended to convey a gentle warning that interpretation of poetry does not demand a study of its anatomy. Yet a conception of the form of blank verse is necessary to an educated person, and those of your class who desire to read expressively may well consider poetic forms. Except for unusually mature pupils (intellectually, not chronologically), a feeling for Shakespeare's poetry is best conveyed by oral reading. Further to emphasize the poetic form, some teachers require the writing of a paraphrase of a famous passage, and ask the pupil to read aloud first his version, then the original. The contrast can hardly fail to be impressive.

In not one of the eight or ten anthologies prepared for high school reading do I find *Romeo and Juliet* included. Perhaps it is omitted because adolescents often turn from a representation of emotions which they themselves are experiencing. The tragic ending to romantic love as shown in this play fortunately lies beyond the knowledge of most high school boys and girls, but the emotion itself is one of which they are becoming conscious. Some groups (but certainly not all) may want to re-create this experience of romantic love. To such as these the lines from the famous balcony scene will give pure pleasure:

> *Jul.* 'Tis almost morning; I would have thee gone; —
> And yet no farther than a wanton's bird;
> Who lets it hop a little from her hand,
> Like a poor prisoner in his twisted gyves,
> And with a silk thread plucks it back again,
> So loving-jealous of his liberty.
> *Rom.* I would I were thy bird.
> *Jul.*   Sweet, so would I;
> Yet I should kill thee with much cherishing.
> Good night, good night! Parting is such sweet sorrow,
> That I shall say good night till it be morrow.

Pearls indeed are these; take heed lest you cast them to be trampled on.

The love scene between Lorenzo and Jessica in *The Merchant of Venice*, Act Five, Scene One, is lyrical also, yet with a whimsical twist which prevents the bashful, self-conscious, or prosaic from light laughter.

> *Lor.* The moon shines bright. In such a night as this,
> When the sweet wind did gently kiss the trees
> And they did make no noise, in such a night
> Troilus methinks mounted the Troyan walls

And sighed his soul toward the Grecian tents,
Where Cressid lay that night.
Jes.   In such a night
Did Thisbe fearfully o'ertrip the dew
And saw the lion's shadow ere himself
And ran dismayed away.
Lor.   In such a night
Stood Dido with a willow in her hand
Upon the wild sea banks and waft her love
To come again to Carthage.
Jes.   In such a night
Medea gathered the enchanted herbs
That did renew old Aeson.
Lor.   In such a night
Did Jessica steal from the wealthy Jew
And with an unthrift love did run from Venice
As far as Belmont.
Jes.   In such a night
Did young Lorenzo swear he loved her well,
Stealing her soul with many vows of faith
And ne'er a true one.
Lor.   In such a night
Did pretty Jessica, like a little shrew,
Slander her love, and he forgave it her.
Jes.   I would out-night you, did nobody come;
But, hark, I hear the footing of a man.

The humor of these last lines might well be noted, for only too often will your pupils consider Shakespeare as a writer so high above ordinary man that common laughter belongs not with him.

This passage also affords opportunity to explain a puzzling matter in blank verse. Often the poetic line, begun by one character, is continued by another:

Lor.   Where Cressid lay that night.
Jes.   In such a night

If your pupils are analyzing the metrical form, smooth their way by removing this stone from their path. Take heed, also, that you select for a beginning study of the lines only those which scan easily and perfectly.

Interspersed with the blank verse and other poetic forms of the play is prose. Your pupils will detect for themselves that Shakespeare employs this medium to express the workaday thoughts of common man: the porter in *Macbeth*, Launcelot Gobbo in *The Merchant of Venice*, the clowns in *Hamlet*. So, too, does he use it when his characters of high estate are engaged in mundane matters: Hamlet's letter to Horatio, his directions to the players, his antics with Polonius. Also, there is that highly dramatic, infinitely pathetic, speech of Shylock too in prose:

> I am a Jew. Hath not a Jew eyes? Hath not a Jew hands, organs, dimensions, senses, affections, passions? fed with the same food, hurt with the same weapons, subject to the same diseases, healed by the same means, warmed and cooled by the same winter and summer, as a Christian is? —

Despite this, as I remarked, Shakespeare ordinarily resorts to prose to depict the common, the ordinary, or the comic. For a contrast, direct your class to Act Three, Scene One, of *A Midsummer Night's Dream*, in which Puck interrupts the rehearsal of the artisans by metamorphosing Bottom into an ass:

> *Quince.* O monstrous! O strange! we are haunted.
> Pray, masters! Fly, masters! Help!
> *Puck.* I'll follow you, I'll lead you about a round,
> Through bog, through bush, through brake, through brier.
> Sometimes a horse I'll be, sometimes a hound,
> A hog, a headless bear, sometimes a fire;

And neigh, and bark, and grunt, and roar, and burn,
Like horse, hound, hog, bear, fire, at every turn.
Bottom. Why do they run away? This is a knavery of
them to make me afeard.

Direct then, the attention of your group to Shakespeare's poetry, but ever keep in mind that major tenet
of your teacher-creed: "I will not force upon my pupils
my own likes; I will not overanalyze; and I will not
demand appreciation of that which is beyond their
years."

Let me give a few warnings and suggestions concerning the teaching of Shakespeare in high school. Do little
with such matters as date of writing or sources of plot
(unless your class has access to a copy of Holinshed's
Chronicles, which older pupils will enjoy reading and
comparing with Shakespeare). A moment's reflection
will convince you that these have nothing to do with
teaching pupils to read. Do not ruin the conception of
the play as a whole by detailed study. This is for mature
students who have capacity for concentrated effort, not
for adolescents who tire of long and exact analysis. In
the language employed by Shakespeare occur many
words, phrases, and allusions unfamiliar to us today. Unless an understanding of these is absolutely necessary, do
nothing with them. It is possible, of course, to spend a
great deal of time ferreting out meanings and possible
derivations, but these are matters of interest to scholars.
To this end, I prefer a text with comparatively few notes,
placed at the bottom of each page for the purpose of
clarifying the meaning of the passage. Except for that,
you should touch lightly on such matters. Students,
however, are usually amused by some of Shakespeare's
anachronisms and are interested in the sports and ac-

tivities of the period. These, by the way, are good material for talks and papers.

As with all pieces of considerable length, you must be concerned with the time problem in teaching drama. Do not give too many periods to each play. You may be tempted to do so; for fresh from your college classes, there is much of Shakespeare that you know and should like to impart. But restrain yourself; think of the limitations of your pupils; remember the restlessness of the adolescent. Three weeks, is, I think, long enough to devote to each play. You should get the actual reading over as soon as possible, but do not require your group to read the entire play before discussing it in class as this procedure is too difficult, even for seniors. Before you begin the play, go over it, dividing it into units, the length of each to be determined by the action of the play, making each sufficiently short so that one can be assigned each day. Usually, your pupils can read an act each day, possibly Acts Four and Five in one assignment. Prepare guiding questions for each. In that way, the actual reading can be done rather quickly, leaving the rest of the time for consideration of the play as a whole: plot, purpose, characters, significant passages, reports on various pertinent topics. You want your boys and girls to think of it as an entire piece, not as isolated bits of conversation. Twelfth-year students may well precede or follow their study of a play by a brief historical outline of the development of drama and by a discussion of the characteristics of tragedy and comedy. With your group, work out a statement of the characteristics of each, determining upon the essentials of each great form by consideration of plays read in high school.

And let me beg you to teach Shakespeare as a writer

familiar with men and the deeds of men; a person loving life yet understanding its conflicts; a person in whose experience tragedy and joy were intermixed. Shakespeare, despite the exalted position given him by posterity, should not be put upon a pedestal, thought of as if he were an idol far above the comprehension of ordinary man. At the time that Douglas Fairbanks and Mary Pickford played *The Taming of the Shrew* more than one student said to me in a shocked voice, "If Shakespeare could have heard how people laughed, he would have turned over in his grave." Well, if people had *not* laughed at his farce, Shakespeare would have been more likely to attempt the gymnastic feat described. Venerate Shakespeare if you will, but teach him as a man, a great student of the heart, the soul, the mind, and the acts of men.

I hope that you are going to be able to use modern drama in addition to Shakespearean. Most anthologies contain examples of modern plays. If you prefer separate classics, try to include in your list at least one non-Shakespearean play. If that is impossible, ask your pupils to read several one-act plays as a part of their outside reading. If you do this, choose your reading list with some care, for you must not forget that high school pupils cannot be fed the strong meat of college students. See that you do not require the reading of a modern play containing anything to which parents may properly object.

Treat modern or non-Shakespearean plays as you do Shakespearean. Because the former are shorter than the latter, they do not need so much class discussion. One-act plays can be handled in one class period, unless you want to add another for dramatization or reports. In general consider plot (including struggle), characters, setting, and purpose. Link dramas with other narratives studied, comparing and contrasting them. Most important of all, present drama as an explanation of life and personality, closely related to the reader and his actions.

ASSIGNMENT

Select a play ordinarily taught in high school and divide it into study units. For the first division, prepare study questions.

FURTHER READINGS

1. LaBrant, Lou L., *The Teaching of Literature in the Secondary School*, Chapter VI.

The author gives an interesting discussion on ways by which you can help your pupils to read drama.

2. Schweikert, H. C., ed., *Five Plays of Shakespeare*.

This contains the most helpful introductory material I have run across.

3. Blaisdell, Thomas C., *Ways to Teach English*, Chapter XXXVII.

If you approve as heartily as I of Mr. Blaisdell's practical suggestions (no abstruse theory here), you will want to read this chapter on "Teaching the Drama."

4. Thomas, Charles Swain, *The Teaching of English in the Secondary School*, Chapter X.

You will want to read this chapter carefully, particularly its plans for teaching Shakespeare. On pages 285–289 you will find test questions aimed to determine the pupils' knowledge after a first, then a third reading.

5. Cohen, Helen Louise, ed., *One-Act Plays by Modern Authors*, revised edition.

As a preparation for teaching modern plays, you may want to consult this volume. A pamphlet called "Teaching Modern Plays" accompanies the text.

6. Brooks, Cleanth, and Heilman, Robert B. *Understanding Drama*.

A college text, this may serve to fill some gaps in your own preparation.

7. Smith, Reed, *The Teaching of Literature*, Chapter XV, "The Drama," pp. 289–327.

Much information on teaching Shakespeare, other long plays, and contemporary one-acts is available here.

8. *Shakespeare for Today*, arranged by Leroy Phillips and Mary Major Crawford, although a simplified version, retains the flavor of the original.

9. Jackson, Elizabeth, "The Kittredge Way," *College English*, IV (May, 1943), pp. 483–487.

The approach of the incomparable "Kitty" is here upheld.

10. Poley, Irvin C., "Keeping Out of Hamlet's Way," *The English Journal*, XXX (September, 1941), pp. 538–549.

"Let Shakespeare speak for himself" is the advice of this experienced teacher.

XVII. LONG AND SHORT PROSE PIECES

Novels, tales of adventure, short stories, essays, biographies — long and short prose pieces — offer themselves next for our discussion. Compared to those just considered, these types afford few problems either for teacher or for pupil, as they do not show the complexities of form of poetry and drama; but do not expect their teaching to be easy sailing, for it won't be. After all, whatever is worth *studying* in class usually presents difficulties that cannot be overcome without the guidance of the teacher.

As in choosing other pieces of literature, base your selection of long prose narratives for class use on the probable interests of your pupils. In making this statement previously, I have tried to qualify it by remarking that this does not necessarily indicate that pupils be allowed to do their own choosing, for of course they cannot know what they enjoy until they have experienced the reading. As the compilers of *An Experience Curriculum in English* remark, selections should not be excluded which would be enjoyed under the guidance of a competent teacher; nor should the dislike of a person or even a group of persons be a sufficient reason for discarding a book. Unless experience has shown that a selection is unsuited to most high school groups, as appears to be true of Burke's *Conciliation with America*, grant your class the privilege of becoming acquainted with the work for themselves and thus sharing vicariously in what may be glorious adventure. Never be disturbed by student whim, but never forget that you are dealing with a group of boys and girls for the most part in their early teens. Consider, too, the difficulty of the selection, its length, and the possibility of its having been studied previously. This last, however, need not disturb you very deeply, for you will discover, only too quickly, that students recall little of what they have read two or three years previously. Furthermore, every teacher approaches a study from a different point of view and with different emphasis. But remember that young pupils tire quickly and read somewhat slowly; therefore, whatever is selected must not be unduly long. Keep in mind, also, that reading which is beyond the capabilities and experiences of the student may produce a dislike, even a definite antagonism, for reading that will continue indefinitely.

Long narratives frequently listed in courses of study are: *Ivanhoe*, *Treasure Island*, *Silas Marner*, and *A Tale of Two Cities*. Let us consider each of these from the points of view mentioned. The great value possessed by *Ivanhoe* consists in its strong appeal to student interests. The normal boy or girl — particularly boy — of twelve, thirteen, or fourteen has a vivid imagination and delights in romantic tales of chivalry and adventure. From the point of view of content, then, *Ivanhoe* holds first place. Next let us consider its difficulty. There we strike a snag. Certain characteristics of Scott's writing (typical of his period) are troublesome points for the twentieth-century boy and girl. Think of the lengthy and frequent passages of description, the long and somewhat involved sentences, the multiplicity of characters — these make for hard reading, do they not? Think also of the history involved — religious, social, and economic — and again you foresee difficulties. Furthermore, *Ivanhoe* is of a length that may tire a twelve- or thirteen-year-old student. Despite these handicaps, this novel often works well with an average or above average group. But you should not attempt it with pupils whose rate of reading and comprehension are below normal. Probably it has not been read previously by your class, and thus it scores again.

What is your opinion of *Treasure Island?* Like *Ivanhoe*, it ranks high from the point of view of subject matter. A story of adventure, written by a boy-man for a boy, it is indeed a thrilling tale. It affords so few difficulties that I have heard teachers disparage it because it is "too easy to teach" and should be used merely as home reading. Its shortness guarantees not boring your students. But it *may* have been read in a previous grade. If it has, you should not select it; for it will probably be remembered better than most and its simple plot structure and straightforward characterizations — although good points in themselves — admit of little value from a second detailed reading. But if it has not been presented, you will find it good for reading with most classes.

Silas Marner is selected, you may think, because compilers of courses of study believe that high school students should know something of George Eliot and because this novel is short enough for use in sophomore classes. Is the subject matter of interest to thirteen- or fourteen-year-olds? That they should be concerned with George Eliot's consideration of the emotional effects of transgression against the moral law is doubtful. Nor do they better appreciate her subtle and delicate sense of humor, her consummate use of detail, her remarkable character delineation. The social and moral implications which interest the adult affect only slightly the adolescent, but the story of Eppie and her grandfather and the account of the sin of Godfrey resulting in his abandonment of his child have, I believe, a somewhat general appeal, sufficiently great to justify the selection of *Silas Marner*. It is short; and, although capable of detailed study, its plot is so clear and its characterizations so definite that even immature pupils can follow the thread of the story. It may not be the best possible choice of novel for sophomore use, but it is more desirable than appears upon first consideration.

A Tale of Two Cities again ranks high in interest. Who could ask for a more thrilling novel, with requited and unrequited love thrown in? It deals too, with a deeply interesting period of history, one with which junior or senior pupils are familiar; for this novel belongs, without doubt, in the upper grades, after students have had enough history to make vivid the account of the Reign of Terror, and after they have had sufficient practice to read quickly this somewhat long novel. Its weaknesses, from the point of view of high school use, consist in the numerous and lengthy descriptive passages, the complicated sentence structure, and the many characters. But for older students it has much to commend it.

Although I have discussed these pieces of literature in some detail, I am not recommending them above all others. That they are frequently read suggests that they

have merit, but it does not mean that you should consider no others. For instance, *Monsieur Beaucaire*, a
charming short novel by that excellent craftsman, Booth
Tarkington, would appeal both to freshmen and sopho-
mores; *Dark Frigate*, by Charles Boardman Hawes, may
substitute for *Treasure Island*, if you desire a thrilling tale
of adventure for a group that has already explored
Treasure Island. *The House of Seven Gables*, *Kidnapped*, and
Splendid Spur may suit your sophomore groups. Juniors
would thrill to *The Red Badge of Courage*, by Stephen Crane,
or to *The Covered Wagon*, an epic of pioneer days, by
Emerson Hough — both now available in a special school
edition published by the D. Appleton-Century Company,
and edited respectively by those leaders in the English
field, Max J. Herzberg and Clarence Stratton. Why not
The Scarlet Letter for seniors; or *The History of Henry
Esmond;* or *Hugh Wynne: Free Quaker;* or *Trent's Last Case*,
that triple-barreled mystery story; or *The Farm*, by
Louis Bromfield? *An Experience Curriculum* will give you
a long list of suggestions from which you must choose
with the limitations of your group and yourself clearly
in mind. Unfortunately, too, much of modern material
becomes prohibitive because of its cost. But send to
D. Appleton-Century Company (New York) for a cat-
alogue of its *Appleton Modern Literature Series;* to E. P.
Dutton and Company (New York) for its *Everyman's
Library* selections; to The Macmillan Company (New
York) for information concerning its *Modern Readers'
Series;* to Allyn and Bacon (Boston) for *The Academy
Classics;* and to D. C. Heath and Company (Boston) for
The Golden Key Series. Often where there is the will, the
way *does* develop, and you should, if possible, give your
boys and girls a taste of the sort of reading current today.

Whatever you select, see that the first book has swift action, clear characterization, and uncomplicated plot. From the foundation determined by a study of such an account you can go on to a novel that contains somewhat complex characters and complicated plot.

Your aim in teaching long prose narratives is, of course, to train the students to read this type with pleasure and understanding. To this end, you will want to keep in mind all that has been said previously concerning the reading of narratives.

As with drama and the longer types of narrative poetry, you must take the time element into consideration in the teaching of long tales or novels. As you cannot discuss every chapter in detail in class, I suggest that you follow the plan outlined for the drama: divide the book into units based upon the plot divisions and prepare guiding questions on these sections. As a preparation for *Ivanhoe*, for example, read aloud chapters from *When Knights Were Bold*, by Tappan, to give your group a picture of how and why men were knighted, what *lists* were like, what *jousts* were, and the arrangements necessary for people to become pilgrims. The information given in that difficult but important first chapter may be elicited by such study questions as these:

1. How many factions were in England at that time? Name them.
2. What was the condition of the lower Saxons? How do you know?
3. Where was King Richard?
4. What language was spoken by the nobles? By the common people?
5. How did our present English language develop? Give some examples.

Take especial pains with the introduction of any novel read, for a great deal depends upon arousing the imagination of your group and upon helping them to understand the opening sections of the novel, often the most involved and complicated portions.

You will, of course, consider setting, plot, and characters as a basis for your plans. The plot analysis given for drama in Chapter XVI is equally applicable here, also the comments on characterization. In fact, everything that has been said pertaining to the teaching of narratives, with the exception of what belongs to the form and nature of poetry and drama, may and should be put into service.

With older students, the elements of surprise, suspense, and foreshadowing often prove of interest. As these are devices common to all writers, it is worth while discussing them. All narratives contain examples which your pupils may like to list. Nothing offers more dramatic illustrations than does *A Tale of Two Cities*, in such episodes as the breaking of the wine cask and the red hue of the coach of the Marquis, as, all unconscious, he drives on to destruction. By the way, do not select an abridged edition of any of these novels. I have in mind one of *A Tale of Two Cities* that begins with an account of Dr. Manette's secret. What, then, becomes of the careful building up by Dickens of the mystery of Dr. Manette? Who wants to read the solution of the major mystery of the novel in the first chapter? If you think a book is too difficult, do not use it at all. No one is injured then, but any cutting that ruins the plan of the author for his book is little short of literary desecration.

Many of the activities previously suggested work very well in connection with the novel. In addition to those already made, such as papers on the historical period, illustrated passages, models or illustrated talks on castles, you might experiment with the following. Have the class prepare a newspaper in which the major events of the book are written up. You should forget time sequence here, preferring news interest. Some students of mine once prepared a paper based on *Silas Marner*. First the class selected a name: *The Raveloe Gazette*. They thought *Gazette* had the proper early nineteenth-century ring. Then I appointed the following heads of departments, and gave to each one assistants, so that each member of the class had his special duty: editor-in-chief; news editor; desk editor; sports editor; society editor; reporters; office manager; business manager. The editor-in-chief was responsible for seeing that all the copy came in and for writing the editorials; the news editor, working with the reporters, saw to the news stories; the sports and society editors had the usual duties; the office manager and the business manager, with the editor-in-chief, planned the copy, made the dummy, and attended to mimeographing the paper. We had news stories on the discovery of the body of Dunstan Cass, on the robbery of Silas Marner, on the finding of Molly and Eppie by Silas, on the adoption of Eppie by Marner. We had a sports story of a wrestling match and of a horseshoe pitching contest; we had an editorial entitled: "War or Peace? Shall England Enter the War?" and one commending the draining of the stone pits. The business manager prepared a number of advertisements: some cows had strayed from Mr. Lammeter's barn; a pitch pipe had been found; a cow was offered for sale; Silas Marner, weaver from North'ard, desired weaving. One reporter wrote an affecting human interest story, called "The Black Spot," in which the death of Molly was described. The society reporter gave a good account of the marriage of Nancy Lammeter and Godfrey Cass; of Eppie Marner and Aaron Winthrop. (As I suggested, we ignored the time element.) Squire Cass's Christmas party also figured in the social news. In a column headed *Locals*, we learned of the staking of Wildfire, of Dunstan's journey to Batherby, of the visit of the peddler, of Silas's trip to Lantern Yard. The writing of this paper is not only the new interest that keeps Jack from being a dull boy, but also practice in composition and a means of review. Such a plan as this can be applied to any long prose narrative.

Similarly, you may have your students prepare a typewritten book, in which are articles on the historical phases of the novel, an estimate of the characters, a description of certain scenes. This may be illustrated by drawings or suitable pictures clipped from magazines and may be an individual or a group project. Or you can have one of the characters write a letter to another, telling an incident that occurred to which the second character was not a party. Pupils often display a considerable amount of imagination in doing this and show an appreciation of the qualities of the person whom they are representing. Again, you can have the students prepare a journal, in which a character relates his experiences, day by day, through some crisis. Mr. Lorry, the onlooker in *A Tale of Two Cities*, would be a good choice. Advanced and rather clever boys and girls may enjoy writing a class novelette, in which each person is responsible for a chapter. To do this, it is necessary to work out very carefully the setting and plot, and to determine upon the type of character that will illustrate the theme. It is evident that this plan demands mature thinking. You may use dramatization, keeping in mind, however, what I have said concerning this device. The many excellent movie and radio versions of outstanding novels provide suggestions for study, writing, and dramatizations.

Probably the first type of prose narrative that you will teach is the short story. In fact, this is probably the first of any type of narrative, for its brevity, its simplicity of structure, its familiarity, all commend it as a good choice for introducing students to reading. You must, of course, base your selections on students' interests. This often means a story of action, although stories of setting and character may also be chosen. The psychological type is frequently least interesting to high school pupils. Indeed, I remember that this is a criticism often made of the reading interests of adults. Almost any red-blooded boy will enjoy such stories as "Gallegher," "Riding the Rim Rock," "The Ransom of Red Chief"; but I doubt a freshman's interest in "The Three Strangers" or "Three Arshines of Earth." When in doubt choose a story of action, is good advice.

Consultation of your course of study will show you that short stories are often listed for reading in all six years. This means that you will have to determine on a means of treatment that will represent growth in a six-year reading of the short story. In junior high school and possibly in the sophomore year, you will be concerned principally that your students grasp the story itself. You will stress, then, the struggle and its result. Thomas C. Blaisdell, in his *Ways to Teach English*, page 431, has a plan for reducing this to an algebraic formula:

> "x" equals the leading character
> "y" equals the problem he must solve
> Does "x" accomplish "y"?

In these years, too, you will want to discuss the purpose of the author with the reasons the students have for their statement. You will want to apply the story to the present-day experiences of the group. And that is about all that you should plan to do with the short story as a type. You should, however, keep in mind what has been said in regard to adding to the vocabulary of the student through reading and to interpreting certain significant passages.

In the sophomore year you should do everything suggested previously, and more. In the first place, the stories selected should be somewhat longer and more complicated both in plot and character delineation than those selected for younger pupils. You can do more with character portrayal than you have previously, pointing out the ways by which the author depicts his characters. We judge a person, you know, chiefly by three means: his appearance and manner; his words and actions; and comments made concerning him by others. Show that an author uses these ways, too. Discuss the effect produced upon character by circumstance and by other characters. Show how the characters and the incidents exemplify the theme.

In the junior year you should use the foundation prepared in the previous years and should add to it a somewhat detailed but nontechnical study of plot. Every piece of writing falls into three divisions: the beginning, the middle, and the end. (I prefer these terms — they are, I believe, Blaisdell's — to the more formal introduction, body, and conclusion, and to the still more formal exposition, rising action, turning point, falling action, conclusion.) With your class, consider what we may expect in the *beginning*. We shall find a portrayal of the setting, the introduction of the characters, an account of the background circumstances (antecedent action), the present situation, and the incident that begins the struggle. The *middle* consists of the struggle itself and gives an account of the incidents that are favorable or unfavorable to the leading characters. In the *ending* we find the resolution of the struggle and its consequences.

Junior students can work out a plan for some short story in which these points are clearly defined. Certainly you will not want to do this for every short story studied, but you will employ it frequently enough so that your students will get an understanding of the way a short story is built.

As an illustration, let us take the short story "Uprooted," by Ruth Suckow. The *beginning* ends with the words: "So they had not got much farther than Jen's deciding that 'Sams' ought to take the old folks if anyone did, for they were certainly best able to afford it. 'But they'll get out of it some way, you just see if they don't,' she had prophesied bitterly." In the *beginning* we learn that the time is the present and the place is a small farm somewhere, probably in the Middle West. The characters, Sam, Hat, and Arthur, and Sam's wife, Lou, Hat's husband, Henry, and Arthur's wife, Jen, are introduced. The background circumstances are that the "old folks," parents of Sam, Hat, and Arthur, are no longer able to remain on the old farm. "The relationship" has met to determine what is to be done. The *present situation* is that none of the children want to take care of their parents. The *struggle* lies between Sam, the well-to-do, and the others, as indicated by Jen's words, "They'll get out of it some way."

The *middle* shows the struggle between Sam and the

others. Sam has a competent ally in Lou, his wife. Until one of Hat's children comes to the door, he makes progress in his plans for forcing Hat to care for the "old folks" on the farm. The sight of the child is such convincing evidence of Hat's poverty and responsibility that Sam is forced to abandon that plan of attack. He begins another but is interrupted by word that his mother is crying in her bedroom. Again this acts as a setback. Sam goes to his mother, who, because of her love for him, her first-born, agrees to leave the old home for some rooms that Sam will add to Hat's house.

In the *ending*, we find matters settled satisfactorily from Sam's point of view. He will break the news to Hat of the arrangements he has made, and he and Lou will take the six-ten for Omaha.

In the senior year, you may add, if you like, a brief account of the development of the short story. You may also do something with types. But as the short story of today offers a great diversity in theme, treatment, and subject matter, you should be satisfied to classify the story as one of character, plot, or setting. For use in the senior year choose somewhat more difficult stories and discuss in some detail the way in which the author chooses setting, characters, and plot to exemplify his theme. If, however, you have a class that has done very little with the short story, you may well limit your analysis to the points suggested for use in the seventh to tenth years. As in composition, so also in literature: you can go no farther than the capabilities and background of your pupils permit.

Senior students, too, may like to evolve a statement of the requirements of a short story. I should prefer to make this a group activity, produced from class discussion, rather than to dictate to the class one of the many definitions of the short story. After the class has listed its points, however, you may like to give them the following requirements used by the judges to determine the winner of the O. Henry Memorial Award, summarized in *Life* and found in F. L. Pattee's *Development of the American Short Story*, pages 372 and 373.

1. The story must have at least two characters; otherwise there is no struggle. A situation with opposing forces must be depicted.

2. The story must be a picture of real life, which gives the reader a definite sensation.

3. It must deal with human beings, either directly or indirectly.

4. In the briefest manner possible, it must reveal a situation that carries the reader beyond it.

5. The supreme test is the climax. The reader feels he is the sole spectator of a supremely interesting human mystery story suddenly made plain.

6. No word in the vocabulary must suggest triteness or the fatal thought that the writer is dependent upon others for his phrasing: "He flicked the ashes . . ."; "A hoarse sound went up from the vast throng"; "With a glad cry she threw her arms about him."

Then let each pupil read a short story in the magazine that he prefers and judge it upon the basis of these requirements. If, without preaching or condemning, you can lead the student to see how false and sentimental are many of the stories in current magazines, you will have accomplished much. Use care and tact, remembering that to the average pupil you are an adult, far removed from your own student days and by your very profession as teacher bound to admire the dull and uninteresting. But perhaps your boys and girls will come to see, if you guide and do not dictate, that life is not one long love story with a happy ending; that the office boy is somewhat unlikely to marry the daughter of his employer; and that success in life demands something more than poor but honest birth and a willingness to work. I do not at all mean that we should emphasize the sordid and unlovely in life. But I do insist that if reading shows us life and human beings as they really are, then we should learn to appreciate short stories that are truthful in their point of view.

Here (as in other types) you should be careful to avoid utilizing your class time for a rehashing of the events of the story. A short check-quiz at the beginning of the period will take care of this. Your class discussion, then, can center about plot, character, and setting; the purpose of the author; the meaning of certain words; the effect of some unusual bit of expression; and the interpretation of a significant passage. You may, too, like to employ some dramatization occasionally. Your students should write their own playlets; then the best can be given in class. O. Henry's stories, because of their use of conversation, are good for this. Try "By Courier," "While the Auto Waits," or "The Voice of the City." You may think one of these good enough for use in an assembly program. And always link all narratives together. At the end of each literature semester, show the common elements of the narratives studied: short stories, novels, dramas, and poems. In this way, the students learn that the various types of literature are only different means for portraying life. As an activity, you might require each pupil to select a story, write a well-worded summary of it, and illustrate it by clippings or drawings, the whole to be combined into a booklet. This same device may be planned for narrative poems or dramas. In connection with the latter, stage plans and costume plates may be included. The amount of writing necessary in this device justifies it.

The novel and the short story are the usual types of prose narratives taught in high school. There are, however, several other sorts of prose to which I wish to call your attention. The first, essays, usually studied in each of the six years of high school, are of three types. One is the simple nature essay, like those of Muir or Burroughs. This is the type generally studied in the first year. As these are informative essays, your principal emphasis should be upon content rather than upon style. Class discussion may center about certain unusual and interesting phenomena described. To motivate this, suggest that your youngsters bring to class pictures of animals, birds, and insects, and have these posted on the bulletin board for all to examine. Probably, however, after determining in some way that your pupils have prepared the assignment, you will want to give most of the class period to projects connected with the essays read. Often your class has a surprising stock of lore concerning birds, bees, insects, reptiles: make use of it. A very diffident student may eagerly volunteer to tell of some experience he has had with beast or reptile. Encourage an expression of observation and knowledge. These talks, you see, which may be prepared or impromptu are really "oral English." You may also have each student read another nature essay by the same or by a different author, and make a report on it. On your desk, have a copy of William Beebe's *Log of the Sun* for your pupils to dip into. A "nature diary" brings very good results, as well as affording training in composition. Ask each pupil to write at least one paragraph every day for a week on his observations of nature. Even the dead of winter in a snow-locked country affords material to the acute observer. You will be delighted by the charming little nature essays that some of your group will write for you.

The second type of essay that you will read — possibly in all six years — is the familiar or friendly essay. With younger students you should emphasize the purpose of the author, asking your pupils to determine what he wants to say to his reader and what is his point of view. With older pupils — juniors and seniors — you may want to do something with style. This matter of style is particularly advisable for seniors, as by the time they have reached their twelfth year they will have completed their study of sentence structure and have some background for commenting upon style. The personality of the author may be noted in all years but is of particular interest to junior and senior students. Someone writes an essay called "The Saturday Night Bath." What sort of person is the author? Any idea of his upbringing, the period in which he lived, his likes and dislikes? In what sort of mood was he when he wrote this essay? What makes you think as you do? In an unsigned essay your class may become concerned with determining the sex of the writer. I have had students become so interested in this (or in proving themselves right!) that they have written to the editor of the magazine in which the essay appeared to ask him concerning the sex of the author. When this sort of thing comes about, you are teaching composition in a thoroughly painless manner. For an activity connected with the familiar essay, your older pupils may write one of their own, and do it very well. After you have read several essays, outline on the board with your class what you and they consider the essential characteristics of a friendly essay. For example, your pupils will suggest: (1) a sense of charm, (2) effective employment of detail, (3) frequent recourse to narrative, (4) a humorous tone, with, however, often an underlying note of seriousness, (5) a wide choice of subject, and (6) indications of the personality of the author. You will want to call to their attention the fact that a friendly essay is not an unformed piece of writing. It may be familiar and light in tone but it is carefully planned. Study the use of narrative and descriptive elements, the ways by which mood is indicated, the purpose of the author. With some such basis for writing as this, your students may surprise you with their efforts. Perhaps the following plan, prepared by a former student of mine, for teaching the friendly essay may prove suggestive:

GETTING ACQUAINTED

Did you get to know someone new today? Or did you get to know better some friend you already had? If you did, you probably stopped to talk to that person for a few minutes about something you both liked. You told him in a friendly way how you had enjoyed a certain moving picture or you discussed with him the exciting ball game of a day or two before. Perhaps you talked about sports and shows for a while and then drifted into telling what you were planning to do that was quite as exciting and wonderful for you as the things professional athletes and actresses were doing for the public. Before you realized it, a new side of your friend's personality had opened up, you had a new intimacy of ideas, you understood each other in some phase where you had been strangers. You left him with the pleasant friendly glow that comes only from having a "good talk."

You don't have to sit and chat with a person to have this

same warm feeling of intimacy. Oftentimes your good talk can come through writing, and you would be surprised at the many new intimacies you may share through reading the message that some man or woman has written to the sympathetic, understanding reader who would like to make a new friend. You are going to have the opportunity to know many of these fine people; how well you get to know them depends upon you. Look for the personality behind the printed words. You may even see a mental picture — the face, expression of joy and sorrow, little mannerisms, ways of doing things as well as saying them, and especially a close-up picture of the person's thoughts and feelings.

Tomorrow you will meet two unusual people when you read the essay which appeared in a Kansas newspaper some years ago called "Mary White," by William Allen White. The portrait of one is clearly and beautifully painted; it's the portrait of the painter himself for which you will have to look closely. Be careful when you read to bring to the article all your sympathy and ability to understand a beautiful affection. When a father talks about an only daughter, he will show his deep pride and joy in her only to friendly hearts.

DISCUSSION QUESTIONS FOR NEXT PERIOD

1. Would you have liked Mary to be your friend? Point out your reasons.
2. For what qualities do you think her special friends — the newspaper men, the Latin teacher, the farmer-politician, the preacher and police judge, the music master and the traffic cop — liked her?
3. What kind of man must Mr. White be to write this about his daughter? Why do you think so?
4. Why did he write the article and have it published?
5. Does Mr. White's tribute to his daughter make you think of people you have known who would react in this same way to such a sad experience?

— FLORENCE HANDY

The third type, to be read only in twelfth-year classes, is the formal essay. Those listed in courses of study are likely to be Macaulay's *Life of Johnson* or Carlyle's *Essay on Burns*, or one of Emerson's essays. Needless to say, you must consider your group before choosing any of these. Because of the difficulty of this type, it demands formal treatment. Outlines of each part may be made. A précis for each section or each paragraph affords a good method of analyzing the content of the essay. You should discuss style with some care, having your students note such matters as sentence variety, paragraph length and means of development, the use of illustrations, examples, anecdotes, the diction used, and the figurative language employed. Both Carlyle and Macaulay afford fine examples: "Granted, the ship comes into harbour with shrouds and tackle damaged; the pilot is blameworthy; he has not been all-powerful: but to know *how* blameworthy, tell us first whether his voyage has been around the Globe, or only to Ramsgate and the Isle of Dogs." (Carlyle's *Essay on Burns*.) Macaulay's remarkable skill in sentence forms, particularly sentence balance, is shown in, "They repelled each other strongly, and yet attracted each other strongly. Sudden prosperity had turned Garrick's head. Continued adversity had soured Johnson's temper." Illustration and anecdote, brilliant employment of detail, all characterize the writing of Macaulay. To complete your unit on the formal essay, you may ask for a report on the contemporaries of the author or of the subject of the essay; on the works of the person concerned; on the period in which these persons (author or subject) lived; and upon some especial interest of the people involved. You can see that Doctor Johnson and his friends afford ample material, as does the period of Burns, or the social experiments of the era of Emerson.

But you will want to do much more than this. Perhaps no greater medium for the expression of ideas has yet been developed than the serious essay. In this type, thinking men deal with problems of the intellect, following them through to their ultimate conclusions, considering their various phases and angles. Because of this, the serious essay, to be appreciated, demands a certain amount of maturity, of reasoning ability on the part of the reader. Do not, then, force it upon immature minds, but as your pupils grow in understanding, open to them this avenue of thought. Concerned with all mental experience, expressed always with grace and charm, it well repays the careful consideration necessary for its appreciation. Over and above the study of form stand the careful and sympathetic character analysis found in Carlyle's *Essay on Burns*, the brilliant, if not always accurate, estimate of the great Doctor made by Macaulay, the philosophic verities of such essays as Emerson's *Self-Reliance*, with its ringing challenge so needed today, "Trust thyself." In reading Emerson with your class, you will want them to determine upon what, in their opinion, are the most helpful and significant ideas which have, perhaps, clarified or influenced their thinking or ideals. Such thought-provoking statements as these your group may be able to illustrate by example or observation: "Whoso would be a man, must be a nonconformist"; "What I must do is all that concerns me, not what people think"; "A foolish consistency is the hobgoblin of little minds."

Statements like the following from Carlyle are provocative of discussion: "Manhood begins when we have in any way made truce with Necessity; begins even when we have surrendered to Necessity, as the most only do; but begins joyfully and hopefully only when we have reconciled ourselves to Necessity; and thus, in reality, triumphed over it, and felt that in Necessity we are free." Today few high school seniors have been so sheltered that they cannot comprehend the wisdom and the strength of these words. The ideas presented, then, be they considered comment on literary personages or philosophical truths, should most concern you.

Soon or late, to everyone comes the astounding realization that he is an individual, unique, a pattern never to be duplicated, the product of many past generations. Newly awakened to this, your pupils may well enjoy the portrayal of human activities, ideals, struggles, as presented in biography or autobiography. In its beginnings, in, say, Plutarch's *Lives of Great Men*, and for many succeeding centuries, this form dealt only with outstanding men, and, occasionally, women. Today we still retain our interest in those who have made their mark, but we have enlarged our sympathies to include portrayal of ordinary men and women who have lived through significant periods of our history or are themselves exponents of certain phases of our civilization. In *Grandmother Brown's Hundred Years*, interest lies, not in Grandmother Brown as a person, but in the growth pictured from pioneer conditions in Ohio to the present. The *Atlantic* prize book, *Old Jules*, also re-creates a period instead of the life of a great man. Through biography, history is interpreted and prejudices removed. Excellent from several angles is this form for all years of high school English.

Today you have many sources of material, from the well-established *Autobiography of Benjamin Franklin* to the more recent lives of Helen Keller, Buffalo Bill, or Al Smith. *Great Inventors and Their Inventions*, by Bachman; *Pete of the Steel Mills*, by Hall; *Andrew Carnegie's Own Story*, by Brochhausen, are a few titles listed in *An Experience Curriculum*. With this type combine letters from great and ordinary people, such as Charles Lamb, Robert Louis Stevenson, and Hilda Rose of the "Stump Farm" (her letters were published in the *Atlantic Monthly*). The dignity and heroism of human endeavor are nowhere more apparent than in personal records concerning flesh and blood people.

The life of anyone, be he prince or peasant, falls into several great divisions: ancestry and birth; childhood and early education; young manhood; maturity; decline and death. Any biography read can be apportioned in this manner for an understanding of the facts of the subject's existence; but class discussion should concern itself with far more than this. What are the achievements of this man or woman? How permanent have they been? How significant to their period? To those succeeding? What outstanding personal qualities are revealed? What preconceived notions are removed? What information gained? What new ideas received? Biography should be thought of and taught as the record of human aspiration and achievement.

Accounts of adventure and travel should also find a place in your plans for enlarging your pupils' experience by teaching them to read. Included either as a part of your classroom activities or your "home reading" program they should certainly be, for through them your boys and girls may sail the seven seas and explore all countries, sharing vicariously in all sorts of glorious adventures. Their daily round may be lightened and the four walls of room or office forced back if you can help them to glimpse the Amazon, the Mississippi sweeping toward the sea, or the great Himalayas reaching toward the stars. With your pupils picture new landscapes, costumes, customs, people. Try to understand and to sympathize with these new ways, so that the different will not seem wrong. Much of our intolerance as a people comes from our failure to accept the fact that other cultures, other peoples, have as great a heritage as our own. By wisely guiding your pupils in their visits to other lands, you will not only be the means of opening to them new doors of experience, but you will also be helping to enlarge the limited point of view that comes from lack of understanding. (On page 45 of *An Experience Curriculum in English* you will find a long list of titles leading to an exploration of the world about us.)

In all types of prose reading — and, indeed, in poetry also — your pupils will encounter a considerable amount of humorous writing. Has it ever occurred to you that students require aid in understanding humor? Let me assure you that they do and that one of your responsibilities in teaching pupils to read with appreciation lies in aiding them to grasp humor expressed through the printed word.

We Americans like to think of ourselves as a humorous people, as indeed we are. But responding to something funny that is seen or even heard requires much less effort than does responding to something *read*. Consider what is required of a child in interpreting a humorous passage read silently. First, he must grasp the *denotation* of each word; next, he must expand its meaning so that he senses its implications. He must respond to the irony which underlies much American humor; he must recognize the devices of exaggeration and understatement; he must identify the incongruous. Figures of speech and allusions he must be able to expand. All this — and more — he must do through *reading* the symbols we call words, unaided by actual vision and hearing.

Because a sense of humor aids in a happy adjustment to living as well as to reading, you should make a deliberate effort to help your boys and girls to enjoy the funny. Although I have mentioned certain aspects of humor, I am not advocating a stereotyped "study" of humorous devices. But see to it that your pupils read humorous material and that they grasp its fun. Cultivate your own sense of humor, both for your own sake and that of your pupils. Do not take for granted that students will respond without aid even to the works of such well-known humorists as Mark Twain. Appreciation of humorous writing can never be taken for granted.

With this, we shall leave our discussion of the teaching of the major types of literature; for, although I shall consider the teaching of the oration and of debate, they belong as properly with extracurricular activities as they do with classroom teaching and will be found in the next chapter. Before I go on, I want to make one comment. Because I have separated composition and literature in my discussion and have suggested that they be taught in different semesters, I do not mean that literature should be neglected during the composition semester, nor *vice versa*. During the period given over to composition, magazines and books of essays may be used, as has been suggested. Not only do these serve to give ideas to your students, but they also offer incidental training in literature. So, too, in the literature semester must composition be considered. You may have noticed that I frequently have suggested written work as a means of rounding out the unit of reading under discussion. Let me urge you to have frequent recourse to oral and written composition during the literature unit. And let me further and forcibly urge you to maintain the same standards for this written work that you hold for themes. Too often students are careless in the form of work done in literature classes. Why? For the reason that we have failed to make them realize that the principles of composition are fundamental to all sorts of writing. We have neglected to show the student that a principle learned in one course should be applied, if possible, in every other. To this end, then, insist that all work handed in be in good form. Ask the students to use only complete sentences, even in preparing their assignments. Demand proper arrangement, endorsement; in fact, see that your students apply what you have so laboriously taught them. If all teachers of English will do this, perhaps the student will acquire the habit of writing accurate papers and will hand in carefully written reports to the teachers of history and of science. And then indeed will your names be called blessed.

ASSIGNMENT

A. Select a long narrative listed in your state course of study. Divide it according to plot divisions. For the first section, formulate questions to be used by your students in preparing their assignment.

B. Select a short story listed in your state course. Following the form you expect your students to use, make statements concerning the points found in the beginning, the middle, and the end of the story. Consult pages 304–305.

C. Read a formal essay listed in your state course of study. Divide it into study units. Make an outline of each unit.

FURTHER READINGS

1. LaBrant, Lou L., *The Teaching of Literature in the Secondary School,* Chapters V, VII, and IX.

These chapters discuss, respectively, how to read a novel, how to read the essay and the biography, and how to read the short story.

2. Thomas, Charles Swain, *The Teaching of English in the Secondary School,* Chapter XI.

In this chapter, "The Teaching of the Essay," Mr. Thomas gives general suggestions as well as specific questions pertaining to structure, style, and personality of the author.

3. Cross, E. A., and Carney, Elizabeth, *Teaching English in High Schools,* Chapter XVIII, "The Short Story in the Secondary School Literature Program," pp. 387–408.

Specific suggestions are given here.

4. Lenrow, Elbert, *Reader's Guide to Prose Fiction.*

This is a bibliography centering around the *needs* of the individual. The introductory material, especially "The Reading of Fiction," pp. 13–16, is valuable. You will want to be critical of the titles listed, for I think you will find that not all are suitable for the average pupil.

5. *The Saturday Review of Literature,* the *Atlantic Monthly, Harper's Magazine, The English Journal,* and many other magazines offer suggestions for reading. As much as possible, keep up to date on your own reading and always call to the attention of your pupils current books and articles of interest to them. "I was reading last night —" will almost always secure the attention of your boys and girls.

6. Woodring, Maxie, and Others, *Enriched Teaching of English in the Junior and Senior High School.*

For many suggestions of illustrative material to enhance effective teaching, consult this book. The sections headed "Maps and Charts" and "Pictures, Posters, Post Cards" will give you the most help.

7. Cross, E. A., *The Book of the Short Story*, Chapters VII and VIII.

In these chapters you will find a discussion of such matters as point of view, titles, conversation, and a plan for the study of a short story.

8. Herzberg, Max J., and Mones, Leon, *Humor of America*. Keep this on your desk for your pupils to dip into.

PART THREE

EXTRACURRICULAR ACTIVITIES; ODDS AND ENDS; READING

XVIII. DEBATES, ORATIONS, SCHOOL
PAPERS, ANNUALS

As a means of transition between the teaching of literature and the management of extracurricular activities, I shall discuss debate and the oration. Both of these may form a part of your classroom activities or may be part of your work outside your classroom, or both. Indeed, both are very versatile, bearing as they do upon composition, literature, and extracurricular activities.

Let us first consider debate. There are two types with which to be concerned: formal and informal. In your classroom teaching you may prefer to use the informal type altogether, which consists in having the students select and discuss a controversial subject. You may arbitrarily determine the length of the speeches and the number of pupils to discuss each side of the question. Each person should prepare an outline similar to the one given on page 156. There need be no decision, or the class may vote as to which side had the more effective arguments. For classroom use, this type of argumentation has much to commend it; however, with junior and senior students you may like to have a unit of formal debate. If so, you will probably give six weeks to this activity. Formal debate, too, is the type generally used as an extracurricular activity.

For a debate to be prepared in the classroom but given before an audience of some sort, I suggest the following procedure. First, divide your class into groups, six students in each group. Next, encourage the whole class to do wide reading on debatable topics. These readings may be reported to the class by means of (1) informal debate; (2) impromptu talks; (3) prepared talks. After this, or during the time you have allotted to reading, give the entire class practice in selecting, stating, and testing a question for debate. For this, assign several topics such as:

1. The general strike should be prohibited by law.
2. Every student should choose his occupation before entering high school.
3. We should have a Secretary of Peace.
4. The gasoline tax should be abolished.

After such practice, let each group decide upon its topic and formulate its statement of the question. Standards for determining the question may be: (1) it must be interesting; (2) it must be on the level of high school students; (3) material on it must be in the school library (there is little point in working on a debate for which there is no accessible material). After the question is selected and stated, it may be tested on the following points: (1) it must be a single assertion; (2) it must not be one-sided; (3) it must be clear and as specific as possible. Furthermore, be careful, even in classroom debates, that the question meets with the approval of your high school principal. I remember assigning as a subject for a classroom debate a question pertaining to the ownership of textbooks: Should the school own them or should the students buy their own books? The subject sounds innocuous enough, does it not? It chanced, however, that the matter was soon to be brought up for action before the local school board and premature discussion would have been somewhat disastrous. Of course I withdrew the question as soon as I learned this. As the classroom teacher cannot be conversant with administrative affairs, it is advisable to consult one's principal before doing anything of a public or semipublic nature.

After the question for debate is selected, it must be carefully analyzed. First, the *purpose* of the debate must be made clear. Exactly what is to be proved or disproved? Next, the *history of the question* must be understood; and, finally, the *terms* used in the statement of the subject must be carefully defined. Then each group is ready to go on to a careful consideration of the question. In analyzing this, the *issues* must be clearly stated and the *points* to be proved must be enumerated.

After this, each group is ready to begin to collect its *evidence*. As preparation for this, you will have to give the class careful instructions in regard to gathering material. You should give the entire class practice in note-taking before you turn each group loose to collect evidence pertaining to its own subject. All the training you have given your pupils concerning the facilities of the library and the taking of notes finds a place here.

During the time that the students are gathering material, you can devote some of your class time to an explanation of different types of reasoning: induction, deduction, example, analogy. As practice, each person can give a brief talk in which he uses one of these types of reasoning. What he learns he may then apply to his own debate problem.

After the evidence is gathered, a careful brief or outline may be made. Today, because of the formality of the brief, many successful coaches advise against its use, preferring strongly the simpler plan. As I have said, you can, find a form for a brief in any book on debate. If you think it advisable, you may have each student make a sample brief or outline before the group prepares one for its own debate. In preparing this, tell the students to give careful consideration to the order in which they place the points, for of course these should be climactic. Also, the conclusion must have particular attention; generally, it should be both a summary and an appeal.

Next your students must consider how they can refute the arguments brought by the opposition, for all good debaters try to foresee and circumvent the arguments of their honorable opponents. As a class activity, let each student select an editorial and prepare a rebuttal for one of the points made by the editor. Each sub-group (the group of six has long ago been divided into two sub-groups of three each, the affirmative and the negative) should try to determine upon what its opponents will submit by way of argument and work out a rebuttal. Of course, this cannot be definitely determined upon, for people do not always act exactly as we expect; but the debaters should prepare themselves as carefully as possible.

After the debate is planned, the members of each team divide the points. Each speaker gives particular attention to his own point but is familiar with every argument to be advanced by his colleagues, for teamwork is most important in debate. When all preparation is done, each person practices his speech. For this, he should use notes prepared on cards and be told by you how to manage these notes easily. You should discourage a memorized speech, but should insist upon careful practice and timing. Timing the speech in practice is vital. It should not be begun immediately, however, for the first two or three deliveries are likely to be slow and halting. After that, the student should watch the time carefully (or you should, if this is to be a public debate), for a speaker stopped by the timekeeper usually fails to make his point. Often, too, an inexperienced speaker becomes "rattled" and may not recover from his fright during the rest of the debate. In the Appendix of this text you will find a carefully prepared plan for a six weeks' unit on debate, which I think will be a very satisfactory guide. It was evolved under the direction of a skilled teacher and tested in the Model High School of the University of North Dakota.

Practically all that I have said pertaining to debate as a classroom project is applicable to debate as an extracurricular activity. You will not, of course, give so much practice as I have suggested here but will start immediately to work upon the question. And if you have anything to do with choosing it, be sure that it is within the comprehension of the high school student. In formal debate, as in so many of our high school activities, we forget the age, interests, and capabilities of our pupils; and then we wonder why debate is an unpopular activity. No doubt this *is* a factor, but there is another, more important one, which you should try to overcome. Debate is not an activity that receives applause. The work is done by a small group of students, in empty classrooms, in the libraries, with none by to see and praise. Very different it is from taking part in athletic contests, or plays, or even in working on the school newspaper.

It takes weeks of quiet work to prepare for a contest in which your team may be eliminated immediately. Try, then, to publicize your group. See that the school newspaper gives space to what the team is doing. Give out such interesting bits of news as you can. Display all the interest and enthusiasm possible in order to encourage your group. Before entering county or state contests, let your debaters appear before the high school assembly or the Parent-Teachers Association, for both the practice and the publicity afforded. Accept work done for public debate in lieu of some of your class requirements, for debate, well done, is very well worth the time spent upon it and needs your co-operation. But see that you give your debate team nothing more than co-operation. Too often has intramural debate become a contest between coaches, not teams. You direct the work of the team, but you cannot, in honesty, do it for them, whether you win or lose. Debate has so dropped into disrepute in certain communities that contests consisting of extemporaneous talks are substituted for it. Although these talks have their place, they are not a substitute for debate. See to it, then, that your attitude as a coach does not bring about such a change in your community.

A first cousin to debate is the oration, except, of course, that it is an individual and not a group activity. But it requires careful investigation, writing, and delivery; it has for its purpose to convince an audience; and it is a public performance. The writing and delivery of an oration are seldom classroom activities; the analysis of an oration frequently is. I shall first consider it from its classroom aspects.

Usually the oration is studied during the junior year, although in schools teaching American literature in the tenth year the oration may be listed for class study. Personally, I consider it a difficult type of reading for sophomore students. Notice some of the orations suggested for the use of thirteen- and fourteen-year-olds who have had, it must be remembered, only the sort of United States history taught in the grades: Washington's "Farewell Address," Webster's "First Bunker Hill Oration" and "Reply to Hayne," Lincoln's "Address at Cooper Union," and Burke's "Conciliation with America." Think back upon your experience with these hoary monuments, and determine, I hope, to select speeches that are more simple, and that deal with affairs of more importance today than do these. And if you can, study the oration in the junior year, where it correlates very well with the plans suggested for both oral and written composition.

In studying the oration with your class, an outline or brief is indispensable. The most simple sort that you can use consists of working out the introduction, body, and conclusion, with the main points given under each. You should give your class these three divisions and let them indicate the points under each. A more complicated form is to outline each section; a still more detailed plan is that of the regular brief. A précis of each paragraph or section is good in securing understanding of the author's plan.

The characteristic of an oration that makes it different from other types of public address lies in its *appeal*. In studying the oration with your class, you will want to determine (1) the purpose of the speaker; (2) the occasion for the speech; (3) the sort of audience that heard it; (4) its material (the logical development of the subject, best got at by means of the outline); and (5) the appeal. To determine the force of the appeal, consider the purpose, the occasion, and the audience. Next determine the impression probably made upon such an audience. Then analyze the means used by the speaker to gain this effect: his references to historical events or to present circumstance; his choice of words; his use of figures; the length and structure of his sentences. (Of course you will not overdo this study of mechanics.) In reading an oration, the tone of the voice — that instrument of many stops, capable of turning the commonplace into the sublime — must be imagined. Possibly, however, you have phonograph recordings of great speeches read by great actors. Certainly you can turn to the radio for examples — not of speeches of the past but of the present. A timely activity would be to have your class listen to political or informative speeches by leaders of this and other countries. Let each student study the method of exposition or argument employed, the occasion and purpose of the speech, consideration of the audience and methods followed to appeal to it, voice control, and special devices utilized. Reports on each of these aspects should be presented in class. Other radio speakers offer good and bad examples for class discussion. But in doing this you must be careful to maintain an impersonal attitude; for the classroom must not deteriorate into a political stumping ground.

In reading a speech in class or in listening to one for the purpose of analysis, be assured that your students (and you) know the historical period referred to. I have observed a cadet teacher blandly permitting students to place Lincoln's "Gettysburg Address" during the Revolutionary War. Of course, eighty years or so may be but a moment in the march of time, but so to telescope them hardly makes for historical accuracy. In order to clarify this point you can well spend a day on the historical period.

To complete this unit of the oration, you may wish your students to read and report on others, or to write orations themselves.

Writing an oration usually precedes the public delivery of one, for orations presented in contests are supposed to be original work of the student. I say "supposed to be," for the same criticism may be made here as was made regarding debates: coaches too frequently rework a student-written oration until it is no longer the production of the student but of the coach. (I wonder what is the significance of this fact? Is it merely the desire to win a contest, or is it an unconscious admission that we are demanding the impossible?)

The study of several orations is of course preliminary to the writing of one. Next, have the students read widely on current questions, with a view to selecting some subject bearing on present interests, a choice definitely preferable to many of the hackneyed subjects appearing perennially in every oratorical contest. Remember that the topic selected *must afford an appeal*. Exposition may and probably must be a vehicle for developing the subject chosen, but the ending must be a peroration, an appeal to thought or action. After selecting his topic, the student should read widely on his subject. He may use for class talks the material he finds, or he may have a conference with you on what he has read. After he has exhausted his field, he should make his brief, or outline, being careful to see that his conclusion contains an appeal. His next task consists in writing his oration and revising it; then he must practice it. Probably he will have to memorize his oration. Notes are not permissible, as in debate, and the chances are he is not sufficiently confident to give an extemporaneous address. But in the delivery of a memorized speech come great dangers: the student is likely to forget, his delivery may be mechanical or oratorical or both. Thorough memorization of his speech, so that his tongue will utter the correct words should his brain fail him, may prevent the first danger; and insistence upon simple, natural, earnest, and sincere delivery throughout practice will guard against the second. Aid your pupil orators to select a timely subject, develop it logically, and present it simply; the judges of the contest will be grateful to you.

To sum up the oration: It appeals to the intellect, to the emotions, and to the will, in that it seeks to influence the hearers toward a decision. Its characteristics are (1) substantial subject matter; (2) coherent development; and (3) earnestness of delivery. Its great days in our country probably passed with the golden-tongued William Jennings Bryan, but as an exercise of the intellect it is worthy of your attention.

As you read these comments, no doubt you are wondering whether you are justified in allotting class time to debate and oratory, as so few of your pupils, either in or out of school, have need for them. My answer to this question is *yes*, for both types provide mental discipline, unfortunately often neglected today. In addition, debate in particular demands self-control, ability to weigh and ponder, the acceptance, without rancor, of another point of view. In order to show the validity, the possibility of honest convictions by both groups, many debate coaches require members of their squad to prepare both negative and affirmative briefs. It may well be, however, that you will discard formal debate from your classroom, being content with argument on some controversial question by means of which you train your pupils to recognize and present points *pro* and *con*, arrived at and delivered (if humanly possible) without malice and prejudice. One of the responsibilities of education lies in aiding pupils to recognize and respect the point of view of others. Both oration and debate co-operate faithfully here.

Closely connected with the teaching of composition and, like debate and oratory, a classroom or an extra-curricular activity, comes the school paper. That the school paper is considered desirable its almost universal use in high schools evidences. That journalistic writing should be the only type taught to high school students (as shown by substitution of journalistic writing for the regular requirements of junior and senior composition in some high schools) is open to question. In my opinion, journalistic writing should occupy part, not all, of the time given to composition. If you follow that plan, the school paper will probably be an extracurricular activity. It may, however, be handled by the class and published "now and then for fun and profit," as one school paper announced.

If an extracurricular activity, it may be managed in the following way. A room should be set aside for the use of the staff. In this should be long tables, if possible a copyreader's semicircular desk, a typewriter, a telephone and a directory, a pencil sharpener, a double-decked wire basket, a bulletin board, a calendar of present and past years, an unabridged dictionary, a book of synonyms (Crabbe's *English Synonyms* may now be had in a dollar edition), a copy of *Who's Who in America*, a city directory, and a newspaper rack. If you can't get all this, don't give up trying to produce a newspaper. Try to get a cubbyhole of some sort, tables, chairs, and a typewriter. The rest of the equipment you may be able to collect by degrees.

Next your staff must be selected. The editor and the business manager should be chosen from among the seniors; the other staff members may be underclassmen. Reporters should be selected from each high school class. Try to have the staff as well balanced and as responsible as possible. Its members may be chosen by a committee composed of the principal, you yourself, and two or three students; or you can select the members by a tryout system. For your own protection, however, I advise the sharing of the responsibility of staff selections, for occasionally pupils not chosen can make you very uncomfortable. Whatever the method, you, as sponsor, should have final choice in regard to the selection of, at least, the editor and the business manager. You must work with these students, and you want pupils who are dependable and will co-operate with you.

After the staff has been selected, plans for the paper may be made. You must first determine what sort of paper can be afforded: printed or mimeographed. Often printing is prohibitive, but mimeographing is comparatively inexpensive, and the use of a Ditto machine is even less costly. Five-cent wax stencils, although not entirely satisfactory, lessen mimeograph expense. Probably the school owns a machine, which you may borrow. It is possible that the school board is willing to pay for the stencils, the most expensive item of the mimeographed paper. Students can do very clever things with a mimeographed paper, even to cutting out cartoons. The cost and your decision concerning the inclusion of advertisements will probably determine your choice of paper. If you expect to support the paper by means of advertising, be certain to consult your principal before you put the plan into effect, for your school may have a policy concerning this with which you are unfamiliar. It is questionable whether merchants should be asked to support this school project. Your principal will give you advice on this.

When you determine what sort of paper you want and how you are going to finance it, the actual work of planning may be begun. You and your staff will have to decide upon the size of the paper, the number of departments, the space to be given to advertising. Most of this will depend upon cost. I suggest that you begin with a small paper, letting it grow if possible. You will have much to say in regard to general plans, and you will be responsible for planning each week's issue. As you are answerable to the public for the paper, you should insist upon these three rules: (1) Never permit anything to be published without your approval. If you are in any doubt, even regarding the good taste of a joke, consult your principal. It is highly desirable that this official read all the copy before it goes to press; for, as I have pointed out, you cannot be expected to know all administrative problems. (2) See that the books of the business manager are audited once a month. (3) Countersign every check yourself. These are simple business practices to which no business manager should object. Put them into effect immediately; do not wait until the horse is stolen to lock the door.

Your greatest problem will be to get the staff members to do the work. But if this activity has any value, the students, not you, must do the writing and managing. Your place is to oversee and with the principal to act as censor, but you will find that the work will devolve upon

you and two or three students, after the first wave of
enthusiasm which always greets the new dies away.
Guard against this by tryouts and promotions. Drop
from the staff anyone who habitually shirks. Give recognition to every member of the staff. Signed articles
may cause reporters to be proud of their work; credit in
English composition may be allowed for actual writing,
(not, however, for operating the mimeograph); staff
membership should be thought of as an honor; pins or
letters may be awarded for excellence and dependability.
Have a "Press Club" with meetings and speakers, and possibly a yearly banquet at which the group is addressed
by a local newspaperman. If you find that none of these
means is effective, you should stop the paper. Perhaps
issuing an edition "now and then," when the students
really are enthusiastic about doing it, is a better way than
to grind out a weekly or semimonthly paper. That only
you can decide. If you are prompt, dependable, and
enthusiastic yourself, the chances are that you will get
co-operation from your staff.

No matter how small and inexpensive your paper may
be, it should conform to the best standards. Become a
member of a press association and exchange papers with
others in the same class. Consider the best features of
other school papers and incorporate them into your own.
Work out a style book, in which you determine upon
matters of usage. (This, a project of some length, may
be assigned to an advanced class in English composition.)
Have as good headlines, leads, news stories, and editorials
as you can. Above all, see that your paper is dignified
in tone, for nothing justifies cheapness or commonness.
To this end, consider jokes and personals with some care.
You will have to learn to be somewhat "hard-boiled,"

using the blue pencil when you think it necessary; for in the eyes of the school patrons you, not the students, are responsible for the paper.

In the appendix of this book you will find a six-weeks' unit on journalistic writing. This is intended for composition classes, but you will find the material given valuable in connection with the production of a school paper. At the end of this chapter you will find suggested books that will help you if you have had no experience in journalism during your college days.

It may be that, after considering this problem, you think a school paper, even a mimeographed one, offers insurmountable difficulties. If so, perhaps you can substitute for it a column in your local paper, which many authorities on high school journalism prefer. By doing this, you will be spared all problems of production, yet will give your students practice in writing, and will build up a very desirable attitude of co-operation between the school and the town.

From time to time in this book, I have suggested journalistic projects. These can take the form of an issue in connection with a piece of literature, as was suggested for *Silas Marner;* or they may be typed or mimeographed special issues for summing up a unit in journalistic writing. Because of its training in effective sentence structure, vivid expression, and succinctness, journalistic writing should have a place in your classroom teaching.

Another of your extracurricular activities may well be the oversight of the high school annual. Usually this is sponsored by the senior class working under your direction, and offers many of the problems of the school paper.

The first step in producing an annual is to select the staff, which may be done by means of tryouts or through selection by a committee. As with the staff of the school paper, you must be the court of final appeal as far as choosing the staff is concerned. Be particularly careful in selecting an editor-in-chief and a business manager. Both should be businesslike and dependable. The editor-in-chief should have some literary ability, and the business manager should be capable of handling funds of some size. As with the newspaper, have the business manager's books audited and countersign every check yourself.

You should begin your plans for an annual early in the fall. With your staff, determine upon its form — printed or mimeographed — and the method of financing it. Printed annuals are very expensive, but an attractive mimeographed annual can be produced by a small group at little cost. You can even bind it yourself. Instead of having photographic plates made, use actual snapshots, or silhouettes. The homemade annual will tax your ingenuity and that of your staff, and affords, I believe, more genuine pleasure in accomplishment than does the more formal printed annual.

After determining the type you can produce, decide upon the divisions you want to have. The person in charge of each section should know exactly what is expected of him, how many pages he is responsible for, and when his copy must be ready. The editor-in-chief oversees the work of each sub-editor, and you must see that the editor-in-chief does his work promptly. If your annual carries advertisements and sells for several dollars a copy, the business manager has a very responsible job. See that he does his work in a businesslike manner, is careful to give receipts, and takes advantage of bonuses for cash payments. In the appendix to this book you

will find a plan worked out by a very businesslike manager
of a high school annual. You will be amused to observe
that he places as one of the duties of the business manager
"to keep after the editor and see that she gets her work
in." Evidently he had the usual male's doubt of the
business ability of a woman!

Often an annual, although of interest to its owners,
seems hardly to justify the time and energy invested.
Most of its departments consist of short write-ups and of
many pictures. If I were you, I should try to have my
annual show some literary merit. In addition to seeing
that the write-ups are well done, have a "literary section"
in which you print the best essays, poems, short stories,
or articles submitted during the year. This plan augments student interest in composition and gives some
justification for the time spent on the book. As with the
school paper, you will want to be assured that the contents conform to the standards of good taste. Furthermore, before the copy is submitted to the printer, you
should ask your principal to read and approve it.

ASSIGNMENT

A. Find out what provision there is in your state and district for furthering high school debate contests.

B. Do the same for oratorical contests.

C. Make a brief for an oration listed for use by your state
course of study.

D. Look up the Northern Interscholastic Press Association,
the National Scholastic Press Association, and the Columbia
Scholastic Press Association. Find out what provision is made
in your state for recognizing the work of the high school paper.

E. Find out what provision is made in your state for contests among high school annuals.

FURTHER READINGS

1. SAVIDGE, ANNE LANE, and HORN, GUNNAR, *Handbook for High School Journalism*, revised and enlarged.

In addition to giving directions for handling a school paper, this book contains particularly good bibliographies.

2. HYDE, GRANT MILNON, *Journalistic Writing*, second edition, revised.

This offers a thorough discussion of student newspapers and magazines.

3. *An Experience Curriculum in English*, pp. 282–284.

Here you will find a plan for an elective course in journalism.

4. DOWLER, C. X., "The High School Paper a Community Service," *The English Journal*, XXIV (November, 1935), pp. 748–753.

This recounts the plan of a small high school for supplying a weekly news column to the local paper.

5. HARRINGTON, HARRY FRANKLIN and HARRINGTON, EVALINE, *Writing for Print*, revised edition.

This practical book offers suggestions on all the problems that confront the teacher of high school journalism.

6. The A. B. Dick Company, Chicago, will gladly send you helpful material on the production of a mimeographed annual or paper.

7. The *New York Times*, Circulation Department, College Service, will send you on request some exercises in newspaper writing called "Patterns for Newspaper Writing."

8. THOMAS, CHARLES SWAIN, *The Teaching of English in the Secondary School*, Chapter XIII, pp. 352–358.

The author comments briefly on the school paper, more fully on debate.

9. ZIMMERMAN, WILMA L., "Debating That's Different," *Washington Education Association Journal*, XVI (1936), pp. 42–43.

This gives a summary of the principles involved in the "cross-questioning" method of debate.

XIX. DRAMATICS AND THE LITERARY SOCIETY

Another of your multifarious activities will no doubt be that of coaching the school plays. We teachers of English must indeed know something of everything!

Your first task will be to select a play. For high school use, choose one with a good plot and with clever lines. As a rule, high school students act best in roles of characters somewhat near their own age. At any rate, you should not select, for high school use, a play that has for its leading character an elderly person. Nor should you choose one in which the delineation is too subtle. Direct, clear, pointed characterizations will carry your play along. As a part of your examination read the play aloud, noting the effectiveness of the dialogue. Few and simple stage settings often prove other determining factors. In order to gain a conception of the problem of settings and action, make for yourself a miniature stage with pieces of paper for properties and characters, moving the latter about as the action or directions suggest. Usually, copies of plays may be borrowed for examination from the library or extension department of your state university or state college.

In many communities your problem will be what to avoid, not what to choose. For a high school production you must eliminate those in which occur swearing, smoking (illegal everywhere for minors), card-playing (only in some communities), excessive love-making, and drinking. You read this list, and you say, "Well, what's left?" When you have examined several plays and have been forced to discard all of them, you are still more discouraged; but be not *too* downhearted, for it is amazing what a little ingenious cutting can accomplish. *Unless the plot hinges* on one of the above-mentioned points, you can always adjust the play to suit your needs. Swearing may be changed to a pointed exclamation (you are not concerned with the intent, you see, merely with the words), smoking may become some rather amusing or significant mannerism, card-playing may be chess, love scenes may (probably should) always be cut, and drinking need not be of intoxicants. So, unless the act is important, see what your blue pencil can accomplish before you give up the play. And be certain to have your principal read the play and agree to its use. Remember always that what may be suitable in college may not be at all good for high school performance. Select plays that have as much literary merit as is possible, but consider always the desires of your community. You cannot produce Ibsen (even if your students were capable of acting it) before an audience whose dramatic taste is formed by "Our Gang" comedies. Determine not to present anything cheap or common, but do not be too insistent upon giving literary masterpieces. Finally, let a student committee read and suggest plays, if you like, but make the decision yourself. It is your task to coach the play, and you are responsible for its success or failure.

After you have selected your play, you must choose a cast. For this, the tryout system is probably preferable, unless the group is small. In a small high school often a coach must select a play not because of its merits, but because of the number in the cast in order that every member of the class may have a part. I have even gone so far as to write in a part, or have introduced an entr'acte in order to accommodate all. If this is the situation, tryouts are still desirable for selecting leads and determining dramatic ability. For this, select bits from the play, have them mimeographed, and give them to the candidates. A committee of the faculty may well act as judges, but you should be present and should make the final decision.

As soon as possible — before interest dies — begin your rehearsals. For a three-act play, allow four weeks; never practice more than five. Pupils of high school age, although capable of tremendous effort, have not the staying power of adults. The shorter and more intense the period of rehearsal, the more spontaneous will be the performance.

You should rehearse daily at a given time. It is not necessary to practice at night, nor should you ever plan to rehearse on Sunday. If you and your cast have a businesslike attitude toward rehearsals, they need not be a burden. Furthermore, you do not want to take so much time for an extracurricular activity that the class work of the student suffers. If you plan carefully, this is not necessary. Insist on promptness at rehearsals and *be prompt yourself*. You cannot expect from a group what you are unwilling to do. As an extreme measure, drop from the cast anyone who is habitually late or frequently absent. Tread carefully here, for you may antagonize an entire group by summary action with one person. It may be the part of wisdom to suffer in silence, but refuse to accept the person in another play until he can convince you he will mend his ways, of course explaining all this to him in private.

During the rehearsals, the persons on the stage must have an earnest attitude. Insist that they keep in character and do their best during each rehearsal, and allow those off the stage some liberties, provided they watch their cues and are not disturbing.

As much as possible, use students on the producing staff. Have a student business manager, who will report to you his plans; a prompter, called on the programs, for obvious reasons, *assistant to the director* (not assistant director). This person, although inconspicuous, is very important. Select a girl, dependable, with good nerves and a clear voice. Try to make this person — who must always be present, may never have any fun, and may never raise her eyes from her book — realize her importance. You should not try to do the prompting yourself. On the night of the performance, someone may faint or have hysterics, or be unable to tie his tie or put in his collar button. You must be free to attend to these emergencies. To return to the production staff — have student property men, costume directors, and make-up committee (if they are trained for this). This group should receive equal publicity with the actors; their names should appear on the programs, and they should be included in all parties given for the cast.

A probable time division for rehearsals is: first week, Act I; second week, Act II; third week, Act III; fourth week, entire play. If you select a four-act play, add another week to your rehearsal time. Insist that lines for Act I be memorized by the end of the week. After your deadline, do not permit anyone to use a book on the stage, even if he has to be prompted for every other word. Say nothing; he will know his lines by the next rehearsal, unless he is one of those undependable, irresponsible persons, whom I pray you may be spared. (You should do more than pray about it, too, by taking dependability into consideration in choosing your cast. The brilliant, irresponsible performer may do very well as an individual on the night of the play, but he may upset the entire cast because they do not know what to expect from him.)

Although many persons persist in memorizing line by line, you should explain to your cast the better method: reading aloud *as a whole* any passage several lines in length. If the speech is very long, it may be divided into two or three main portions and this procedure followed for each. After several careful readings with particular attention to the meaning, the book should be closed and the thought reproduced. The parts in which the wording cannot be recalled should be examined again, and another attempt should be made to recall the whole. Although this method may seem tedious at first, in the end it will prove more efficient than the old "line by line" plan. Once memorized, the passage should be allowed to rest for some hours; then it should be repeated for permanent retention. *Meaning*, not *words*, is stressed in this system of memorization.

Toward the end of the fourth week have at least one dress rehearsal, *with all properties*. A good way to manage this is to give a matinee on the day of the performance, to the grade school children, at a very low price. This makes unnecessary the long, evening, dress rehearsal, rightfully objected to by parents, and reduces the period of responsibility for borrowed articles. Before presenting the play at home, if you can, give it before a group outside your own community. Sometimes you can go to a near-by small town. In one school in which I taught, we always took our plays to the state penitentiary, providentially located near the city, thus assuring, as the boys used to say, an audience that would not walk out on us.

Expect great enthusiasm at first, then a slump. When that drop comes, discuss such matters as costumes and stage settings and the possibility of giving the play somewhere else. Such talk will arouse lagging interest.

There are certain responsibilities that you, the coach, have, aside from producing the play. In the first place, you must watch over expenses, such as for tickets and advertising. With the business manager, plan all expenditures carefully. After the play, you or some other faculty member — perhaps the principal — must count the box office receipts, pay the costs, and turn over the remainder to the proper person.

You are also accountable for all borrowed furniture and costumes. Shops in the town are often glad to lend furnishings (always see that the group presenting the play sends a letter of thanks and that the names of these firms appear on the program). Because women's clothes are more easily harmed than are those of men, you should discourage the girls from borrowing from shops. Usually their friends can lend them suitable dresses. The boys may be permitted to borrow suits with the understanding that each individual is to be responsible for the clothing borrowed. You must see that such clothing and furniture are carefully taken care of and *returned promptly*. In the height of enthusiasm it is easy to borrow; but in the let-down after the play it takes will power to return. A steady, reliable property manager will be a tower of strength here.

You must also see that the royalty on any royalty play produced is paid. Probably you will not be sent to jail if you ignore this payment, but training in honest business methods is far more important than is a ten or twenty-five dollar royalty fee. Do not, as I have known coaches to do, change the name of the play to avoid paying royalty. If you cannot afford to pay the premium asked, use a nonroyalty play, many very acceptable ones being on the market if you take the trouble to hunt for them.

If you have had no experience in coaching, I suggest that you send for one of the books on play-directing mentioned at the end of this chapter. With such a guide and your own common sense you will be able to produce plays that will please you. Make-up will offer some problems, but written directions and much practice will work wonders in this. As a general principle, remember that make-up is used merely to counteract the effect of strong lights. To the audience an actor should look natural. Men, except for eccentric or old-age characters, should have very little make-up, never any on the lips, a little on the cheeks and about the eyes. Women should have somewhat more; the lips should be done, but delicately. No one is beautiful with a vivid gash for a mouth. It is far better to use too little make-up than to produce caricatures of the human face. Shadows and lines for older faces are difficult to produce, but practice and careful scrutiny of the effect under strong lights will help you to get the natural effect desired.

The National Council of Teachers of English has published a pamphlet called "Guide to Play Selection," by Milton Smith, which I commend to your attention as containing a list of plays and much valuable supplementary material. You will find in the appendix to this book the names of companies publishing plays. I think you will enjoy coaching plays. Students have a great deal of fun out of it, and so may you — as well as work — provided you plan your procedure carefully.

Perhaps your boys and girls so enjoy "play-acting" that they will want to have a dramatic club. If so, make some definite and progressive plans for it, each meeting marking a stage in the development of your program. You may begin, perhaps, with pantomime. A committee may work out somewhat dramatic situations — brief ones — to be indicated by pantomime, in which gesture, facial expression, and movement all come into consideration. Next you could work on some definite problems: for example, given a man, a girl, and a bench, what possible positions are there in this grouping? Telephone conversations offer excellent material for variety in position; other situations can be worked out similarly. Show your students what strong and weak stage positions are; let them observe the effect of persons in those positions. Work also on stage balance, experimenting with the placing of large and small groups. Effective exits and entrances may well occupy you for an evening.

Make-up constitutes a project that may be carried along in a dramatic club throughout the year. A big problem here is the expense. Ideally each student should own a kit, but as these are costly, the best you can do, possibly, is to buy one for use by the entire group. Try to guard against waste, for an open make-up kit affords a great temptation to alter the face that nature gave one.

Your final objective is production of one-act plays. These need not be memorized but the action should be carefully planned and the reading of lines effective. By the way, if, the day before you give a play your leading man is quarantined for mumps, do not waste time in having a substitute learn the lines, as at best his delivery will be halting. Instead, drill him in the *action* of the play and in reading his lines. After the first shock, the audience will forget all about the book in the hands of the actor. A "Play Festival," consisting of several one-act plays directed by pupils who have taken part in a three-act play and presented before an audience of high school pupils and their friends, provides excellent training for future play directors and includes a large number of the members of the student body. Although a student project, this, like everything else, needs your guiding touch.

Activities connected with the dramatic club may include going in a body to a movie or to see some legitimate drama. The group should look for definite points: perhaps the way exits and entrances were handled, perhaps the management of the love scenes. At the next meeting of the club there should be constructive criticism. Another interesting project is to have reports on certain actors, living and dead, and on methods of stage production. There is much that is very educative concerning the stage and famous actors.

Why not make use of shadow plays as one of your activities? For these, the group may select its own episode for portrayal by means of shadows — perhaps a nursery rhyme: Jack Spratt who would eat no fat and his wife who would eat no lean, each being fed with morsels to suit his taste; or the misadventures of Jack and Jill with their pail of water. These require skill in selecting the incident, effectively timed reading of the lines to explain the picture, and experience in such mechanical aspects as hanging the sheet behind which the actors appear, placing the light, and timing the action. Simple work with marionettes offers much in the way of choosing and handling dramatic situations as well as experience in the mechanical aspects necessary. Almost anyone soon becomes fascinated with this phase of dramatics. Perhaps you may be so fortunate as to live near some institution offering courses in marionette making, and what a thrill your group would receive from going in a body to see one of the productions.

Another type of club — perhaps not so usual as in an earlier period but still found in many schools — is the literary club. Make this more than a hodgepodge by selecting some central theme upon which to base the programs for the year or the semester; for example, the period of the Civil War may be chosen: talks could be given on modes of living both in the North and South just previous to the war; the music of the time might be discussed and presented; cartoons, if available, would furnish excellent material for talks (*Harper's Weeklies* of the Sixties provide a mine of information); plays centering about the era might be presented; debates on the issues of the moment could be given; books could be read and reviewed. By such a plan the literary society will be given the dignity that is often lacking in unplanned meetings.

In this, as in any other club you sponsor, either in or out of class, see that the meetings follow the proper procedure. This is an excellent chance to put into practice the fundamental principles of parliamentary law.

A practical application of composition principles develops from writing minutes. (I was amused not long ago, by the way, to hear these referred to as "seconds" — a further evidence of the necessity of emphasizing *terms*.)

We have now discussed most of the major extracurricular activities that fall to the lot of the teacher of English, but a few minor ones remain to be noted. You may have to coach students for entrance into a declamatory contest but this is an individual matter. Use good taste in selecting readings and insist upon simple, direct interpretation. The day of bombastic delivery is past, although everyone does not yet realize it; and among these bombast-loving people may be your judges. You must, then, steel yourself to accept defeat in order to further good standards. You will certainly be asked to chaperon picnics, dances, hikes, and parties. It is not a bad idea to have in mind games and entertainments of various sorts that you can resort to. Be on the alert for classroom activities suitable for presentation before the assembly. Debates or arguments; dramatizations of poems or short stories; cuttings from dramas; illustrated talks (perhaps on shawls or antique furniture); group singing of early ballads; the book pageants and shadow pictures suggested on pages 473–497 — all are interesting to an audience outside the classroom. Also you should gather as many suggestions as possible for brief programs, to be given before the high school group or at parties or carnivals. Selections which are brief and need little practice (an important factor) are difficult to find. Sometimes a pantomime such as "And the Lamp Went Out," "Lord Ullin's Daughter," or shadow pictures serve the purpose. If you begin a notebook now in which you jot down every suggestion from college entertainments, including toast programs, you will find it a lifesaver when a group of students rush in to exclaim breathlessly, "Oh, Miss ——! We're going to have a party tonight and we can't dance! Tell us what to do!"

All these extracurricular activities mean work both for you and the students. They are enjoyable and for the most part desirable. But you and your pupils should remember that after all they are *extra*curricular activities. In no way do they substitute for the academic subjects of the curriculum nor should these suffer because of enthusiasm for debate, dramatics, or the school paper. To guard against this, scholastic standards should be set, preferably by your school, for participation in any extracurricular activity except athletics or for any other activity for which there are conference rules. I make this exception for the reason that it is probably unfair for one institution to have higher standards than those set by the state. This, an administrative problem, however, has no real concern for you. It *is* your concern to work toward definite scholastic standards for extracurricular activities that are not under conference rulings. I suggest that every pupil taking part in any sort of extracurricular engagement (with of course the above exception) shall be passing in all subjects and have an average of eighty. This numerical average may be a little too high or too low for your school, but experience will decide what it should be.

One person should be discouraged from holding two executive positions. In a small high school particularly, one energetic, capable pupil will be in every activity sponsored by the school, including athletics, and may be president of two or three organizations. That is attempting too much; furthermore, it prevents others, who may have concealed merits, from obtaining experience in management. Since there is considerable value to the individual in holding executive positions, that privilege should be shared among many.

If you like the idea, after you have become established in your school system, suggest to your principal a plan for school letters, whereby participation in other extracurricular activities besides athletics may have the recognition it deserves. I am not belittling athletic contests — I enjoy them thoroughly — but I know that hours of work and sacrifice go into the preparation of a debate, the production of an annual or a newspaper, the performance of a play. Why not recognize this in some public manner? Letters might be awarded on the point basis: so many points for scholarship, for committee work, for singing in the glee club, for participation in any extracurricular activity. Such a plan would give an opportunity to recognize students who are as important as are the members of the second team — those reliable, substantial persons, not brilliant enough to attract public attention, but whose steadfast efforts really make possible much of what attracts the eye of the public. During the six years of high school life, these worthy students and the more brilliant ones would be gathering points, until, perhaps at the middle of the senior year, each would receive a letter awarded at a special meeting of the high school assembly. In addition a letter might be presented to the faculty's choice of the best all-round student in the high school. I should like to see you experiment with some such plan as this. Not long ago I read that we Americans do not appreciate, as do Europeans, the value of a decoration, of a bit of ribbon to wear in the buttonhole. We have no "Order of the Garter" and perhaps

we do not want one, but a recognition of work well done
can hardly go amiss.

ASSIGNMENT

A. Find provisions in your state for dramatic contests.
B. Write a plan for a literary society.

FURTHER READINGS

1. HACKETT, WILLIAM ARTHUR, "Advice to the Frantic,"
The English Journal, XXIV (December, 1935), pp. 817–823.

Formerly a professional actor, now Professor of Speech,
Western State Teachers College, Michigan, Mr. Hackett gives
excellent advice to the bewildered play director.

2. WOOLBERT, CHARLES H., and WEAVER, ANDREW T.,
Better Speech, Appendix A, "The Nature of Acting," Appendix
B, "Directing a Play for School or Class."

These sections afford practical help on many problems.

3. BRADY, FLORENCE A., "The Use of Marionettes in
Literature," *The Elementary School Journal*, XXII (May, 1945),
pp. 182–185.

Although designed for third-grade pupils, the plan and suggestions are applicable to the upper grades.

4. ANGUS, WILLIAM, "Some Practicable School Plays,"
The English Journal, XXI (May, 1932), pp. 395–398.

Here you will find a list of one-act plays and phantasies.

5. *Encyclopaedia Britannica*, Fourteenth Edition.

You will find valuable information under "Marionettes."

6. WOODRING, MAXIE NAVE, JEWETT, IDA A., and BEN-
SON, RACHEL T., *Enriched Teaching of English in the Junior and
Senior High School*, "Dramatics."

This section provides titles, names, and addresses that will
aid you greatly.

7. CRAIG, ALICE VIRGINIA, *The Speech Arts*, second revised
edition.

Chapters XXVII and XXIX define stage terms and give
suggestions for acting and stage settings.

XX. ODDS AND ENDS

THROUGHOUT this book I have touched lightly upon various aspects of your teaching which I now want to consider in detail. I am taking it for granted that you have had some background courses in the principles of education. For that reason, I am not going to discuss fully these matters I have in mind; I am merely going to describe briefly some points that are particularly applicable to the teaching of secondary school English.

The first of these concerns the use of tests and scales. As you will remember, I suggested that you first find out what your students know and build your teaching program upon the results of your test. I have said that you may devise your own tests or you may use one of the standardized objective tests on the market. In the appendix you will find lists of reliable tests for use both in composition and in literature. Some publishers furnish tests with the text you select.

All this is valuable, but I want to point out to you one or two dangers, as I see them. In the first place, too much dependence must not be placed upon the results even of standardized tests. They are *suggestive* merely, and should be supported by less formal methods of testing, observation, and your own good sense. Don't think of them as final, then; think of them as indicative.

In the second place, not everyone knows how to administer a test or how to evaluate the findings. A little knowledge is a dangerous thing. Unless you understand objective testing you should not use it except informally.

Nor does everyone know how to make an objective test. Frequently, you may very well want to test the factual knowledge of your group, for which nothing is better than an objective test. Very well; but do not think that you can make such a test on your way to school. The principles of testing must be applied and the test tried out several times before it can be accurate. You will be amazed at the possible interpretations of what you have thought to be perfectly obvious. You can get standardized tests on pieces of literature (these are listed in the appendix), but the cost may force you to prepare your own.

It is possible to buy on the market certain scales for determining achievement in writing. If you use one of these, keep in mind that its purpose is to measure the progress of a group, not of an individual. Such a scale has value in indicating to you the improvement of your class after a period of teaching, or in comparing your pupils with others; but it should not be used to indicate the mark earned by an individual student for a particular theme.

Finally, and most important, although objective testing has its place in the teaching of English, *it can never be a substitute for the essay type of examination.* By the time a student is graduated from high school you want him to be able to select a subject, to limit and define it, to analyze it, and to express his ideas concerning it clearly and effectively. None of these is taught him by means of objective testing. When he writes the essay type of examination, he must do all of these. It is possible of course to say that he gets such training in theme writing. He does; but the whole process is so complicated that he needs all the practice that he can obtain. I suggest that you use objective testing to determine factual knowledge, but that you do not substitute it for the essay type of examination. Objective tests may be easy to mark, but they are not easy to compose, and they do not give training in the essential aspects of composition.

Occasionally I have used the term "unit." There seems to be considerable division of opinion in regard to this term. As I employ it, I mean it to indicate a block of work. To plan one's teaching in units or blocks, allotting a definite period of time to cover the work in each unit is always desirable. The unit may consist of the matter to be covered, activities connected with the material, and an examination to test the students' mastery of the content included in the unit. For example, you might plan a unit on the writing of a friendly letter. You would first have your pupils write a friendly letter in class. You would then teach them the essentials of a letter, basing your class procedure upon the needs indicated by their letters. You would also give them practice in writing letters. Perhaps you would have the pupils read and analyze well-known friendly letters; or you might arrange an exchange of letters with students living elsewhere. You would then test the knowledge of your group on the writing of a friendly letter.

The general plan of the unit system is to test, teach, test. This procedure I have suggested several times: find out what your students know, teach them whatever is necessary, and test them upon their accomplishment.

The unit system has definite advantages in that it enables one to plan his work intelligently, to stay within the time limits set, and to test the student over each phase of work. It is particularly adaptable to working out a flexible plan of procedure; that is, although with one group it may be wise to begin with a certain type of work, with another it might be better to delay this study. The unit system permits one to change with ease one's order of work. (For a suggestion as to how to plan a unit of work in literature, consult Robert C. Pooley's *A Year's Course in English Literature*, Scott, Foresman and Company, 1929.) A weakness lies in the failure of some teachers to correlate each block of work with what has been and will be studied.

Your plan for a unit may well include the division of the material into contracts. The employment of the contract system provides a minimum of work for slow pupils, more work for average boys and girls, and the most work for superior students. An attempt to provide for individual differences, it is particularly good for use in unsectioned courses. I can, perhaps, do no better than to quote Dr. Robert C. Pooley's statement concerning the theory underlying lesson units.

> Each study unit is based upon a general theory. Group D, the first section, contains the minimum essentials of the unit: that material which every pupil should master. Group C is built upon the work of Group D, and contains supplementary reading and some form of pupil-response calling for a comparison with the work of Group D. Group B is unifying and expressive, calling upon the pupil to express himself in a written essay or an oral report on the general theme and the specific contents of the unit under study. Group A is critical

and creative: it should challenge the pupil either to do original work, or to interpret the material under consideration in terms of life experience. This last group calls for a high grade of response of which only a few students in a normal class are capable.

Upon these principles rests the contract method. Doctor Pooley's outline is for literature, but the same principles may be applied to composition. In preparing such a unit, one would decide upon minimum essentials in the work in composition for the year under consideration, calling this Group D (or C, if you plan for only three groupings). Group C should include the work of D, with additional and more difficult material; B should demand more theme writing than is asked for in C; and A should demand, not only more writing, but writing that lays some claim to originality in thought and expression. As your particular purpose in teaching composition is to aid students to communicate their ideas, you should increase the number of themes asked for in the successive units. Not until the requirements of all four contracts —A, B, C, and D — have been met will a pupil receive a grade of A.

A number of your assignments have been to make lesson plans based upon the following points: (1) your aim, (2) your approach, (3) your assignment, and (4) five questions you would ask. For your daily lesson plan I believe these are the points to keep in mind. If I were you, I should write a plan for each class period. You should begin this with "routine procedure," jotting down under this heading the daily matters to which you must attend: taking the roll, accepting or rejecting excuses, collecting absence slips, making announcements. Unless you write these down, you will probably forget them entirely, or be forced to interrupt your class procedure with, "Oh, yes, I forgot to tell you that you are to go to assembly immediately upon the close of this period." Such interpolations are most disturbing to the forward movement that your class period should have.

Although in planning your work you do not need to write down your aim for each class period, to do so is desirable. This aim must be specific and of such a nature that you can accomplish it in one class period. For example, your general or remote aim in teaching freshman composition may be "accuracy of expression," but your specific or immediate aim may be to teach the recognition of the verb. Undoubtedly the immediate aim has a bearing upon the remote, but it is the specific end of teaching this grammatical point that you should keep in mind for use in that class period, not the remote aim. Upon your decision as to what you want to accomplish in a given period depends your class procedure. Therefore it is necessary to have clearly in mind a specific objective for each class recitation.

Similarly, in teaching literature, your aim may well be "appreciation of literature" (although it seems to me that this aim without qualification is too general to be valuable). But this is far too broad to set as an aim for a single class period. When you consider the implications of "appreciation of literature," you realize that you cannot hope to accomplish it in one class period. Therefore it is a poor objective for use in a class period, although acceptable, possibly, for a remote end in teaching literature. Much better are the following, selected from papers of prospective teachers: "To give the necessary background for the reading of *The Lady of the Lake*," and "To have the students understand the story of the poem and

to have them appreciate some of the visual images."
(This last is not a statement of aims for *The Lady of the Lake* but for another shorter poem in which both objectives suggested may be attained in one reading.)

The next point in class procedure that I have listed is the *approach*. This, of course, means the way in which you introduce the subject at hand. Without straining for effect, try to lead up to the subject in such a manner as to interest the students. You "approach" or introduce an assignment, and you "approach" or introduce the class discussion of the assignment. This latter is often a summary of what has been accomplished in the preceding class period. The purpose of the approach consists in arousing interest and showing the connection between what has been discussed and what is to be discussed. It may be either an introduction or a transition. To illustrate what I mean, let me offer two methods of approach to the reading of *The Rime of the Ancient Mariner*, both suggested by students:

(1) Begin with an informal discussion of the author. Follow this with a review of the following figures of speech: simile, metaphor, alliteration, onomatopoeia.

Let us see what is wrong with this introduction. In the first place, why begin with a "discussion of the life of the author"? Does Coleridge's life have any bearing upon an appreciative reading of the poem by ninth-grade students, twelve- and thirteen-year-olds? Mr. Lowes, in *The Road to Xanadu*, has, it is true, pointed out the personal aspects of this poem, but Mr. Lowes's point of view is not for the high school student. An easy, but not always a desirable, approach to any piece of literature is by way of discussing the life of the author. But unless the incidents of the author's life have a bearing upon the meaning of the poem I suggest that you try another method. In teaching Shelley's "Ode to the West Wind" a knowledge of the life of the poet is essential, but not in teaching *The Rime of the Ancient Mariner.*

Consider the next point: a review of figures of speech. Will this arouse the interest of the students? Will it make them yearn to read this vivid poem? I doubt it. Furthermore, can you determine the *aim* in the mind of the cadet teacher who planned this approach? A discussion of the life of the author indicates that the poem is being introduced to the students. But emphasis on figures of speech suggests that the poem has been read, for surely one would not start students on a hunt for figures of speech before they were familiar with the content of the poem. Do you note, too, that all the items mentioned are *not* figures of speech? The cadet teacher who planned this approach admitted, without realizing it, "I am too lazy to think of a way of introducing this poem that will interest my students. I am not concerned with taking into consideration the age, abilities, and previous interests of my students. I have in mind no aim; I don't know what I want to accomplish in my first assignment of this poem. I have to write a lesson plan including a statement of my approach in order to get credit from the course. Well, I've done it."

(2) The second cadet teacher tells his students that they are about to read a poem concerning a sailor. He reminds them that sailors are superstitious folk, and he gives some examples of superstitions connected with the sea. He then suggests that his pupils be alert for such superstitions in reading the poem.

Now this teacher *is* considering student interests. He knows the fascination of the sea for most people, particularly for boys; he knows their interest in superstitions; he knows the lure of the search. If he tells his tales of super-stition well, he is certain to interest the students in their reading — he has given them something to look for. Fur-thermore, he has in mind the discussion of the purpose of the author which will come after the class has read the poem; for Coleridge wrote to show the result of killing a bird of good omen, not, as many think, to point a moral against the ill-treatment of dumb creatures. All this indi-cates that the cadet teacher knows and understands the poem himself and that he remembers the age and interests of the group with which he must deal.

I often think that the most important part of our teaching is the *assignment*. Class discussion clears up difficulties, affords drill, offers (sometimes) inspiration, but the assignment guides the student by showing him what to look for. It directs his work without doing it for him; through it he is forced to think and act for him-self, which is valuable training. Let us, then, consider with some care this important factor of teaching.

One of the difficulties that confronts you is the *length* of the lesson, for of course it must be sufficiently long to insure a certain amount of work from the student yet short enough for him to "see his way through" without being discouraged by its mere length. Unfortunately, it is impossible to be definite concerning this important point. It is necessary to keep in mind the age, ability, and background of the students; whether the material to be covered is old or new; whether it is difficult or easy. In assigning exercises, one can ask for many more if the student is required merely to fill in a blank than one can if he has to copy each sentence in order to make a correc-tion or to use a certain form. Find out how much time each pupil is expected to give to each preparation. Plan to make the assignment of a length proper for the average student. If you have time, experiment upon yourself, keeping in mind the fact that you are familiar with the material. Remember that you are not the only teacher that your students have and remember, also, that high school assignments must be prepared *daily*. Fresh from college, where you have taken two-, three-, or four-hour courses you forget that your high school pupils have only a few hours instead of days in which to do their work. Many modern texts are arranged in such a way that each lesson is the proper length for an assignment. As this is more characteristic of composition than of literature texts, your particular problem comes in making assignments in literature.

Next consider the material to be included in an assignment in the field of composition. In teaching *grammar*, it is important to assign only *one* phase of the work at a time. As has been pointed out, the principle of teaching one thing at a time must never be forgotten. You may, however, group two allied phases. For example, you could assign for diagraming ten sentences illustrating the use of the appositive and twenty or twenty-five sentences containing appositives for punctuation. If the students have to copy these sentences, you must reduce the number to, say, ten; if not, you may assign twenty or twenty-five with a clear conscience.

Spelling assignments should be brief, planned to occupy only a few moments of the class period. Except in a general review exercise, *punctuation* is best combined with grammar, as suggested above. *Sentence structure* is so difficult that exercises pertaining to it should constitute the whole of the lesson. The number of illustrative sentences for each of these must depend upon the factors mentioned above.

The writing of a *theme* should be the only requirement made for that day. Properly done, it is long enough to occupy the time set aside for preparation in English. Its importance should not be underemphasized by using it in connection with another aspect of teaching, unless the theme is so brief that it is actually only an exercise. As suggested previously, every theme should be assigned several days in advance.

In oral composition the speech with its outline comprises a sufficiently long assignment.

In the field of literature the assignment is less defined than in composition. I can make only one particular statement concerning it: It should *never* be "Read so many pages." I am convinced that this is a poor type of assignment, for it offers no challenge or directions for reading; beyond that I cannot speak with such decision.

As far as the *short story* is concerned, you can probably assign two of average length for each class period. If, however, you are asking for any sort of analysis, one story is sufficient. You must judge by the length and difficulty of the story and by the personnel of your class. Questions to be answered by the student are usually highly desirable as a part of the assignment. If these questions are to be written on — and I think you will find this a good plan — you will have to make allowance for the time required for writing. Assignments for the *novel* should be according to plot divisions, as has been said. Each daily assignment must be of a manageable length, and again, answering questions in writing must be considered. The *drama*, *long narrative poems*, and *formal essays* require the same sort of management as does the novel. *Short poems* are comparable to the short story; make your assignment conform to the length and difficulty of the poem. To give an entire class period to Edward Sill's "A Fool's Prayer" means overemphasis and overanalysis, for there is not enough in this poem to demand an hour or so of preparation on the part of the student. The reading of two or three *familiar essays* may be asked for, but probably only one nature essay, for the students reading this type are usually younger than are those studying the familiar essay and the subject matter is likely to be somewhat difficult. The best advice that I can give you is that you try to put yourself in the place of the pupil and then determine the length and difficulty of the assignment.

Several specific suggestions have already been made regarding the nature of the assignment. In general, you should give the students definite points to look for. Help them to read by asking questions that will make them see, think, and feel with the author.

Furthermore, the requirement must be of such a nature that you can tell whether or not it is done. This is one of the values of asking the pupil to do some written work as a part of each lesson. Consider this assignment, suggested by a cadet teacher: "Read the poem aloud several times, putting as much expression and interpretation in as you find necessary or desirable." How are you going to check on such an assignment as that, unless you go back to the procedure of the "blab" school? And is not such an assignment far too easy? For you cannot expect such careful reading as a student of speech would give a poem. I have noted several times in discussing the assignment with beginning teachers that they are likely to emphasize oral reading. I approve of training in oral expression, but I think our purpose in teaching literature is to enable the student by means of *silent* reading to understand the thought of the author, for this method is most employed by adults.

Again, the assignment must be clear and it must be accurate. In writing an assignment, a student of mine once asked her hypothetical class to read John Masefield's *The Rime of the Ancient Mariner*. No doubt this was a slip of the tongue or pen, but such lapses should be guarded against. And the assignment *must* be clearly worded; otherwise your students cannot possibly do good work. What do you make of this, an assignment presumably carefully thought out: "Look up John Dryden; each pupil to pick out one thing about him he considers interesting other than where and when born and give these to two pupils who volunteer"? Try to prepare this assignment and see what you make of it! Consider the long, hazardous, and I fear impossible journey that you would have to take to "look up John Dryden." After you find him, what are you going to give to "two pupils who volunteer"? Aside from its deficiencies as an assignment in literature, isn't it a very poor example of English composition? Is there any excuse for such abuse by a person planning to teach English?

Let your assignment, then, be definite, reasonable, and couched in good form. Give it your careful attention, for by its means your students grow in grace.

Next to the assignment in importance is the art, or possibly I should say the *science*, of questioning. At any rate, questioning is more than simply asking someone for information. Like the assignment, it requires your earnest consideration.

Questions may be placed in two classes: fact and thought questions. Fact questions have for their purpose the unearthing of information; thought questions seek to develop the power to reason, analyze, judge, compare. Both have a place in your teaching.

Fact questions are to be used primarily in ascertaining whether or not the students have read and understood the assignment. They are of particular use in objective testing and in the little "check quiz" that you will frequently give at the beginning of the class period. They should not be used in an attempt to further discussion, as, by their very nature, this they cannot do. Only if a statement of fact is necessary before proceeding to discussion should it be considered in class. A friend of mine once observed a cadet teacher conducting a class in *Ivanhoe*. Asked the teacher, "And what was Ivanhoe doing then?" "Ivanhoe," replied the student, "was lying on the bed." "Yes," said the teacher, "he was lying on the bed." Interesting? Provocative? Hardly. The only purpose in doing this is to kill time. This the teacher was proceeding to do. She was also killing interest by insulting, unintentionally, of course, the mental capacity of her students. Fact questions have their place but they seldom promote discussion.

Thought questions, on the other hand, are the type to serve as a basis for discussion. What is the purpose of this? The meaning of that? Can you think of a way in which this applies to our problems of today? What makes this story worth reading? How does this compare with what we read yesterday? Good thought questions are an exercise for your wit as well as for that of your students. By skillful questioning you can make a piece of literature vivid and alive; by dull questioning you can reduce it in the mind of your students to the veriest piece of drivel.

Let me illustrate what I mean by "fact" and "thought"

questions by quoting from Mabel Irene Rich's text for high school use, *A Study of the Types of Literature* (The Century Company, 1923). Those I have selected refer to *A Tale of Two Cities* and may be found on pages 398, 399, 403, and 404.

FACT QUESTIONS

(Book the Third, "The Track of the Storm.")

Chapter II. "The Grindstone."

(1) What were the headquarters of Tellson's Bank in Paris?

(2) What advantages were gained from its location?

(3) Why did Dr. Manette and Lucie come to Paris?

Chapter V. "The Wood-Sawyer."

(2) What example of Lucie's faithfulness is there here?

(7) What was the carmagnole?

(8) What was the popular Revolution song of 1792?

THOUGHT QUESTIONS

General Questions.

(1) Select from the book six incidents to reveal character.

(3) Name a character that was developed by adverse circumstances.

(7) Name a person who helps to unravel the plot. Show how.

(13) Try to determine the reason the author had for the introduction of each character in the story. For instance, what use is made of Stryver, Mr. Lorry, Jerry, Miss Pross, etc.?

(21) What important changes in the ending of this novel would be necessitated if the following circumstances were changed:

    (a) If Defarge had not succeeded in his search on the day of the storming of the Bastille?

    (b) If there had been room for Miss Pross and Jerry in the carriage with the family?

(22) Do the characters seem to do things of their own will, or do you feel that the author is moving them to suit himself?

Formulate your questions with great care, especially for written work. They should be specific, capable of only one interpretation, and not be answerable by "yes" or "no," unless you follow such a question with the useful word "why?" Otherwise you should give full credit for an answer of "yes" or "no." In testing students, consider the element of time. Sometimes instructors ask questions that cannot be answered with any degree of adequacy in an entire class period. If you want a subject discussed, you will get best results if you subdivide the topic yourself, saying, "Discuss under the following heads." Your questions should always be fair — trick or catch questions have no place in your teaching; they should be specific; and they should be carefully worded.

Before making out your first (and succeeding) set of examination questions, you should ask yourself "What is the purpose of examinations?" I hope you will reply immediately: "They are *not* primarily for the purpose of determining grades." Then what are they for? In my own thinking, I look upon them as a means of examining and systematizing the content covered during the period over which the pupil is to be tested. Although, in your mind, the class work of each day may be a clearly defined step toward a future goal, to most students the daily work appears somewhat isolated, divorced, unrelated. In preparing for his test, he is forced to re-examine the material of the unit, to place together related thoughts, to distinguish between main and subordinate ideas. Under no circumstances would I abolish examinations if I could, not because the grade earned by this means weighs heavily in my estimate of a student's progress, but because of the great advantages afforded him by this opportunity to sit down and think back upon the material presented to him. Perhaps an understanding of this purpose of testing will go far toward removing the fear unfortunately present in the hearts of some pupils, as well as giving them a suggestion as to *how* to review.

Of course, then, your questions must bear upon the aim of examinations — synchronization of ideas. Trick or catch questions must be shunned, as should those bearing upon unimportant details. Many instructors like to include one "fact" question, for the purpose of testing the pupil's retention of important facts, but such a question, if used, should include *only* significant points and the credit given it should be less than that accorded other types of questions. After your group has read a play, for example, you are thoroughly justified in expecting them to remember the main characters, the principal settings, the name of the author, and so forth. For this question you may use any objective type of test: recall, completion, matching.

Your other questions should bear upon the phases you have emphasized in your class discussions. By this I do not mean that an examination need be merely a rehashing of what has been given out in class. With maturity, students should show an increasing knowledge of how to apply their information. Ideally, testing should require the pupil to *think*, *correlate*, *eliminate*, and *write;* within the limits of their age, experience, and capabilities, this your pupils should learn to do. An examination on details can be justified only if the pupil understands and expects this type of question. Provocative of cheating, open to the criticism of testing *unrelated* pieces of knowledge, this type should be resorted to sparingly.

Let me make clear by illustration what I mean by these generalities.

Fact Questions in Composition

I. Define (1) complete subject, (2) predicate, (3) degrees of comparison, (4) transitional expression, (5) compound sentence.

II. State the rule for punctuating: (1) words or phrases in a series, (2) the two types of compound sentence, (3) a phrase in the initial position, (4) an imperative sentence.

III. (a) Name three functions of the adverbial clause.
(b) Name three uses of the noun clause.

Thought (or Applied Knowledge) Questions in Composition

I. State the errors in the following sentences. Correct each.
(a) Altogether, he looked wretchedly in the dim light.
(b) Due to illness, I was absent from class.

II. Illustrate, using complete sentences: (1) an adjective phrase, (2) *there* as an expletive, (3) a compound sentence containing a transitional expression.

III. Punctuate the following sentences. Give the reason for your punctuation:
1. A kind old uncle Mr. Caldwell is paying most of my expenses otherwise I could not be in college.
2. The entire Byrd party saw the pictures they had made in the Antarctic.

IV. Write a descriptive paragraph, using general terms. Rewrite it, changing the general words into specific ones.

V. Justify the use of the italicized expressions:
1. It was *she whom* I met at the dance.
2. The black kitten was *lying* in the corner.

VI. Comment, from the point of view of word choice, on the following:

1. Depart for home.
2. It was pleasant to see the food spread on the grass before us.
3. Her hat was trimmed with tan wings like two slices of cold chicken.

FACT QUESTIONS IN LITERATURE

I. Place the following according to century. Name one work of each: (1) Browning, (2) Shakespeare, (3) Housman, (4) Wordsworth.

II. Give concise information about five of the following (include the approximate time): Landor, Jane Austen, Lamb, Dickens, Scott, Coleridge, Byron, Pope, Swift.

III. What traits of Burns's personality are reflected in his poems? Name the poem or poems in which each trait you mention is reflected.

IV. What is the struggle and its result in: (1) "The Secret Sharer," (2) "The Open Boat"?

V. Match five of the following titles and authors:

1. The Christmas Carol   Davis
2. The Gold Bug   Shelley
3. The Romance of a Busy Broker   Crane
4. Gallegher   Van Dyke
5. The Luck of Roaring Camp   Poe
6. The First Christmas Tree   Dickens
7. The Open Boat   O. Henry
8. Frankenstein   Harte

THOUGHT (OR APPLIED KNOWLEDGE) QUESTIONS IN LITERATURE

I. Apply this definition — "Poetry is the rhythmic creation of beauty" — to the following:

To Autumn

Who hath not seen thee oft amid thy store?
Sometimes whoever seeks abroad may find
Thee sitting careless on a granary floor,
Thy hair soft-lifted by the winnowing wind;
Or on a half-reaped furrow sound asleep,
Drowsed with the fume of poppies, while thy hook
Spares the next swath and all its twinèd flowers:
And sometimes like a gleaner thou dost keep
Steady thy laden head across a brook;
Or by a cider-press, with patient look,
Thou watchest the last oozings hours by hours.

— JOHN KEATS

II. Discuss the following poem for (1) imagery, (2) figures of speech, (3) onomatopoeia, (4) type:

The Eagle

He clasps the crag with hookèd hands:
Close to the sun in lonely lands,
Ring'd with the azure world, he stands.

The wrinkled sea beneath him crawls;
He watches from his mountain walls,
And like a thunderbolt he falls.

— ALFRED, LORD TENNYSON

III. Answer the following questions on the poem given below:
1. What is the connection of the title to the poem?
2. What struggle is referred to here?
3. From what part of England is Sir Byng?
4. What is the meaning of the term "crop-headed Parliament"?
5. Who were the Cavaliers?
6. How many compose the troop?
7. Of what is the rhythm suggestive?
8. What is the mood of the author? How do you know?

Marching Along

Kentish Sir Byng stood for his King,
Bidding the crop-headed Parliament swing:
And, pressing a troop unable to stoop
And see the rogues flourish and honest folk droop,
Marched them along, fifty-score strong,
Great-hearted gentlemen, singing this song.

God for King Charles!   Pym and such carles
To the devil that prompts 'em their treasonous parles!
Cavaliers, up!   Lips from the cup,
Hands from the pasty, nor bite take nor sup
Till you're —
   Chorus. — Marching along, fifty-score strong,
            Great-hearted gentlemen, singing this song.

                              — ROBERT BROWNING

IV. As fully as time permits, explain the meaning of the
    following.   Show the connection of the passage to the
    piece as a whole:

    1. O, my offense is rank, it smells to heaven;
       It hath the primal eldest curse upon't,
       A brother's murder.

                         King Claudius, in *Hamlet*.

    2. In the first days of January he died, and in the de-
       lirium of his death agony, he protested his innocence,
       repeating: "A little piece of string — a little piece
       of string — see, here it is, m'sieu' mayor."

                         From "A Piece of String."

V. Show the connection of the following titles to the story:
   (1) "The Purloined Letter," (2) "The Revolt of
   'Mother,'" (3) "The Luck of Roaring Camp."

VI. Explain the significance of these details taken from "The
    Ambitious Guest":

    1. The daughter had just uttered some simple jest
       that filled them all with mirth, when the wind came

through the Notch and seemed to pause before their cottage — rattling the door, with a sound of wailing and lamentation before it passed into the valley.

2. Then, starting and blushing, she looked quickly around the circle, as if they had caught a glimpse into her bosom.

In these illustrations, I have tried to give examples of different sorts of questions you may use, but I have not indicated the years in which they may best be used, as *type* and *nature* of questions, like any other phase of your teaching, must be determined by the need of your class. I suggest, too, that you turn to the questions quoted from Miss Rich and examine them for type. If you consider an examination a means of composition training, you will allow time for careful planning and writing. Pupils should understand that arrangement and expression constitute part of their responsibility in writing examinations.

As a means of consolidating a unit of work, many teachers use some means of *review*. Review is, in my opinion, difficult. Unless carefully planned, it is likely to result in a monologue by you delivered to an indifferent class. To prevent such waste of time, plan a review that will compel the class to do the work. This means that the subject matter itself should not be rehashed, but that an activity should be planned that will compel a rereading or a concentrated study of the material included in the unit. To that end, some teachers ask each member of. the class to prepare questions covering important phases. Those given under "Thought Questions" on the preceding pages are samples of questions designed for review of the whole — not, however, prepared by pupils. A newspaper project makes necessary the rereading of a piece of literature; sentences illustrating the application of a rhetorical or grammatical principle give assurance that the student understands the principle. An "identification test," for which you give no credit, transforms review into a game. For this, often you can use the index of your text. Check whatever is listed there pertaining to the work under discussion. During the class period have a sort of "bee," in which the students choose sides and the side scoring the greater number of correct answers wins. Even "dignified seniors" are not above enjoying this occasionally. A paper comparing, contrasting, and discussing an important subject is also good.

Some time during the course of your teaching you will have to *select texts* for the use of yourself and your pupils. I hope you will not have to do this before you have taught the group for which a text is to be selected; for what is suited to one group may be very poorly adapted for use in another. Obviously the interests, background, capabilities, age, and, alas, the weight of the purse of your students all have a bearing on the choice of text. Whenever possible, you should put off selecting a text until you have taught for at least a semester in the school. If you must choose before you begin work with the group, find out as much as possible about the preparation, activities, and background of your students-to-be.

In the appendix to this book you will find a form for evaluating both composition and literature texts. Although the questions in the form are, for the most part, self-explanatory, I want to comment on some of them. In the first place, let me repeat, try to find a text that suits the needs *of the students whom you have in class*. Study them carefully and test the books you are considering as to their use *with this particular class*. Before leaving college, you should examine as many as possible of the more recent books for high school use. Then, when you are considering a new text, consult your file and send for a copy of two or three of the texts apparently best adapted to your use. Publishers are glad to send you examination copies provided you will seriously consider their product. Do not take advantage of their kindness, but feel free to ask for sample copies when your need is legitimate. Keep these books on your desk and experiment with them as you can. In this way, you can determine the text best fitted for your use.

The first comment that I want to make is concerning the author or authors of the text. Note whether or not they are high school teachers; note also the part of the country from which they come. As a rule, teachers who are actually working with high school students write the most satisfactory texts. College instructors, even administrators, are likely to be too far removed from the field of high school interests to be sufficiently conversant with the point of view of students in secondary schools. I do not, of course, say that this is invariably true; I only mean that it is *likely* to be. Also, the background and experience of pupils in different sections of the United States are so varied that usually (not always) it is wise to select a text of which at least one of the authors is from the part of the country in which your school is located. Theme topics pertaining to the sea are all very well in some sections of our land; but there are many high school students living in the arid or semiarid parts of our country who have had no experience with boats or with a body of water larger than the town swimming pool. Furthermore, the point of view may be so different that students are unnecessarily confused. We want, naturally, to enlarge the experience of our pupils; but we do not want them upset by a text in which too much is taken for granted.

In selecting a composition text, you should note particularly the exercises included. If you have to think of and dictate sentences for correction or analysis, you will find that your work is greatly increased and that your students must use their time in writing sentences from your dictation, rather than in applying principles. A text that has with it an exercise book is no doubt most efficient. Do not, I beg of you, *substitute* a workbook, no matter how good, for a text. The art of composition, let me reiterate, consists in much more than mechanical accuracy. A good workbook, however, used in connection with a text, may be desirable.

A special problem in choosing texts in literature is whether to select an anthology or separate "classics." On the market today you will find a number of anthologies prepared for high school use. These are listed in the appendix to this book. Any of the publishing companies publishes separate classics. In choosing between these, you will want to consider such matters as cost (unfortunately of great importance), opportunity for progressive teaching, library facilities (as an anthology includes much more material than you can read in one semester, its use affords supplementary reading material), and the possibility of appeal to student interests. The publishers whose names are listed in the appendix will be glad to furnish you with information concerning both kinds of textbooks.

An activity that you will be concerned with during both the composition and the literature semesters is that of *home reading*. As we have noted, wide reading should be encouraged in all grades and on all levels. Hard and fast requirements — such as the reading of a certain number of books a semester — may defeat their purpose. It is perhaps better to use a carefully selected anthology or group of separate "classics" as a basis for the literature course, and then to develop a desire and a will to read through all the devices at your command than it is to *require* what should be *pleasure* reading. Yet truth dictates that all your pupils who would profit from wide reading will not read, left to their own devices. Perhaps these pupils have reading disabilities which can be corrected, possibly they are so active that they resent "taking time" to read, or perhaps they have been conditioned against reading for some reason. You will have to study your pupils as individuals and aid them to develop a desire to read.

Closely akin to requiring the reading of a certain number of books is the making of formal, written book reviews, for which you give a grade. All experienced teachers agree that pupils cheat readily in writing such reports and that they are not above reporting on the same book year after year. Such facts lead me to suggest that you lend your energies to *encouraging* reading rather than dissipating them by reading and grading long reports written outside of class.

There may be times, however, when you will wish to check on the reading of members of your class. Methods which you may find satisfactory are as follows. Have a card for each student. After he has read the book, ask him to list the title and author, and rate the book as a one-, two-, three-, or four-star book. In conference or in class, ask the pupil to justify his rating. Some pupils will enjoy writing "blurbs," similar to those found on the dust covers of trade books. You may well have written reports *in class*. It may seem impossible to you so to word questions that they may be used as a basis for a report on a number of books. You can, however, do this very easily if you require the students to read the same *type* of book. Questions pertaining to plot, character, and setting work well with any novel; questions on characteristics, life, and accomplishments pertain to any biography. You will find that class reports are quite easily handled and you are, I believe, justified in using a period for this. Like any piece of written work, these should be in good form to be acceptable.

The following outline, suggested by Miss Ethel Bryce, Reference Librarian of the State College of Washington, may be given to each pupil as a guide for his estimate of a piece of fiction:

I. Discover the *theme*, the germinal cell, the nucleus, the egg from which the work grew. Few good books "just growed," like Topsy, but rather, they are the result of a *purpose* in the author's mind.

II. Determine the *major interest* to the reader.

Is it *plot* — the story?
Is it *setting* — the place?
Is it *character* — the people?
Is it *theme* — the idea back of it all?

III. Discuss the *plot* very briefly, for it is the bare bones of the story, but tell

A. Any unusual structural feature, or
B. Any storytelling device, i.e., discuss craftsmanship without technical terms.

Any high school pupil can see that *The Bridge of San Luis Rey* is planned as a five-pointed star with the theme idea centered; that some novels are merely chronological, like biography, for example, *Hugh Wynne, Free*

Quaker; that others have a pattern like the blueprint of a factory.

IV. Recognize the setting. Discuss the *time* and *place*. Is it a modern period or is it a specific, identifiable locality and date? Does environment influence plot or people's conduct in any way? Does it matter where or when action occurs?

V. Discuss *characters* specifically. Do not give long descriptions of them, but show how they affect the reader: i.e., are they as real as your friends, or more so; or are they mere marionettes jerked by the author?

VI. Determine the book's *values*.

A. Would the story or the author's central idea be of interest in any age and to any race or nation, or — like polygamy, dueling, the caste system — is it of immediate or restricted interest? Will it last? Do you remember it pleasurably or thoughtfully?

B. Is the novel a kodak picture of life, or is it a "retouched" photographic study, more satisfactory than the ordinary picture? Analyze the type of story as real or "fairy-storyish"; as serious or light.

C. Does the book give you the joy of familiar experience, or joy of surprise, or the emotion of sympathy, or the shock of new ideas, or a wider outlook?

VII. Tell about the *author* only what is relevant to the book, i.e., the part of his life spent in a region about which he wrote a novel of setting or exploration; or experiences that produced a problem-theme like a social wrong or labor troubles.

VIII. Analyze the *style*.

A. Is the manner of telling simple or difficult to follow? Are you aware of *how* it is told — its clever wording — or is the method not apparent, like looking through glass?

B. Do you have the feeling of intense sincerity, as if it were written with the heart's blood; or does it seem written with ink, casually?

Another good plan is the oral book review. These may be given to the teacher in private. This takes a great deal of time and does not benefit the members of the class, but in the opportunity afforded both teacher and pupil to exchange opinions and to become better acquainted, it yields big dividends. Oral reviews may also be given before the class. These you can handle very easily by having one or two a day until every student has given his report. You will have to work out an outline for these reports and you will have to set a time limit, and abide by it. You should allow for a few minutes of discussion and questioning after each report. Oral reviews are most successful with older students who have had some practice in speaking. As a preparation, analyze several reviews in magazines such as *The Saturday Review of Literature* to see how competent reviewers manage to suggest the content of the book and interest the reader, yet withhold such exact information that the reader finds it unnecessary to peruse the book. (Radio book reviews offer models, also.) Like any other piece of exposition, reviews fall into three divisions: introduction, body, and conclusion. In the introduction your pupils will find necessary information concerning the book: kind, author, and title. But, because the attention of the reader must be attracted and held, all this is given as interestingly as possible. I quote a few opening sentences from reviews in the *Atlantic Monthly* for April, 1936:

"It is inevitable that Mr. Farson's book, *The Way of a Transgressor*, should be compared to recent autobiographies that preceded it. . . ."

"I suspect that the experience of many readers of that superb novel, *Josephus*, was not unlike mine. Until I had read it, my acquaintance with the remarkable man whose later life is now told in *The Jew of Rome*, was, I must confess, very slight."

"*The Son of Marietta* is a leisurely but never dull portrayal of humble life in Todi, in Italy, during the second half of the eighteenth century, supplemented by scenes in the decadent Venice of that day."

The body of the book review suggests the general content of the book, retelling, perhaps, a few significant incidents. Often the conclusion evaluates the book, or compares it with others by the same author or with those on a similar theme by other authors. To quote again from the *Atlantic Monthly:*

A Duranty or a Sheean seemed part of the events in which they lived. They had concern and appreciation for more than was merely on the surface. Mr. Farson has written material which is entirely factual — and incomplete. He saw the wheels go round, but he gives no hint that he knew what made them turn. He has come through life undaunted and undented.

These suggestions, planned by Miss Ella E. Clark of the State College of Washington, offer a guide for an oral review of non-fiction.

Preliminaries:

1. Name the title and author of the book distinctly. If any words are difficult, spell them or write them on the board.
2. Give the date of the book unless it is unimportant.
3. Identify the author — what are his special qualifications for writing this book? How did he get his material?

Motive of the review: Share your reading experience with your listeners. Say mentally as you plan and as you give your review, "I have read this book; you have not. I want to share my reading with you." Or say, "You and I have both read this book. Let us enjoy it together." Remember that a review cannot be a substitute for reading a book but that it can be a very helpful introduction to a book. In that introduction include as many as possible of the following:

1. Tell us briefly but definitely the author's purpose in the book.
2. Inform us about the general nature or scope of the book. Don't give a prolonged summary of the contents but enough of the organization and scope to enable us who have not read it to see the book *as a whole*.
3. Select some central theme and build your review around it. Such a theme might well be the thing which impressed you the most. For example, in reviewing *Madame Curie* you might build your review around the character of Madame Curie; or you might build your review around the achievements of Madame Curie.
4. Select incidents or other details *throughout the book* that bring out that central theme. For example, select incidents that show Madame Curie's perseverance, her unselfish devotion to science, etc. Without illustrations a review is dull because it is general instead of specific. Use facts that make your listener see and feel. (Points 3 and 4 will probably constitute the major portion of your review.)
5. Tell us what you think about the book, how it made you feel. We will be interested in your opinions even though we have read the book and disagree with you. There is no reason why you should be impersonal; even personal experiences that parallel the book are often effective.

6. Compare or contrast this book, if you can, with other books by the same author or other books in the same field or on a similar subject.

7. Suggest the personality of the book — its uniqueness (if it has any), its special tone and flavor, the quality or qualities which make it distinct. For some books you can do this best by reading a few passages aloud.

8. If you decide to read in order to suggest the style and the atmosphere, select your passages carefully. Use only a few. Practice reading them aloud so that you can read smoothly and effectively with proper interpretation of the thought. Have them marked so that you don't have to leaf through the book. Hold your book and your chin up, so that we, not your collar, will catch your words.

9. Prepare carefully a conclusion which will leave with us the impression you want us to carry away concerning the book.

Note that these are suggestions for reviewing biographies, histories, travel books, and other books of facts — not novels. They can be used for some fiction, particularly for historical and sociological novels. When reviewing a novel, be careful not to reveal too much of the plot, not to spoil the suspense for the reader. It is better to concentrate on the theme or on the characters than on the plot of a novel.

In *The English Journal* for April, 1930 (High School Edition), XIX, pp. 324–326, Miss Marie Luck writes on "Varieties of Book Reports." Among her unusual suggestions are:

1. Dramatizations of scenes from a book read by several members of the class. A brief explanation of the situation must be made before and after the dramatization, in order to fill in the outline.

2. An imaginary dialogue between two contrasted characters. This requires more cleverness in preparation and delivery than does the former.
3. Interviews by the student with one or several characters. These may be given as a monologue, dialogue, or a newspaper story.
4. A telephone conversation by two members of the class in which several books are mentioned and discussed.
5. Book pageants and shadow plays.
6. A friendly letter about a book, perhaps illustrated by sketches.

The National Council of Teachers of English publishes two annotated reading lists that should be in the hands of every student. These are called *Books for You* and *Victory Corps Reading List* and are so charmingly illustrated that almost any boy or girl will experience a desire to read some of the books described. If finances do not permit each pupil to have his own copy, send for one of each book yourself and keep them where your students can have easy access to them.

Try to make this reading a pleasure, not a chore. If we are to have more leisure in the future than we have had in the past, we need to learn to read. May you be successful in showing your students the way to this never-ending pleasure.

One of the purposes of the *bulletin board* (easily made from a piece of beaverboard) that you should have in your classroom is to encourage reading. On this you and your pupils can post clippings pertaining to new and interesting books, photographs of scenes, characters, and authors. Your local playhouse may provide you with advance material pertaining to the screening of well-known novels and dramas; magazines and newspaper supplements often afford attractive and suggestive material. Advertising agencies and publishing houses often provide artistic materials such as posters, literary maps, photographs, sketches, and calendars. Sometimes a "Guess Who" contest provides good fun. Pictures of famous authors may be posted and a contest held to see how many pupils can identify the pictures. On a special board, a group of boys and girls may post reviews or advertisements under the heading "Books I Have Read and Like." Short and to the point, these provide excellent experience in composition. Artistic students may prepare a frieze to top the board, perhaps using "No Frigate Like a Book."

Not only does the bulletin board promote interest in reading, but it also enhances knowledge of current affairs. If you like, you can appoint a committee whose duty it is to post each week significant clippings from books or magazines. One alert teacher whom I once knew had a weekly quiz over the material posted on the board. In this way she insured the reading of the clippings posted. Whether or not you make a board a part of your classroom activities, you will, I know, want one as a part of your classroom equipment, because of the part it plays in enlarging the interest and knowledge of your boys and girls.

Several times I have referred to the value of magazines in the teaching of English, and I know you have wondered what magazines to use and how to handle them. At present, as far as I know, the only magazines prepared particularly for high school use are *The Scholastic* and *Junior Scholastic*, published by the Scholastic Publishing Company, Pittsburgh, Pennsylvania. You should be familiar with these magazines and with the other material for high school use published by this firm. It has, for example, briefs for a number of debates. I suggest that you write to the company for information concerning its publications and for sample copies of *The Scholastic*. If possible, you should plan to use the magazine.

Although the material in either of these magazines is varied, you may wish to use other magazines to supplement it. Some well-prepared, advanced groups enjoy the *Atlantic Monthly*, the *Free World*, *Encore*, and *Harper's Magazine*. *Life*, *Look*, *Time*, and *Coronet* (this last provides teacher aids) are four magazines dealing with current happenings. The best newspaper published near you should be available. All these may be kept on a table in your classroom so that the class may have easy access to them. Keep a card for each magazine and employ a library system for lending magazines to students. Always encourage wide reading.

Many teachers discard the suggestion of using magazines because they think the expense prohibitive. You will not find it so if you follow this plan. Instead of asking each student to subscribe to the magazine or magazines, decide upon the minimum number for classroom use. Two or three persons can use one copy. Then find out the cost of the necessary magazines, divide this by the number of students in your class, and ask each pupil to bring his share, usually ten or fifteen cents. If you can, select one magazine, probably *The Scholastic*, for classroom use and subscribe for one copy of as many other magazines as your group can afford. Often the teacher of social sciences or of geography will join you in this. Because many of the standard magazines offer special classroom prices, you will want to inquire about such rates.

You will find a magazine useful in every phase of your teaching. In written composition, it will afford examples of types of writing, give material for outlining, for précis writing, for illustrations of diction, sentence structure, and punctuation, and will be provocative of class discussion that will serve to motivate theme writing.

In oral composition, a magazine will supply material for talks and for debates. Your students may like to form a "Magazine Club" in which the magazine is used as material for club meetings. If you do anything with oral reading, the magazine will offer a number of suitable selections.

It is no less useful in teaching literature. Short stories, essays, articles of all sorts, poems, plays, are some of the types found in current magazines. Often, too, there are biographies of living and dead authors and literary criticism. *The Scholastic* also publishes examples of student writing, an incentive toward creative composition.

I urge you to use magazines, especially in a community in which books are few.

As you read the suggestions in this chapter, you have probably noted the many visual aids suggested. Like plans for correlation, visual and audio aids have always been employed by good teachers. But improved mechanical devices and methodology serve to strengthen classroom use of such devices.

In the area of visual aids, maps, cartoons, models, reproductions of paintings, graphs, charts, and so forth can easily be utilized. Many schools today make provisions for using moving pictures. City schools usually have a library of suitable films, but smaller schools must rent films they desire to show. This, however, can be done at minimum cost.

In the field of the language arts less has been accomplished than in other areas. But films designed for other classes may be utilized by the English instructor. For example, pupils may be asked to see a film portraying the location and products of the Western states and may then be quizzed on their ability to observe and remember. Some films to show grammatical usages are now available and others will be forthcoming as time goes on. In the field of literature,. a number of films are readily obtainable. Audio aids, such as recordings, may be secured from many sources.

Although you can and should employ these aids to understanding in your classroom, they are not intended as substitutes for teaching but as adjuncts to it. This means that both you and your pupils must prepare before you see a film or listen to a recording. The following outline suggests your responsibility.

I. *Teacher* preparation consists in knowing the content of the film or recording and in determining upon the teaching purpose.

II. *Pupil* preparation includes knowing what to look for through prediscussion and specific questions given by the teacher.

III. *Procedure* consists in presenting the film or recording, followed by drill on content, a test, written composition, discussion.

IV. *Evaluation* by teacher and pupils completes the presentation.

Certain other problems require consideration. For you to preview a film requires planning. But insist upon doing this if at all possible, for you cannot make seeing the film a *teaching* device unless you have time to study it. Occasionally you are justified in permitting the class period to be relegated to entertainment purposes only, but such periods should be few. Another problem lies in the presentation of unauthentic films dealing with literary periods or persons. I have in mind one on the life of Shakespeare which is historically inaccurate, yet successfully conveys mood and tone. Should you present such a film? Not long ago I saw a most attractive film designed to present some aspects of grammar. The approach was contrary to my own methodology. Despite that, had it sufficient merit to be shown? Should films based on plays or novels be given pupils before or after they have read the piece? A cutting of the screen play "A Tale of Two Cities," although it minimizes the love story, shows the murder of Monseigneur Evrémonde and the execution of Sidney Carton. Do you want to spoil your students' enjoyment in *reading* these dramatic episodes in order to help them visualize the characters and the period?

Although visual aids, particularly, present these and other problems, I believe you will want to employ these teaching aids. Because this field, as a formal educational procedure, is relatively new, you will wish to be alert to new developments.

Some years ago the National Council of Teachers of English sponsored "Better Speech Week." Because many teachers considered that better speech should be emphasized throughout the year and not for a week only, observance of "Better Speech Week" was often set aside. Occasionally, however, I receive inquiries concerning ways of observing it; I am, therefore, making a few suggestions.

As a preparation for this week, you can have several of your artistic students prepare posters. These should be placed on bulletin boards in classrooms, in the halls, and in the assembly rooms. By means of class discussions of the purpose of the week, you can stimulate interest in the pupils, who, in turn, will interest their parents.

Activities for the week itself may be the following: Tell each pupil to select some person living in the town. Have the student interview this person informally, asking him or her in what ways English is important. Then, during "Better Speech Week" each student can report briefly to the class. (This has been suggested previously as a project for a group of freshmen.) Another plan consists in having your pupils write brief papers on words — their history, definitions, etc. These should not be at all technical; necessary material can be found in a good dictionary and in such reference books as Fowler's *The King's English* or Greenough's *Words and Their Ways in English Speech*. During one or two class periods you may have spelling or pronunciation matches. In one school that I know of, words to be pronounced were thrown on a screen and representatives from each class took part in the contest. In this way, it was made a school and not a classroom project. An interesting variation of the spelling match is to require the naming of a synonym of the word given and its correct spelling. You may like to have a "tag day," on which anyone, faculty member or student, detected in making an error in English, is tagged. Although the object, of course, is to be tagged as little as possible, you may find that some wags will reverse it, proudly decorating their persons with as many tags as possible. The week may well culminate with a play, such as "The King's English," by Herbert Bates, or "Nevertheless," by Stuart Walker, given in the assembly.

ASSIGNMENT

A. Plan a unit of work for use in a class in literature, which includes contracts for three groups.

B. Do the same for a class in composition.

C. Prepare an assignment for a class in literature and one for composition.

D. Prepare a set of examination questions for a class in literature.

E. Do the same for a class in composition.

F. Review a text for use in literature. Follow the plan given in Appendix I.

G. Do the same for a composition text.

H. Make a set of questions for use as a test on home reading.

FURTHER READINGS

1. Hovious, Carol, "Book Reports and Book Reviews," *The English Journal*, XXII (November, 1933), pp. 736–741.

Here the author suggests a plan for listing and evaluating *all* reading done by her pupils, from Edgar A. Guest to Robert Frost.

2. Francis, Helen M., "Book Reports — A Bane or Blessing?" *The English Journal*, XV (April, 1924), pp. 304–307.

This gives questions for use in reporting on various types of reading.

3. Thomas, Charles Swain, *The Teaching of English in the Secondary School*, Chapter XII.

Here you will find a set of questions used in an oral book report on Dickens's *Hard Times*.

4. Haines, Helen E., "Reviewing Books Carefully," *Library Journal*, LXI (1936), pp. 754–757.

This is valuable reading for the teacher, especially the sections headed "What Is an Open Mind?" and "What the Reader Wants."

5. MIRRIELEES, LUCIA B., *Teaching Composition in High School*, Part II, Chapter III, pp. 200–231.

Here the unit method is defined, several sample units are given, and some pertinent comments on assignments are made.

6. BLAISDELL, THOMAS C., *Ways to Teach English*, Chapter XLI.

A series of challenging questions on such subjects as the use of magazines, modern material, examinations, a bulletin board, and reading is here presented.

7. ROWE, J. WYNANT, "The Bulletin Board as a Vital Project," *The English Journal*, XXV (May, 1936), pp. 403–405.

This article provides good suggestions for the use of the bulletin board in stimulating pupils to read.

8. WOODRING, MAXIE NAVE, JEWETT, IDA A., and BENSON, RACHEL T., *Enriched Teaching of English in the Junior and Senior High School*.

Again, consult this book for all sorts of suggestions: names of "Better English" playlets; materials to be had for the asking for use on bulletin boards; models, exhibits, lantern slides that may be borrowed.

9. The *Publisher's Weekly*, with its announcements of new books, sales, etc., will provide clippings for your bulletin board.

10. GREY, LENNOX, "What Communication Means Today," pamphlet on communication, prepared for the National Council of Teachers of English.

This pamphlet affords background for the responsibility of the teacher of English toward communication and should be read by all.

11. FINCH, HARDY R., and CHILDS, ELEANOR D., "Producing School Movies," monograph of the National Council of Teachers of English.

Practical suggestions for making your own movies are given here.

12. HERZBERG, MAX J., "Radio and English Teaching."

Another publication of the English Council, this monograph shows how radio can be utilized by the English teacher.

13. *Coronet Magazine* sponsors a non-profit visual aid service consisting of eight of its timeliest and most educational Picture Stories reproduced on 35 mm. slide-film and in reprint form.

14. ADAMS, HARLEN M., "Speak, Look, and Listen."

This publication of the National Council of Teachers of English explains how audio-visual aids may be utilized effectively.

XXI. READING: YOUR PROBLEM

Previously we have said that your purpose in teaching literature should be to help your students to read. That aim we have interpreted in its broader sense to include not only an understanding of content but also a grasp of the wide horizon surrounding the printed word. Now let us consider what is referred to in discussions as the "reading problem."

When and why did reading become a "problem"? As usual, war is responsible. World War I exposed the ignorance of great numbers of adults; World War II emphasized the need for intelligent reading; for, even more than World War I, it demanded literate soldiers and officers. In the period between these wars, much research was done; but even yet, teachers and administrators lack consciousness of the extent of the need for relating reading to the entire school curriculum and to democratic living, nor do they realize that pupils *can* be *taught* to read.

Schools, then, are confronted with a problem. What responsibility have you, a teacher of English, toward it?

In the first place, the responsibility is not yours alone, for reading is a *school* problem. *Every teacher should consider himself a teacher of reading.* An understanding of words, sentences, paragraphs, and the whole is demanded in every course taught in our schools. Each teacher should recognize this and should aid his students in the reading problems inherent in his own subject. The mathematics teacher must help his students to read the problem under consideration. (It has been found that some pupils who are unable to follow the written instructions in their text can do so with ease when the problem is read to them.) He must also teach them to read signs and symbols; he and others must teach interpretations of maps, charts, and graphs. All instructors must be responsible for teaching the special vocabulary of their own fields. All must be on the alert for physical and emotional causes of poor reading.

No, you are not entirely responsible. Yet reading must receive special emphasis in some field, and we may as well admit that English is the logical one. So, you, English teacher, must assume first responsibility. To aid you, this chapter presents a synthesis of the most recent thinking in the field.

What are some general aspects of the problem? First, keep in mind that educators no longer consider the teaching of reading a responsibility of the elementary schools *alone*. It is now known that the acquisition of reading skills can and should be cumulative. Elementary schools provide a certain foundation; the junior high schools, the high schools, and the colleges add to that. Everyone — no matter how adept — can improve his reading skill. Indeed, as one professor of education remarked, "the sky's the limit — and no one knows what *is* the sky."

Training in reading, then, should never cease. But it may well be emphasized at certain transitional periods.

Miss Carol Hovious, authority on reading, suggests that these points may be during the seventh grade, when a pupil is entering the junior high school; then during his sophomore year, when he is entering senior high school; and during his first year in college. An adaptation of this consists in giving specific training in the last part of the seventh grade and the first of the eighth; the last part of the ninth and the first of the tenth; and the last semester of the senior year. By giving special training just before the student graduates, you assure the sharpening of a tool essential for those going on to college and for those entering directly into their life occupation.

Perhaps some statistics will serve to illustrate the scope of reading needs. According to figures quoted in the *Seventh Yearbook* of the Claremont Colleges Reading Conference for 1942, required reading for college graduates has increased since 1920 by 183.5 per cent. These findings show, too, that many college students are equipped with only third-, fourth-, or fifth-grade reading ability to grapple with the amount of reading required of them. Since 1900, reading offered adults has increased over 170 per cent. In 1936, according to the "March of Education" *News Letter*, published by the Office of Education, Washington, D.C., there were over 2167 daily newspapers in the United States and 10,805 weekly papers. According to this same publication, the required reading of officers and executives has increased 500 per cent since this century began. Figures showing reading variation are significant, too. Ruth Strang, writing in *Problems in the Improvement of Reading in High School and College*, states that reading ability among high school students varies from third-grade reading proficiency to that of the superior adult. In other words, some high school pupils display greater reading ability than do some of their teachers. Miss Strang also states that the reading age ranges from below nine years to above seventeen years. Rate shows similar spread; at the University of Chicago, for example, studies revealed that freshmen in that institution read from two words a second to more than seven words a second.

We shall now assume that you are convinced of the importance of reading, that you realize that it *is* a problem, and that you accept your special responsibility toward it. Now let us consider it in detail.

Perhaps we should begin in the time-honored manner with a definition. William S. Gray, in *The Teaching of Reading: A Second Report* (36th Yearbook of the National Society for the Study of Education), presents this definition: "Reading involves the recognition of the important elements of meaning in their essential relations, including accuracy and thoroughness of comprehension." He further states that "reading is also a form of experience that modifies personality."

Let us examine briefly these statements. Probably you first notice the absence of emphasis upon *word recognition*. This omission, however, does not suggest that a knowledge of words — their spelling, pronunciation, and meaning — should be neglected; it merely stresses that reading is a *thought* process. Meaning is arrived at by an understanding of the denotation and connotation of individual words in relation to one another. To illustrate, consider this sentence from a recent magazine article: "For lesser folk, though, it is better to be dead in Washington than to know the wrong people." To read this intelligently, the reader must understand that "dead in Washington" is a figure of speech; that the idea of the sentence, as indicated by the word "though," is contrasted with something said previously; that the term "wrong people" has a special meaning; and that the tone of the whole is ironical. A good reader, true enough, does not stop to think out all these implications; but somewhere in his reading training he has developed the power to think through the word to the idea beyond. What a contrast is this conception of reading to the "word by word" approach of our forebears!

Mr. Gray's second statement deserves some thought also. Modern educational theory recognizes that the school should become a training ground offering pupils experience suited to their age yet affording a basis for future growth. Teachers of English should recognize that reading affords such opportunities. The psychological factors involved in teaching adolescents and their relation to reading are suggested in the phrase "modifies personality." Look back upon your own reading for interpretation of this thought. Perhaps you are teachers of English because of some reading experiences. Not long ago a young man told me that his determination to become a minister had crystallized upon reading Lloyd C. Douglas's *The Robe*. If you will keep in mind, then, these and similar definitions, your conception of reading and your sense of responsibility toward it will be greatly enlarged.

Next, we should "classify" reading, should we not? Educators divide reading experiences into two main groups: pleasure or recreational and informative or work types. The first we can dismiss rather briefly by reminding you that this is the type we call "literature." Suggestions for aiding your students in sharing literary experiences have already been made, but later the relation of this type to the "reading problem" will be discussed. "Work type" reading is designed primarily to gain information. Although much of it deals with the acquisition of facts or with such stodgy concerns as understanding directions, oftentimes the "work type" delves into the realm of ideas. You can readily see that the "recreational" and the "work types" frequently overlap. Both of these are aspects of "developmental" reading, which seeks increased growth in reading skill for all pupils.

These are the two main classifications. But, unfortunately, a third type must be considered. As you read the statistics concerning the reading levels of high school and college students, you recognized at once that students who read at a third- or fourth-grade level can never compete on equal terms with their fellows whose reading ability is average or superior. Training in reading which is designed to correct glaring reading deficiencies is referred to as "remedial."

To bring your formal background to a fitting close, let us consider certain objectives laid down in the "Second Report on the Teaching of Reading," referred to previously. The Committee engaged in preparing this report first named four broad objectives which students in this field had determined previously. These are: (1) to enrich experience; (2) to broaden interests; (3) to develop appreciations; and (4) to cultivate ideal and appropriate attitudes. These the Committee retained. But in 1937, it added these specific aims: (1) to broaden the vision of readers; (2) to make their life richer and more meaningful; (3) to make them meet the practical needs of life more effectively; (4) to develop social understanding; (5) to develop ability to use reading in the intelligent search for truth; (6) to promote a broad common culture; (7) to promote a growing appreciation of the finer elements in contemporary life; and (8) to stimulate wholesome interests in reading.

Let us consider briefly some implications in these objectives. Underlying all, we recognize a strong sense of social consciousness. Most teachers, I believe, accept the thesis that their first duty as educators rests in fitting the individual into the social scheme. The place of reading in this formula is admirably represented in these objectives. Note, however, that the importance of reading as a practical skill is not neglected. To find truth and to appreciate finer elements of contemporary life through reading represent worthy goals in a period in which human beings are again turning to a realization that man does not live by bread alone. To attempt wisely to counteract the pernicious influence of cheap magazines and books constitutes an imperative objective. The aims stated, then, serve to recall to teachers of reading their responsibility of fitting individuals for their place in a democratic society.

Now let us turn to the classroom application of these general principles. As a conscientious teacher, you are alert to the reading program and are employing part of your summer vacation in planning your attack upon the problem. You will, in your thinking, keep in mind the goal of improvement for *all* your pupils. You will also recall the sensitiveness of adolescents, their desire to conform, and their consequent unwillingness to admit a defect that sets them apart from their fellows. You understand that one of your main considerations must be the psychological factors involved.

We shall assume that your class is the usual unsectioned group and that you are dealing with the reading problem in one of the "key" years, possibly the freshman, in which class procedure centers about reading. What shall be your plan of action? For the first few days, do nothing except attempt to become acquainted with your group. During this period, notice unobtrusively what you can about reading habits and background. Then plan as an assignment a piece of reading which is somewhat factual. As an approach, discuss rather generally the importance of reading skill. You might lead the class into a consideration of what uses they have made of reading during the previous period. Then suggest that they read a certain portion of the assignment for the following day and note the time necessary to read this. In class, comment on their findings casually. The next day, do the same, but suggest that this time they check in the margin of their book (very lightly, so that the mark can be erased) ideas that appear to them important. Again, discuss the results. Class members will notice a variation in reading rate and a difference in the number of ideas marked. Perhaps you are then ready to administer a reading test. Upon the results of this test you can plan your procedure. Individual conferences with the student are indispensable at this point, for he must understand his problem in order to improve. Tact and sympathetic treatment are required in large measure, especially with those whom the test has shown to be poor readers. Remember that high school pupils who are below-average readers also have problems in other courses. They have failures behind them, and, they fear, failures ahead of them. They have an overwhelming desire, moreover, to keep pace with the group. It is your task to show them that their reading ability can be bettered, and that with it will come improvement in other abilities.

The results of the test will show that between five and twenty per cent of your class are "reading illiterates" who will require individual guidance. We shall leave this problem for the moment to comment on what can be done to improve (for all *can* and *should* improve) the reading ability of eighty or ninety per cent of your pupils.

As has been said, much depends upon your relation to your class and theirs to you. We shall assume, however, that it is good. Such being the situation, the pupils will not be averse to discussing the importance of the reading problem. They may enjoy making a study of the use made of reading by their parents — mother's reading of recipes and dad's examination of his commuter's ticket must not be overlooked. The statistics given earlier and others which the students and you can find may prove suggestive. Let the bulletin board do its share in displaying findings.

Next, causes of poor reading may be determined. Obviously, some are physical: poor eyesight and hearing. Glandular disturbances and malnutrition, being much less obvious, probably will not be presented by the class, but the teacher should privately consider these possibilities. In a general way — class discussion must be impersonal — advice to see a physician could be given.

Poor reading conditions, both at home and at school, may be discussed. What sort of artificial lighting is most satisfactory? Has posture anything to do with reading skill? Can a person read effectively if he is disturbed by noises? How responsible is the radio for poor reading habits? What are ideal study conditions? Are they the same as or different from conditions when we read for pleasure? Can a person, by deliberately exerting self-control, force himself into a satisfactory reading attitude? Such questions as these, as well as others occurring to you, can well be answered in a round-table discussion.

Personal experience can be utilized here, but some questions require investigation before a satisfactory reply can be made. The physics, home economics, and physical education instructors may have helpful suggestions for the asking, and electric light and gas companies willingly furnish information. Older pupils may like to glean from your own books on reading problems. The time spent on this project is justified, for many of the physical obstacles to reading can be removed simply by a recognition that they exist and by a resulting determination to overcome them.

Next, more subjective causes of poor reading may be presented. Undoubtedly, one cause lies in failure to consider the purpose in reading. Why do we read? To this question pupils will present different answers. List these on the board, seeing to it that they include the following: to derive pleasure, to grasp a specific piece of information, to understand a process, to analyze a point of view, and to comprehend a definition. Next, show the class that each of these purposes demands a somewhat different technique. For example, in reading fiction for pleasure, the reader attempts to see, think, and feel with the writer, and to understand what he is saying by means of plot, characters, and setting. In reading for a specific piece of information, the "skimming" technique is employed. For example, the reader wants to find the name of the college that Sinclair Lewis attended. He glances rapidly through a biographical sketch of Lewis until his eye lights on the words "Yale University." He has "skimmed" to get the information needed. To understand a process, the technique of skimming would be inadequate and wasteful. This, and the other purposes mentioned, all require a methodical plan of approach.

Help your class to see that reading *methods* depend upon reading purposes.

Now the group is probably ready to return to a discussion of the findings so lightly passed over during the first few days — the techniques known as rate and comprehension. Most educators agree that these are closely related — that an increase in one automatically augments the other. Most agree that a rapid reading rate tends to increase comprehension, but not all agree that rate, as such, should be drilled on. More students in the field concur, I believe, in the statement that the study and practice of comprehension techniques will result in added speed in reading. If your class has continued to cooperate in this study, they will be concerned with examining their own reading habits and will welcome aid in improving them.

Aside from physical disabilities (which cannot, of course, be discussed or cured in class), causes for a low reading rate usually considered are: (1) faulty reading habits, such as lip movement, pointing at words with a finger, and "back tracking" (regressive) eye movements resulting in an uneven and diminished reading rate; (2) failure to phrase properly; (3) attempts to employ the same reading rate to all types of reading, instead of adapting rate to purpose; (4) lack of the will to read, with the result that reading is done lackadaisically and therefore ineffectively; (5) inadequate vocabulary. Let us consider each of these trouble points.

The first listed is faulty reading habits. Lip moving (we are considering here, you recall, students with average and above-average reading ability) can be overcome by conscious effort, as can pointing at words with a finger. In conference with those addicted to the latter habit, suggest an oculist, however, for if eyes don't "track," the finger guide may be employed. Faulty eye movements afford a different problem. Many students in the reading field consider that rhythmic eye movements will develop through improvement in reading comprehension. Indeed, Dr. Ernest Horn, in *Methods of Instruction in the Social Subjects*, states: "The classroom teacher needs to be concerned with movements of the eye little more than with the movements of the bones of the inner ear." Some, however, place faith in mechanical devices. Of these, the most scientific is the Ophthalmograph, a machine developed by the American Optical Company. A device for analyzing faulty eye movements, the Ophthalmograph is supplemented by the Metronoscope, a machine for the practice of controlled reading, also developed by the American Optical Company. A certain easily acquired technique is necessary to operate these machines, and, of course, they must be purchased by the school, not by the individual teacher. A "homemade" device for eye-stretching exercises is included in Appendix F, *Reading: Silent and Oral*, on page 510. The theory upon which this is based is that if the eye can be trained to take in more words as it travels along a line, comprehension will be improved and there will be less tendency for the eye to return to a word already covered. If you use any type of mechanical process in teaching reading, be careful that you understand what you are working with and that you do not overuse it. Like other parts of the human body, the eye is a delicate instrument which can be injured through misuse.

A second cause for slow reading rate is faulty phrasing. Because of its importance both in rate and comprehension, phrasing should be attacked with vigor. An amazing number of adults read one word at a time; an even more amazing number fail to think — and therefore to read — in intelligent groupings. In such a sentence as this: "If you are a young woman not engaged in essential war work, apply at once," poor phrasing might result in these groupings: If you — are a young woman — not engaged. As the reader proceeded with the sentence, he would recognize that he was not grasping its meaning and would be forced to reread it.

To make pupils conscious of the importance of intelligent phrasing, Carol Hovious in "Suggestions for Teachers of Reading" offers a number of ideas. Among these are: (1) Have the pupil hold his finger in front of his nose, perhaps a foot away, and look at his finger. Although his attention is concentrated on his finger, he can see more than that. So it is in reading; the eye can see more than one word. (2) Explain that the eye moves in a series of "jerks." To test this, have one pupil sit opposite another, holding a mirror so that he can see his partner's eyes. As the partner reads, the watcher observes the jumps of his eyes. (3) Hand the pupil two copies of the same paragraph, one poorly phrased, the other intelligently phrased. The pupil will readily observe how much more rapidly he can read the properly phrased paragraph than he can the other.

Such devices as these serve to call the pupils' attention to the problem. To supplement, some teachers employ "flash cards" on which are printed phrases. As time goes on, these cards are flashed more and more rapidly, until the pupils find they are reading groups of words with increasing speed. But the principal emphasis should rest upon practice in the intelligent grouping of words into phrases in material your students are reading. With practice, this grouping becomes mechanical and rate will improve.

Our next point deals with failure to realize that different types of reading require different reading rates. An important kind of reading is "skimming." As has already been stated, this is done very rapidly. Another study technique consists in obtaining a preview of given material. Reading for this is also rapid. After the principal thought divisions have been located, however, *studying* them is a relatively slow reading process. Recreational reading, especially of fiction, tends toward a gallop; but the recreational reading of poetry slows to a walk. Physical conditions also affect reading rate: the comfort of the reader, the speed with which twilight is approaching, and the imminence of dinner. Considering these and other factors that occur to you, you can help your pupils to understand that *rate* varies with purpose.

Next, let us consider the somewhat subjective element of lacking the will to read. When you and I think of the worlds opened by reading, we cannot understand why anyone should deliberately deprive himself of the joys and values awaiting him. Yet the fact remains that many students see no use in reading. Faulty reading habits may be responsible for this. But possibly the student has never been directed to reading for a purpose. Give your pupils *something to look for* in their reading and note how interest and rate improve. Adults are too often inclined to think that boys and girls will grasp the central thought, note details, or understand the steps in a process without guidance, whereas frequently they read words and nothing more.

Last in your list of factors tending to produce low reading rate comes vocabulary. Puzzling over unfamiliar words retards speed immeasurably. This fact suggests an increased emphasis upon helping students to enlarge their stock of words. As plans for doing this have been given at length in Chapter IX, suffice it here to call to your attention the fact that an adequate stock of readily recognized words affects reading rate.

Turn now to the other blade of the shears — comprehension. As has been said, educators differ as to which should be stressed first — speed or comprehension — but all agree that both are very important.

Placed first by many as a cause for poor comprehension is lack of "reading readiness." As the term suggests, this means that pupils are required to read material before they are competent to do so. According to a comprehensive study reported in "Reading Instruction in Secondary Schools," a publication of the National Education Association, correction involves (1) developing many new concepts; (2) improving pupils' language habits; (3) extending the range and accuracy of the pupils' vocabulary; (4) cultivating familiarity with the literary and cultural background assumed to be the common heritage of pupils of that age and grade; (5) stimulating more grown-up interest when pupils have been slow to mature physically, mentally, or emotionally; (6) helping pupils to understand more complex language forms than those which they themselves use; (7) leading pupils to discover new and more vital purposes for their reading; and (8) helping pupils to understand the organization of selections more difficult and complex than those used in the earlier grades. Teachers sharing in this study emphasized that pupils coming from homes in which a foreign language is spoken are often less "ready" than are others, but they also stressed that *all* students, even superior ones, need help at some time or another on one or more of these problems.

In "Suggestions for Teachers of Reading," previously referred to, Miss Hovious presents several specific suggestions for helping pupils prepare for certain reading experiences. For example, before *Vanity Fair* is read, satire may be studied by means of current cartoons; a discussion of figures of speech in slang and current songs as well as in more formal writing could precede the reading of *Macbeth*. Not long ago, an experienced teacher told me that before beginning a unit of literature with her class, she attempts to foresee trouble points and to forestall them by giving some preliminary help as provided in *Flying the Printways* or *Following Printed Trails* by Carol Hovious. Before reading poetry, for example, she worked with material involving the recognition of details. Realization of the need for reading readiness and aid on your part will go far toward assisting your students to comprehend what they read.

Aside from lack of reading readiness, many other factors hinder comprehension. A number of these we have considered under *rate*, for faulty eye movements, excessive vocalization, weak vocabulary, and the reading of single words rather than thought groups enter into this aspect of reading, also. But there are other causes, too. In *How to Read Rapidly and Well*, a very useful little book by C. Gilbert Wrenn and Luella Cole, four trouble points are noted: (1) An inadequate vocabulary, both general and technical, is a great handicap. No teacher should assume that technical terms in any field are understood. Today a high school student may well read of "sanctions," "rehabilitation," and "reconversion." But does he know what these terms mean? Until he does, he cannot comprehend what he is reading. (2) Another basic difficulty lies in inadequate general background. One reason, I believe, that girls generally have more difficulty than do boys in comprehending the principles of economics is that girls seldom listen to talk of stocks and bonds, supply and demand, or seasonal employment. (3) Wrenn and Cole also list a point less frequently considered than it deserves to be: failure to look ahead, to anticipate the author's meaning. Ability to do this will result in increased speed as well as comprehension, and will develop mental alertness. (4) Poor concentration, perhaps because of a littered desk or some intermittent sound, prevents comprehension. Wrenn and Cole state that subjective factors also weigh heavily. Vagrant thoughts that come between the reader and the written word, a sudden recollection of some duty to be performed, a sense of injury at being forced to study — these and others like them interfere with intelligent reading. As a means of preventing wandering ideas from crowding out the work at hand, Wrenn and Cole suggest keeping a memorandum pad on which to jot down — and thereby dispose of — these transitory thoughts.

Shortly we shall consider at some length techniques required for good reading, such as reading in thought groups, understanding the main idea of a selection, grasping details, and reproducing the central thought of a passage. Obviously, failure to acquire these interferes with comprehension. In your teaching be alert to these stumblingblocks.

Now let us consider certain techniques in teaching reading. As a part of all reading programs, even remedial, authorities recommend that "wide" or "free" or "recreational" reading be encouraged, rightly thinking that the way to learn to read *is* to read. But let me say again that *undirected* reading often defeats this purpose. If students are required to read, with no help given them in book selection and reading techniques, it may well be found that pages of cheap material have been devoured or that good reading has not been comprehended. In undertaking any program, you see, the teacher must be more than an ornament.

Under the developmental plan for reading, two types (work and recreational) are listed. Let us examine the recreational type. From the beginning of your reading program, this kind should be encouraged. Such reading experiences should be as wide and as pleasant as possible. In no circumstances should the teacher condemn the student's choice or impose his own choices upon him. In this, as in other aspects of your teaching, begin with the pupil *where he is*. If he likes cheap Westerns, do not condemn them, but suggest for his next book a Western which is less cheap. As he goes on, you may encourage him to read more desirable materials. As an aid to the teacher in advising books, both Miss Hovious and Miss Dora V. Smith suggest a "book ladder." In this plan books on the same topic are listed according to their interest or literary values. In Appendix F, you will find some samples, but for the most part, you will have to compile your own. Older students may well enjoy working on this project with you. If you are being successful in the other aspects of your reading program, you may have good hope for the majority of your pupils, for it is a truism that taste improves with experience. I recall hearing Deems Taylor remark that the way for the untrained to enjoy symphonic music is simply to listen to it. So it is with reading, provided you supply the aids we have mentioned.

Your particular duty, then, lies in furnishing an ample supply of the right sort of reading. How may you do this? In the first place, you must work closely with the librarian. If, as often happens in a small school, you are librarian, so much the better. In any event, you must be familiar with the books on the shelves. You must be prepared to provide your superintendent with lists of suitable books and magazines, and — as much as is humanly possible — you must read the books yourself. Only by doing this can you stand on common ground with your boys and girls. A number of teachers suggest a "browsing library" in the classroom, ranging in number of volumes from twenty to fifty. I have heard teachers object to such a plan, for, they say, their pupils "read too much, anyway." Can this be? Is not this objection a confession that class procedure is poorly handled, with the result that students read instead of giving their attention to other class activities? No, I doubt that students ever read too much, but I am not so naïve as to think that class activities should be uncontrolled. Have your "browsing library," then, but let reading in it bear its proper place.

If you are the librarian — or perhaps if you are not — you may utilize a device for arousing reading interests suggested by an experienced teacher. Have piled on your desk a new shipment of books, to be unpacked and "checked in" for the library. Who can resist the lure of unopened packages? Who can fail to open and glance through a new book? Even the male sex exhibits a considerable Pandora-like quality under such conditions. And some boys and girls will do more than glance through — they will sample, and often they will devour.

Other plans for arousing interest frequently mentioned are the "bookmark" device, in which a bookmark is kept in each book with room on it for the name of each pupil reading the book, and a word or two of comment; acquaintance, particularly on the part of older pupils, with professional book reviews and advance notices sent out by book clubs; listening to some of the many excellent radio programs dealing with books and reading; enjoyment of recordings made by authors and actors; and attending moving pictures, both professional ones and those available for school production. But the most potent motivation of all is the teacher's own enthusiasm for reading; no "device" can achieve good results without this.

Should some record be kept of pleasure reading? Usually, yes, for several reasons. Without some notation, you cannot expect to recall the reading interests and levels of all your boys and girls. To this end, as explained in Chapter XX, a card for each pupil may be made. Boys and girls — like the rest of us — enjoy sharing experiences, both in written and oral forms. Give them an opportunity to do this. A number of suggestions are provided in this same chapter. Modern opinion, having turned against the old-fashioned, written report, tends toward discussions, panels, written "blurbs," and so forth. If you can aid your pupils to enjoy sharing experiences, you will find that they will have many plans for so doing. But keep in mind that, although the class procedure may and should be student planned and activated, yours must be the guiding touch. Do not, for example, let your boys and girls be satisfied with "I liked" or "I did not like." Show them that such a statement demands from the reader or listener a "Why?" Help them to answer this question intelligently. In their "Manual" to accompany *Elements of English*, Center and

Holmes offer Goethe's formula: What did the artist try to do? Was it worth doing? Did he do it? Such questions as these help students to think, read, and express ideas specifically.

Elsewhere in this book, emphasis has been placed on the principle "*We enjoy what we understand.*" In considering plans for recreational reading, do not overlook your responsibility in helping pupils to understand. Centering attention on what the author attempted and his success or failure constitutes one facet; recognition by the pupil that different types of reading fill different reading demands is another. To read a biography expecting to experience a series of thrilling adventures would prove deeply disappointing to a reader and would make him dislike biography. In *You and Your English*, a text for eighth-grade pupils, three specific purposes are given the students: to read an interesting story (applicable to narratives such as *Treasure Island*, to short stories, and to the occasional novel read by this age group); to become acquainted with the life of a famous person (applicable to biography, autobiography, and some travel books); to read for pleasure at least three poems. For older pupils, related reading purposes may be added. It goes without saying that, to be understood, reading must be within the mental and physical power of the reader.

What should your own attitude toward recreational reading be? What do you hope that it will accomplish? In *Teaching High-School Students to Read*, the authors, Stella S. Center and Gladys L. Persons, suggest the following purposes in reading: (1) to share experiences intelligently; (2) to satisfy and stimulate emotions; (3) to find material for reflection; (4) to develop a philosophy of life; and (5) to experience esthetic delight. By keeping these objectives in mind as you help boys and girls select books, as you talk to them about their reading, and as you guide their classroom reading activities, you will help cultivate a desire to read and a critical attitude toward reading. Today, as perhaps never before, all of us need to grow in wisdom and understanding. To do this, there can be no substitute for books, the written records of mankind.

Turn now to the second aspect of developmental reading, that referred to as the work or informational type. As its name suggests, the purpose of this type is to gather information designed particularly to aid in the activities of living. It differs primarily from recreational reading in that the latter has no motive other than pleasure, whereas the former provides guides for one's activities. It is evident that some would read a novel for pleasure and others would read the same novel for information. *Huckleberry Finn* and *Gulliver's Travels*, for example, are read by children for pleasure, but adults may read them for a statement of social ideas. Books may even be read by the same person for pleasure or for profit, depending upon the reader's maturity and needs. The types may overlap, then, but, on the whole, the reading of newspapers, technical writings, directions, textbooks, and so forth, belongs primarily to the work type category.

Like recreational reading, the work type revolves about certain purposes. Those usually listed are the following: to acquire information, to form opinions, to find answers to questions, to visualize details, to discover new problems, and to evaluate materials. The *Experience Curriculum in English* divides informational reading into four fields: (1) discursive reading, which is guided by curiosity, a desire to keep informed regarding such matters as current events and to know the opinions of others on civic, social, moral, or economic problems; (2) problem reading, such as following directions, recipes, and road guides; (3) reading for reports, such as talks, lectures, or investigative papers; and (4) reference reading, for the purpose of securing the types of information found in dictionaries, encyclopedias, glossaries, and so forth. In each of these divisions, the *type* of reading is determined upon by the *purpose* in reading. As you consider these divisions, note the mental maturity required by many of them and recall that reading is basically a *thought* process.

Among the techniques particularly applicable to this type may be listed summarizing, outlining, answering questions by teacher or class, recognizing and being able to state the central idea of the piece being read, discovery of details developing the main idea, recognizing key words (an essential technique in phrasing), skimming, following directions, applying one's own experience and knowledge as a means of interpretation or in order to form an opinion, finding answers to questions, reviewing systematically, and preparing a précis. Naturally, these techniques are not to be poured into the students, to be swallowed in one gulp. As teacher, you must decide what principal technique is needed for a certain reading purpose. Discuss the principle of this technique with the class or individual student and show him how to utilize it. Perhaps the pupil has been asked to answer certain questions based on several pages of reading. The "skimming" technique should be applied here to *identify* passages which answer the assigned questions, and identification of the main ideas and their supporting details may be the techniques demanded for answering questions. (Have I made it sufficiently clear that "skimming" is not synonymous with rapid reading? When a reader "skims," he reads only key words or sentences; when he reads rapidly, he reads each sentence, but with great speed. Neither should skimming be confused with sloppy reading — a procedure to be warred against, as it is destructive to thought.)

A type of work reading of particular concern to students is textbook reading. C. Gilbert Wrenn and Luella Cole offer a number of practical ideas for this type. These writers suggest that the first step consists in exploring the book — in examining the table of contents, the title, the author's name and position, and the date of publication. Next, they advise examining each main section as a unit. The student should then look through the book for subheadings. Then he should read each subdivision and think about it. By so doing, the student will be able to identify the author's outline or plan. Next he must determine whether there are introductory and closing paragraphs; if so, he should read and digest them. These four steps constitute the preliminary survey. After that, careful reading should begin. As the reader now understands the author's plan, reading consists merely in filling in with details. Although your pupils may object at first to this somewhat leisurely procedure, assure them that in the end it actually saves time.

Wrenn and Cole suggest these additional methods in attempting to master an entire chapter. After making the preliminary survey just outlined, let the student read for ideas, stopping occasionally to recapitulate, orally or silently, what has been read. Then, if necessary, reread *selectively*, omitting sentences and paragraphs understood or transitional. After this, notes may be taken. With practice, notes may be combined with the rereading, but they should never be made during the preliminary survey.

In connection with reading paragraphs, Wrenn and Cole suggest examining the paragraph structure. If the paragraph contains a topic sentence, it should be identified and marked. If it does not, one should be written. By these means the purpose of each paragraph becomes clear. (You note, as you read this, how closely co-ordinated are reading and writing skills.)

Finally, these authors emphasize the necessity of reading by means of phrases. Like all students of the reading field, they advise the pupil to break up the sentence into thought units, and encourage him by saying that with practice a sentence may be read with only two or three pauses.

Much of the work type reading of your students will be done in scientific fields. Without your help, your pupils may not realize that the reading techniques enumerated here apply to scientific reading as well as to history and other "reading" subjects. To understand how ice is prevented from forming on windshields, for example, the reader must master the *details* given; if he wishes to grasp the basic principle of humidity control, he must read for identification of this principle; if he wants to understand a paper on motor fuels, he must identify the author's organization. Thus work techniques are readily applicable to all types of scientific writing.

Because of the popularity today of newspaper reading, you may well devote class time to helping your pupils to read intelligently. As you consider reading purposes, you note how many of them apply to newspaper reading. From this source, we gain much information, we are aided in arriving at conclusions, in forming opinions, and in answering questions. Reading techniques that we utilize frequently are skimming, rapid reading, and thoughtful reading. Graphs, maps, charts, scales, and cartoons often must be interpreted. Certainly we must weigh all editorials and many news stories against our own judgment and experience. Even comic strips and cartoons demand attention. In every recent presidential election, some voters have cast their ballots for Andy Gump, and Colonel Blimp has earned a place for himself in our thinking and vocabulary.

Suggestions for reading a newspaper made by Zenna L. Serrurier in the Claremont Colleges *Seventh Yearbook* include a study of how news is gathered and transmitted, and of the difference between news columns and editorials; an examination of headlines; identification of the purposes of the various features and departments; knowledge of who own and manage the newspaper, their political affiliations and background; a consideration of the policies of the paper as indicated through the owners, the editorials, the headlines, the special features, and the news stories; and a study of propaganda. In order to be fair in their study, students should examine at least two newspapers and attempt to analyze attitudes on current issues. Perhaps at first glance some of these suggestions seem far removed from the process of reading; yet a little thinking will show that an understanding of the political bias, say, of the owner of the paper is essential in interpreting editorials and even news stories. Your common sense will also tell you that under some circumstances such a reading survey as this requires tactful handling; but your sense of responsibility as a teacher in a democracy will require you to help your students to read newspapers intelligently.

Many words ago we began our discussion of plans for handling intensified study of reading in one of the "key" years, perhaps the ninth. We commented on how to begin such a program and we talked over, in some detail, desirable purposes and techniques. But you probably wish specific information for divisions of such a course. Let us turn to Miss Hovious for a plan. This is what she presents in "Suggestions for Teachers of Reading":

First Quarter:

First Week: Getting under way, somewhat as we have suggested. Oral reading to detect handicaps. Many will be indicated.

Second Week: Reading test, to be given on Monday and returned to on Friday. (If the class personnel is fixed and if teacher and students feel at ease with one another, the test may be given toward the end of the first week.)

Remainder of the Quarter: A basal reading program, involving as many of the techniques referred to as the class can assimilate. Speaking and writing activities which develop from the reading should be encouraged. In general, so-called "classics" should be avoided, directed individual reading being substituted.

Second Quarter: Continuation of the basal reading program, including reading and writing situations as they develop. Toward the end of the Quarter, some of the simpler classics may be read, either as individual or group reading.

Third Quarter: A more orderly and carefully planned composition program than that which develops naturally from reading activities. If the teacher desires, this may be substituted for plans for the second quarter.

Fourth Quarter: Return to the basal reading program, with particular attention to the more difficult classics.

As Miss Hovious emphasizes, this is only one plan. But it offers a starting point, from which you can branch out as your good sense dictates. Perhaps I should reiterate here that this procedure is for a *planned* program of developmental reading for boys and girls who offer no particular reading problem.

What to do with the small group in every unsectioned class who *do* afford a serious problem must now concern us. Actually, these pupils fall into two groups: retarded readers and nonreaders. The latter group consists of those who have never learned to read because of inability to learn through ordinary visual techniques but who are average or above average in intelligence; and those who are mentally incapable of learning. As these mentally inferior pupils ordinarily drop out before they reach high school, they need not concern you. Whether or not to segregate slow readers depends upon their age and the extent of their reading disability. In dealing with grade-school boys and girls, it is probably advisable to keep them with other children of their age. With older students, the problem should be presented to them and those who desire aid in reading be asked to volunteer. Nonreaders, however, require such individualized instruction that they cannot be taught in a group.

Let us consider first what to do for the retarded readers. Miss Harriett Carmody, reading diagnostician for the Reading Clinic, the State College of Washington, suggests the following procedure. Keep in mind, as you read it, that the pupils for whom it is designed are not subnormal in *intelligence*, but that they rank well below average in muscular control and in visual and auditory responses.

Miss Carmody's program for attacking their reading problem consists of the following steps:

1. Find out at what stage in reading development the pupils are. For this, the Gates Silent Reading Test, published by Teachers College, Columbia University, for grades 3 to 10, is excellent, as it indicates whether the weakness lies in vocabulary, level of comprehension, or reading rate.

2. After this test is given and the results interpreted, begin the reading program. Except for slow learners and non-readers, students should not be segregated.

3. Begin with readers two or three grades below that of the pupil — for pupils in the seventh or eighth grades select fourth- or fifth-grade readers; for freshmen pupils, choose books on the sixth-grade level. On the fourth- or fifth-grade level, Ernest Horn's *Reaching Our Goal*, published by Ginn and Company, is excellent; for the sixth-grade level, *Wings for Reading* by Carol Hovious, published by D. C. Heath, is a wise choice. Provide also additional readers, such as *Finding New Trails*, *Exploring New Trails*, and *Traveling New Trails*, published by Lyons and Carnahan; or the *American Adventure Series*, published by Wheeler Publishing Company.

4. Continue reading on the pupil's level until he has grasped the techniques. Two books ordinarily supply sufficient foundation.

5. At some point the student will "jump" in his reading skill. When this occurs, he is ready to be advanced to his regular class.

Let us turn next to the comparatively small group of nonreaders. As we have said, in the grades they should be kept with their fellows, but in junior high school (they seldom advance beyond the eighth grade), they will require individualized attention. This means that, through tests, observation, talks with the pupil, his parents, former teachers, and others, you will attempt to understand the basic causes — psychological, social, or physical — for this lack of reading ability. Gain the confidence and liking of the child. Never forget that he is not subnormal in intelligence but normal or even superior. Avoid using or even *thinking* the term "remedial," for psychological factors affect teachers as well as pupils.

A nonreader can do nothing in a group. He must begin on the primer level and be taught to recognize letters and their sounds, singly and in combination. In short, devices used by the first-grade teacher must be employed with this boy or girl. As these children are intelligent, progress will come quickly, after confidence has been established and basic weaknesses identified. Satisfactory primers for such a group are *Fun with Dick and Jane*, Scott, Foresman, and Company; *At Play* and *Fun in Story*, Winston Publishing Company; *Day In and Day Out* and *The Wishing Well*, the Row-Peterson Company. These primers should be followed by readers on succeeding levels. Sooner or later the pupil will reach a point at which he can read advanced material. Then he should be given opportunity to do so. In this, as in other reading programs, provide supplementary reading material.

In this remedial reading program you will notice a marked increase in physical disabilities: uncorrected sight, poor hearing, marks of malnutrition, and evidences of glandular disturbance. Deportment may be poor, for often these boys and girls have developed a defense mechanism to hide their weaknesses. Their physical handicaps, too, contribute to misbehavior. One of your first responsibilities lies in recognizing these facts and in having as a long-range aim growth in personal development.

As you work with these boys and girls, you will observe an intensification of the weaknesses previously noted as

well as several in addition: vocalization; finger pointing at each word; word by word reading; inversion of
letters within a word; substitution of letters, such as *b*
for *d*; inability of the eye to return to the beginning of a
line. You will wonder, and rightly, how and why such
handicapped readers ever reached the junior or senior
high school level. But do not fall into the trap of blaming
someone else. There are many reasons for this condition;
recognize it as part of your present responsibility and
attack it with vigor.

In addition to suggestions made previously, you may
profit from examining the plan followed by Mrs. Serrurier,
to whose experiences you have already been referred.
She begins by stressing the need of arousing in the poor
reader a desire to read and notes that the techniques she
advises center about this purpose. Next, she comments
upon the necessity of putting these pupils at their ease.
As a means toward this, she suggests employing very
simple word drills, which all but actual nonreaders can
do successfully. No class discussion should follow these,
for retarded boys and girls dread having their errors
called to the attention of the class. The scores made
should be recorded, however, by the teacher.

As the span of attention of this group is short, class
activities should be varied. After a few minutes of written
work, books should be distributed, and the teacher should
read aloud the opening pages of a story. The choice of
this first story naturally is most important and must be
carefully considered. Ettie Lee's adaptation of *Les Mi-
serables* is recommended by Mrs. Serrurier. In addition
to this book, there should be a well-selected classroom
library. Books in it must be short, with many illustrations, large print, and cheerful bindings. Ten-cent stores

afford many suitable books. Boys like adventure and mechanics; girls like stories of love. A few fairy tales may be included.

For about two weeks, the class works on exercises and silent reading while the teacher gives his time to personal interviews. The ostensible purpose of these interviews is to hear the pupil read aloud. A book of simple short stories or the book the boy or girl is reading supplies the material. The pupil reads a page without interruption from the teacher. During this time the teacher makes mental notes of the pupil's probable background (judged by clothing, mannerisms, and so forth), his personality, and obvious reading difficulties. Regardless of the quality of the performance, the reader is praised by the teacher. Often this results in the boy or girl becoming communicative. If so, some of his reading problems may be discussed and suggestions for improvement made immediately. Often, however, the pupil returns to his seat with the words of praise ringing in his ears. After he has gone, and before another student is called on, the teacher records on a card his first impressions of the pupil. These should be filed and additions and alterations made as time goes on.

During this exploratory period as well as later, one period a week should be devoted to reading aloud by the teacher (never by the pupils) or to word games. Oral reading by the teacher becomes the highlight of the week, for boys and girls enjoy material they cannot read themselves, they receive valuable object lessons in phrasing and pronunciation, and they learn that reading can be enjoyable. In this oral reading, the teacher should present different types of writing. Humor which is not too subtle is popular. A simplified version of O. Henry's

"The Ransom of Red Chief" and the Paul Bunyan stories, especially if they are illustrated, are always favorites.

Word games selected must be very simple. "Sides" may be chosen, and each pupil in turn be required to name an animal, a plant, or an object in the room. Within limitations, geographical terms may be substituted. Oral spelling is almost impossible with low groups.

As these children like to receive "credit" for their class work, Mrs. Serrurier advises keeping individual cards, on which are noted what grades are made in each exercise and whether mistakes have been corrected. Titles of all stories and articles read also are recorded. Despite the tremendous amount of paper work involved Mrs. Serrurier considers this plan worth the effort demanded, because of the improvement in morale of these pupils whose record hitherto has been little else than failure. In this lies the whole value of the card, for the teacher bases his grading on entirely different factors.

After these preliminary interviews have been held, the teacher gives most of his time to individual aid. Only a very few activities can be followed by the class as a unit. Visits to the library may be made and simple instructions for drawing books from it may be given, but these pupils must not be expected to show much interest in a library. With some classes, instruction in using a dictionary may be given, but usually this should be explained individually. Some class time should be spent on the alphabet, the use of a telephone directory, and the reading of clock and calendar. Pupils of junior high school age frequently are ignorant concerning these, yet are ashamed to admit it. These, plus the weekly oral reading, constitute the bulk of class activities.

Individual help by the teacher includes correction, if possible, of the most glaring reading faults. Books from other classes should be used, so that the teacher can give aid in preparing assignments. Much time must be allotted for selection of books of interest to the pupil. Many written assignments must be at hand for pupils to do while waiting their turn for individual aid. These must never be "busy work," but must provide drill needed by the student. Fortunately, even a class of slow readers falls into two or three groupings, so that exercises will suit several members of the class.

Tests should be given at least twice during the semester, primarily as guides to the teacher concerning his procedure. As with the first test, students must be reassured regarding the purpose of the test. Pupils who have improved may be shown the result of the test. Others should be put off if they inquire. Probably they will soon forget that a test has been given.

Tests will show three groups: those who improve almost miraculously; those who reach a certain level, upon which they rest; those who show no progress or who (alas for the teacher's morale!) actually decline. The first group will take their place with others of their age; the second may be encouraged to utilize efficiently their reading ability; the third may try again, under a different teacher. In most cases, a start has been made toward showing pupils the advantages that come to them from increased reading ability.

Another remedial reading program reported on in the *Seventh Yearbook* involves a group of boys who were not only poor readers — they were also disciplinary problems. Ten points comprise the program as presented by Mr. Leonard Christensen:

1. Creation of an incentive to improve in their ability to read the printed page.
2. Easy but interesting reading material.
3. Records for charting individual progress.
4. Providing interesting and varied classroom activities.
5. Integration of school work with industrial occupations.
6. Motivated drill for short periods of time in reading, English, grammar, spelling, penmanship, and vocabulary development.
7. Adequate reading material for the students to read for pleasure and project work in the classroom.
8. Free reading periods with good books available in the classroom.
9. Opportunities to develop character through reading and discussion.
10. Rapport gained with the individual pupil through interest in his problems.

Such are plans for programs designed to occupy a quarter or a semester. To supplement them, you will want to read widely the material published recently and make adaptations to suit your needs.

And now a word about a group of students at the opposite end of the scale from those we have been discussing — the superior readers. These boys and girls read well, show interest and curiosity, sift the wheat from the chaff, and evince creative and inventive powers. Have you any responsibility toward this group? I wish I could assure you that you may forget them, but the consensus appears to be that they, too, need guidance. Strangely, they tend to read below their ability and to confine themselves to one type of reading. Your task with them lies in helping them to read intensively and broadly. Fortunately, they are easily motivated and are capable of individual work. These and other above-average pupils may profit from the following program, taken from Johnson, Bessey, and Ryan's *English Patterns:*

1. Check your eyes; see that you have a proper reading light.
2. Provide yourself with paper and pencil for jotting notes.
3. Read rapidly, but with concentration.
4. Pause from time to time to think back over what you have read.
5. Either orally or in writing summarize the author's thought.
6. Select material other than fiction so that it will be necessary for you to focus your attention.
7. Eliminate physical motions such as pointing at words and forming them with your lips.
8. Hold yourself rigidly to a time schedule, checking yourself for rate and comprehension at the end of the appointed time.

As you have read these pages on silent reading, you have wondered, no doubt, just what materials you can find for use in your developmental and remedial reading programs. It is impossible to give you a comprehensive list, but most of the publishing houses named in Appendix K print textbooks and workbooks designed for the developmental program. A letter to any of these firms explaining your problem will result in immediate aid. For the 22 to 25 per cent of high school freshmen who rank on or below the sixth-grade level, select a good fifth- or sixth-grade study reader that will give training in word analysis techniques, comprehension skills, and meaning vocabulary. Notice that these books should be on certain *levels*. This means that the subject matter is sufficiently mature to interest older boys and girls but that the techniques belong to lower grades. You should not, then, select any fifth- or sixth-grade reader for these boys and girls, but should choose a book especially designed for them. Magazines offering suitable material are *Popular Mechanics*, *Popular Science*, *The Scholastic*, *The Junior Scholastic*, *Science News Letter*, and similar periodicals. *Collier's* frequently prints a short short story. You yourself can rewrite material that is suitable except for its vocabulary and length. Modern textbooks abound in exercises you can use. Manuals prepared for the teacher by many publishers of high school texts provide excellent ideas. *The English Journal* and *The Elementary English Review* reward you monthly. There is so much in this field that your problem may well be one of selection. But beware of employing poetry and other "literary" types of writing as subject matter in diagnostic work. As has been pointed out in these pages, overanalysis can completely ruin literary experience. For practice material, then, find interesting, well-written, logically organized pieces of factual writing, and leave other types for recreational reading, either under the free reading program or in a literature class.

We have now discussed the silent reading program under a number of aspects. Although much attention has been given to plans for administering this program throughout one of the "key" semesters, you should not ignore it during the semesters in which you teach conventional classes in composition and literature, for adaptations should be employed in all your teaching experiences. If you consider suggestions given elsewhere in this book, you will note how many of them are for reading techniques. Consider outlining, preparing a précis, summarizing, identifying the central idea, and noticing details — to mention only a few. Reading, speaking, writing — and their base, thinking — must never be divorced one from another. Even though you may not be *emphasizing* developmental reading in your classes in composition and literature, you nevertheless *encourage* it by means of your teaching techniques. The "reading cripples," as we have said, should be removed from the class for individual instruction.

All these suggestions deal with a planned program. But suppose that your school sponsors no such program. What can you do then? A little thought will show you that application of these techniques — as has been said — may and should be made in all your teaching. In any class you can discuss the value of proper reading techniques and can aid your pupils in applying them. Taking time from the regular class proceedings for this sort of guidance is entirely legitimate. You will be gratified at how much you can accomplish even without the advantages of special instruction. If you discover that your classes include one or two who read so poorly as to require individual aid, provide for them privately. Do not penalize such pupils by withdrawing them from school activities, which they both need and like; but plan, somehow, to fit this labor of love into your daily schedule.

According to Miss Carmody, ten or fifteen minutes a day given over to individual work with the child will produce amazing results. She suggests that the teacher should: (1) Have the pupil read on the level at which he can read successfully, even though it is that of a second- or third-grade reader; (2) Be sure that the child learns to analyze his words by detailed visual analysis, phonics, visualization techniques, and so forth, for he is the child who lacks visual aptitude to such an extent that he was not able to learn by the sight methods; (3) Guide his eyes by sliding the finger in a continuous movement under the line and have him slide his finger himself; (4) Have him work with a remedial spelling group where word analysis techniques, spelling rules, and so forth are being emphasized.

Let me end what I have to say about silent reading with a few warnings. Do not overemphasize this program. Good as it is, fundamental as you consider it to be, it is not, after all, the only important part of your teaching. You have other obligations to your students which must not be crowded out. Simply because tests must be administered to your pupils, do not place complete dependence upon them. Consider the various factors that may invalidate a test, and resolve to employ your findings in conjunction with your judgment, records on file for each pupil in your principal's office, and class performance. Mechanical aids to reading must be carefully handled and may be omitted without great loss. Above all, do not let *techniques* in reading crowd out enjoyment in reading. Without question, however, silent reading deserves your energetic co-operation.

Timidly slipping out of the darkness in which it has been hiding for some time comes oral reading. Because all of us today employ the techniques of silent reading many more times than we do oral, the latter has received less and less emphasis in the classroom, particularly in the upper elementary grades and the high schools. As with silent reading, teachers have had a tendency to think of oral reading as belonging to the beginning years of a child's education. Now we are realizing that oral reading, like its silent partner, involves a complex technique requiring maturity of thought, that it too is a means of understanding ideas, and that it bears main responsibility in sharing reading pleasures. We have, then, unwittingly deprived our pupils of a useful tool and a means of pleasure. Perhaps the Friday afternoons of our grandfathers, devoted to "speaking pieces," were much more beneficial and pleasurable than we have been willing to admit.

In all reading programs — developmental and remedial — oral reading is a useful handmaiden. By means of it, a teacher can diagnose physical weaknesses, such as inversion of words and letters, substitution of letters, telescoping of words and syllables, and inability of the eyes to swing back easily and quickly to the beginning of each line. So, too, may mental causes for failure in comprehension be detected, such as word-by-word reading, substitution of words (such as "fairy" for "ferry"), failure to phrase properly, overlooking of punctuation marks and inability to interpret these guides to a writer's meaning, and failure to recognize and therefore to respond to an author's mood. Personally, I go even beyond these generally accepted values in that I believe that training in oral reading increases ability in public speaking and that it may even aid us in our attack upon our foe — poor spelling.

You are, then, justified in spending class time upon oral reading. It may well enough form a part of your reading program and will afford an opportunity for variety in class procedures. In presenting oral reading, you should, I believe, emphasize reading for *ideas*. To this end, you should aid your students in recognizing main and lesser thought divisions as indicated by punctuation marks; you should explain, and let your pupils identify, figures of speech; you should see that they recognize the mood and the point of view of the author. In other words, all that has been discussed previously regarding the teaching of poetry and prose may be applied to oral reading. Of course you will consider the mental age of your group, physical handicaps, interest span, and so forth, before choosing selections for oral reading. In this phase of teaching, as in all others, your careful observation of the needs and capabilities of your class must guide you.

In addition to helping boys and girls grasp the thought of whatever is read aloud, you should stress the aspect of *communication*. In silent reading, ideas are shared by writer and reader; in oral reading, ideas are shared by writer, reader, and *listeners*. In either type the reader has a responsibility toward the writer to understand what the latter has said. In oral reading, the reader adds to his responsibility the sharing of ideas with others. He must, then, not only understand what the author is saying, but he must also *transmit* these ideas to others. To that end, he must learn how to control his voice so that what he is reading can be understood in every corner of the room; he must indicate the mood and tone of the selection by rate of reading and by variations of voice; he must enunciate and pronounce words with exactness, yet with naturalness; and he must assume a sitting or standing posture which will not detract from the sharing of ideas which constitutes oral reading.

One of the most pleasurable devices that you can utilize is choral reading. This group activity possesses many of the values of group singing, yet does not demand so much native ability. Boys or girls who hesitate or refuse to read aloud individually derive great pleasure from choral reading. Indeed, this serves excellently as an introduction to oral reading by the individual.

Although you should read on this topic and enroll in a

class in choral reading yourself, the following suggestions may help you until you have the opportunity to enlarge your background.

1. Select poetry with strong rhythm, such as "Pirate Don Durk of Dowdee." Poems utilizing the devices of repetition and refrain are good beginning choices.
2. Divide your group into two or three parts, according to voice quality.
3. Divide the poem into parts, each to be read by a different group.
4. With the class, analyze the poem carefully. Pupils must understand the meaning of each word and must see the picture back of each word. Thought units must be recognized, and marked off by vertical lines. The mood of the poem and its relation to the rate of reading must be determined on. If dialogue occurs, an attempt to portray character through reading must be made. Careful pronunciation and enunciation should be stressed.
5. Avoid a "sing song" effect by having someone act as leader to direct the reading, very much as a choirmaster directs singing. At first, you should be that leader, but later some member of the group can and should serve.
6. Practice, but avoid boring the pupils.
7. Present a particularly finished product before an audience.

All these suggestions you can impart to your students, even though you may have had little training in interpretative reading yourself. If you will think of this process as one facet of communication and if you can lead your pupils also to consider it in this way, you will provide your boys and girls with a skill that will aid them in silent reading and that will afford them life-long pleasure.

As testing must occupy a prominent place in any reading program, let us now consider purposes and types of tests. In general, they show two purposes: (1) to test a student's reading ability and (2) to diagnose particular reading ills. Most authorities consider that the first type of test should be given to all students at the beginning of the reading program. With a normal group, another form of this test may be administered later to test progress. Subnormal readers, however, should be given diagnostic tests, including oral reading, in an attempt to discover particular trouble spots.

To attempt to enumerate the many tests obtainable is impossible. Lists of tests, with comments upon their reliability and type, may be found in these publications, among others: *Problems in the Improvement of Reading in High School and College*, by Ruth Strang; *Developmental Reading in High School*, by Guy L. and Eva Bond; *Teaching High-School Pupils to Read*, by Stella S. Center and Gladys L. Persons; "Reading Instruction in Secondary Schools," the National Education Association; and "Suggestions for Teachers of Reading," by Carol Hovious. Appendix F contains a list of popular tests.

You can see from the number of tests on the market that your problem is one of selection. Miss Hovious suggests considering these questions: (1) Does the test cover suitable grade levels? (2) How many parallel forms are available? (3) Does it produce valid scores? (4) Is the test easy to give, score, and interpret? In addition to these, cost must often be taken into consideration.

As you consider this testing material, you realize that its application can be time-consuming and burdensome to the classroom teacher. Ideally, a reading program should be school-wide, its administration a problem for the superintendent and principal to grapple with. But you know that teaching is not always done under ideal conditions and that you, as an individual, may have to plan and administer the program. Shall you attempt a testing plan? If you can afford the cost, you might buy copies of one test and let it serve for both measuring and diagnostic purposes. If you can arouse your students' co-operation, each might contribute enough for his own test. (I recognize objections to this and realize that provision may have to be made for pupils unable or unwilling to co-operate.) But if you cannot obtain copies of standardized tests, do not abandon the program, for you can compile your own. Examine a copy of a standardized test and follow a simplified plan. (Be careful not to utilize the same material, for these tests are copyrighted.) Also you can make out tests on special aspects: vocabulary, paragraph comprehension, and so forth. These "homemade" tests must be much less significant than commercial tests and, as you know, they are only *one* means of aiding pupils to read skillfully. In fact, if you decide it wise to omit testing altogether, you can still direct a reading program that will produce desirable results.

We have now touched on the main aspects of a reading program. To attempt to discuss the reading problem adequately in one chapter imposes an impossible condition. But I hope that these few pages, in addition to outlining the main divisions of a reading program and suggesting some methods of procedure, have inspired you to continue your study and have increased your determination to do what you can to aid your boys and girls in acquiring and developing this prerequisite to the good life.

ASSIGNMENT

A. Prepare for a panel discussion (a) several of the objectives listed on page 402; or (b) the definitions of reading found on page 400.

B. After you have examined the sample "reading ladders" in Appendix F, select a general subject (such as "hobbies") and prepare a "ladder," listing at least ten titles.

C. Read several books designed for junior or senior high school students and review them orally.

D. Rewrite an article or a story for use by immature or poor readers.

E. Select a reading test and describe it as you would to a class. Consider its purpose, norms, and administration.

F. Check your own reading ability by: (1) "skimming" this chapter to find references to Gray; (2) summarizing the section on remedial reading; (3) defining recreational and informational reading types; and (4) selecting a section and noting your rate and comprehension. (You should be able to read about 325 words a minute.)

G. Consult such books as *Flying the Printways*, *Young America's English*, and *You Can Read Better;* and such magazines as *The English Journal*, *The Elementary English Review*, *The Scholastic*, and *The Junior Scholastic*, and summarize plans for "word games" you consider suited to retarded and to normal readers.

FURTHER READINGS

1. These publications, referred to in this chapter, justify further examination:

a. *An Experience Curriculum in English.*

   Part III. Chapters VI, VII, and VIII consider reading procedures.

b. BOND, GUY L., and BOND, EVA, *Developmental Reading in High School.*

   Addressed to the high school teacher, this book discusses, simply and practically, all aspects of the problem.

c. CENTER, STELLA S., and PERSONS, GLADYS L., *Teaching High-School Students to Read*.

A publication of the National Council of Teachers of English, this is an account of a program undertaken in Theodore Roosevelt High School, New York City.

d. HOVIOUS, CAROL, "Suggestions for Teachers of Reading," Grades VII to XII.

A recognized authority, Miss Hovious approaches this problem with her usual simplicity and practicality.

e. "Reading Instruction in Secondary Schools," a Research Bulletin of the National Education Association, January, 1942, 1201 Sixteenth Street, N.W., Washington, D.C.

This "overview" of the reading problem is well worth its cost of twenty-five cents.

f. *Seventh Yearbook* (1942) of the Claremont Colleges Reading Conference.

For a number of years, Claremont Colleges and Alpha Iota Chapter of Pi Lambda Theta, National Education Association for Women, have sponsored a reading conference. All yearbooks offer practical suggestions.

g. STRANG, RUTH MAY, *Problems in the Improvement of Reading in High School and College*.

Discussing all aspects of the reading problem, this book recognizes the relation between high school and college reading problems.

h. *The Teaching of Reading:* A Second Report (36th Yearbook of the National Society for the Study of Education).

If possible, read this authoritative discussion.

i. WRENN, C. GILBERT, and COLE, LUELLA, *How to Read Rapidly and Well*.

This is a practical little book by two reading authorities.

2. LAMOREAUX, L. A., and LEE, DORRIS MAY, *Learning to Read through Experiences*.

Although this book deals particularly with beginning techniques, it is of value to junior and senior high school teachers.

3. McNALLY, H. J., "Developing a Junior High School Reading Program," *Teachers College Record*, XLIII (January, 1942), pp. 264–276.

The importance of selection of reading material is here stressed.

4. BOND, GUY L., and BOND, EVA, *Developmental Reading in the High School;* WITTY, PAUL, and KOPEL, DAVID, *Reading and the Educative Process;* and MONROE, MARION, and BACKUS, BERTIE, *Remedial Reading*.

Taken together, these three books afford an excellent background on reading. *Developmental Reading* discusses the entire field, *Reading and the Educational Process*, psychological aspects, and *Remedial Reading*, a specific area.

XXII. THE TEACHER IN AND OUT
OF THE CLASSROOM

N<small>O DOUBT</small>, as you think of your prospective teaching, you have often wondered to yourself, "What am I going to do on the first day, before there are any regular assignments?" And you are right to think of it, for this opening day is important to you. For the first time your students will meet you; they will observe you, "size you up." You want to come out of this examination with confidence. You should, then, consider your appearance. Select something that is simple yet becoming (if you are a woman); if a man, take note of your necktie and general appearance. You do not want to be judged a fop by your students, but neither do you want to be carelessly dressed. In manner, be pleasant, friendly, but firm. Much depends upon this first impression and certain problems of discipline may become acute or may completely disappear after this first day. There will be certain routine matters for you to attend to, such as taking the roll, making announcements (you should announce no rules of your own this first day), giving the pupils your name, telling them the textbooks they are to use or buy, and making the assignment. Do this in a businesslike manner. If your class shows signs of being disorderly, ask them courteously for their attention and wait until you get it. If the periods are shortened, this will occupy the time; if not, you will have to do something else for twenty minutes or so. You should take the opportunity to show the class, as clearly as possible, the reasons why this course is given and its practical value to them. As a part of your preparation for·this first day, think this out with care. Not long ago I heard an educator say that one of the duties of a classroom instructor is to show his class the reason for their studies. I think this person is right. Very few of us study for study's sake; we like a practical reason for our labor.

Now this is not particularly difficult in composition classes. Anyone should be able to see that in every activity of the adult world we need to express our ideas clearly, accurately, and effectively. But students (and adults) find more difficulty in seeing why they should study literature. In these courses, you should emphasize the importance of knowing people and should point out how great an aid to understanding human beings is reading. Using incident and example as much as possible, comment upon the social and, indirectly, the business advantages resulting from a knowledge of the background common to educated persons. Any such discussion as this should precede your assignment. Watch the time, and try to plan your work so that you complete the assignment as the dismissal bell rings. In this way, you will hold the attention of your class, and this, as you will soon learn, is essential. You should plan this first day with care, having in mind more to do than you think you can accomplish. You should talk to the group, not read to them, exerting yourself to be pleasant and charming, yet letting the students know that you are in control.

And now let me close these informal remarks on the teaching of English with some comments on matters that do not pertain to the teaching of any particular subject, yet that are important to every teacher.

In the preceding paragraphs I have made suggestions for the first day and I have said that you must lay plans with care, for by the conduct of your classes then you will be judged and your disciplinary problems will be augmented or lessened. I sometimes wonder whether much can be said on this subject that is particularly helpful, as apparently a teacher either is or is not a good disciplinarian, for reasons difficult to determine. Yet lack of discipline can mar or indeed ruin your teaching career. You must control your class or you cannot teach them anything. And, in these days, your control must be moral, not physical, always much more difficult. A woman teacher can make no greater mistake than to attempt to use force, and a man teacher should always resort to some other means. Hence, no matter how tempted you may be, keep your hands off and control your group in other ways.

Much of good discipline resolves into a matter of good manners. If you are unfailingly polite to your students, most of them will be courteous to you. Not all — there are always "problem cases" — but the majority will respond. You should put the class procedure, then, on that basis. A courteous person does not talk while another is speaking, he does not move about noisily, he does not conduct himself in a way which is disturbing to his classmates. Almost all acts that become disciplinary problems are those of discourtesy, and the right attitude on your part will go far toward avoiding trouble. You should resolve — although, being human, you will break this resolution — never to speak or to act in a way that you yourself would resent if you were the student concerned. If you can, put yourself into the pupil's place. Remember his age, realize his sensitiveness and his self-consciousness; respect his rights as an individual. All this you must try to do, and at the same time you must retain your authority.

There is nothing, I believe, that boys or girls so resent as injustice, or what they think is injustice. Severity, merited, they can understand. They will respect you if you insist upon observance of rules. They may like you if you do not, but they will not *respect* you, and upon respect is based your discipline. They will not resent, then, the infliction of penalties if *these are fair*. But they will be indignant at injustice to themselves, and worse, to their classmates. Remember that you are dealing with pupils who have worked and played so long together that they are like a large family. And, running true to form, injustice to one is injustice to all. Any teacher can cope with *one* insubordinate; no teacher can contend with a roomful. Be fair, courteous, and firm, then, in your classroom proceedings.

Teachers often resort, in dealing with students, to sarcasm. I say to you that there exists no weaker weapon and none better calculated to anger an entire class than this. Do not have recourse to it; it is invariably unkind and often unjust — on a par with making personal remarks. If you have a tendency toward this rhetorical device, stifle it.

I spoke, a few moments ago, of rules. Now, regulations are usually necessary, but they should be as few as possible; for you must never make a rule that you cannot enforce. Otherwise, your discipline will become a farce in no time. Now, how are you, a high school teacher, going to compel obedience? Not by physical force, certainly. By sending the culprit to the principal? Only in extreme cases, after you have exhausted every means within your power. By sending the rule breaker to study hall? Have you the right to interrupt that august body by the introduction of an unruly member? By sending a student into the hall? The principal will soon object to that, especially if several are dismissed simultaneously. By "keeping students in"? Possibly, but that is childish and results, of course, in keeping yourself in. What is left? Well, not much. Private conferences in which you appeal to the student's sense of fair play; consultation with the principal when nothing else serves. I believe you will do better without *rules*, depending instead upon fair and courteous treatment. In any event, you should not begin with issuing mandates. Let the few you have develop because of a need — real, not fancied.

As I said, there are always problem students who will not respond to the treatment accorded others. These persons you will have to keep in class as long as the law, or their parents, or the principal insists. You will have to get along with the minimum amount of friction. Usually, the troublesome girl or boy is an exhibitionist. He likes to "show off." Very well, put him in a corner, on the back row. There he cannot reveal his cleverness except to you and his next-door neighbor. And you aren't interested, and his next-door neighbor, if properly chosen, isn't either. Much of the pleasure is thus taken out of the antics of the troublemaker. This placing of the problem student you can accomplish, often, by seating your class in alphabetical order. In beginning teaching, you should do this, for it will enable you to learn the names of your students promptly — an invaluable aid in discipline — and will make it possible to break up undesirable groups. Wait for a day or two to do this, for by that time, if you have observed carefully, certain students and groups will stand out to you. Break these up by seating arrangements. You don't have to place the *A*'s on the front row; perhaps one of them is much better on the back. Very well, begin there. If you think it out, you will see that there are several ways to seat a class alphabetically. Use the one that places the exhibitionist most advantageously — of course from your point of view. If this does not prove successful, try isolating him; that is, leave vacant chairs near him. But, because public and therefore humiliating, this method should be only a last resort. Unless you have the permission of your principal, you should never forbid a student to attend class. Remember that the law requires attendance and that the setting aside of that law is a problem of the administrator, not of the classroom teacher.

Probably the best method of obtaining order in the classroom consists in keeping students busy. You have heard that "Satan finds some mischief still for idle hands to do." He does; you will be convinced of that. And this leads me to a statement of the best advice that I received as a cadet teacher, and I pass it on to you, knowing, through my years of experience, its value. *Never go to class unprepared and always have in mind more than you can finish.* Provide yourself with a lesson plan, brief, possibly, but adequate. Using it as a guide, proceed systematically with your teaching. *Be certain that your plan is adequate.* Because of their tendency to do too much of the work themselves, beginning teachers often complete their work before the period is half over. Then come questions of discipline. So arrange your work daily, not only for the sake of efficiency in teaching, but also as a means of minimizing your problems of discipline, that rock upon which many a well-prepared student teacher goes down. There is nothing that makes one feel so helpless as to gaze into the eyes of thirty or forty youngsters who are, as a janitor I once knew expressed it, "rarin' to go," and to know that you have nothing planned to use up that surplus energy.

Classroom teaching usually offers few problems in comparison to study hall discipline. In your classroom you are dealing with a small group, who know you, and who have their own reasons for wishing to stand in well with you. In the study hall, you are dealing with a large group, perhaps two or three hundred, many of whom you have not had in class and whose names you do not know. Even here you should make few rules, but should apply the principles of courteous and fair treatment. But you will have to be more strict than you are in your classroom. You cannot, for example, permit talking, for it is far too disturbing. I found that a good substitute was to allow the students to write notes, delivered by me. It was surprising how little garrulous students have to write about! Instead of permitting one student to ask another for the assignment, I got that information myself and delivered it. Only one person at a time should leave the room; only one person should consult the dictionary. Don't lay aside your sense of humor in the study hall or in the classroom; a good laugh hurts nobody. Be particularly controlled on days of excitement, such as just before a game or a holiday. You will be interested and a little frightened to note how quickly students react to *your* moods. You need *say* nothing at all, but the pupils know immediately whether you are cross, or cheerful, or indifferent. And, good readers of human nature that they are, they will act accordingly.

Possibly the most serious breach of discipline that you have to handle is cheating. For your comfort, let me hasten to say that I think there is less cheating in high school than there is in college, but there will be some, and for the sake of the honest students you must try to prevent it. A good deal of cheating results from the indifference or carelessness of instructors. As I have suggested, you should use, whenever possible, *original* theme subjects, should handle book reports in class or conference. As examination questions that are largely factual provoke cheating, why not give pupils factual information and let them apply it? Inattention during examinations on the part of the instructor promotes cheating, for you cannot sit at your desk, marking papers, and expect your students, all of them, to do honest work. Seat your pupils apart; if possible, use mimeographed questions; stand at the back or the side of the room (*stand*, don't *sit*), and discourage questions. I find it a good policy in examinations to read the questions with my students before they begin writing and answer queries then. (If your examinations are carefully thought out and clearly worded there will be few questions from the students.) If someone has a comment during the writing of the test, I ask the student to raise his hand. I then go to him quietly, he puts his question in a whisper, and I reply to him in the same way. These precautions will reduce, although probably not prevent, cheating in tests. A teacher is not a policeman and should not be unduly suspicious; on the other hand, fairness to the honest student demands oversight on the part of the teacher. You must, moreover, be convinced that a pupil has cheated before you accuse him of it. No matter how suspicious you may be, say nothing until you have proof. If you give a person enough rope, he will hang himself, you know, and you must not run the risk of treating a pupil unfairly.

Now, if you do detect a person cheating, what are you going to do about it? Your school may have rules pertaining to this and by these rules you must abide. You cannot accept the work, of course; it must be done over for you. What credit you give depends somewhat upon circumstances. You should talk the matter over with the culprit and try to find out *why* he cheated. You may be able to help him acquire a more honest point of view or you may learn that you must share the responsibility because of some laxness on your part. You should take no extreme steps, such as failing the student in the course, without consulting your principal. And that leads me to say that in all important matters of discipline and classroom management, you should always know and respect the point of view of administrative officers. The principal is there to help you and the students. Consult him freely, but handle your own problems whenever possible.

This comment suggests a consideration of the matter of working with the administrative officers of your school. I am of the opinion that you owe them loyalty and co-operation as long as you are in the school system. If you cannot honestly give it (and sometimes this is impossible), you should try to say nothing and get another position as soon as possible. In any event, do not discuss your principal and superintendent in public. Outwardly, at least, there should be harmony. In judging administrators, too, keep in mind their problems, many of which you do not have. Remember that they act as a buffer between you and the patrons of the school, and that policies of theirs which you question may be best under the circumstances.

Members of the same school system owe a certain loyalty to one another also. It is unkind and usually inadvisable to discuss teachers with parents; it is inexcusable to discuss them with students. Be on friendly terms with your immediate associates. I recall a comment made by a pupil concerning the attitude of co-operation existing among the teachers in a school system of which I was a member. We knew that we got along well, but we had no idea that our students noticed it, until a senior girl told us of the inspiration it was to the members of the high school. We were not, all of us, on intimate terms; but we all tried to be helpful to and considerate of our colleagues.

Often there is an unfortunate gulf between grade and secondary school teachers. We all know that a college degree does not necessarily make a person a more valuable teacher than the one without such a degree. Any feeling of mental and social superiority is to be deplored. High school instructors need very much to understand the problems and methods of grade school teachers. At present, we teach in isolation: grade school, high school, and college instructors. Only in certain city systems does a more co-operative method exist. This is unfortunate for we need, especially in English, to make our teaching progressive. Try to know what is being done in teaching English in the grades and the teachers who are doing it. This effort will have to come from your side.

You must consider, also, the town in which you teach. Small communities are usually very closely in touch with the schools, and in principle this is desirable. Your attitude toward the place in which you teach should be one of friendliness and helpfulness. To that end, find out as much as possible concerning the community before you begin teaching. One excellent source is the census report, available in any library. From this you can learn the industries, educational and religious facilities of the community, and the racial and national background of the people with whom you will live and work. A subscription to a local paper will acquaint you with names and community interests — valuable assets to a newcomer. Enter into the social activities of the town; take part in whatever interests the community; accept gratefully any invitations from parents that you receive; and try to be a pleasing guest. Teachers often complain that they have too little social life in the town in which they are teaching; and to this I agree. But often instructors themselves are to blame. The teacher who spends all his week ends out of town is hardly a force in his community; the one who accepts invitations ungraciously, or whose conversation centers about his pupils and his problems in the classroom, will probably receive few invitations. Often, too, teachers of the present suffer for the sins of those of the past. Try, then, without being presumptuous, to enter into the life of the community as fully as your time permits. You and the school patrons should remember, however, that teaching is a full-time job and comes first in your interests. But you can do much to make a place for yourself in the town life if you so desire.

One of the duties that you owe to school patrons is to be willing to discuss with parents the work and attitude of their children. All teachers must do a certain amount of this, although a good principal often acts as adviser himself. In dealing with parents, remember that to each his own child is of tremendous importance. You may be blamed for the failure of the student. If so, meet the attack with courtesy and prove your position by reference to your class book. More than one parent has been convinced by a glance at a carefully kept record book. Do not resent this interest on the part of the parent; it is only natural and should receive a sympathetic response.

I have said the patrons in a small community take a great interest in their teachers. You may think that this concern is often too deep and too personal. With this I fully agree; but I believe that we teachers must remember that we are employees of the state, of the people. We should try, therefore, to adjust our mode of living to the standards set by the community, and if we do not like those restrictions, we should leave as soon as another position opens. The parents of your students are going to be concerned with your dress. I once knew a teacher who said that she always selected clothes she thought would be approved by the parents of her students. Perhaps you think that too severe a standard; at any rate, the informal clothing worn by many college men and women is usually out of place for wear by instructors. People who meet the public day after day should dress tastefully, neatly, and conservatively. Perhaps you can think back upon your own high school days and remember the impression made upon you by the clothes of your instructors. I have in mind a teacher who, at the close of a review, said, "Now, is there anything else you want to know?" "Yes," replied a student; "show us how you tie your tie." Pupils *do* notice and they *do* imitate. Give them models of good taste.

Another matter that the public is going to be concerned with is your amusements. I hope that you do not teach in a town in which the school patrons object to your dancing or playing cards, but if you do, there is nothing for it except to bow to public opinion for the length of time that you remain in that district. You may be surprised that such "blue laws" still exist, but I assure you that they do. The public will be critical also of your friends. Young women teachers are often tempted to accept attentions from high school boys. It is true that these pupils are often as old as the teacher and that they may be more entertaining than some of the eligible young men of the town (if such there be). I have not, however, known such relationships to bring anything but trouble to the teacher — usually dismissal or failure to be re-elected. Men teachers may go with high school girls with less danger, but even for them it is by no means advisable.

And do you smoke? If so, I trust that smoking is not such a habit that you cannot set it aside, for even today there are some small or medium-sized communities in which women who smoke would be severely criticized, with the probable result of failure to be re-elected. Men may smoke with more freedom than women, but there are still communities in which men teachers should not smoke. Many communities would also criticize teachers who drink intoxicating liquors in public. You may not think of yourself as an example to your boys and girls; you may consider that your whole duty consists in con-scientious teaching; but a community almost invariably places upon you far more responsibility than arises from your classroom duties.

You should, then, give heed to your appearance, your demeanor in public, your choice of amusements, your friends, and your habits, trying to judge them as they will appear to the community in which you teach. After all, these people are your employers. I hope that their sense of values is true; but if it is not, there is nothing for you to do except to conform or resign. Teachers who are human beings, not machines, who enjoy all sorts of healthful pleasures, are usually the best leaders, for they bring to their teaching the breadth of experience and zest for living that make teaching a joy. At present, however, standards of what constitutes normal, healthful pleasures are so different that the wise beginning teacher moves slowly upon entering a new community.

I know, as you have read these pages, that you have thought that a great deal is demanded of you. And right you are. Because teaching is so exhausting, you must plan your work efficiently and keep well in mind and body. Otherwise you will become a drudge or will break down entirely. From time to time I have noted ways by which you can conserve your strength. Let me now make some further suggestions.

One of your exhausting tasks is the marking of papers, particularly test papers. The objective type of test affords little strain in marking, but, as I have pointed out, in your teaching you will usually prefer the essay type. Even this sort may be made comparatively easy by making the questions definite; that is, by asking the class to discuss them under a certain number of heads. If you will see that each question has a numerical value in round numbers you will save time and energy. For example, three questions with a value of $33\frac{1}{3}$ per cent each, subdivided into five parts each, becomes a problem in mathematics. You can just as easily have four questions with five points each or five questions with five points and avoid adding in fractions. I find that I do this clerical work more quickly if I deduct from each question the number of points necessary, add my minuses, and subtract the total from one hundred, than I do if I give positive credit for each question. In other words, it is easier for me to add −2, − 3, − 7, − 5, subtract from one hundred for the final mark, than it is to add 18, 17, 13, and 15 to arrive at the total. But you may be better at simple arithmetic than I. Students, I believe, are better satisfied with the marking I suggest than they are with the other, for by this means they can determine exactly what each error cost. The final mark you should place on the outside of the paper for ease in recording.

All records should be kept neatly and accurately, and at all times a student should be at liberty to know his standing. You should have an adequate number of marks for each class member. It is not convincing to a pupil or to his parents for him to receive a *D* based on two or three marks. You should have, then, a number of grades; but work out for yourself an easy system of marking. Some instructors prefer to use *ten* and not *one hundred* as the basis for class quizzes, computing and recording figures under ten. You might use figures for classwork and tests, letters for themes, letters encircled or written in a different medium for notebooks and reports, a check for work not handed in, and a question mark for work handed in but returned, for some reason, uncorrected. Then a glance will show you the record of the pupil in each phase of the work.

You may doubt that the public has a right to dictate to you how you are to occupy your free time; but no one will question the privilege of the public to demand teachers with good health and rested nerves. Now, with the burden of work that you will carry, this becomes somewhat of a problem. Regular hours, an adequate amount of sleep each night, sufficient exercise and diversion you must have. If you find yourself tired and nervous, forget your work for a week end — papers always keep — and go away to the mountains or to the nearest city. Put your responsibilities completely behind you. You will come back with a different outlook and find that you can do your work more quickly rested than tired, or that some of the work you thought essential actually is not and can be thrown aside. Keep yourself fit; it is your duty. We teachers give of ourselves freely. Daily we meet and control several hundred persons. In itself, this is exhausting; we have to replace each night the energy that we have burned up during the day. To be conscientious is good; to be ultraconscientious is bad, both for yourself and for your pupils.

Much of this stimulation, this renewing of old wine, must occur during the summer vacation. As a progressive teacher, a "growing soul," you will realize, I know, that graduation from college actually marks the beginning, not the end, of your education. During some summers you will want to travel, freeing yourself completely from responsibility, steeping yourself in new experiences, and coming back, as a wise superintendent under whom I once taught used to remark, "a better teacher in the fall." Again, you will plan to attend a summer session, perhaps at the Bread Loaf School of English in Vermont or the Banners Elk School of English in North Carolina, where in beautiful mountain surroundings you refresh yourself physically and mentally. Or you may enroll at one of the great universities, such as Chicago, or Columbia, or California, where city experiences augment those of the classroom. Wherever you go, plan to take such courses as will carry you as far as possible from the daily round of the school year and will give you a new outlook upon human activities. Perhaps courses in international relations, in various phases of sociology, in philosophy will best supplement a too restricted undergraduate education.

In your classroom, do everything with the minimum of labor. Have a desk calendar; let it remind you of the special duties for each day. A timepiece of some sort is essential. Use carbon paper for your absence reports and stick your copy on a spindle for ready reference. Have your files in order and easily accessible. To get papers out of your way, return them as soon as they are marked. Have a certain drawer for marked papers; another for those yet to be graded. There are many ways to save your time and energy; a little planning will give you, in the course of the year, several hours of time.

During World War II, many colleges turned their efforts to instructing soldiers. Much has been written regarding lessons to be learned from this concentrated type of teaching — lessons that can and should be applied to the activities of the peacetime classroom. As I look back upon my own brief experience in teaching soldiers and as I consider the experience of others, it seems to me that the army program offers the classroom teacher of any subject several specific suggestions. First, both pupil and teacher must recognize the *need* — the importance — of every classroom activity. Second, fewer aspects of a subject should be presented, but these should be taught thoroughly. Third, both teacher and students should have a businesslike attitude toward class activities. Fourth, each week's work should be carefully planned in advance. Fifth, more conscious emphasis should be placed upon the old basic teaching methods of demonstration, application, practice, and supervision. Finally, the plans for each subject should be carefully integrated with those in other fields. This demands frequent meetings of the entire faculty, as well as consultation among members in subject matter fields.

As you recognize, none of this is actually new. But the speed and effectiveness with which soldiers were trained — you note I do not say *educated* — has served to focus the attention of the public upon the techniques employed. Therefore you should be conversant with the strong points of the program.

As a teacher, you have certain professional duties. I hope that you have been told, in some of your courses in the principles of education, of the accomplishments of the various educational organizations in our country. That our schools and the expenditures for the schools are being challenged is known. What is being done to protect the school children and teachers is not so well recognized. In my opinion, it is the duty of every teacher — in the grades, secondary schools, and colleges — to belong to the bodies that are working for the betterment of the schools *as a whole*. I have known teachers to refuse to belong to organizations because, they say, none has benefited them as individuals. That statement, in addition to being false, is an evidence of selfishness and shortsightedness. None of us is any stronger, actually, than is our profession, as these last few years have demonstrated. I suggest, then, that you join the following groups. First, be a member of the National Education Association. This organization works for the whole profession. Next, belong to your state education association. This body makes a study of local conditions and endeavors to better them. Next, as a teacher of English, you should be a member of the National Council of Teachers of English. Membership in this includes a subscription to *The English Journal* or *The Elementary English Review*, the official organs of teachers of English, which no classroom English instructor should be without. Membership in the Council also permits purchase of professional monographs and pamphlets at a reduced price. There are many other professional groups to which teachers may belong, but they are all secondary to these three. If you investigate the work of these organizations, I believe you will agree with me that to support them is an essential.

If you are reading these words shortly before graduation from college, your mind is filled, I know, with thoughts of the future — a realization of your responsibilities, a hope that you can rise to them, a dread of making a wrong initial decision. What each of you, as an individual, should plan for your future, of course I cannot say; but two choices you have, either leading to a satisfying, but different, future. Some of you — the majority — will obtain positions in small high schools, will stay there a year or two for the sake of the experience gained, will go on to other, larger schools, finally settling down as a member of a community in which you are liked and respected. Others will enter large city systems as cadet teachers, will work for several years under careful supervision, finally, if progress is satisfactory, being placed on the regular teaching staff, with permanent tenure and systematic salary increases. Which way do you prefer? Study yourself, your background, interests, capabilities, and choose your way advisedly. But you must remember that, if your path leads cityward, your choice must be made now, for as a rule, only young, inexperienced teachers are selected for cadet service in large school systems. Both plans have defects and compensations; your choice must rest upon your knowledge of yourself.

My final word to you is to ask you to remember that you are a member of a profession, one of the greatest and oldest in the world. But it has fallen upon evil days. Teachers in large numbers have left the profession, and fewer and fewer high school and college students are preparing to enter it. Why? Teaching can be a most satisfying experience; but until we go into it seriously, with the intention of remaining in it permanently; until we understand and support its policies; until we are proud to be known as teachers, it will not regain its former position of power. Perhaps the first and last of your many duties is to work for the betterment of the students and the teachers of our land.

ASSIGNMENT

A. Make a plan for your first meeting with a class in composition.

B. Do the same for a class in literature.

FURTHER READINGS

1. CROSS, E. A., "Painless Education," *Atlantic Monthly*, CLVI (December, 1935), pp. 740–746.

In this a former dean of a teachers' college analyzes both the teacher and his "job."

2. "Leadership," *The English Journal*, XXIV (September, 1935), pp. 587–588.

This unsigned editorial contrasts the teacher who drives with one who leads.

3. *An Experience Curriculum in English*, "Teacher Education in English," pp. 312–323.

Perhaps you think it a little late to read recommendations for teaching training, yet summer sessions lie before you in which you can supplement your preparation. In this connection you will want to read these pages.

4. "Shall I Become a Teacher?" *Journal of the National Education Association*, XXV (January, 1936), pp. 5–6.

This is a leaflet to serve as a guide to those contemplating entrance into the teaching profession.

5. TOWNSEND, M. ERNEST, "Supplying Teachers for Young America," *Journal of the National Education Association*, XXV (May, 1936), pp. 143–144.

Suggested by the foregoing, the article stresses the importance of careful selection of those preparing to teach.

6. WOODRING, MAXIE NAVE, JEWETT, IDA A., and BENSON, RACHEL T., *Enriched Teaching of English in the Junior and Senior High School*, "Travel," pp. 332–336.

This affords references leading toward both "real and vicarious" travel experiences.

7. BAKER, FRANK E., "Discipline," *Progressive Education*, XXI (February, 1944), pp. 57–60; 98–99.

Here you will find a common-sense discussion of the modern attitude toward discipline.

8. "Letter to a Seventeen-Year-Old Son," *Harper's Magazine*, CXCI (August, 1945), pp. 167–174.

If you ever doubt the value of your profession, read this letter.

9. KLAPPER, PAUL, "Teacher Education — A Forward Look," *Bulletin* of the American Association of University Professors, XXXI (Spring, 1945), pp. 36–41.

Teachers of tomorrow will constitute a group of public servants, with broad training and acute social conscience.

APPENDICES

A. CORRELATING ENGLISH WITH OTHER SUBJECTS

As a help in correlating English with other subjects of the curriculum, the following suggestions by teachers in the fields noted are included. The teachers in your own high school will no doubt offer you many more ideas such as these.

MUSIC

1. Provide your class with several magazines devoted to music. Let each pupil select a musician — composer, performer, or conductor. Throughout the semester, each student should peruse his magazines and report to the class any item he may find concerning his subject.
2. Term papers written for the music instructor may be marked (for expression) by you.
3. Assign current events pertaining to music or musicians.
4. By means of the phonograph or the radio, become acquainted with the musical settings of poems.

FOREIGN LANGUAGES

1. Make translations from a foreign language.
2. The class may select a country, and, in a series of oral or written reports, give a picture of its customs, traditions, and history.

3. Compare France's Bastille Day with our Fourth of July.
4. Study the school system of a foreign country (such as England or France).
5. Courtship and marriage customs of another land are always interesting.

INTERNATIONAL AFFAIRS

1. Interested pupils may analyze means by which they, as individuals, may help to keep their country out of war. Direct their thinking toward such matters as selection of legislators and Congressmen, an intelligent knowledge of public affairs, and freedom from prejudice. Although only advanced pupils can comprehend the significance of international affairs, surely this effort to determine one's personal responsibility toward world affairs is preferable to writing a theme on "How to Keep the United States Out of War," which even experts cannot determine.

2. For eleventh- or twelfth-grade pupils an interesting assignment is a comparative analysis of the characters and policies of national leaders. The sources, whether magazines or books, should be criticized in respect to their authority and impartiality.

3. Write or give a talk on one of the following subjects:

> Expand the following statement made by Felix Frankfurter, Justice of the Supreme Court of the United States: "Democracy is not a safe harbor; it is a perilous journey."
> Why should we help to feed Europe and China?
> Shall our school adopt or help to adopt a devastated school in a war-torn country? See "Practical Education in Sharing," by J. W. Mace in *New York State Education*, XXXI (June, 1944), pp. 653–655.
> What can our schools do to promote better understanding among Americans of different nationalities, races, and religions?
> Get acquainted with the Springfield Plan for overcom-

ing prejudices. See *The Story of the Springfield Plan*, by Clarence L. Chatto and Alice L. Halligan, Barnes and Noble, Inc., 1945, and *The Springfield Plan: A Photographic Record*, by James Waterman Wise and Alexander Alland, Viking Press, 1945. How can the Springfield Plan be adapted to our school or community?

What can be done in our school to make us better acquainted with other countries and people?

What social and religious prejudices are there in your family and community? What causes them? How can they be overcome?

What evidences do you find in your community of the American traditions of tolerance, equality, opportunity for all people?

What can American boys and girls do for the thousands of war orphans in Europe and Asia?

The Social Studies

1. Investigate the types of social insurance in your state.
2. Determine the type of insurance policy desirable for a sixteen-year-old boy.
3. Describe, orally or in writing, a visit to a nursery school.
4. What can Parent-Teachers Associations accomplish for parents, teachers, pupils, and community?
5. Study the work of the Red Cross in your community.
6. Discuss the position of women in colonial society, with special reference to their independence and legal rights.
7. Write or give a talk on one of the following subjects:

"Gentlemen of the jury, what is your verdict?"
Buying a wagon for the Oregon Trail
The roads we now use: Who made them? When? How have they been changed?
Adobe houses, sod huts, and log cabins
Tomorrow's centers of travel; landing fields of today
The oldest buildings I know — and the newest
Campfires, kettles, and stoves — a lesson in the history of cooking
Dams and ditches: Power and irrigation in (Washington, Oregon, Tennessee)

A western "Promised Land" — Salt Lake City as a "New Jerusalem"

History in newspapers: the United States and the front page of yesterday's ——

Report orally on issues of *Building America* (published at 425 West 123 Street, New York)

The French Huguenots in America

The Wilderness Trail

An underlying cause of the French Revolution

Two outstanding historical events of the year

Historical allusions in Lincoln's "Gettysburg Address"

The American pioneer (colonial period, Revolutionary period, early nineteenth century, later nineteenth century, on the Atlantic seaboard, in the Southwest, or in the Northwest)

Why I should like to know (Theodore Roosevelt, Mahatma Gandhi, or Franklin D. Roosevelt) personally

A personality in the White House (Mrs. Franklin D. Roosevelt, Woodrow Wilson, or "Ike" Hoover)

Games of (the Chippewas, Nez Percés, or Navajos)

How our Constitution came to be

What patriotism means to me

What my country means to me

MATHEMATICS

1. Select from your mathematics text five words, such as *triangle, denomination, digit, equation, tangent, power, formula, ratio, velocity, circle, parallelogram, cylinder,* and explain them. Illustrate your point.
2. Explain to the class a problem or theorem.
3. Explain the English, French, German, Swiss, Greek, or Egyptian coinage system and illustrate if possible.
4. Write or give a talk on one of the following subjects:

> Why I should like to know (Galileo, Euclid, or Pythagoras)
>
> The contributions of (Napier, Descartes, or Newton)
>
> "Shooting the sun"
>
> Tricks with figures: How to find your victim's age; the magic clock
>
> Possibilities for a mathematician

How to forecast the weather
What a housewife should know about mathematics
What (or how much) arithmetic do I use daily?
The story of numerals
My study of mathematics has helped me to think
How a sundial tells time

BIOLOGICAL SCIENCE

1. A study of General Gorgas's fight against yellow fever will afford interesting oral or written reports.
2. Several pupils may report on sections of De Kruif's *Microbe Hunters* or *Men in White*.
3. The story of the development of vaccination against smallpox is an absorbing study.

PHYSICAL AND NATURAL SCIENCES

1. Expand the definition of a thermometer found in a physics text — "A thermometer is an instrument for recording temperatures" — into a long composition, using the following plan from *Writing Craftsmanship*, revised edition, compiled by Maurice Garland Fulton.

    I.   What the thermometer is. (Perhaps the starting point may be the sentence definition.)
    II.   Short description — bulb, stem, etc.
    III.   One of the uses of the thermometer — the determination of the freezing point. (Description of the experiment.)
    IV.   The determination of the boiling point. (Description of the experiment.)
    V.   The system adopted for the Fahrenheit and Centigrade thermometers. (Comparison of the two.)
    VI.   The uses of thermometers.

2. Tell the story of rubber.
3. Describe the manufacture of glass.
4. Investigate new types of glass and their uses.
5. Explain how to make a barometer.
6. Give the story of the Curies.
7. Investigate trust control of the manufacture of plastics.

8. Give an account of a field trip.
9. Make a report of demonstration experiments, the report to include observations and conclusions.

MANUAL ARTS

1. Boys, particularly, may like to gather information concerning the various kinds of lumber used, habitat of trees, characteristics of trees, appearance of wood, physical qualities, common uses.
2. Investigate a source of material and treatment in making varnish.
3. Study the source of material for making shellac.
4. Report on kinds of glue and their uses.
5. The history of various period furniture will interest both boys and girls.
6. The evolution of a hammer, a saw, or a file may be developed either by exposition or narration.
7. Tell how to repair a broken insulation plug, to replace the heating elements in an electric iron, or to renew the carbon plugs in an electric motor.

HOME ECONOMICS

1. Name some laborsaving devices of the modern home and discuss (in oral or written form) their influence on the social life of the home.
2. Pupils may review *Grandmother Brown's Hundred Years*, by Harriet Connor Brown; *A Son of the Middle Border* or *A Daughter of the Middle Border*, both by Hamlin Garland.
3. Describe a "sod house."
4. Investigate and report on the financial plans available for persons who want to own their own homes.
5. Let a pupil interview an insurance representative and report on fire, theft, and automobile insurance rates in his own town.
6. An investigation of the air-conditioning systems on the market will be of considerable interest.

B. ACTIVITIES

Some of the following projects — for example, those on debate and journalism — will help you in planning units of work; others, such as those of the Byrd expedition, are included to illustrate how a happening of current interest may be adapted to classroom activities. Be on the alert to add to your store of suggestions; for your own sake, as well as that of your pupils, you want to guard against falling into a rut and being unable or unwilling to climb out.

DEBATE PROJECT OF SIX WEEKS FOR AN ENGLISH III CLASS

(From the School of Education *Record* of the University of North Dakota, Grand Forks, XVI [Feb., 1931], No. 5, pp. 141–154. This project, prepared by Miss Mayme Bach, was a part of the regular work of the Special Methods and Practice Teaching Course under the direction of Miss Mary J. Laycock of the University High School and the School of Education of the University of North Dakota. Craig's *Speech Arts* was the chief source of information.)

GENERAL OUTLINE

First week: A study of parliamentary law
Second week: Organization of an Open Forum
Third week: A study of argumentation and debate
Fourth week: A general survey of the debate
Fifth week: Brief making and the study of delivery
Sixth week: Debates proper

FIRST WEEK: STUDY OF PARLIAMENTARY LAW

First Day

Discuss the meaning of parliamentary law. Call upon several students to give their prepared definitions of parliamentary law. Have an informal discussion of these, and let the students select the best for copying in their class notebooks.

Show the value of parliamentary law. Call upon various

students for examples of organizations where such law is necessary: class meetings, clubs, legislatures, and Congress.

Discuss the practical advantage of a knowledge of parliamentary law. "The chain is as strong as the weakest link." Thus parliamentary law enables the most timid and the least resourceful to have a voice in a meeting. It also develops initiative and assurance. "The chief function of parliamentary law is to make possible the orderly conduct of an organization's business."

Second Day

Discussion of steps in parliamentary practice (Appendix E):

I. Method of obtaining the floor: The president or chairman is addressed as "Madam" or "Mister." Only one member is recognized on the floor at a time. If several demand recognition, the chairman gives the privilege to the one who rises first.

II. Introduction of business
    A. The form of a motion
    B. The difference between a suggestion and a motion

III. Voting
    A. Kinds: viva voce, raising of hands or standing, general consent ("The minutes stand approved —"), ballot, and roll call (for the recording of the vote)
    B. Majority versus the two-thirds vote — under what circumstances each is used

IV. Chairman and speaker courtesies
    A. The impersonal manner of conducting a meeting: the chairman is always referred to as "the chair."
    B. Speakers rise to address the chair and to make their motions.
    C. No more than one motion can be under consideration at one time, that is, main motions.

V. Main motions
    A. Definition: A main motion is one that brings before the meeting any particular subject for discussion and consideration.

B. Steps of a motion:
1. Presentation — "I move that —"
2. Seconding — a motion is lost for want of a second
3. Statement of the question by the chairman
4. Putting the question to a vote
5. Announcement of the result — whether the motion is carried or lost

VI. Amendments
A. Principal motions can be amended in the following way: "I move that the motion be amended by —"
1. Striking out certain words
2. Inserting certain words
3. Striking out and inserting other words
4. Adding certain words

For practice, this second day, let the teacher take the chair and begin a meeting in the middle of its business, to provide the proper motivation. She can stimulate the class activity by saying, "The question before the house is: All students having a grade above ninety in any subject shall be exempt from final examinations in it." The discussion and the business that follows must be according to what has been discussed previously. In a short while the teacher may appoint another chairman, so that she can observe the proceedings and later make suggestions. By rising to points of order, she can make suggestions at the time a mistake is made.

Third Day
Discussions of kinds of motions.

I. Main motions

II. Subsidiary motions (those that are applied to other questions for the purpose of modifying or disposing of them)
A. Lay on the table (set aside for more important business)
B. Limit or extend discussion
C. Postpone to a certain time
D. Refer to a committee
E. Amend
F. Postpone indefinitely

III. Incidental motions
    A. Point of order
    B. Appeal from the decision of the chair
    C. Suspension of rules
    D. Request for information
    E. Permission to withdraw a motion

IV. Privileged motions
    A. Time of adjournment
    B. Recess
    C. Orders of the day
    D. Question of privilege (to have a window opened, etc.)

As these points are discussed, a student may be outlining them on the board, and the rest of the class taking down the outline in the class notebooks.

Practice should follow, as before. The teacher must be ready with a number of suggestions or devices to stimulate pupil activity — remarking to herself that the room is too warm, professing ignorance, or violating rules.

Fourth Day

Discuss precedence of motions. Although there can be only one main motion before the meeting at one time, there are other motions that either pertain to it or to the welfare of the organization, and can, therefore, take precedence or supersede the original motion.

An illustration of precedence in traffic regulation will be good: train, streetcar, automobile, motorcycle, and pedestrian.

Make out a table with the class illustrating the order of precedence of motions.

Fifth Day

Oral drill and written review of the week's work. The pupils can be required to reproduce the chart which was made on the previous day.

First Day

Preliminary steps: Let the students report upon the duties and privileges of the following officers: president, vice-president, secretary, treasurer, and sergeant-at-arms. The teacher must be prepared to add suitable, or remove unsuitable, material.

The duties and privileges of the officers should be copied in the students' notebooks.

The order of business should be discussed next: call to order, roll call, reading of the minutes, reports, unfinished business, and new business. The purpose and forms of resolutions should be discussed next, and several examples given.

Second Day

Organization proper: The nature of an Open Forum should be explained, and a chairman elected by the class. A set of by-laws can then be formulated. The question must be brought before the meeting by moving the orders of the day. The by-laws should include:

I. Three minutes is the time limit for each speaker.

II. Every member must speak before any one member will be allowed to speak twice.

III. Each speaker must be recognized by the chair.

IV. The Open Forum may be adjourned by a motion from the floor, or if no time remains, by a declaration from the chair.

After the final discussion of each of the above, the decision of the members can be taken by voting on the question in the form of a resolution.

As a member of the Open Forum, the teacher may move that a certain prepared list of timely and suitable subjects be adopted for the next three days' discussions. This motion may be amended to include any student suggestions.

Third, Fourth, and Fifth Days

Open Forum discussion of the selected subject for the day. Each member is expected to take part in the discussion. He may choose his own time and occasion to volunteer, and should be well informed on some definite point for or against the subject. Remarks are to be extemporaneous.

THIRD AND FOURTH WEEKS: A STUDY OF ARGUMENTATION AND DEBATE

First Day

Let the students bring to class definitions of argumentation and debate. The difference between them should be clearly understood. Following this discussion, the best definitions should be copied by the students in their notebooks.

Discuss the two methods of reasoning: inductive and deductive. Put on the board examples of the wrong and right methods for each division. This will be an excellent place to teach the form of deductive reasoning — the major and minor premises, and the conclusion.

Have a discussion of the three methods of argumentation: generalization, analogy, and causal relation. Under the latter there are three subdivisions: (1) cause to effect, (2) effect to cause, and (3) effect to effect.

All methods of argumentation involve inductive and deductive reasoning, and they should be explained simply for practical use in argumentation and debate.

Second Day

Have the students bring original examples of all the kinds of argument and reasoning studied the previous day. Most of the period should be devoted to discussing these examples in form and logic and to reviewing the kinds of arguments and reasoning.

Read portions from the great historical debates, such as Lincoln and Douglas's Dred Scott debate, Sherman and George's Anti-Trust Law debate, and the Webster and Hayne debates. The students and the teacher can point out various examples of reasoning and argumentation from these.

Third Day

Oral argumentation by the students. In these talks they must use the various forms of reasoning and argumentation that have been discussed before.

Fourth Day

A general survey of debate: Debate as a science and an art should be discussed informally. Quote Jevons, "A science teaches us to know, and an art teaches us to do." Debating is a science because it deals with systematic knowledge; it is also an art because it involves the application of this knowledge.

From the definitions of the following terms brought to class, have the best selected and copied in the students' notebooks: *proof, evidence, burden of proof, fallacies,* and *brief.* Show that there are two kinds of evidence — direct and indirect — and that direct evidence is usually the more valuable, since it is usually based on some kind of authority. Read to the class the story of how Lincoln freed an innocent man by his use of the almanac. In a discussion of refutation, explain its two forms: (1) *reductio ad absurdum* and (2) dilemma.

Fifth Day

Have the students bring to class examples of evidence, burden of proof, the various kinds of fallacies, and the various kinds of refutation. Many of these can be found in such debates as are mentioned for the second day's work and in other debates such as: "Neutrality of the Isthmian Canal" by Douglas and Clayton, and "Ship Subsidies" by Hanna and Clay. If these debates are not available, let the students make up their own examples.

Show the relation of evidence, burdens of proof, fallacies, and refutation to reasoning and argumentation.

Sixth Day

Theory of briefing: Explain that the brief is the plan of the argument, not only an outline of the speech, but — if properly made — the debate itself in condensed form.

Illustrate the construction of a brief by putting on the board and outlining a specimen form. It should have three parts: the introduction, the body, and the conclusion. The introduction should include a definition of terms, a statement of the question (in the light of these terms), and the determination of issues. In the proof, or body, explain that each issue must be proved by advancing three types of reasons: evidence, authority, and example. The conclusion is a statement of why the question is true or not true, and includes a summary of the issues proved.

In formulating the several issues, the following terms can be suggested as definite aids to organization: *beneficial, desirable, justifiable, necessary, practical, successful where tried,* or the negatives of these adjectives, as the case may warrant. There should be but three or four main issues in the proof, and these should be arranged in a logical and climactic order. All statements should be complete.

Every point that is made should bear a definite relation not only to every other point in the chain of the argument and to the proposition as a whole, but it should also bear a definite relation to the opposing side of the argument.

Seventh Day

Each student will previously have selected one specific phase of a general question which has been selected by the class for a composite debate. (This question should be one on which source material is abundant, to permit extended debate.) During the class period, "let each student present his division of the debate definitely and wholeheartedly as if he were taking part in a regular, formal debate." His choice is his own:

1. Introduction
2. A point proved by inductive reasoning
3. A point proved by deductive reasoning
4. A point proved by example
5. A point proved by analogy
6. A point proved by cause
7. The issue that —— is justifiable
8. The issue that —— is desirable
9. The issue that —— is beneficial
10. The issue that —— is practical
11. The issue that —— is unjustifiable
12. The issue that —— is undesirable
13. The issue that —— is detrimental
14. The issue that —— is impractical
15. A rebuttal for the affirmative
16. A rebuttal for the negative
17. The conclusion or summary of the debate for the affirmative
18. The conclusion or summary of the debate for the negative

Eighth Day

Choosing the question: The matter of the question for debate is an important one. Choice should be left to the students, but their choice should be wisely guided. It should be explained that a question must have two features: (1) it must be debatable, and (2) it must be interesting. Give to the class the following points by which to judge and select a question for debate:

1. The proposition should involve one central idea.
2. It should have two sides that involve a clash of opinion.
3. It should be neither too broad nor too narrow in scope.
4. It should be of present-day, vital interest.
5. It should still be unsettled.
6. It should be one that depends upon facts for its proof rather than upon opinions.

With the foregoing rules in mind, let the class discuss and criticize the questions of debatable subjects which the members of the class have brought. These debatable subjects should pertain to each of the following (two from each class): school affairs, city affairs, state affairs, and national affairs. All questions that cannot meet the requirements will be discarded.

Ninth Day

The final choice of questions and speakers: This class period should be conducted as an Open Forum under the regulations previously formulated. The purpose of the forum is to select questions for debate from those that survived the test at the last recitation. Each student is to come prepared with several good arguments to support *one or two* proposed questions. He should also have an idea of where he may secure reliable data further to uphold his side. If during a meeting a conclusion is reached as to the best solution of the problems (all the members agreeing to the truth of the question by vote), the question is dropped. If not, it is put in the form of a resolution for debate. Several of these questions should be of a sufficiently controversial nature to become debatable, so that no one group needs to have a resolution similar to that of another group.

The students themselves should volunteer as to which side they will uphold, since no one should debate against his convictions. However, the final selection may be made by the teacher, if he is careful to discriminate between those who show interest in the affirmative and negative sides.

Tenth Day

Preliminary work in the method of preparing for debates: Emphasis should be placed on the fact that preparation of one of the opposing sides of a debate requires much intensive study and demands great accuracy.

Let the student suggest possible sources of information, and then amplify this information they have.

During this period, a definite system of gathering and keeping debate material can be worked out. The value of a bibliography should be emphasized, and at this point a review of library science could be brought in. The use and knowledge of cross reference is especially valuable in debate work.

Prepare the way for eliminating useless and irrelevant quotations by pointing out that quotations are of service in debate only when they are the words of persons "whose opinions and statements are granted to be unimpeachable, because of their direct association with the subject under consideration."

Initiate the practice of writing notes on filing cards of uniform size. A separate card for each fact should be used. The card should contain the topic, the information of the subtopic, and, at the bottom, the sources of information. Put on the board an illustration of a card as it should be blocked out.

FIFTH WEEK: BRIEF MAKING AND THE STUDY OF DELIVERY

This week should be devoted to making the briefs for the coming formal debates, and the study of the delivery of a speech. The class should take on as socialized an aspect as possible, the groups of students making up the affirmative and negative sides of a debate working together. A greater part of the information should be gathered before the making of the briefs is attempted, and it would be very desirable if the class could meet in the city or school library at the beginning of the week for at least one recitation. On other days the material, which has been found during after-school hours, could be organized and incorporated into the brief. The teacher should always be at the service of any group desiring his assistance and advice.

The last day of this week could be used for the study of debate delivery. With the class, work out a set of standards by which the debates ought to be judged. These should include logic and weight of the arguments presented, correctness and appropriateness of the English used, and the manner of delivery — voice, directness, sincerity, and posture.

If notes are to be used they should be on small cards. Extra notes to be used if the opponent brings up certain issues should be readily accessible.

As much as possible, create an atmosphere of friendly rivalry between the various squads of debaters. In this way, the students can be induced to work more wholeheartedly and the classroom atmosphere can be dispelled.

SIXTH WEEK: ACTUAL DEBATES

All the debates should be conducted in a smooth and orderly fashion. More interest will be aroused if a chairman can be another member of the faculty. After the meeting is called to order, the chairman must announce the question to be debated, the names of the speakers and their respective sides, and the length of time for each speech and rebuttal.

There should be one debate a period, and the members of the class who are not debating may act as judges. Another plan for selecting the judges may also be used: the affirmative chooses a judge from the class, and the negative chooses one. These two judges then select a third.

Typewritten sheets of instruction may be given to the judges. On the blank lines for the speakers of each side, the judges are to write (or vote) *affirmative* or *negative*. Either of the two following judgment scales may be used: Argument, 60 or 70 per cent; delivery, 20 per cent; English used, 20 or 10 per cent.

LESSONS ON JOURNALISM FOR NORTH DAKOTA HIGH SCHOOLS

(By Lawrence W. Murphy, *English Syllabus for North Dakota High Schools*, 1928.)

A. THE COURSE

1. A study of the newspaper. History of journalism. Some of the great journalists. What some of the men of literature have contributed toward journalism. What the

newspaper contains. Comparison of make-up. Criticism of the American newspaper in comparison with the foreign newspaper. (*Time:* 1 week.)

2. Ethics in newspaper work. Canons of journalism. Some high school codes. Attitude of leading dailies. What high school press associations have done. Forming a code for the high school paper. (*Time:* 3 days.)

3. News values and sources. What constitutes news? Where may we find news? Essentials of a news story. What gives news value? Press associations. Sources of school news. How to check a story for news value. (*Time:* 3 days.)

4. Requisites for news reporting. A "nose for news." The cub reporter. Qualifications of a reporter. (*Time:* 1 day.)

5. Steps in news gathering. News "runs," in dailies and for school paper. "Future" book. The expected and the unexpected news. Getting the assignment. Reading the paper for news. Organization of the run. Securing an appointment for the interview. Covering the beat. (*Time:* 2 days.)

6. Interviews. Requirements for making the interview. Use of notebook. Questioning in the interview. Recognition of news values. Types of persons to be interviewed. Libel. Scoops. Making interviews. (*Time:* 4 days.)

7. Organization of notes or news materials. Purpose in organization. Types of news stories. Picking the feature. Orders of organization. Application to organization of notes previously secured. (*Time:* 2 days.)

8. Writing the story — the lead. Story told three times. Three parts of a story. Order of writing them. Types of leads. Lead arrangements. Tone in the lead. Length of sentence and paragraph. The feature. Grammatical constructions employed in beginning the lead. Practice in writing leads of different types and with different constructions, and different emphasis and tone. (*Time:* 1 week.)

9. Writing the story — the body. Purpose of the body. Review of essentials of journalistic style. Order of arrangement. Editorializing as a fault in high school journalism. What "play" to give the story. Interest at beginning of each paragraph. Clearness, coherence, and unity in composition. How to close the story. The "cutoff" test. Actual practice in writing the body, and combining it with the lead. (*Time:* 1 week.)

10. Writing the story — the head. The head schedule. Mechanical problems involved in head writing. Purpose of the headline. Heads as index of character. Kinds of heads. Style in headlines. Rules to be observed in head writing. Common faults of heads in high school papers. Actual practice in writing heads for schedule adopted by the school or local paper. (*Time:* 1 week.)

11. Athletic and sport stories. Qualifications of the sport story writer. Use of sport slang. Types of sport stories. The sport story lead. The body. The conclusion. Football, basketball, track, tennis, baseball, and other athletic stories of local interest. Sport page features. Athletic stories should be taken up as they come into season. The time will need to be divided. (*Time:* 2 weeks in all.)

12. Journalistic styles. The style book. Word usage. The sentence in journalistic writing. The paragraph. These practice drills should be scattered throughout the course. Regular weekly drills might be used advantageously. (*Time:* 1 week in all.)

13. Feature stories. Place of features in school paper. Human interest stories. Signed articles. Personality sketch. Subjects for stories. Sources of materials. Style of composition used. The lead, body, and conclusion. Heads for feature stories. (*Time:* 1 week.)

14. Special types of news copy. Reports of meetings. Speech stories. Advance or advertising stories. Followups. Re-writes. What to feature in these types of stories.

Style of composition used. Actual writing of each sort. (*Time:* 1½ weeks.)

15. Editorial writing. Style of the editorial. Classes of editorials. Choosing subjects. Editorial essentials. Beginning, developing, and closing the editorial. Literary editorial. Paragraphs. (*Time:* 1 week.)

16. Publishing a high school newspaper. The policy of the paper. The editorial staff. The business staff. Duties of staff members. The name. The style sheet. Financing the project. (*Time:* 1 week.)

17. Getting acquainted with newspaper terms. Become familiar with terms used in the print shop. See the newspaper in actual process of composition and preparation for the press and when run. Make necessary shop terms a part of the student's vocabulary. (*Time:* 2 days plus drill.)

18. High school newspaper make-up. Study the different sizes and column make-up of typical high school newspapers. Determine upon a definite make-up for the local project. What should the front page contain? Material for the editorial page. Departmentalizing of news such as sports, organizations, etc. (*Time:* 3 days.)

19. Newspaper advertising. What constitutes a good advertisement for the high school paper. Laying out the ad. Placing the ads in the paper. Use of space. Use of illustrations in advertising. The appeal of the advertisement. Actual ad-writing practice. (*Time:* 1 week.)

20. Copyreading and proofreading. Actual practice in copyreading should be done by each student as copy is turned in for the paper. Rules for copy should be adopted and required of all work. Learn the significant marks for proofreading and those employed by your printer. Practice in proofreading comes when copy has been returned as galley proof by the composer. (*Time:* 1 week in all.)

21. Criticism. As the students become acquainted with good journalistic practice, criticism of the high school paper

and of the weeklies and dailies should be done constantly to acquaint the student with practical newspaper style and to enable him to recognize poor newspaper work.

B. AN ORAL ENGLISH PROJECT

Twelve lessons for high school journalism:

1. A study of the newspaper. What the newspaper contains. How it is of help to us. Important things in yesterday's edition. (*Two-minute talks.*)

2. What a reporter does. Funny mistakes that reporters have made. Serious mistakes that reporters have made. (*Three-minute talks.*)

3. The editor and his paper. The duty of an editor. Big things that editors have done. (*Three-minute talks.*)

4. Literature and journalism. Place of Addison, Steele, Defoe, Poe, Thackeray, Bryant, Dickens, Twain, in literature; their place in journalism. Conclusion: Literary ability is one quality of value to a journalist but it does not determine his value to journalism. (*Five-minute talks — different writers assigned to different students.*)

5–6. What a journalist should know. Analysis of the pages and stories of a daily newspaper to see what the journalist deals with, e.g., politics, science, government, death, marriage, society, athletics, school, church, music, drama, etc. Analysis of pages of a daily to see how he deals with such things as reporting, editing, proofreading, editorial writing, feature writing, advertising, financing the publication, etc. Analysis of the pages of a daily to see the relation of importance, interest, and reliability to the material used. (*Three-minute talks.*)

7. The life of a great journalist. Greeley, Bennett, Dana, Watterson, Nelson, Raymond, Bowles, White, Northcliffe, Bok, Lawson, Stone, Ochs, Pulitzer; also journalists who won distinction as public men: Franklin, Clemenceau, Harding. (*Five-minute talks.*)

8. A good magazine. What the magazine contains and why it is worth while. (*Two-minute talks.*)

9. Staging a news story. Class divided into two parts, each part having rehearsed a simple news scene in secret, and each scene to take about four minutes and to contain something unexpected. The half which is not taking part should take notes as the scene progresses and then try to write a news story based on what happened. This gives an opportunity for observation of the chance for inaccuracy and the need for accuracy. Suggested scenes to include necessary action and conversation: (1) A "wedding" scene interrupted by robbers. This furnishes chance for confusion which will be shown in student stories. (2) A scene showing the "coach" of the football team giving a talk to the "team" interrupted by two of the boys talking and making a disturbance. The boys are reprimanded by the real teacher and one of them talks back, etc. Order is restored and the class asked to write the story instead of the talk that had been "spoiled." If each move of this faked disturbance has been carefully rehearsed, the accounts, distorted under the unusual emotional strain, will be easily checked. It will be found, for example, that "screams rent the air" when only one girl screamed once; that the offending boys were accused of making noises and of saying things that were not said; and that the teacher glared when she was very careful not to glare, etc. Pupils should hand in papers and not take them home.

These exercises should be accompanied by having the necessary names written on the blackboard. Students will make mistakes in copying them or will try to write the story without mentioning them. They should be checked for Kipling's six honest servingmen — who, what, when, where, why, and how — and such other points as may have been indicated — writing for an afternoon paper, for example.

10. The stories should be handed back and read aloud in class to give the class a chance to see the inaccuracies. A correct version, prepared by the teacher — not necessarily in news form — should be presented and a short talk given on the need for absolute accuracy.

11. A final exercise might be the organization of the class as a newspaper staff and the preparation of all material for a paper, the paper to be made up on the blackboard. Class organization might be perfected at the close of one hour and the reporter's assignments and editorials, etc., brought to the next meeting of the class at which time the copy would be corrected and the dummy made.

12. A desirable exercise would be publication of an issue of the student newspaper, the class to take it over for one issue. In this case the teacher should act as supervisor and check all copy after it has passed through the hands of student editors. The supervisor need not make changes but may pass imperfect copy and proof back to the editor to be changed.

Sources of information:

1. The newspaper.

2. The newspaper, parents, teachers, reporters, printers, etc. Books on journalism.

3. Books on journalism, teachers, parents, newspapers, magazines.

4. Books on literature, encyclopedias, biographies.

5–6. The newspaper. Measure length with rulers and classify. Study process by which information gets from source to reader. Test stories for importance, interest, and reliability of news sources referred to.

7. Books on journalism.

8. Library and current issues in the homes and stores.

9. Scenes to be written by teachers: to include two or three pages of speeches and directions. All must be staged as for a psychological test.

10. Correct version to be prepared by teacher, each inaccuracy to be checked and classified to determine what errors were most frequent, etc. Checking can be done at the blackboard.

11. List of news sources and suggested assignments to be made by class and compiled by the teacher. Teacher to make assignments after class has discussed sources for each story — regular source — real stories.

12. Regular sources — real stories.
Books, periodicals, and representative newspapers.

AUTOBIOGRAPHICAL UNIT FOR HIGH SCHOOL FRESHMEN

(From Pullman, Washington, High School)

DIRECTIONS TO STUDENTS

Theme subjects for the term will be so assigned that together they will compose an autobiography. From two pieces of cardboard or a large sheet of heavy manila paper you will make the covers for your book, with a title and suitable decorations. Illustrate the chapters of your autobiography with kodak pictures, picture post cards, or illustrations clipped from magazines. Make a title page and a table of contents. Each theme will be a chapter. The following subjects are suggested, but you will attempt to secure more attractive titles:

CHAPTER I

An incident (before my birth) from the history of my family

An interesting ancestor of mine

A happening (before my birth) which tested the character of my mother or father

How my family came, many years ago, to this state, country, or community

CHAPTER II

My first toy

My earliest recollection

My first punishment

A bright saying or performance of my infancy

CHAPTER III
My first day in school
How I learned to read
My first spelling lesson

CHAPTER IV
My brother
My sister
Being one of a large family
Being an only child

CHAPTER V
Our home
A picturesque scene we visited

CHAPTER VI
My chum
My hobby
My pet aversion

CHAPTER VII
My first night away from home
My first night away from my family
My narrow escape

CHAPTER VIII
The kind of book I like to read
My favorite form of recreation
My favorite holiday
My pet superstition

CHAPTER IX
My favorite study and why
The kind of boy (or girl) I admire
My opinion of girls' smoking
My opinion of politics

CHAPTER X
My future vocation and why I chose it
Why I want an education

CHAPTER XI
My habit that I tried to break
My habit that I tried to form

CHAPTER XII
A practical joke in which I participated
The meanest act I ever did

CHAPTER XIII
The first money I ever earned
My first appearance on the stage

CHAPTER XIV
The most exciting moment of my life

CHAPTER XV
How I help with the work at home
My most difficult study and why
How I study

CHAPTER XVI
My next summer — What shall I do with it?

CHAPTER XVII
What I think of term examinations
What I think of high school football

CHAPTER XVIII
My worst fault
My chief virtue
The thing I am proudest of

CHAPTER XIX
The pet I like best

CHAPTER XX
My club
My gang
What I am making of life

Study of Periodicals

(Activity of Spokane, Washington, high schools)

Name of student...

Name of magazine...

1. Publisher................ Editor...................
2. Where published?....... How often published?........
   Price........
3. Subjects covered. Answer by underlining words in following list.

Current events	Travel	Household matters	Editorials
Stories	History	Science	....
Poems	Biography	Arts	....
Essays	Social reform	Literary subjects	....
Humor	Education	Book reviews	....

4. Name two important articles and their authors.

   ....
   ....

5. Name any special departments or sections.

   ....

6. Illustrations?........ Many?........ Kind?........
7. Are the articles of literary excellence?.................
8. In what school subjects would this magazine be useful?

   ....

9. Is it more valuable as a reference book or for pleasure reading?

   ....

10. What proportion of the magazine is devoted to advertisements, and what is the character of those advertisements?

    ....

11. Underline the groups to which this magazine makes a special appeal.

    Men   Boys   Average reader
    Women   Girls   Students

12. Which article or feature most interested you?

An Activity on the Byrd Expedition

(A report by Alice M. Worley on an activity conducted in one of the Spokane, Washington, high schools)

An interesting activity I observed in Spokane was one on the Byrd expedition. This was undertaken by a class of juniors.

Miss Catton, the teacher, first made a very thorough study of the expedition and listened to the Byrd broadcasts each Saturday night, at the same time having her students listen to these broadcasts and collect all the newspaper and periodical material they could find which was relevant to the expedition. When she and the pupils had completed this study, and Admiral Byrd's expedition had become an interesting topic of conversation for the students, Miss Catton made a list of topics bearing not only upon the actual expedition but also upon weather conditions in Antarctica: geography, previous explorations, means of transportation, food supplies — in fact anything to make the study more interesting.

The students then selected from the list of topics the ones which appealed to them most and each began a search for material on his own particular subject. The interest of the students was evidenced by the search for material in all the libraries, public and private, scanning of periodicals, etc. Many of the pupils became conscious for the first time that the *Readers' Guide* could actually be of great service when correctly and carefully used. They learned also that much valuable material has to be dug out in small bits rather than handed to them on a silver platter. Every Monday the report of the radio program from Antarctica on Saturday night was given.

Finally, when each had apparently selected all the facts possible, every student prepared an oral report on his topic. These reports were organized and delivered as an oral theme, and sometimes illustrated by drawings on the blackboard.

When the oral themes were all delivered and commented upon, each student gave a written report based upon the oral. Stress, but not too much, was placed on the mechanics of composition. The result was in many cases a work of art, since the illustrative drawings were even more elaborately carried out on paper.

The final step in the project came in the compiling of a bibliography, which, at present, is not complete, but which, according to Miss Bacon, the librarian, is one of the most worth-while she has seen. The material has been carefully classified under four heads and so made usable.

This activity has successfully combined interest in current affairs with a practical knowledge of using the *Readers' Guide*, and writing and giving themes.

ACTIVITIES ON *THE LADY OF THE LAKE*

I. Make:
    1. Weapons
    2. Castles
        a. From soap
        b. From paper
        c. From wood
    3. The fiery cross
    4. Highland huts
    5. Ellen's lodge
II. Costumes:
    1. Draw costume plates
    2. Dress dolls
III. Make a cookbook of Scotch recipes
IV. Scotch music
    1. Piano
    2. Readings
    3. Group singing
    4. Scotch dances
V. Write in booklet a brief history of Scotland

Activity I should be accompanied by oral and written reports. The costumes report carries a similar requirement. Activity IV requires a written report. The history report is, of course, written.

SUGGESTED READING FOR ACTIVITIES

The activities listed here merely hint at the many available. On the whole, *The English Journal* and *The Elementary English Review* afford the most suggestions; but most recent high school texts offer useful material. Of course you must not fail to apply to projects as well as to other classroom activities the principles of choice which we have frequently discussed.

WATTS, MARJORIE S., "Intercultural English: An Experiment," *The English Journal*, XXXIV (February, 1945), pp. 81–87.

This article tells of a successful attempt by a class of juniors in the Senior High School, Bloomfield, New Jersey, to practice cultural and racial tolerance. It contains, too, some useful bibliographies.

McBRAYER, B. LEONE, and LINDSEY, ALETHEIA, "Cooperative Reports on Current Topics," *The English Journal*, XXXIII (October, 1944), pp. 421–424.

A plan for co-operation between the history and English departments at the Roseville, California, Joint Union High School, this paper presents in detail steps in the preparation and presentation, in oral and written form, of a formal "term paper."

RANOUS, CHARLES A., "A Sample Lesson in Reading," *The English Journal*, XXXIV (October, 1945), pp. 428–434.

How to help your students to recognize and follow "clues" in reading is the purpose of this article.

ARMSTRONG, DAVID T., "Dictionary Work," *The English Journal*, XXXIV (November, 1945), pp. 490–492.

Here you will find specific suggestions for a five-day unit designed to improve students' vocabulary.

GOLDBERG, MURRAY A., "Constructing a Short-Story Index," *The English Journal*, XXXIII (December, 1944), pp. 558–560.

The plan described here offers a suggestion for correlation of the activities of the English classroom with those of the library.

DUFFY, MARIE E., "A Unit in Reading and Thinking," *The English Journal*, XXXV (January, 1946), pp. 43–45.

Junior high school boys and girls planned and executed a program which culminated in an auditorium presentation.

BERGFELD, ANNABELLE WAGNER, "A Creative Writing Project," *The Elementary English Review*, XXIII (April, 1946), pp. 157–159, 177.

If you possess a burning desire to write, you will find here a plan for including your pupils in your hobby.

SIMONSON, EVELYN, "The School Assembly Program," *The Elementary English Review*, XXII (November, 1945), pp. 257–260.

This account of a composite type of assembly program as presented in the Madison, Wisconsin, public schools, although designed for young pupils, offers suggestions for pupils on the high school level.

CUDDINGTON, RUTH ABEE, "Assembly Programs," *The English Journal*, XXXIV (October, 1945), pp. 448–449.

If you are responsible for an assembly program, why not follow the plan given here and make the program a class project?

C. CONTRACT PLAN FOR LITERATURE

Below you will find a plan for a contract dealing with literature. The plan provides the pupil with four choices: *A* contract, in which he does a minimum amount of work; *B* contract, in which he does additional work; and *C* and *D* contracts, in which he does still more work. In contracts *B*, *C*, and *D* the work required is in addition to that of the lowest ranking contract; for example, students undertaking *B* contract would first prove their mastery of the story (the basis of the *A* contract) and would also write a paper on one of the topics suggested; those electing the *C* contract would first complete the requirements of *A* and *B*, then would add those of *C*; and pupils contracting for *D* would complete the requirements of the preceding agreements before assuming those of *D*. The final contract offers provision for creative writing.

A TALE OF TWO CITIES

A Contract   Mastery of the story (use objective type test)

B Contract   Theme on historical background of novel:
  Social conditions in England and France
  Famous buildings: the Bastille, La Force
  The Reign of Terror
  Leaders of the Revolution

C Contract   Report on one of Dickens's shorter pieces:
  A Christmas Carol
  Sketches from Boz
  American Notes
  The Cricket on the Hearth

D Contract   With three or four others, write part of a novelette

D. INTEGRATION OF THE "TOOLS OF EXPRESSION" WITH COMPOSITION

Because of the arrangement of many textbooks in which the "tools of expression" are separated from written and spoken activities, many teachers find it difficult to decide on what principles to teach, especially in the seventh, eighth, ninth, and tenth years. Accordingly, I have prepared a list of grammatical principles, arranged progressively, for use from the seventh through the tenth years, and centering about the sentence as a unit of expression. Punctuation should be taught in relation to the grammatical principles presented, and spelling should always be considered. At no time throughout these four years should grammar or any of the "tools" be presented in a separate unit. Instead, pupils should be encouraged to speak, read, and write; and their study of the tools should grow from and be considered with these activities. A few such activities are listed below, to suggest the basic class procedures from which should grow an understanding of the sentence, the paragraph, and the composition as a whole.

If your students have mastered the expression techniques planned for the seventh through the tenth grades, no special stress need be laid on these in the eleventh grade. Instead, plans should stress composition experiences, possibly with an emphasis on speech. The "tools of expression" should not, however, be neglected, but should be reviewed as the class needs indicate.

In the twelfth year — your last chance to aid your pupils — you will probably plan a review of the "tools." Contrary to the suggestions made for the preceding years, this review may be a unit in which concentrated attention is given to grammar, punctuation, and sentence forms. Following this, the class emphasis should be upon speech, reading, and writing activities in which application of the principles of grammar, sentence forms, spelling, punctuation, and word choice is expected. If you plan your teaching in some such way as this, your students will grasp the relation of these aspects to the transfer of thought from writer to reader, known as "composition."

Tools of Expression for the Seventh, Eighth and Ninth Grades

Seventh Grade

Grammar: Kinds of sentences (declarative, interrogative, exclamatory, imperative)

Simple subject; nouns and personal pronouns as subjects

Simple predicate: verbs, verb phrases

Recognition of prepositional phrases

Nouns and pronouns as predicate nominatives

Correct use of personal pronouns in the above constructions

Singular and plural forms of nouns and personal pronouns

Recognition and simple uses of adjectives and adverbs

Possessive forms of nouns and pronouns

Words of direct address

Eighth Grade

Grammar: Nouns and pronouns as direct objects

Use of prepositional phrases (adjective and adverbial modifiers)

Nouns and personal pronouns as indirect objects

Appositives

Agreement of subjects and verbs; of pronoun and antecedent

Ninth Grade

Grammar: Continuation of functional grammar; memorization of declensions, conjugations, and principal parts of verbs

Recognition and analysis of simple, compound, and complex sentences

Parenthetical expressions

Verbals

Parts of speech

Punctuation: To be taught in connection with the grammatical principles listed above, but from the angle of meaning

Spelling: To be taught directly and indirectly throughout these years

Activities: Writing of short papers, one to three paragraphs in length

Letter writing

Oral reading, including choral work

Oral composition, individual and group

Dictionary study

Library exploration

Book reviews, written and oral

Vocabulary study

Diagramming

Tools of Expression for the Tenth, Eleventh, and Twelfth Grades

Tenth Grade

Grammar: Study of the sentence

Recognition

Subjects and predicates

Complements

Modifiers

Phrases

Verbals

Clauses

Kinds of sentences

Sentence errors

Punctuation: Review as needed; continued emphasis upon meaning conveyed through punctuation

Spelling: To be considered as the problem of the individual student

Activities: Vocabulary growth

Dictionary study

Paragraph development

Short themes, oral and written

Letter writing: formal and informal notes, business letters, friendly letters

Eleventh Grade

This year may be given largely to oral composition if desired. If not, more oral work may be given in grade ten and part of the material on the sentence transferred to grade eleven. Unless needed, no special emphasis is placed on the "tools of expression."

Twelfth Grade

Grammar:
Review of fundamentals

Study of the sentence

Diagramming (the individual teacher must decide how much stress to put on this)

Activities:
Paragraph and theme writing

Vocabulary development

Letter writing

Outlining

Dictionary study

Library theme

Note taking

Oral composition of various types, including book reviews

Writing definitions

Instruction in writing examination questions

E. TWO CORRECTED THEMES

For your consideration, I have included two high school themes, one good, one bad, each marked according to the suggestions made in the chapter on *Theme Correction*. The second, "Moonlight Reverie," needs little additional comment; but the first, "Going to the Mts.," requires some explanation. Written by a poorly prepared freshman, this is the sort of paper I pray you may be delivered from. Yet almost certainly you must grapple with at least a few. You will notice that my corrections and comments deal mostly with mechanical errors, although much could be suggested concerning the plan of the theme. But until fundamental errors are eliminated, it is futile to make written comments about subject limitation and selection of incidents. You will note, too, that I have not marked all mechanical errors, merely those most flagrant. I assume class instruction in the recognition of verb and subject — nothing more.

> *Always use ink and write on one side only [Bob Backer] On back of the paper. Please follow form of sheet of endorsement given you.*

Write out.   *Going to the Mts.*

Verb in this sentence   *One day some boys and I planning to go to the [Mts.] We want to go to cold Hill. We took lots of food*

Only one?   *with us. We all had car so the transportation was nothing for us.*

?
Past time?   *Going there one of the car broke down and some run out of*
Subject of had?   *gasoline. Had one flat all the way up there.*

Don't you mean past time?   *We got as far as the car could go and then we [walk] for 2 or 3 mile* *Write out.*
sp.   *and carried our pack. The trouble we had one boy got his foot hurt* *was that*

503

and we had to help him along. We
got there all right by night.

Put a period after the first information you have given here.

We all had work to do in
fixing supper we got it done all right

Do the same here.

sp.

We had to fix our bed we had
bed all over. Fixing our bed was easy
but going to slept. that might we

Past time

all (wish) we were home in bed but
we got to slept someway.

sp.

Verb in this sentence?

Getting up the next day and
fixing breakfast and then going to and

sp.

old mine We found a gold nugget *Bring?*

Why the capital?

Going back to camp and Packing to
go home is not so much fun going
back to the car went just fine.
Fixing our pack in the car
went just fine.

Two sentences?

Write out.

Going home was not so good
a flat tire and run out of water we
got home all right *Does this give any particular information?*

Verb?

Getting over the trip and all
the blisters on our feet and we all

sp.

bruses all over our bodys.

Your first concern is to express your
ideas exactly. You have good material in
this, but you have made so many errors
that you greatly mar the effect. Work first
on sentences; remember that *every* sentence
must have a verb and that no word ending in *ing* is a verb unless it has a helping
verb with it. Make a list of your misspelled words. When you want to tell
of something in the past, use the past form
of the verb: walk, _walked_, walked.

margin

Should be on outside of paper.

Moonlight Reverie — by (Audrey Goods)

word corrections

Silvery moonlight shone in through the window and
reflected brilliantly on the polished floor. Shadowy, uncertain shapes filled the darker corners of the room.
The only sound was the roar and thunder of
the breakers.

There was something fairy-like and unreal in this summer midnight. Usually the breeze sang me to sleep,
but that night a vague restless feeling filled me.
Obeying an impulse, I arose from bed, slipped
on a robe and slippers, and crossed to the French doors.
I stepped out onto the wide terrace perched on the
edge of a rugged precipitous cliff — against which the
waves eternally beat and splash, battling to break
down this mighty barrier — untiring, unyielding, gradually succeeding as the centuries rush by and ledge after
ledge crumbles and falls into it, the greedy triumphant ocean.

Do something about this margin.

Before me stretched the sea, shimmering and sparkling, a silver pathway across it, beckoning enticingly.
At the end of it was the moon, a great white disk which
had never looked so near. Then, as never before, did
I want to take the fabled "trip to the moon." It
would be so easy to follow the pathway — in a fairy
boat — but alas, I would go on and on — my goal would
seem farther and farther away — would fade — and
finally dawn would come, and Lady Luna would not
return until the next night.

Do you like the effect of these dashes?

P. ~~While~~ in the midst of my reverie the gentle *dangling*
salt sea breeze softly caressed my cheeks, and I
felt a strange feeling of peace steal over me. I was
so glad to be alive on this wonderful magic night.

Suddenly I was sleepy, and yawning, I said
goodnight to the ocean, the moon, and the myriads
of stars shining in the dark blue heavens, arching above.
Turning, I left the solitary terrace, went inside to
my warm, cozy bed awaiting me, climbed in, and
pulled up the covers.

Necessary?

Crowded

The moonlight had faded and now shone faintly on
the wall beside my bed. Before I knew it I was in Dreamland and   P.
in a fairy ship bound for the moon for my adventure there — that's another story.

Upon reading a paper as good as this, your first thought will
probably be, "There's nothing for me to suggest!" But isn't
there? Consider the form of the paper: The writer's name
should appear on the back of the sheet only; the margin is
inadequate; the writing is crowded at the bottom of the page;
and the closely placed lines leave no space for your comments
and the pupil's corrections.

Excellent as the paper appears to be mechanically, it nevertheless contains two examples of the "feminine intensive" use of *so:* "so glad, so easy"; "while in the midst of my revery" does not refer logically to the subject "sea breeze"; "awaiting me" is redundant; "before I knew it" and "while in the midst of my revery" should be set off by commas. You might call attention to the effect made on the reader by the dashes in paragraph four.

All these points you could call to the attention of the writer by brief remarks on the paper itself and by the use of symbols, such as P for punctuation.

On the back of the paper you might write:

This is carefully planned; every idea pertains to the subject and one leads easily to another. Your sentence structure shows good variety — I was particularly pleased with the sentence beginning each paragraph. Some of your expressions, such as "greedy, triumphant ocean," are vivid. You have made me share the experience with you.

For your next paper write something more vigorous, an account of Saturday's game or your downfall last week in skiing. See whether you can make your reader enjoy this experience, too.

A busy teacher cannot be expected to write such an extended comment on all themes. I am merely indicating by this the aspects of writing to keep in mind in your marking — accurate and effective expression of ideas.

F. READING: SILENT AND ORAL

1. UNIT IN READING [1]

FOLLOWING DIRECTIONS

Class: Tenth-grade students of average ability.

Time: Three weeks.

Philosophy: Students fail to follow directions either (1) because they have no deep inner conviction that following them is really important (thus war workers disregard safety directions that they understand perfectly well) or (2) because they do not know exactly how to go about a businesslike and efficient execution of orders.

UNIT OUTLINE

I. Class discussion of what happens — the waste in human life, energy, and resources — when people fail to follow directions.

> *Purpose:* To make students aware of the fact that accurate adherence to directions is really important.
>
> Discuss numerous examples (first proposed by the teacher, later supplemented by students) drawn from newspapers and from personal experience — the train wreck caused by erroneously noted signals, the explosion caused by the woman who used gasoline in her washing-machine, etc.

II. Class discussion of two questions: (1) What causes these errors in following directions? (2) What can be done to prevent such errors?

> *Purpose:* To provide students with a working pattern to use in following directions.
>
> Answers to the first question finally boil down to "undue haste." For the second question the class work out a basic procedure pattern designed to prevent errors. The pattern is sevenfold:

---

[1] From "Lesson Plans in Reading" by Carol Hovious, *The English Journal*, XXXII (November, 1943), pp. 499–501.

1. Read directions through first, from beginning to end, trying to understand them as well as possible and to ascertain the goal (main idea).
2. Re-read to check meanings of all unfamiliar words.
3. Re-read to note every important detail, since in following directions even minor details may achieve major importance.
4. Re-read to be sure the goal is now clear (if it was not on first reading).
5. Re-read to visualize procedures, a sort of mental roughing-out, to detect any errors and correct them while they are still in a state to be easily corrected. Make tentative pencil sketches if necessary.
6. Act, but keep an eye on the written directions, re-reading them step by step. Do not trust to memory.
7. Check finished results to be sure they achieve the goal set in step 4. If they do not, recheck the entire procedure.

III. Preliminary supervised class experiment using the seven-point pattern.

Purpose: To provide supervised class practice in following directions according to the seven-point pattern (not too arduous at first) and to demonstrate concretely the fact that by their results shall you know those who have followed wisely and those who have not.

The teacher provides string, scissors, and written directions (suggested by Leeming's *Fun with String* [1]) for knotting or braiding with string; the class try, step by step, their seven-point plan.

IV. Application projects of various types.

Purpose: To provide a variety of situations (as nearly related to immediate student needs as possible) requiring directions to be followed. In each case, a student's efficiency is judged *by his results*, by his ability to translate words into concrete action.

During this period (1) all assignments are written on

[1] Joseph Leeming, *Fun with String: A Collection of String Games, Useful Braiding and Weaving, Knot Work and Magic with String and Rope.* Stokes, 1940. $2.00.

the board, to be followed without further oral amplification (a class check, daily at first, points out those who have followed directions, those who have not), and (2) the class hour is conducted according to written "Orders of the Day" received by the class when it convenes.

"Orders of the Day" includes directions for such projects as: (1) Instructions (to coincide with a grammar lesson) for playing a game called "Adverbs," in which a student elected as "It" leaves the classroom while the class choose an adverb, then returns to the room and asks various students to perform some action "in the manner of the adverb" until he can guess the right adverb. (2) Demonstration lessons in which a student reads aloud directions for doing something, chosen either from his hobbies or from his regular schoolwork (cutting out a dress according to pattern instructions, building a model airplane, charting the course of an airship, mounting specimens for botany) and at the same time carries out the directions, step by step, under class observation. (3) Questionnaire unit in which students fill out blank forms — post-office change-of-address cards and money order forms, applications for charge accounts at department stores and checking accounts at banks, questionnaires (school registration blanks, college application forms, war-factory applications, etc.). (4) "Etiquette" unit in which each student writes a question to which he would like the answer (How do you introduce two boys? What do you say when you acknowledge an introduction?). Questions are distributed by lot, each student writing the answer to the question he has drawn. In class, students act out impromptu scenes in which action is determined by written directions. (Girl introduces two boys, following directions on her slip, and the boys acknowledge the introduction according to their written instructions.) (5) A luncheon, for which a committee issues all directions in written form (advance directions on what to bring, where to leave contributions; directions issued at time of luncheon on setting tables, placing food, etc.; directions during luncheon on refilling plates, making impromptu speeches, etc.)

2. Developing Eye Span

As an aid to pupils desiring to improve their reading ability, most authorities suggest "eye stretching" exercises. These follow four steps: broken lines to train the eye to take in a span longer than a single word; single words; short phrases; longer phrases. These you can set up for yourself by following the directions given below. Place each exercise on a sheet of regulation-size paper ($8\frac{1}{2}'' \times 11''$). See that the length of each line is from $4\frac{1}{2}$ to 5 inches, the usual length of a line in "easy reading" material. In the exercises containing phrases, use material easily understood, as your students should not be puzzled over vocabulary when they are working to increase their eye span. If you compose your own examples, make them as interesting and clever as possible.

EXERCISE ONE

On a sheet of paper, arrange 17 broken lines, about $\frac{1}{2}$ inch apart. Put the symbol x at the beginning and at the end of each group. The eye of the pupil should jump from x to x. When the pupil first begins to use this exercise, he may like to move his finger along the lines to guide his eye and to direct it from the end of one line to the beginning of the other. See to it that he does not *point* to the symbols.

x ---------------------- x   x ---------------------- x

x ---------------------- x   x ---------------------- x

EXERCISE TWO

Arrange this sheet similarly, but eliminate the x's and substitute an easy word for the x at the end of each broken line. In this exercise, the pupil not only "stretches" his eye span to take in at a glance a line approximately two inches in length, but he also reads a word as he does this.

---------------------- driver   ---------------------- whip

---------------------- horse   ---------------------- pulled

EXERCISE THREE

In this, you eliminate all lines and substitute phrases.
These should not be isolated phrases, but easy sentences
broken up into phrases. The lines may now be somewhat
longer, about 5 inches.

> In the nest   were 600 pounds   of honey.
> This honey   was made   by ants,
> not by bees.   In Mexico   the Indians eat
> this honey.   It tastes   like bee honey.

EXERCISE FOUR

Continue to follow the plan of Exercise Three, but make the
phrases slightly longer. Prepare several of these exercises.

Bob looked   down the long cabin aisle   of the airplane.
Along one side   ran a row of seats,   upholstered in blue.
By each seat   was a small window   shaded by curtains.

3. ADOLESCENT LITERATURE BOOK LADDER

As a teacher concerned with the development of your pupils,
you will wish to encourage more and better reading. You
must, however, begin where your pupils are, for criticizing
the reading preferences of your students defeats your purpose.
But you can encourage the reading of worth-while material
by leading the pupil to higher levels. One method for ac-
complishing this consists in preparing a "Book Ladder,"
similar to the one given below. To prepare this, examine the
books in the school library, grouping them according to
themes, such as "Adventure," "Animals," "Mystery," and
so forth. Under the heading "Step One," place the titles of
least distinction; under "Step Two," those of more value;

"Step Three," those of greater distinction; and "Step Four," very desirable books. When you note a student reading a book on one level, suggest for his next reading one from a higher level. In this way, you can lead him gently and unobtrusively toward greener fields. If your "Book Ladder" is arranged on cards, you can add or remove titles easily.

With some groups of seniors, preparation of this "book ladder" would be an interesting and helpful activity.

ADVENTURE STORIES

Step One

Alger, Horatio, *Ben, the Luggage Boy*
Appleton, Victor, *Tom Swift Series*
Burroughs, Edgar Rice, *Tarzan Series*
Curwood, James Oliver, *Kazan*
Grey, Zane, *Riders of the Purple Sage*
Hope, Laura Lee, *Bobbsey Twins Series*
Porter, Gene Stratton, *Freckles*, etc.
Rockwood, Roy, *Bomba, Jungle Boy Series*
Wright, Harold Bell, *The Winning of Barbara Worth*

Step Two

Adams, Julia Davis, *Mountains Are Free*
Baker, John, *Shasta of the Wolves*
Buchan, John, *Prester John*
Clemens, Samuel L., *Tom Sawyer*
Duncan, Norman, *Adventures of Billy Topsail*
Fox, John, *Little Shepherd of Kingdom Come*
London, Jack, *The Call of the Wild*
Pyle, Howard, *Otto of the Silver Hand*

Step Three

Bennett, John, *Master Skylark*
Bill, Alfred Hoyt, *Clutch of the Corsican*
Churchill, Winston, *The Crisis*

Clemens, Samuel L., *The Prince and the Pauper*
Cooper, James Fenimore, *The Deerslayer*
Crane, Stephen, *Red Badge of Courage*
Dana, Richard Henry, *Two Years before the Mast*
Davis, William Stearns, *Beauty of the Purple*

Step Four

Blackmore, Richard, *Lorna Doone*
Bojer, Johan, *The Emigrants*
Boyd, James, *Drums*
Conrad, Joseph, *Lord Jim*
Dickens, Charles, *A Tale of Two Cities*
Dumas, Alexandre, *The Three Musketeers*
Hugo, Victor, *Toilers of the Sea*

4. PLAN FOR CHORAL SPEAKING [1]

Not every person can recite poetry well all by himself, but many people enjoy taking part in a "speaking concert," when a whole group recites poetry in choral fashion. In choral speaking, voices that are naturally high and soprano in pitch form one group and those that are low and deep form another. An in-between group may also be formed for three-part reading. Poems for choral reading are often marked

> (1) high, light voices
> (2) in-between voices
> (3) low, deep voices

To which group does your voice belong?

PREPARING FOR CHORAL SPEAKING

To prepare for choral speaking follow these steps:

1. Read the poem silently. Discuss its meaning in class. Have several pupils read the poem aloud so that all may have a better understanding of its meaning.

[1] From *You and Your English*, by Roy Ivan Johnson, A. Laura McGregor, and Agnella Gunn; Ginn and Company, pp. 342–343.

2. Study the pronunciation of any difficult words until you can say them easily.

3. Read the poem aloud, the whole class reading in concert. Do this as many times as necessary to feel the rhythm and swing.

4. Divide into two or three voice groups according to the needs of the poem. Decide which parts of the poem are to be read by each group. In doing this, think whether the high, light voices or the deep, low voices are more suited to the stanzas. In-between voices are able to carry all other parts. Occasionally, it is effective to have all the groups join in reading a line or stanza.

5. Each voice group should practice its part before the full choral reading is given.

6. When choral speaking is to be part of an entertainment, the poem should be memorized by all.

PRESENTING POEMS THROUGH CHORAL SPEAKING

1. Use the following poem for your first attempt at choral reading in your classroom. Numbers at the left show what voice group is reading.

A Boy's Song

(2)   Where the pools are bright and deep,
      Where the grey trout lies asleep,
      Up the river and over the lea,
(All)   That's the way for Billy and me.

(1)   Where the blackbird sings the latest,
      Where the hawthorne blooms the sweetest,
      Where the nestlings chirp and flee,
(All)   That's the way for Billy and me.

(3)   Where the mowers mow the cleanest,
      Where the hay lies thick and greenest,
      There to track the homeward bee,
(All)   That's the way for Billy and me.

(1)   Where the hazel bank is steepest,
(2)   Where the shadow falls the deepest,
(3)   Where the clustering nuts fall free,
(All) That's the way for Billy and me.[1]

5. BIBLIOGRAPHIES

REMEDIAL READING

Elson-Gray Basic Readers, pre-reading, pre-primer, primer, and six grade levels, Scott, Foresman and Company.

HILDRETH, GERTRUDE, and OTHERS, *Today and Tomorrow*, 4th grade level, The John C. Winston Company.

——, *Looking Forward*, 5th grade level, The John C. Winston Company.

HOVIOUS, CAROL, and SHEARER, ELGA M., *Wings for Reading*, 6th grade level, D. C. Heath and Company.

HORN, ERNEST, and OTHERS, *More Adventures*, 4th grade level, Ginn and Company.

——, *Following New Trails*, 5th grade level, Ginn and Company.

——, *Reaching Our Goals*, 6th grade level, Ginn and Company.

SPENCER, PAUL R., and HORST, HELEN W., *Finding New Trails*, 4th grade level, Lyons and Carnahan, 1943.

——, and FRITSCHLER, LOIS DUFFIE, *Exploring New Trails*, 5th grade level, Lyons and Carnahan, 1943.

——, *Traveling New Trails*, 6th grade level, Lyons and Carnahan, 1943.

STOVALL, EVELYN, *You and Your Reading*, 6th grade level, Ginn and Company, 1940.

WALPOLE, ELLEN WALES, *You Can Read Better*, 6th grade level, Silver Burdett and Company, 1945.

DEVELOPMENTAL READING

BESSEY, MABEL A., and COFFIN, ISABELLE P., *Active Reading*, D. Appleton-Century Company, 1941.

---

[1] *A Boy's Song* by James Hogg (1770–1835). This well-known poem can be found in numerous anthologies for the younger student.

BISHOP, MERRILL, and OTHERS, *They Also Serve*, Steck Company, Austin, Texas, 1938.

HOVIOUS, CAROL, *Flying the Printways*, D. C. Heath and Company, 1936.

——, *Following Printed Trails*, D. C. Heath and Company, 1936.

JORDAN, RACHEL, and OTHERS, adapters, *Lorna Doone*, Scott, Foresman and Company, 1936.

KNOLLE, DOROTHY N., *Adventures in Reading*, 3 books, John C. Winston Company, 1945.

MODEROW, GERTRUDE, and OTHERS, adapters, *Six Great Stories*, Scott, Foresman and Company, 1937.

NORVELL, GEORGE W., and HOVIOUS, CAROL, *Conquest Series*, 3 books, D. C. Heath and Company, 1946.

POOLEY, ROBERT C., and OTHERS, *Growth in Reading Series*, 3 books, junior high school level, Scott, Foresman, and Company, 1939.

ROBERTS, HOLLAND D., and OTHERS, *Let's Read*, 4 books, Henry Holt and Company, 1937–1941.

ROBBINS, ZILA, and MEDARY, MARJORIE, *All in the Day's Work*, D. Appleton-Century Company, 1944.

WITTY, PAUL, and OTHERS, *Reading for Interest Series*, Books IV–VI, D. C. Heath and Company, 1942.

READING TESTS

GATES, ARTHUR I., "Gates Reading Survey for Grades 3 (second half) to 10," Bureau of Publications, Teachers College, Columbia University, 1942.

"Iowa Silent Reading Tests," World Book Company, Yonkers, New York.

MONROE, MARION, and SHERMAN, EVA EDITH, "Group Diagnostic Reading and Achievement Tests," Houghton Mifflin Company, Boston, Massachusetts.

"Nelson-Denny Reading Tests for Colleges and Senior High Schools (Self Marking)," Houghton Mifflin Company.

For further lists of tests consult Bond and Bond, *Developmental Reading in High Schools;* Hovious, *Suggestions for Teachers of Reading*, and other texts on reading.

GENERAL BIBLIOGRAPHY

An Experience Curriculum in English, Part III, Chapters VI, VII, VIII.

BOND, GUY, and BOND, EVA, *Developmental Reading in High School*, The Macmillan Company, 1941.

CENTER, STELLA S., and PERSONS, GLADYS L., *Teaching High School Students to Read*, D. Appleton-Century Company, 1937.

COLE, LUELLA, *The Improvement of Reading*, Rinehart and Company, Inc., 1938.

GRAY, WILLIAM S., *Recent Trends in Reading*, University of Chicago Press, 1939.

HOVIOUS, CAROL, *Suggestions for Teachers of Reading, Grades VII to XII*, D. C. Heath and Company, 1939.

"Reading Instruction in Secondary Schools," a Research Bulletin of the National Education Association, 1942.

STRANG, RUTH MAY, *Problems in the Improvement of Reading in High School and College*, Science Press, 1940.

The Teaching of Reading: A Second Report (36th Yearbook of the National Society for the Study of Education), Public School Publishing Company, 1937.

WRENN, C. GILBERT, and COLE, LUELLA, *How to Read Rapidly and Well*, Stanford University Press, 1937.

Yearbooks of the Claremont Colleges Reading Conferences, issued annually by Claremont Colleges and Alpha Iota Chapter of Pi Lambda Theta.

G. PRODUCING AN ANNUAL

To the inexperienced adviser, the problems presented by the production of an annual seem almost insurmountable. This chart, prepared by a former high school pupil of mine — a systematic, businesslike boy — indicates the time divisions necessary in preparing a printed annual.

CALENDAR

December 1		Conduct first Annual drive.
December 25		Let contracts for printing and engraving.
January 1	(a)	Begin soliciting for advertisements. Plan to have all advertisements contracted for by the first of April.
	(b)	Begin collecting insertion fees. Have all insertion fees collected before the senior panels are sent in to be engraved.
January 25		Conduct second Annual drive.
February 15	(a)	Send *all* cuts in to be engraved not later than this date. Send all of the cuts to the engraver at once so that he can do the work uniformly.
	(b)	Select and send for covers. (Through the printer.)
April 1		Complete the dummy of advertising and turn over to the printer. Also give the printer the editor's dummy.
April 10		Send out bills for advertising.
April 10 to May 20		Collect for advertising — keep in touch with the printer so that if he needs anything you can supply it.
May 10 to 20		Collect remaining amount due on Annual subscriptions.
May 20		Distribute Annuals. *Do not give out the Annuals later than May 25.*
May 20 to 30		Finish collecting money for advertising. Pay printing and engraving bills — all other bills.
May 30		Turn books over to junior business manager.

Instructions

1. **Keeping Books** Be sure to keep books correctly. Balance the books once a month. Whenever money is received or paid make a note of it in the book. *Do not rely on your memory.*

2. **The Editor** Keep in constant touch with the editor to see that copy will be ready on time for the printer and engraver. Be sure to have both dummies ready on April 1.

3. **Letter File** Keep in a file a duplicate of every letter written. It is important to keep a copy of the letter in which you give instructions or pay a bill.

4. **Engravers** When cuts are sent out, keep a copy of the instructions. Make instructions clear. If there is enough money, pay the engraving bill before the 15th of the month after the date of invoice. You then receive the additional 3% discount. Ask for receipted bill of all money paid.

5. **Management** *Cut down overhead.* Before going into a deal, consult the principal or superintendent.

Important

1. Send all cuts to be engraved by February 15.
2. Have all advertisements contracted for by April 1. Have dummy completed also.
3. Turn advertisement dummy and editor's dummy over to printer not later than April 1.
4. Be sure to keep in touch with the editor and hurry her editorial work along.

H. PARLIAMENTARY PROCEDURE FOR BEGINNERS

If you cannot give your pupils a book on parliamentary law, the following guide from Brewer's *Oral English* will serve.

TABLE B

Not Debatable and Not Amendable	⎰ Adjourn ⎱ Lay on the Table Stop Debate = Previous Question	2/3
Debatable and Amendable	⎰ Postpone to a Definite Time ⎱ Refer to a Committee Amend Main Motion	

DIRECTIONS FOR TABLE B

1. When any motion in Table B is before the house (moved and stated but not yet voted upon), any other motion which is above it in the table may be regularly moved, and will temporarily supplant the first motion.
2. Any motion which is below the motion before the house is out of order and may not be moved.
3. When the motion of higher rank is decided, the meeting proceeds to the consideration of the motion which was supplanted, unless the vote already taken disposes of both.

DIRECTIONS FOR TABLE C

1. *Amend* and *Postpone indefinitely* are bracketed; neither may supplant the other.
2. The six incidental motions are bracketed:
   a. Any motion of the group may supersede any motion below the group.
   b. The *Objection to the Consideration of a Question* may be applied only to a principal motion.

   c. Any motion within the group, except the objection, may be applied to any other motion within the group.

   d. Any incidental motion, except the objection, may be applied to any other motion outside the group, whether such motion be above or below the group in the table.

3. In all other points Table C is used as in Table B.

TABLE C

A — Time for Next Meeting.
    Adjourn.
A — Recess.
DA — "Question of Privilege" (treat as a principal motion).
    "Orders of the Day."   NS

    ⎧ "Appeal."
    ⎪ "Point of Order."
    ⎪ "Objection to the Consideration of a Question."
    ⎨   NS — 2/3
    ⎪ Reading Papers
    ⎪ Withdrawal of a Motion
    ⎩ Suspension of Rules   2/3

    Lay on the Table
    Previous Question — Stop Debate.   2/3
DA — Postpone to a Definite Time.
DA — Refer to a Committee.
       ⎧ Amend (change wording, substitute motion, divide
DA — ⎨   question).
       ⎩ Postpone Indefinitely.
DA — Principal Motion (main motion, rescind, expunge, etc.).

KEY

D = debatable
A = amendable
NS = no second is required
Quotation marks (" ") = in order when another person has the floor

2/3 = two-thirds vote necessary to carry. See directions under Table B

I.   EVALUATION OF SECONDARY SCHOOL TEXTBOOKS

Composition

1. Give the title, author, date of publication, publisher, address, price. Is the book one of a series?
2. What background for the preparation of this text have the authors?
3. Is the book arranged in units, or areas, or is the material presented progressively?
4. Is the format attractive and durable? Is the book illustrated? If so, are the illustrations photographs, drawings, or reproductions?
5. How are grammar, spelling, punctuation, and so forth presented? Are they an integral part of the plan of the book, or are they considered separately?
6. What teacher and pupil aids — activities, bibliographies, evaluation exercises, and so forth — are provided?
7. Are there sufficient exercises? Are they challenging or stereotyped?
8. What provisions for improvement in reading are made?
9. Does the book conform to modern educational theory? How?
10. Are there ample opportunities provided for group and individual activities? Do these activities help the pupil to acquire knowledge and understanding and "to stand on his own feet"?
11. What means are taken to develop the pupil as a member of a democratic society?
12. Is the book actually one on composition, in which written and oral activities, treatment of punctuation, grammar, spelling, and so forth combine to develop the principles of communication and self-expression?
13. Is the book suited to your needs?
14. Summarize your opinion of the book.

LITERATURE

1. Give the author, title, date of publication, publisher, address, price. Is the book one of a series?
2. What background for the preparation of this text have the authors?
3. Is the arrangement chronological, national, structural, or upon some other basis?
4. Is the format durable and attractive? Are there illustrations? Of what type?
5. Has the book notes? If so, where are they placed? Are they adequate or confusingly numerous?
6. Are selections complete? Note the number of incomplete selections.
7. Is there a variety of reading types, selected for different reading levels and offering ample material to suit individual differences and problems? Are the selections based on pupil interests?
8. Is there a satisfactory balance between traditional and modern material?
9. Are there teacher and student aids, such as vocabulary helps, bibliographies, reading guides, and suggested class activities?
10. Are there suggestions given for improving reading techniques?
11. What efforts are made to develop the pupil as a member of a democratic society?
12. Is the book suited to your needs?
13. Summarize your opinion of the book.

J. LETTER OF APPLICATION

Probably the most important business letter you will ever write is one of application. Before starting such a letter, equip yourself with a transcript of your high school and college credits (do not depend on your memory); sheets of bond paper, plain, size $8\frac{1}{2} \times 11$; a dictionary; and a book of usage, such as the *New Handbook of Composition*, by Edwin C. Woolley (D. C. Heath and Company). If you type your letter, see that your typewriter is in good condition, the ribbon (black or blue-black) new, the keys clean; if you write in longhand, use black or blue-black ink. The appearance of this letter means much to you; take time to make it right. Let it express your personality, as well as give information about your attainments. Don't neglect the appearance of the envelope — twenty-five per cent of application letters are tossed into the waste basket unopened because of the careless appearance of the envelope. Always enclose a self-addressed, stamped envelope for a reply, and *remember to sign your letter*.

Follow the usual business form. Find out the name of the superintendent or other officer to whom you are applying and address him thus:

> Mr. George D. Long
> Superintendent of Schools
> Johnson, Minnesota
>
> Dear Mr. Long:

Sign yourself:

> Very truly yours,
> (*Miss*) *Matilda Smith*

Make your letter long enough to say what it should, but not so long as to be burdensome to the reader. In the first paragraph state that you are applying for the position and give the name of the person or agency from whom you learned of the vacancy. In the next paragraph give your most significant qualifications; in the third state your experience. In the closing paragraph express your willingness to call or to send further information. Do not, as a student of mine once did, say you would like to interview the superintendent. If you are enclosing a data sheet or if you have obtained an application blank previously and this letter is to accompany it, the information you give need not be so complete as it must be if you do not have means of giving additional information. Whether or not you use the data sheet is a matter of choice; personally I prefer it.

In this letter, apply all the knowledge of composition principles which you possess: word choice, sentence variety, plan. Be concerned with the impression you create; you want to be modest, yet sufficiently confident in your own powers to impress your ability. Write as you would talk if you were making a personal application. Of course, spelling, punctuation, and grammatical forms must be faultless.

Either at the close of your letter or at the end of the data sheet, give the names of six people who know you in different capacities and who have given you permission to use their names as references. Never enclose letters of recommendation in your letter, for superintendents prefer to write for information directly.

After you have written your letter, revise it with great care. Check the mechanics of letter writing. What of the tone? Have you included everything pertinent, and have you eliminated everything not pertaining to your application, such as the salary, opportunity for advancement? Is the material on your data sheet complete; is it neatly arranged? Be a severe critic of your own letter. Never write it hurriedly. More than one person has lost a position through failure to give time and thought to his application letter.

Below you will find a sample application letter and data sheet, put there, not to be copied, but to serve as a guide. Note how the first paragraph immediately establishes a contact, and how the succeeding paragraphs show what has been gained from the experiences listed on the data sheet.

1729 Winter Street
Somerville, Connecticut
August 1, 1936

Mr. Charles A. McGuire
Superintendent of Schools
Manchester, New Hampshire

Dear Mr. McGuire:

Through my critic teacher, Mr. E. W. Shoeder, a graduate of Manchester College, I have become very much interested in applying for a position in the Manchester High School. The high standards you have set for the work in English and the interest in dramatics evidenced by your pupils make me desire to become a member of your high school faculty. A data sheet and my photograph are enclosed for your consideration.

I believe that my six months in the Naturalization School, Jewish Center, gave me an insight into working with the foreign-born and taught me to deal sympathetically with underprivileged persons. Throughout the period of my cadet teaching, I taught average and above-average pupils under the careful supervision of such skilled teachers as Mr. Shoeder and Miss Esther Mynatt. Through this training, I have strengthened my disciplinary power and my ability to present subject matter clearly and forcefully. My experience as assistant to Mr. John A. Conover in the Theatre Workshop gave me exceptional training in play production, costume design, and make-up.

My training in extracurricular activities — gained either as a cadet teacher or as a college student — has given me a feeling of confidence concerning the management of the activities often directed by the teacher of English.

If you wish, I shall be very glad to call for an interview with you, or with someone whom you may appoint, at a time convenient to you.

Very truly yours,

Matilda Smith

(Miss) Matilda Smith

Data Sheet

of
Matilda Smith
1729 Winter Street
Somerville, Connecticut

EDUCATION

INSTITUTIONS ATTENDED	DATES OF ATTENDANCE	MAJOR AND MINOR SUBJECTS
Somerville High School	1927–1931	College Preparatory Course
University of Pennsylvania	1932–1936	English, Education, Dramatic Arts
Bread Loaf School of English	Summer, 1936	Dramatics, Creative Writing

DEGREES

A.B. in Education
Five-year diploma for high school teaching
Graduate Study

TEACHING EXPERIENCE

Six months, September 1931–February 1932, Naturalization School, Jewish Center, Philadelphia.

Cadet teaching of English, Edison High School, Philadelphia, fall and winter quarters, 1933–1934; assisted with debate, glee clubs (boys' and girls'), dramatics.

Assistant to John A. Conover in Theatre Workshop and Costume Design, University of Pennsylvania, summer sessions, 1934–1935.

BUSINESS EXPERIENCE

File clerk, Somerville Medical Clinic, June, July, August, 1931.

MEMBERSHIP IN CLUBS AND SOCIETIES

Writer's Guild, The Thespians (actors' club), Phi Beta Kappa (liberal arts honorary), Pi Lambda Theta (women's honorary in education), Gamma Mu Phi (social sorority), International Relations Club.

PUBLICATIONS

"The Retainers" (one-act play), *Young Writer's Magazine;* "Sonnet to Youth," *Writer's Guild Journal.*

ACTIVITIES

Assistant editor, *The Breeze* (university annual), 1935–1936; day editor, *The Journal* (university daily paper), 1934–1935; board member, Y.W.C.A., 1935–1936; glee club member and assistant director, 1932–1936; debate team, 1933–1936; dramatic productions, 1934–1936.

PERSONAL INFORMATION

Age, 23; *height*, 5 feet, 4 inches; *weight*, 125 pounds; *sex*, female; *church affiliation*, member of the Episcopal Church.

REFERENCES

Mr. E. W. Shoeder, Critic Teacher, College of Education, University of Pennsylvania, Philadelphia.

Mr. George W. Rankin, Superintendent of Schools, Somerville, Connecticut.

Mr. John A. Conover, Assistant Professor of Speech, University of Pennsylvania.

Miss Esther Mynatt, Critic Teacher, College of Education, University of Pennsylvania.

Mr. Philip Nelson, Office Manager, Somerville Medical Clinic, Somerville, Connecticut.

Dr. Hubert D. Smithson, Dean of the College of Education, University of Pennsylvania.

Dr. Wilfred T. Magnus, Head of the Department of English, University of Pennsylvania.

K. BIBLIOGRAPHIES

Although it is not possible to list all items in any field, I hope the following bibliographies will prove helpful to you. Before ordering any title listed, however, it would be well to write the publisher for information, as changes in all fields are frequent and rapid.

1. SECONDARY SCHOOL TEXTBOOKS

WRITTEN COMPOSITION

ADDISON, GERTRUDE M., and GARRISON, BLANCHE L., *Language for Living*, First and Second Books (senior high school), Charles Scribner's Sons, 1942.

These books, graded for ninth and tenth or tenth and eleventh years, are based upon the conviction that language development and personality development must go hand in hand. Guidance themes are merged with language activities.

BELL, JOHN W., and OTHERS, *The English We Need*, Books One and Two, John C. Winston Company, 1945.

Training in composition and a procedure in reading constitute the core of these books. In addition there are directions for enjoyment of newspapers, magazines, radio programs, moving pictures. Tools of expression are both integrated and presented separately. Individual differences are provided for by means of A and B activity programs.

CANBY, HENRY SEIDEL, and OTHERS, *A Modern English Course*, 4 books, The Macmillan Company, 1943.

This series is based on the purposes stated in "Basic Aims for English Instruction in American High Schools" (National Council of Teachers of English) through emphasis upon purposeful activities. In the first three books attention is given to individual differences. Tools of expression are presented separately. A handbook of English usage is designed for the twelfth year.

DARINGER, HELEN FERN, and SWEENEY, FRANCES G., *Young*

America's English, Books One, Two, and Three (junior high school), World Book Company, 1942, 1943.

Helping the student to take his place in a democratic society is the underlying philosophy of this series. Tools of expression are integrated.

GODDARD, MABEL, and OTHERS, *American English Series*, 4 books, J. B. Lippincott Company, 1939.

The underlying philosophy of this series recognizes the development of the English language. The approach is a simple and practical one. Tools of composition are integrated.

HATFIELD, W. WILBUR, and OTHERS, *Junior English Activities*, Books One, Two, and Three, American Book Company, 1940.

——, *Senior English Activities*, Books One, Two, and Three, American Book Company, 1938, 1939.

——, *English, Your Obedient Servant* (Advanced Book), American Book Company, 1939.

English is considered as a social subject in this series. Scientifically, the books are based on the *Experience Curriculum in English*. Tools of expression are presented separately.

JOHN, NELLIE, *Natural English* (Grade Nine), Row, Peterson and Company, 1943.

——, *English for You* (Grade Ten), Row, Peterson and Company, 1943.

The language arts — speaking, writing, reading, and listening — are considered important tools for individual learning and living. Teaching starts with the individual, not with the subject matter. "Mechanics of Communication" constitutes a separate section.

JOHNSON, ROY IVAN, and OTHERS, *Daily-Life English Junior Series* (junior high school), Ginn and Company, 1943.

——, *Daily-Life English Senior Series* (senior high school), 3 books, Ginn and Company, 1941, 1945.

Emphases in this series lie upon thinking, socialization, individual attainments, and guidance toward worth-while living. Tools of expression are integrated, but are summed up in a section called "Tests and Measurements," which ends all but the final volume.

PAUL, HARRY G., and OTHERS, *Junior Units in English*, Books One and Two, Lyons and Carnahan, 1940.

——, *Units in English*, Books One (ninth year), Two, Three, and Four, Lyons and Carnahan, 1940.

These books aim to help the pupil toward correct speaking and writing. They are organized into units, almost all of which are planned under the "test-teach-test" principle. Suggestions for dovetailing the tools of expression and composition activities are given in the text, but grammar is treated separately.

SALISBURY, RACHEL, and LEONARD, J. PAUL, *The Thought Program*, 4 books, Scott, Foresman and Company, 1941.

These books represent the "thought approach" to reading, writing, and speaking. Instead of being "grammatical and analytical," the presentation is designed to be scientific and constructive. Considerable emphasis is given throughout to the tools of expression.

STRATTON, CLARENCE, and OTHERS, *English for Meaning*, 3 books, Houghton Mifflin Company, 1944.

Designed for junior high school, these books offer an organized program.

TANNER, WILLIAM, and PLATT, FRANK J., *My English*, 4 books, Ginn and Company, 1941.

These books are designed to help the pupil to help himself to acquire new skills in speaking, writing, reading, and listening, or to correct bad habits in these aspects. Tools of expression are integrated and presented in a separate section.

TEUSCHER, RUTH H., and OTHERS, *Language Skills*, 3 books, Harcourt, Brace and Company, 1946.

A revision of the former *Growth in Using Language* series, these books show a careful integration of the tools of expression with composition.

TRESSLER, and OTHERS, *Junior English in Action*, fourth edition, 3 books, D. C. Heath and Company, 1945.

——, *English in Action*, fourth edition (four- and two-book editions for grades nine to twelve), D. C. Heath and Company, 1945.

This series rests upon the principle that all experiences, both in and out of school, which call for communication and stimulate self-expression offer an opportunity for building language habits and skills. Tools of expression are presented in a separate section.

WARD, C. H., *Sentence and Theme*, third edition, Scott, Foresman and Company, 1929.

——, *Writing Craft*. Scott, Foresman Company, 1932.

——, and MOFFATT, H. Y., *The Junior Highway to English*, revised edition, Books One and Two, Scott, Foresman and Company, 1931.

This series puts into practice the principles of composition for which the senior author is noted.

WOLFE, DON M., and GEYER, ELLEN M., *Enjoying English*, revised edition, 4 books, Newson and Company, 1944.

The distinctive feature of these books is that activities are based upon the pupil's own past and present experiences at home, school, and elsewhere. Tools of expression are given in a separate section.

LANGUAGE AND USAGE

BRYANT, MARGARET M., *A Functional English Grammar*, D. C. Heath and Company, 1945.

This textbook assumes a foundation of elementary grammar on the part of the student. The author has attempted to distinguish between grammar and rhetoric and to present as much historical background as is necessary to adequate comprehension. Abundant exercises are included in each chapter.

CANBY, HENRY SEIDEL, and OPDYCKE, JOHN BAKER, *Handbook of English Usage*, The Macmillan Company, 1942, 1943.

Designed as a permanent part of the student's working library, this book is applicable to twelfth-year review or to reference during any or all of the high school years.

Cosper, Russell, *This Is Your Language*, D. Appleton-Century Company, 1944.
This little book evolved from the desire to write a course based on a *descriptive* approach to language study. It is usable in any year of the senior high school.

Daringer, Helen Fern, *Grammar for Everyday Use*, World Book Company, 1938.
You may use this book as a text in English grammar or as a supplementary book in an integrated course.

Hermans, Mabel C., and Shea, Marjorie Nichols, *New Studies in Grammar*, Henry Holt and Company, 1946.
In this book, fundamental facts of grammar are related to interest themes, such as airplanes, radio, and television. Students are given assignments to prepare, and a key with which they may check their own work is provided.

Patterson, Sophia H., and Semmelmeyer, Madeline, *Know Your Language* (A High School Grammar), Silver Burdett Company, 1941.
This book presents the principles of English grammar, exercises for their application, and "Progress Checks" to determine individual growth.

Pribble, Evaline, *Correct English Usage*, Lyons and Carnahan, 1942.
This study and practice book concentrates on principles habitually misused in the oral and written expression of a considerable number of students. The "Pribble-McCrory Diagnostic Tests in Practical English Grammar" (published by Lyons and Carnahan) are designed to accompany the text.

Radke, Frieda, *Living Words*, The Odyssey Press, 1940.
Increased emphasis upon democratic processes has stimu-

lated concern with composition. This book aims to increase the student's facility with a basic tool — words.

STERLING, EDNA L., and EMERY, DON W., *Guide to English Usage*, Henry Holt and Company, 1940.

A handbook, suitable for use in any high school year, this "Guide" includes only those aspects of expression needed in everyday speech and writing.

WALSH, J. MARTYN, and WALSH, ANNA KATHLEEN, *Plain English Handbook*, new edition, The McCormick-Mathers Publishing Company, 1946.

This book is designed as a guide to sentence correctness. The Reed-Kellog system of diagramming is employed throughout.

WEBSTER, EDWARD HARLAN, *Daily Drills for Better English*, enlarged and revised, World Book Company, 1939.

This book is a "self-help" text in that the student is enabled to drill himself in matters of usage. Emphasis is placed on oral expression. To accompany this book is a manual containing oral tests.

WOOLLEY, EDWIN C., SCOTT, F. W., and TRESSLER, J. C., *Handbook of Writing and Speaking*, D. C. Heath and Company, 1944.

Clear, correct expression in speaking and writing is emphasized, and exercises furnish correlation with the social studies and science. Training in the use of the library and in the selection of reference books is provided, together with practice in handling common language situations.

SPEECH

BORCHERS, GLADYS LOUISE, *Living Speech* (Grades Eight, Nine, and Ten), Harcourt, Brace and Company, 1938.

This book presents fundamental speech training through many activities based on everyday speech situations. Checks for the student to rate his own progress are provided.

PAINTER, MARGARET, *Ease in Speech*, revised edition, D. C. Heath and Company, 1943.
This book rests upon the fundamental principle that youth demands training in speech that brings immediate returns. General principles and suggestions for speeches for special occasions are presented.

SEELY, HOWARD FRANCIS, and HACKETT, WILLIAM ARTHUR, *Experiences in Speaking*, Scott, Foresman and Company, 1940.
The authors hope, through this book, to help high school students to realize the significant part played by oral expression in the everyday life of a democracy. The organization centers about formal and informal speech experiences.

WEAVER, ANDREW THOMAS, and BORCHERS, GLADYS LOUISE, *Speech*, Harcourt, Brace and Company, 1946.
This book stresses the importance of communication in social relationships, civic participation, and business.

JOURNALISM

HARRINGTON, HARRY FRANKLIN, and HARRINGTON, EVALINE, *Writing for Print*, revised edition, D. C. Heath and Company, 1929.
Designed to aid the pupil in understanding the public press and its functions, this book considers the school as a community and offers samples of journalistic practices with suggestions for their application in high school classes.

MERRIMAN, LEE M., *Between Deadlines*, Benjamin H. Sanborn Company, 1941.
This book is a realistic study of journalism.

SAVIDGE, ANNE LANE, and HORN, GUNNAR, *Handbook for High School Journalism*, D. C. Heath and Company, 1940, 1944.
This book, designed for use by high school classes in journalism, presents briefly but adequately the various aspects of journalistic writing. Many helpful bibliographies are included.

SPEARS, HAROLD, and LAWSHE, C. H., *High School Journalism*, The Macmillan Company, 1940.

The "laboratory" approach of this book makes possible a year's schedule of production. The technical aspects of writing and management are stressed.

LITERATURE

BARNES, WALTER, and OTHERS, *The Realm of Reading Series*, 6 books, American Book Company, 1940, 1941.

Principles upon which this series rests are the selection of pieces good as art and interesting to the age group for which each volume is intended; organization according to theme; editing to increase appreciation and understanding; and an attractive format. Illustrations are in black and white, with a colored frontispiece.

BLANKENSHIP, RUSSELL, and OTHERS, *Our Literary Heritage Series*, 5 books, Charles Scribner's Sons, 1940.

Designed to bring social values into prominence without sacrificing literary worth, these five books (one for each of the four high school years and *Contemporary Literature* to supplement reading in any high school year), present various aspects of life and culture. Organization of all books (except *English Literature*, which combines the social and historical approaches) centers about social and personal themes. Each book contains a colored frontispiece. All other illustrations are in black and white.

BOLENIUS, EMMA MILLER, *Literature in the Junior High School Series*, 3 books, Houghton Mifflin Company, 1929.

Aims in this series are to develop pupils' reading ability, appreciation of literature, self-reliance, and judgment. Organization is according to themes and types. Illustrations are in black and white, with a colored frontispiece.

BRIGGS, THOMAS H., and OTHERS, *Literature in the Senior High School Series*, 3 books, Houghton Mifflin Company, 1934.

Aims are a continuation of those for the junior high school

series. Selections are increasingly mature. Organization is according to types and historical development. The volume containing examples of contemporary literature centers about man at work, at play, in society, and in the world. Illustrations are in black and white, with a colored frontispiece.

BROENING, ANGELA M., and OTHERS, *Best-Liked Literature*, Ginn and Company, 1945.

In this junior high school series, modern selections are emphasized, although standard ones are not omitted. Organization is based upon interest themes.

CAMPBELL, GLADYS, and THOMAS, R. B., *Reading American Literature* and *Reading English Literature*, D. C. Heath and Company, 1944.

These books contain both "standard" and modern selections, chosen to develop the student's ability to understand and appreciate the best in American and English literature. Organization is chronological within types.

CHAMBERLAIN, R. W., *Beacon Lights of Literature Series*, 6 books, Iroquois Publishing Company, 1940, 1944.

This series, based upon recommendations of *An Experience Curriculum* and designed for junior and senior high school reading, contains examples of both standard and modern writings. Organization centers about themes and types, although Book Twelve contains a summary of the history of English and American literature. Each book is illustrated with drawings and photographs.

COLLETTE, ELIZABETH, and OTHERS, *The World in Literature Series*, 4 books, Ginn and Company, 1946.

Designed to replace the *Good Reading Series*, these books seek to serve the cause of peace through increased understanding of other peoples. Organization follows the unit plan. Illustrations are drawings, photographs, and full color. At present, only the first two books — *Within the Americas* and *Beyond the Seas* — are available. Books Three and Four of the *Good Reading Series* may be used with these.

CROSS, E. A., and OTHERS, *Literature*, 7 books, The Macmillan Company, 1944, 1945, 1946.

This series aims to provide basic literary materials selected to enlarge the realm of the students' interest, knowledge, and understanding. Selections, from both modern and standard authors, are of high literary merit, related to other secondary school subjects and to problems of living in the world today. Junior high school books are arranged according to theme; senior high school volumes include one containing types of literature and another of world literature. Volumes of English and American literature show a "reverse" approach, beginning with modern literature and progressing to earlier writings. A history of literature is also included. Illustrations are pen and ink drawings by Maud and Miska Petersham.

HAGGERTY, MELVIN E., and SMITH, DORA V., *Reading and Literature*, 3 books, World Book Company, 1937.

This series aims to provide material helpful to junior high school pupils in developing their reading skill. Choice of selection is intended to appeal to adolescent boys and girls. Both standard and modern material is included. Photographs are used as illustrations.

LYMAN, ROLLO L., and HILL, HOWARD C., *Literature and Living*, revised edition, Junior High School Series, 3 books, Charles Scribner's Sons, 1940.

Organized into reading units, this series is designed to correlate with community living and other social studies. Both standard and modern authors are included. Illustrations, many of which are photographs, are in black and white.

MILES, DUDLEY, and OTHERS, *Literature and Life*, 4 books, Scott, Foresman and Company, 1943.

The underlying philosophy of this series is that literature is not a collection of facts, but rather a gateway into civilization. Material is from the writing of both standard and modern authors. Organization is developed around themes in the earlier books and historically in the volumes dealing

with English and American literature. Illustrations are in
black and white.

NEVILLE, MARK A., and PAYNE, LEONIDAS W., Jr., *Enjoying
Literature*, 3 books, Rand, McNally and Company, 1942.

This junior high school series centers about experiences
which stimulated or prompted expression in various literary
forms. Although some of the selections are "standard,"
many are from modern authors. Illustrations are in black
and white.

NORVELL, GEORGE W., and HOVIOUS, CAROL, *Conquest Series*,
3 books, D. C. Heath and Company, 1946.

Based on a ten-year study of pupils' likes, these seventh-
and eighth-grade books contain an anthology — a collection of
favorite stories, poems, and plays; and special units on such
topics as motion pictures, choral reading, and library skills.

PAYNE, LEONIDAS W., and OTHERS, *Enjoying Literature Series*,
4 books, Rand, McNally and Company, 1941.

These books constitute a program of experiences in literature, designed to aid the student in enjoyment of reading and
to make reading a part of his equipment for life. The student
is brought into contact with a variety of human activities with
a view to helping him understand the progress of mankind.
Organization of all four books centers around themes, with,
however, some attention in the volumes dealing with English
and American literature, to types and historical development.
Illustrations are in black and white, with a colored frontispiece.

POOLEY, ROBERT, and OTHERS, *Growth in Reading Series*,
3 books, Scott, Foresman and Company.

These books are designed to precede the *Literature and Life*
series. A developmental reading program, they offer reading experiences. Organization centers about interest areas.
The selections, all of which are short, are taken for the most
part from modern authors. Illustrations, in black and white,
are drawings or photographs.

Ross, J. M., and Others, *Adventures Series*, 6 books, Harcourt, Brace and Company, 1941, 1943, 1944.

Four of these books are for use in the last four years of high school. *Adventures in Modern Literature* may be used in either the eleventh or twelfth years. They aim to conform to modern educational theory through the selection of subject matter, and its relationship to present social, political, and economic trends. Arrangement in the first three books is largely according to types; *Adventures in English Literature* combines types with the historical approach. *Adventures in Modern Literature* also centers around types, arranged chronologically. Each book contains a colored frontispiece. Other illustrations are photographs.

Witty, Paul, and Others, *Reading for Interest Series*, Books IV, V, and VI, D. C. Heath and Company, 1942.

Although designed for Grades IV–VI, these books contain selections of a variety and interest that will appeal to high school pupils needing remedial work in reading. An increasingly wide range of experience is presented in the choice of subject matter and emphasis is placed on the development of reading techniques. A glossary is included in each book and there are many illustrations in color and black and white.

DICTIONARIES

Thorndike Century Junior Dictionary, Scott, Foresman and Company, 1935.

Thorndike Century Senior Dictionary, Scott, Foresman and Company, 1935.

These dictionaries were prepared with the child using the book in mind. Hence definitions, examples, and illustrations are adapted to pupil interest and knowledge.

New Comprehensive Standard School Dictionary, Funk and Wagnalls Company, 1937.

This book may be used by pupils on both the elementary and high school levels. It contains 50,000 words, based on frequency and range of occurrence in children's reading matter.

Webster's Elementary Dictionary, American Book Company, 1941, 1945.

Webster's Students Dictionary, American Book Company, 1938, 1945.

These dictionaries are designed to precede the adult book, *Webster's New International Dictionary*. Therefore, although the words listed and their definitions are based on pupils' interests, needs, and abilities, pronunciations, spellings, and so forth conform to the standard Merriam-Webster usage.

Winston Dictionaries for Schools, the John C. Winston Company, 1946.

These include volumes for all grade levels.

2. WORKBOOKS

It was thought best not to attempt to list workbook titles. You will find that most of the textbook houses publish workbooks based upon their particular textbooks. Too, there are many special kinds of workbooks independent of texts.

3. PUBLICATIONS OF THE NATIONAL COUNCIL OF TEACHERS OF ENGLISH

You should be familiar with these publications of the National Council of Teachers of English, issued by special committees of the National Council under the direction of the Publications Committee. They may be obtained from the National Council headquarters, 211 West Sixty-eighth Street, Chicago 21, Illinois, or from the D. Appleton-Century Company.

MONOGRAPHS

APPY, NELLIE (Editor), *Pupils Are People*.

A collection of lively, experiential essays on means of discovering and ministering to pupils' individual differences.

BROENING, ANGELA M. (Editor), *Conducting Experiences in English*.

Condensed accounts of successful long and short units of English based on pupil experiences.

CENTER, STELLA S., and PERSONS, GLADYS L., *Teaching High School Pupils to Read*.

The story of a successful attack upon reading disabilities in a great city high school.

FINCH, HARDY R., and CHILDS, ELEANOR D., *Producing School Movies*.

A practical manual of moderate-cost procedures based upon the authors' successful experience.

FRIES, CHARLES C., *American English Grammar*.

The first analysis of Modern English usage to be based on objective evidence, this work is one of the most original and important linguistic studies of the past decade.

HATFIELD, W. WILBUR (Editor), *An Experience Curriculum in English*.

This outline of an English program from kindergarten through high school is the most generally approved presentation of modern English curriculum and method. Effective statements of principles and hundreds of instruction units.

HERZBERG, MAX J. (Editor), *Radio and English Teaching*.

In this striking overview of the field, experienced broadcasters give detailed hints as to the way in which teachers of English may employ radio as an educational ally.

JACOBS, IDA T., and DEBOER, JOHN J., *Educating for Peace*.

A timely monograph for teachers of English, who have a unique opportunity to help build ideals and attitudes necessary to making and keeping the peace.

KENNEDY, ARTHUR G., *English Usage*.

Gives a broad foundation for building an understanding of general principles of usage and for making intelligent decisions about troublesome problems of usage.

LEWIN, WILLIAM, *Photoplay Appreciation in American High Schools*.

An important experiment in modifying and directing the choice and taste of a high school audience.

MARCKWARDT, ALBERT H., and WALCOTT, FRED, *Facts About Current English Usage*.

A re-study of the controversial language items contained in Leonard's *Current English Usage*, which is reprinted as a part of the present volume.

RAND, HELEN, and LEWIS, RICHARD, *Film and School*.

Designed as a pupil text, with an abundance of effective class activities and excellent illustrations. Well balanced between the techniques and the content of photoplays.

SMITH, DORA V., *Evaluating Instruction in Secondary School English*.

This book is a keen analysis of typical American high school work in English, with definite practical suggestions for improvement.

SMITH, MILTON (Editor), *A Guide to Play Selection*.

A descriptive list of available plays.

WEEKS, RUTH MARY (Editor), *A Correlated Curriculum*.

This pioneer study of correlation, fusion, and integration of English with other subjects supplies abundant positive suggestions and points out pitfalls.

READING LISTS

CROSS, NEAL, and OTHERS (Editors), *Victory Corps Reading List*.

A reading list of nearly 325 recent books on issues of the war, preparation for military service, and activities on the home front. Classified into helpful categories. Brief annotations, dates of publication, and publishers.

NEVILLE, MARK (Editor), *Books for You*.

A reading list for grades 9–12, containing nearly 2000 titles carefully classified by topics and by types within topics, annotated, and graded for reading maturity. Attractively illustrated and fully indexed.

WHITFORD, ROBERT C. (Editor), *Good Reading*.

This guide for college students and adult readers briefly describes 1500 especially significant, enjoyable books, most of them available in inexpensive editions. Titles classified by periods, types and subjects.

ADAMS, HARLEN M., *Speak, Look, and Listen.*

A list of the best current audio-visual aids for English classes, with information as to manufacturer, price, and educational use. The aids include recordings and radio transcriptions, motion pictures, slides, speech-reproduction machines and other equipment in common use in schools.

GREY, LENNOX, and CONSULTANTS, *What Communication Means Today.*

The first in a series of pamphlets dealing with the language arts as communication in the modern world, this pamphlet points up the importance of the communicative arts in war and in peace. Part I is entitled "First Definitions"; Part II, "Charting Our Resources"; and Part III, "The Future of English and the Communication Arts."

HANLON, HELEN G., and BOOTH, MIRIAM B., and COMMITTEE, *Junior High School English — in Wartime and After.*

The authors emphasize American ideals and ways of living; understanding our world, America, and ourselves; co-ordination of English with other subjects and school activities. Eighty per cent of the pamphlet is devoted to accounts of successful practices in widely distributed schools.

RAGLAND, FANNIE J., *Children Learn to Write.*

Ten authors have contributed to this excellent bulletin which contains descriptions of practices and underlying philosophies of master teachers of children.

SALT, GEORGE, *Thinking Together: Promoting Democracy through Class Discussion.*

The difficult techniques of guiding group thinking and of building language concepts essential to life in a democracy are outlined. The principles of language communication in relation to literature and life are made clear.

SAUNDERS, KAY MONOGHAN, and OTHERS, *Skill in Listening*.

A pioneer publication in a field of language activity the importance of which has come home to us through needs of the army and through the addiction of children and adults to radio and sound pictures.

SMITH, DORA V., chairman Basic Aims Committee, *Basic Aims for English Instruction*.

This forward-looking document states and discusses thirteen basic aims in a manner that will inspire new faith in the profession and its leaders.

4. FOR YOUR BOOKSHELF

Suggested by authorities in the fields represented, each of the books listed here deserves a place in your library. Why not plan to buy a book a month until you have acquired an adequate library?

BABENROTH, A. CHARLES, revised by PARKHURST, CHARLES CHANDLER, *Modern Business English*, third edition, Prentice-Hall, Inc., 1942.

This is probably the best book on business English to be had.

BEARD, CHARLES A., and BEARD, MARY R., *A Basic History of the United States*, New Home Library Series, Blakiston Company, 1924.

This is a well-written one-volume history of our country by two famous authors.

BLANKENSHIP, RUSSELL, *American Literature*, Henry Holt and Company, 1931.

Here you will find an account of the facts of American literature, from its beginnings to the present, with interpretations of these facts.

BROOKS, VAN WYCK, *The Flowering of New England*, E. P. Dutton and Company, Inc., 1940.

——, *New England: Indian Summer*, E. P. Dutton and Company, Inc., 1940.

BROOKS, VAN WYCK, *The World of Washington Irving*, E. P. Dutton and Company, 1944.

These volumes, the first three of a history of American literature, are filled with biographical, historical, and critical facts.

BUCKINGHAM, BURDETTE ROSS, *Research for Teachers*, revised edition, Silver Burdett Company, 1935.

Here you will find explanations of statistics needed by modern teachers, testing, objective type examinations, classifying and grouping students, and so forth.

BUSHNELL, NELSON SHERWIN, *The Historical Background of English Literature*, Henry Holt and Company, 1930.

The author aims to present a readable account of the chief events in the political history of the English nation, and to indicate the most obvious points of contact between English history and English literature.

CAMPBELL, WALTER S., *Professional Writing*, The Macmillan Company, 1945.

This book is valuable as offering suggestions to those desiring to write for publication.

CHISHOLM, LESLIE L., *Guiding Youth in the Modern Secondary School*, American Book Company, 1945.

You will find in this book the best modern theory on guidance.

COLE, LUELLA, *Psychology of Adolescence*, revised edition, Rinehart and Company, Inc., 1942.

This is one of the most helpful recent books on adolescence.

CUNLIFFE, J. W., *Pictured Story of English Literature*, students' edition, D. Appleton-Century Company, 1933.

This is a readable account of the growth of English literature from its beginnings to the present, beautifully illustrated with authentic plates to show what writers really looked like and what their surroundings actually were.

DOUGLASS, A. A., *The American School System*, revised edition, Rinehart and Company, Inc., 1940.

This should be read in connection with *Principles of Teaching* for a comprehensive view of our American school system.

DREW, ELIZABETH, *Discovering Poetry*, W. W. Norton and Company, 1933.
This book analyzes delightfully the experiences provided by poetry and suggests ways by which poetic insight may be gained.

——, *Enjoyment of Literature*, W. W. Norton and Company, 1935.
The pleasures of reading prose and poetry are discussed in this book, and essays on the various types are presented.

EARNEST, ERNEST, *A Foreword to Literature*, D. Appleton-Century Company, 1945.
This little book attempts to explain some of the fundamentals of literary criticism.

FARGO, LUCILE F., *The Library in the School*, third edition, American Library Association, Chicago, Illinois, 1939.
One of the Library Curriculum Series, prepared under the direction of W. W. Charters, this book offers authoritative suggestions to those concerned with the school library.

FAULKNER, RAY, and OTHERS, *Art Today*, Henry Holt and Company, 1941.
This book introduces the reader to fine and functional arts.

FESSENDEN, SETH A., *Speech and the Teacher*, Longmans, Green and Company, Inc., 1945.
This book affords a guide to any teacher, whether or not he teaches "speech."

FISHER, HERBERT A. L., *A History of Europe* (1 or 3 volumes), Eyre and Spottiswoode, 1938.
A well-written and authoritative history of Europe.

GASSNER, JOHN (Editor), *Twenty Best Plays of the Modern American Theatre*, Crown Publishers, New York, 1939.
A historical and critical comment by the editor precedes this collection of twentieth-century plays by such authors as Maxwell Anderson, Lillian Hellman, and Archibald MacLeish.

GRAF, MAX, *Composer and Critic: Two Hundred Years of Musical Criticism*, W. W. Norton and Company, Inc., 1946.

This book is a history and criticism of music from the eighteenth century to the present.

GREENOUGH, JAMES BRADSTREET, and KITTREDGE, GEORGE LYMAN, *Words and Their Ways in English Speech*, The Macmillan Company, 1931.

This is a very readable history of our language.

JOHNSON, CLAUDIUS O., *Government in the United States*, fourth edition, Thomas Y. Crowell Company, 1947.

This is a very readable and authoritative account of our government, based upon the executive-legislative-judicial type of approach.

The Kittredge Shakespeare, (individual or one-volume editions), Ginn and Company, 1946.

This gives the Kittredge reading of the text and the Kittredge notes.

KUNITZ, STANLEY J., and HAYCRAFT, HOWARD, *Twentieth Century Authors*, the H. W. Wilson Company, 1942.

In this reference work you will find 1850 biographies and 1700 portraits.

LANDIS, PAUL H., *Adolescence and Youth: The Process of Maturing*, McGraw-Hill Book Company, 1945.

This book discusses the development of the adolescent in relation to his experiences in his social environment: urban, town, and rural.

LATOURETTE, KENNETH S., *A Short History of the Far East*, The Macmillan Company, 1946.

Written by a well-known authority, this book offers a readable history of an important section of the world.

LEE, J. MURRAY, and LEE, DORRIS MAY, *The Child and His Curriculum*, D. Appleton-Century Company, 1940.

Although particularly helpful to elementary school teachers, as "the child is father to the man," this book is valuable to teachers on all levels.

LEGOUIS, EMILE, and CAZAMIAN, LOUIS, *A History of English Literature*, revised edition, The Macmillan Company, 1929. This is a standard one-volume history of English literature.

MANLY, JOHN MATHEWS, and RICKERT, EDITH, *Contemporary American Literature: Bibliographies and Study Outlines*, second edition, revised by FRED B. MILLET, Harcourt, Brace and Company, 1929.

——, *Contemporary British Literature: A Critical Survey and 232 Author-Bibliographies*, third revised and enlarged edition, revised by FRED B. MILLET, Harcourt, Brace and Company, 1935. If you desire to continue your study of American and English literature, these books will be very valuable, as they suggest materials, outlines, and methods of work, designed to help the student to form intelligent judgments.

OSGOOD, CHARLES GROSVENOR, *The Voice of England*, Harper and Brothers, 1935. This is a delightful history of English literature, as well as an authoritative one.

REYNOLDS, GEORGE F., *English Literature in Fact and Story*, revised edition, D. Appleton-Century Company, 1946. This book provides excellent background material.

SCHERMAN, DAVID E., and WILCOX, RICHARD, *Literary England*, Random House, 1943. A book of photographs of some of the scenes made famous by English writers.

STILES, DON, *High Schools for Tomorrow*, Harper and Brothers, 1946. An account of new procedures, reflecting community life, as seen by the author in visiting one thousand high schools in thirty states.

STITES, RAYMOND, *The Arts and Man*, Whittlesey House, McGraw-Hill Book Company, 1940. Literature, music, and the fine arts are shown in their relation to man.

STRAYER, GEORGE D., FRASIER, GEORGE W., and ARMENTROUT, WINFIELD D., *Principles of Teaching*, American Book Company, 1935.

To be used with *The American School System* for a general survey of principles of American education.

TITUS, HAROLD H., *Living Issues in Philosophy*, American Book Company, Cincinnati, 1946.

This book seeks to show the part of philosophy in interpreting current tensions.

TSCHAN, FRANCIS J., and OTHERS, *Western Civilization*, J. B. Lippincott Company, 1942.

Here you will find a readable account of European history from the fall of Rome to the present.

TURNER, W. J. (Editor), *The Romance of English Literature*, Hastings House, 1945.

A fine collection of modern essays. The illustrations are outstanding.

WAGENKNECHT, EDWARD, *Cavalcade of the English Novel*, Henry Holt and Company, 1943.

This is a history of the novel from Shakespeare's time to the present.

WEBSTER, MARGARET, *Shakespeare Without Tears*, McGraw-Hill Book Company, 1942.

Director and producer of Shakespearean plays, the author makes Shakespeare live.

Webster's Biographical Dictionary, G. and C. Merriam Company, 1943.

Here are listed names, their pronunciations, and brief biographies of famous persons.

Webster's Dictionary of Synonyms, G. and C. Merriam Company, 1942.

This contains antonyms and analogous and contrasted words.

WILSON, MARTHA, and CURRIN, A. M., *School Library Management*, sixth edition, H. W. Wilson Company, 1939.

This is an authoritative text in this field.

WOODRING, MAXIE N., JEWETT, IDA A., and BENSON, RACHEL
T., *Enriched Teaching of English in the Junior and Senior High
School*, revised and enlarged, Bureau of Publications,
Teachers College, Columbia University, 1941.

This is a handbook listing and annotating free and low-cost
materials that will enrich the teaching of English. You will
want it at your elbow.

To this list should be added at least one text on the teaching of English.

5. THE TEACHING OF ENGLISH

Listed below are most of the recent books on the teaching
of English. Starred items were available when this volume
was published. For the others, you will have to depend on
library copies.

BLAISDELL, THOMAS C., *Ways to Teach English*, Doubleday
Doran and Company, 1930.

This book offers detailed and practical suggestions for the
teaching of English from the second through the twelfth years.

BOLENIUS, EMMA M., *The Teaching of Oral English*, J. B. Lippincott Company, 1920.

Not a new book, this is nevertheless a practical one.

*——, *The Teaching of Literature in the Grammar Grades and
High School*, Houghton Mifflin Company, 1929.

Specific suggestions for the teaching of many "standard"
selections are given here.

CHUBB, PERCIVAL, *The Teaching of Literature in the Elementary
and Secondary Schools*, revised edition, The Macmillan Company, 1929.

One of the first books to plead for unity and continuity in
the teaching of English, this book discusses the needs of both
the pre-school child and the high school senior.

COX, SIDNEY, *The Teaching of English*, Harper and Brothers,
1928.

Perhaps you will not gain greatly in "methodology" from this book, for it offers no hard-and-fast panaceas, but you will enhance your enthusiasm for teaching.

CRAIG, VIRGINIA, *The Teaching of High School English*, Longmans, Green and Company, 1930.

Here you will find specific instructions, based on the author's wide experience as a high school teacher.

*CROSS, E. A., and CARNEY, ELIZABETH, *Teaching English in High Schools*, The Macmillan Company, 1939.

Two experienced teachers of English offer suggestions for adaptations of subject-matter to modern educational theory. A chapter on Basic English is included.

FRIES, CHARLES C., HANFORD, JAMES HOLLY, and HARRISON, ROSS STEEVES, *The Teaching of Literature*, Silver, Burdett and Company, 1926.

Literature as a means of liberal culture is discussed in this volume by three experienced teachers.

FRIES, CHARLES C., *The Teaching of the English Language*, Thomas Nelson and Sons, 1927.

Although some of the material in this book is outdated, it contains many helpful suggestions for teaching one's mother tongue.

*GLASER, EMMA, *On the Teaching of Junior High School English*, D. Appleton-Century Company, 1935.

In this book all the phases of junior high school teaching are presented as centering around child development.

*HAWLEY, HATTIE L., *Teaching English in Junior High School*, Houghton Mifflin Company, 1924.

Pleasantly written, this little book offers specific suggestions for teaching both composition and literature.

HITCHCOCK, ALFRED M., *Bread Loaf Talks on Teaching Composition*, Henry Holt and Company, 1927.

——, *Bread Loaf Talks on Teaching Literature*, Henry Holt and Company, 1927.

Consisting of lectures delivered at the Bread Loaf School of English, Vermont, these delightful little books afford enjoyment as well as instruction.

LaBrant, Lou, *The Teaching of Literature in the Secondary School*, Harcourt, Brace and Company, 1931.

An easily read little book, this affords suggestions for teaching the usual types of literature.

*Miles, Dudley, and Pooley, Robert, "Teaching Literature," Scott, Foresman and Company, 1943.

Designed to accompany the *Literature and Life* series, this little book offers information regarding the teaching of literary types, methods of review, formulation of examination questions, and so forth, which may be utilized by all teachers.

*Mirrielees, Lucia B., *Teaching Composition and Literature in the Junior and Senior High School*, Harcourt, Brace and Company, 1943.

A practical book, this gives specific teaching suggestions as well as discussions of such allied problems as minimum essentials and the encouragement of reading. The material in the Appendices is particularly valuable.

*Neville, Mark A., and Others, "Resources in Teaching English," Rand, McNally and Company, 1942.

*——, "Resources in Teaching Literature," Rand, McNally and Company, 1942.

These paper-backed books are designed to aid teachers using the Rand, McNally texts in composition and literature. But much in the books offers aid to all teachers, as, for example, the discussion of the unit method of teaching, answers to questions frequently asked by teachers of literature, and biographical sketches.

Parker, Roscoe Edward, *The Principles and Practices of Teaching English*, Prentice-Hall, Inc., 1937.

Dealing largely with modern *theory* regarding the teaching of English, this book nicely balances others that emphasize method.

*PERRY, BLISS, *A Study of Poetry*, Houghton Mifflin Company, 1920.

*——, *A Study of Prose Fiction*, Houghton Mifflin Company, 1920.

Do not turn from reading these books because of the date of their publication, for a skilled teacher and delightful writer such as Bliss Perry has much to say to you.

*ROBERTS, HOLLAND D., KAULFERS, WALTER V., and KEFANNER, GRAYSON N. (Editors), *English for Social Living*, McGraw Hill Book Company, 1943.

Twenty-five projects and practices for junior and senior high school, covering every important phase of "English," are presented here.

*ROSENBLATT, LOUISE M., *Literature as Exploration*, D. Appleton-Century Company, 1938.

A publication of the Progressive Education Association, this book presents the reading of literature as a social experience.

SEELY, HOWARD F., *On Teaching English*, American Book Company, 1933.

Much of this book presents the theory of composition teaching in relation to pupil experiences. A valuable section contains examples of student writing.

*SMITH, REED, *The Teaching of Literature*, American Book Company, 1935.

Twenty-five years of classroom experience have enabled the author to present practical plans for the teaching of literature.

STRATTON, CLARENCE, *The Teaching of English in High School*, Harcourt, Brace and Company, 1923.

Although some of the material in this book is "dated," such as the chapter dealing with courses of study, the suggestions given for teaching both composition and literature are still fresh.

THOMAS, CHARLES SWAIN, *The Teaching of English in the Secondary School*, revised edition, Houghton Mifflin Company, 1927.

A skilled teacher and a popular lecturer presents in this book suggestions for teaching composition and literature. Although some of the material is outmoded, you will find the book surprisingly modern and helpful.

*TRACY, HENRY C., *English As Experience*, E. P. Dutton and Company, 1928.

Here you will find presented one of the several approaches to teaching English.

*WARD, C. H., *What Is English?*, revised edition, Scott, Foresman and Company, 1925.

*——, *Grammar for Composition*, Scott, Foresman and Company, 1933.

Readers either strongly approve Ward's theories or as strongly disapprove them. Read the books of this teacher whose ideas influenced the trend of composition in the twenties, and judge for yourself.

WEBSTER, EDWARD H., and SMITH, DORA V., *Teaching English in the Junior High School*, World Book Company, 1927.

As supervisors, the authors watched the demonstration, with hundreds of junior high school pupils, of the plans for teaching composition presented in this book.

6. TESTS

WRITTEN COMPOSITION

BARRETT, E. R., and OTHERS, *English Test*. Grades 9 to 16; 2 forms; $1.10 for 25; 15 cents per specimen test; 2 cents per machine-scorable answer sheet; 40 (50) minutes; World Book Company, 1938.

This tests sentence structure, diction, grammar, and punctuation. It may be used successfully by a teacher unfamiliar with testing procedures.

Cleveland English Composition and Grammar Test. Grades 7 to 12; 2 forms; 50 cents per 25 copies; single specimen set free; Houghton Mifflin Company, 1931–32.

An easily administered test, this emphasizes the functional aspects of grammar.

Co-operative Effectiveness of Expression Test, Tests B1 and B2. Grades 7 to 12, 11 to 16; 2 levels; Form Q; 5 cents per test for 10 to 99 copies; 1½ cents per machine-scorable answer sheet; 25 cents per specimen test; answer sheet; 40 to 45 minutes; Co-operative Test Service, 1940.

Co-operative English Test: Mechanics of Expression. Grades 9 to 16; 4 editions; 25 cents per specimen set of any one edition; 6 to 8 cents per test for 10 to 99 copies; Co-operative Test Service, 1932–39.

Co-operative Vocabulary Test. Grades 7 to 16; Form Q; 5 cents per test for 10 to 99 copies; 25 cents per specimen test; nontimed (10 to 30 minutes); Co-operative Test Service, 1940.

Although somewhat complicated to administer, these tests are reliable and attempt to correlate with modern educational theory.

CROSS, E. A., *Cross English Tests.* Grades 9 to 12; 3 forms; $1.20 per package of 25; World Book Company, 1924.

These cover spelling, pronunciation, sentence structure, punctuation, verb and pronoun forms, idiomatic expressions, and miscellaneous faulty expressions.

High School Spelling Test. Grades 7 to 12; 4 forms; 25 cents per specimen test; Turner E. Smith and Company, Atlanta, Georgia, 1929.

The aim of this test is to determine whether students should be excused from special spelling classes.

HUDELSON, EARL, *English Composition Scale.* Grades 4 to 12; $1.00 plus postage per 25 copies; World Book Company.

Using this scale, you can judge how your pupils' writing compares with the samples in the scale.

Leonard Diagnostic Test in Punctuation and Capitalization. Grades 5 to 12; 2 forms; 90 cents per 25 copies; 20 cents per specimen set; nontimed (20 to 40 minutes); World Book Company, 1931.

This is a well-constructed test, requiring knowledge and judgment from the student.

Lewis, E. E., *Lewis English Composition Scales*. Grades 3 to 12; World Book Company, 1923.

These scales are helpful in judging class progress.

Nelson's High School English Test. Grades 7 to 12; 2 forms; $1.65 per 25 copies, including 25 answer books; specimen set free; 40 to 50 minutes; Houghton Mifflin Company, 1932.

Although a self-correcting test, this requires careful attention from the pupils in order to follow directions.

Pressey, L. C., *Diagnostic Tests in English Composition for Junior and Senior High Schools*. 4 forms; 15 cents per sample set; Public School Publishing Company.

This test diagnoses errors in capitalization, grammar, and sentence structure.

Smith, Dora V., and McCullough, Constance, *Essentials of English Tests*. Grades 7 to 12; 3 forms; 45 minutes; 25 cents per specimen test; $1.00 per complete package of 25 copies; Educational Test Bureau, 1939.

Pupils are tested in spelling, grammatical usage, word usage, sentence structure, punctuation, and capitalization.

Tests of General Educational Development (G.E.D. Tests), United States Armed Forces Institute. Test One: Correctness and Effectiveness of Expression, High School Level, Form B; 60 minutes; self-scoring; test booklet, 10 to 99 copies, 7 cents each; 25 cents per specimen test; American Council on Education, 1944.

Prepared by the Examination Staff for the United States Armed Forces Institute, this test is now being used in high schools. It is in two parts: spelling; and four themes, written by high school students, to be corrected by means of the multiple-choice technique.

TRESSLER, J. C., *The Revised Tressler English Minimum Essentials Tests*. Grades 8 to 12; 3 forms; Public School Publishing Company, 1941.

Grammatical correctness, vocabulary, punctuation, sentence structure, sentence sense, inflection and accent, and spelling are tested through use of the latest testing techniques.

LITERATURE

ABBOTT, ALLAN, and TRABUE, M. R., *Abbott-Trabue Exercises in the Appreciation of Poetry*, Forms X and Y; 5 cents per copy; Teachers College, Columbia University.

These serve excellently to stimulate an interest in poetry.

BARRETT, E. R., and RYAN, TERESA M., *Barrett-Ryan Literature Tests*. High school and college levels; 4 cents per copy, 70 cents for 25 copies; C. A. Gregory Company, 345 Calhoun Street, Cincinnati, Ohio.

These test knowledge of English and American "classics."

BURCH, MARY, *Stanford Test of Comprehension of Literature*. 2 forms; 75 cents for 25 copies of one test; Stanford University Press.

Designed to classify students of junior and senior high school groups according to ability, these tests are in three parts: (I) Narration and Description; (II) Character and Emotion; (III) Exposition.

CARROLL, HERBERT A., *Prose Appreciation Tests*. Junior and senior high school forms; nontimed (35 minutes); $1.50 per package of 25 copies; 35 cents per specimen set; Educational Test Bureau, 1935.

In this test the student reads various selections and rates them according to their literary merit.

Co-operative Literary Comprehension Test, Form Q. Grades 9 to 16; 40 to 45 minutes; 5 cents per test for 10 to 99 copies; 25 cents per specimen set; Co-operative Test Service, 1935–40.

This requires the student to read closely and interpret precisely; it tests both speed and comprehension.

LOGAN, CONRAD T., and PARKS, CARRIE BELLE, *Study Tests for Literary Understanding*. Grades 11 and 12; 56 cents for 15 tests and 15 retests; D. C. Heath and Company.

This test is designed to determine the kind of reading the students are doing.

LOGASA, HANNA, and WRIGHT, MARTHA McCOY, *Logasa-Wright's Six Tests for Appreciation of Literature*. 10 cents per set of 6; 20 cents per sample set; Public School Publishing Company.

These require pupils to discover the theme; to react to sensory impressions; to recognize comparisons and rhythms; and to distinguish between trite and fresh expression.

Tests of General Educational Development (G.E.D. Tests), United States Armed Forces Institute. "Interpretation of Literary Materials — High School Level"; Form B; self-scoring; 7 cents per test for 10 to 99 copies; 25 cents per specimen set; The American Council on Education, 1944.

By means of multiple-choice questions, the students' ability to interpret selections of prose and poetry is tested.

PUBLISHERS OF TESTS

The American Council on Education, 15 Amsterdam Avenue, New York 23, New York.

Bureau of Publications, Teachers College, Columbia University, New York 27, New York.

Co-operative Test Service of the American Council on Education, 500 West 116th Street, New York, New York.

Educational Test Bureau, 720 Washington Avenue S.E., Minneapolis, Minnesota.

D. C. Heath and Company, 285 Columbus Avenue, Boston 16, Massachusetts.

Houghton Mifflin Company, 2 Park Street, Boston 7, Massachusetts.

Public School Publishing Company, Bloomington, Illinois.

Scott, Foresman and Company, 623–633 South Wabash Avenue, Chicago, Illinois.

Stanford University Press, Stanford, California.

Teachers College, Columbia University, New York 17, New York.

World Book Company, 33 Park Hill Avenue, Yonkers-on-Hudson, New York.

7. AUDIO-VISUAL AIDS

Prepared by Catharine Williams, Teaching Aids Laboratory, the Ohio State University, and published in *The News Letter*, XI (April, 1946), edited by Edgar Dale, this represents a comprehensive bibliography in audio-visual aids. It is used with the permission of Mr. Dale.

REFERENCES ON UTILIZATION

ABC's of Visual Aids and Projectionist's Manual, by Philip Mannino. New York: Educational Film Library Association, 1946. $1.00.*

A brief discussion of types of visual aids and their uses; guidance in selection and care of equipment; sources of material and equipment.

Audio-Visual Methods in Teaching, by Edgar Dale. New York: Dryden Press, 1946, $3.90.

Comprehensive treatment of audio-visual materials in terms of the particular contribution of each type, and their application to various subject-matter fields.

Audio Visual "Tools" That Teach for "Keeps," by Bruce A. Findlay. Los Angeles, Calif.: Office of the Superintendent, Los Angeles City Schools, School Publication No. 395, 1944.

Suggestions for making the materials serve the teacher, not the teacher serve the materials.

* The price of each publication, or its free distribution, is indicated wherever known.

"The Bulletin Board as a Teaching Device," by J. R. Stolper.
Teachers College Record, 4:407–10, February, 1939.
Effective use of bulletin boards.

"Filmstrips as an Educational Aid," by Thomas R. Wright.
Visual Review, 1940.
Suggestions on use of filmstrips.

Focus on Learning, by Charles F. Hoban, Jr. Washington, D.C.:
American Council on Education, 1942. $2.00.
Summarizes a five-year evaluation study and relates the
findings to the teaching field. Many practical suggestions for
using supplementary aids.

How to Read Pictures, by Bartlett, Lemler, Clark. Grand
Rapids, Mich: Informative Classroom Pictures, 1943. 25¢.
Excellent suggestions on use of pictures.

An Information File in Every Library, by Delia F. Ovitz and
Zana K. Miller. Buffalo, N.Y.: Library Bureau, Division
of Remington Rand, Inc., 465 Washington St. Free.
Concise suggestions and clear-cut directions for ready reference filing of materials.

Making Films Work for Your Community, prepared by The Committee on Community Use of Film. New York: Educational Film Library Association, 1946. $1.00.
A handbook on use of educational films in the community.

Materials for Instruction, Eighth Yearbook, Department of
Supervisors and Directors of Instruction. New York:
Teachers College, Columbia University, 1935. $2.00.
Excellent source of guidance in the selection and evaluation
of materials.

A Measure for Audio-Visual Programs in Schools, by Helen H.
Seaton. Washington, D.C.: American Council on Education. 40¢.
Discussion of current problems, with recommendations regarding essential planning for expanded use of teaching aids.

Movies That Teach, by Charles F. Hoban, Jr. New York: Dryden Press, 1946.

New conceptions and uses of motion pictures in education that were developed and tested on a mass scale in the war-training program.

Opaque Projection, A New Frontier in Teaching, by J. Y. Taylor. Buffalo, N.Y.: Spencer Lens Co., 1941. Free.

Suggestions and directions for use of opaque projection with various age levels and learning areas.

Opportunities for Teachers in the Use of Visual Aids in Instruction. U. S. Office of Education Pamphlet 89. Washington, D.C.: Supt. of Documents, Government Printing Office, 1940. 5¢.

Brief suggestions and guidance.

Phonograph Records as an Aid to Learning in Rural Elementary Schools, by Effie G. Bathhurst. Albany, N.Y.: University of New York, State Education Department, 1943. 60¢.

A handbook for teachers and supervisors; gives annotations and details regarding utilization.

Radio and the School, by Norman Woelfel and I. Keith Tyler. Yonkers-on-Hudson, N.Y.: World Book Co., 1945. $1.88.

The findings and judgment of experts who spent five years investigating the school use of radio, transcriptions, and recordings. Comprehensive treatment of sources and selections.

A School Uses Motion Pictures, by Tower Hill School Staff. Washington, D.C.: American Council on Education, 1940. $1.00.

Helpful guidance in using motion pictures as an aid to learning.

Sources of Visual Aids for Instructions in Schools. Washington, D.C.: Federal Security Agency, U. S. Office of Education, Pamphlet No. 80, revised 1941. 15¢.

Sources of films, filmstrips, lantern slides, charts, pictures, posters, maps, globes, exhibits, and specimens.

Teaching through Radio, by William B. Levenson. New York: Rinehart, 1945. $3.00.

An account of unique work carried on in Cleveland, Ohio, which operates its own FM broadcasting station for schools.

BASIC SOURCES

Teachers will find their own state university and state department of education the best sources of information concerning educational films. For example, the Ohio Slide and Film Exchange of the State Department of Education serves the schools of that state. In many states, colleges and universities have established excellent film libraries, and distribute films on a rental basis both within and outside the state. A few of these are: Visual Aids Extension Division, Indiana University, Bloomington, Ind.; New York University Film Library, 71 Washington Square South, New York, N.Y.; University of California, Extension Division, Berkeley, Calif.

Castle Films Catalogs. New York: 30 Rockefeller Plaza. Free.

Catalogs describing the U. S. Office of Education Visual Training Units, Army and Navy Training Films, and U. S. Dept. of Agriculture films.

Educational Film Guide. New York: H. W. Wilson, 950 University Ave. Cumulated annual catalog with two-year supplement service, $4.00; catalog without supplement service, $2.00.

Lists 2,370 films in alphabetical order.

Educators Guide to Free Films. Randolph, Wis.: Educators Progress Service. $3.00. Revised annually. Lists 2,165 films and 203 slidefilms.

Title index, subject classification, cross-index, and brief descriptions.

Keystone View Company Catalogs. Meadville, Pa.: Keystone View Company. Free.

Extensive listing of $3\frac{1}{4}'' \times 4''$ slides; materials and directions for slide-making.

Ohio Slide and Film Exchange Catalog. Columbus, Ohio: Ohio Slide and Film Exchange, State Department of Education. Free to schools.

Annotated list of films, filmstrips, and lantern slides available only to Ohio schools.

One Thousand and One (The Blue Book of Non-Theatrical Films). Chicago: The Educational Screen, 64 East Lake St. $1.00; 25¢ to *Educational Screen* subscribers.

Annual listing of films, classified in 162 subject groups.

S. V. E. Educational Motion Picture Catalog. Chicago: Society for Visual Education, Inc., 327 S. LaSalle St. Free.

Brief descriptions of educational films, filmstrips, and 2″ × 2″ slides under topical headings.

U.S. Government Motion Pictures and Filmstrips. Washington, D.C.: Division of Visual Aids, U.S. Office of Education, Federal Security Agency. Free.

RADIO PROGRAM LISTINGS

American Broadcasting Company, New York, N.Y.
Periodic outline of programs.

Columbia Broadcasting System, 485 Madison Ave., New York 22, N.Y.
Advance programs and teacher's manuals for American School of the Air series. Monthly service schedules. Free.

Mutual Broadcasting Company, 1440 Broadway, New York, N.Y.
Monthly service schedules. Free.

National Broadcasting Company, RCA Building, Radio City, New York, N.Y.
Advance program schedules and teacher's handbooks for University of the Air programs. 25¢ per handbook. Monthly service schedules, free.

Radio Station WOSU, Ohio State University, Columbus 10, Ohio.
Program bulletins for Ohio School of the Air. Free.

Copies of broadcasts. Printed copies of the following series are available for a small fee, usually 10¢: "University of Chicago Round Table," American Broadcasting Company's "America's Town Meeting," Mutual's "American Forum of the Air."

EDUCATIONAL RECORDINGS

A Catalog of Selected Educational Recordings. New York: Recordings Division, New York University Film Library, 1944.
Annotated lists of recordings, organized under subject matter headings. Includes a discussion of recordings as an aid to teachers, methods of use, and operation of playbacks.

Recordings for School Use: A Catalog of Appraisals, by J. Robert Miles. Yonkers-on-Hudson, N.Y.: World Book Company, 1942. $1.25.
Annotates and appraises the recordings listed. Also deals with utilization of recordings, facts about recordings and equipment, selection and operation of record players.

Transcription Exchange Service. Washington, D.C.: Transcription Exchange, U. S. Office of Education. Free.
Catalog of transcriptions and recordings available to schools for rent or loan; many recorded broadcasts.

Other Catalogs. Some large companies producing and distributing 78 r.p.m. phonograph records — Columbia Recording Corp., 1473 Barnum Ave., Bridgeport, Conn.; Decca Records, Inc., 50 West 57th St., New York, N.Y.; General Records Co., 1600 Broadway, New York, N.Y.; RCA-Victor Records, Inc., Camden, N.J.

FREE AND INEXPENSIVE TEACHING AIDS

Bibliography of Economic and Social Study Material. New York: National Association of Manufacturers, 14 West 43rd St., 1943.
Brief descriptions of booklets, motion pictures, slide-films, lantern slides, transcriptions, and posters.

Bulletin of Free and Inexpensive Teaching Aids for Junior and Senior High Schools. Cumberland, Md.: Allegheny County Board of Education, September, 1939.

Lists a number of inexpensive books, pamphlets, and pictures, arranged alphabetically by sources under each school classification.

Carroll-Miller List of Teaching Aids and Educational Materials from Commercial Sources. Sacramento, Calif.: Dept. of Education, Bulletin No. 20, October, 1939. 25¢.

Sources of pamphlets, exhibits, charts, and other visual aids, arranged alphabetically under topical headings.

Catalog of Business Sponsored Educational Material. New York: Committee on Consumer Relations in Advertising, Inc., 420 Lexington Ave., 1945. $2.00.

Annotated lists of pictures, posters, movies, exhibits, etc., which are distributed without cost.

Educator's Directory. Harrisburg, Pa.: Continental Press. $2.50.

Classified list of free materials, including pamphlets, catalogs, booklets, exhibit materials, pictures, posters, maps and charts, magazines, motion pictures, and slides.

Educators Index of Free Material, by Guy Fowlkes. Randolph, Wis.: Educators Progress League. Semi-annual service, $24 per year; three-year rate, $36 cash or three-year payment plan. Comprehensive annotated listing of all types of free materials.

Enrichment Materials for Teachers, compiled by Robert De Kieffer. Evanston, Ill.: Curriculum Laboratory, School of Education, Northwestern University. Service Bulletin No. 7, 1941. 50¢.

Comprehensive bibliography of pamphlets, maps, charts, posters, movies, slides, exhibits. Chart form, sources, age levels for which most suitable. No descriptions.

Free and Inexpensive Learning Materials, compiled by Martha C. Crigler. Nashville, Tenn.: Curriculum Laboratory, George

Peabody College for Teachers. Bulletin No. 79, 70¢. 1942 Supplement, 25¢.

Selected and annotated list of pamphlets, charts, maps, pictures.

Free and Inexpensive Learning Materials. Chicago: Quarrie Reference Library, 35 E. Wacker Drive, 1940. $5.00.

Listings with brief descriptions — pamphlets, flat pictures, charts, booklets, etc., under general classifications.

Government Documents: A Selected List of Teaching Aids. New York: Library, Teachers College, Columbia University. The Library Consultant, No. 4. 15¢.

Lists material issued by the federal government; gives information regarding selection and ordering.

Handbook of Inexpensive Resources and Services for Ohio Elementary Teachers, compiled by the Department of Elementary School Principals of the Ohio Education Association. Columbus, Ohio: Ohio Education Association, 215 E. Broad St., 1944. Free.

Index of Free Teaching Aids, by Brose Phillips. Harrisburg, Ill.: Free Teaching Aids Company, 1945. $2.60.

Lists by topics a variety of free teaching materials.

Index to Visual and Auditory Aids and Materials. Eugene, Ore.: Curriculum Laboratory, University of Oregon. Curriculum Bulletin No. 17, May, 1940. 30¢.

List of publications issued by research associations and foundations, arranged according to agencies concerned.

Industrial Arts Cooperative Service, 519 West 12th St., New York, N.Y.

A nonprofit organization which makes available at minimum cost directions for making some visual materials, accounts of teaching units, etc. Membership fee varies with services desired.

Inexpensive Book Service, by R. L. Reynolds. New York: The Author, 586 West 114th St. 25¢.

Classified lists of books and booklets selling for 10¢ to $1.00.

New Tools for Learning, 280 Madison Ave., New York 16, N.Y.

Information on co-ordinating use of pamphlets, radio transcriptions, recordings, and motion pictures.

One Dollar or Less: Inexpensive Books for School Libraries. Washington, D.C.: U. S. Office of Education. Pamphlet No. 88, 1940. 5¢.

Lists bibliographies of ten-cent booklets and other inexpensive books.

"Other Aids to Learning (Bibliography)," by M. E. Kirk et al. *42nd Yearbook*, National Society for the Study of Education, Part II, 1943, pp. 176–218.

The Picture Collection, by Margaret Frebault. New York: H. W. Wilson Company, 950 University Ave., 1943. $1.25.

A list of sources of pictures, with information on processing, filing, and giving effective service.

Public Affairs Pamphlets. U. S. Office of Education Bulletin No. 3, 1937. Washington, D.C.: Supt. of Documents. 10¢. Supplement No. 1, 1938, 10¢.

This bulletin and supplement give annotated listings of 1212 pamphlets on political, economic, social, and international affairs.

Source List of Audio-Visual Aids. Albany, N.Y.: Bureau of Audio-Visual Aids, New York State Department of Education. Circular No. 5, revised 1943.

Sources of Free and Inexpensive Teaching Aids, by Bruce Miller. Ontario, Calif.: The Author, Box 222. $1.00.

Sources of all types of aids, including those which pupil and teacher can make.

Sources of Free Teaching Materials, by R. M. Holmes. Lock Haven, Pa.: State Teachers College, 1941. 50¢.

Bibliography of free teaching aids which may be obtained from various manufacturing companies.

"Teaching Aids for Teachers," by M. H. Davis. *School Life*, 24:144–7, February, 1939.
Bibliography of teaching aids.

Teaching Aids Service of the Library, Lili Heimers, Director. New Jersey State Teachers College, Upper Montclair, N.J. Issues booklets on various subjects, each booklet giving annotated listings of pictures, exhibits, recordings, films, charts, publications, etc., with prices indicated. An excellent source of information. Send for list of available booklets, which range in price from 25¢ to $1.00.

KEEPING CURRENTLY INFORMED

Associations

Department of Visual Instruction, National Education Association, 1201 Sixteenth St., N.W., Washington, D.C. Membership in this department is a valuable aid to any teacher or school. Membership fee includes a subscription to the magazine *Educational Screen*.

Educational Film Library Association, 45 Rockefeller Plaza, New York 20, N.Y. A clearing house for audio-visual information and a sale center for 16-mm. films produced by membership agencies. Issues monthly *Film News* which contains lists of evaluated films. Fee varies with size of film library. Highly recommended.

Periodicals

Business Screen, 157 E. Erie St., Chicago 11, Ill. Eight issues, $2.00.

Educational Screen, 64 E. Lake St., Chicago, Ill. Ten issues, $2.00.

Film and Radio Guide, Educational and Recreational Guides, Inc., 172 Renner Ave., Newark, N.J. Nine issues, $2.00.

Film News, Educational Film Library Association, 45 Rockefeller Plaza, New York 20, N.Y. Twelve issues, $2.00.

Film World, 6060 Sunset Blvd., Hollywood 38, Calif. Twelve issues, $3.00.

Hollywood Quarterly, 350 Royce Hall, University of California, Los Angeles 24, Calif. Four issues, $4.00.

Movie Makers, Amateur Cinema League, 420 Lexington Ave., New York 17, N.Y. Twelve issues, $2.00.

See and Hear, E. M. Hale Co., Eau Claire, Wis. Nine issues, $2.00.

Visual Review, Society for Visual Education, 100 S. Ohio Ave., Chicago, Ill. Annual, free.

Service Bulletins

Federal Radio Education Committee (FREC) Bulletin, Federal Security Agency, U. S. Office of Education, Washington, D.C. Monthly, free.

Deals with new programs, uses of radio in education in various places; reviews books and articles in the field.

Film Information Service, 535 Heart Tower Bldg., Baltimore, Md. Twelve issues, $1.00.

Monthly service list of new teaching films.

The News Letter, Edgar Dale, Editor, Bureau of Educational Research, The Ohio State University, Columbus, Ohio.

Monthly news about audio-visual aids. Free.

Program Information Bulletin, Program Information Exchange, 41 Maiden Lane, New York, N.Y. Ten issues, $2.00.

Describes new films, recordings, radio programs, pamphlets, sources of visual aids; lists available speakers; reports educational experiences.

Program Information Service, Program Information Exchange, 41 Maiden Lane, New York, N.Y. Annual subscription, $5.00.

An addition to the *Bulletin* — carefully selected lists of sources of material issued several times a year.

Wilson Bulletin, H. W. Wilson Co., 950 University Place, New York, N.Y. Twelve issues, $1.00.

Lists of pamphlets and posters which can be obtained free or at low cost.

Other

The Education Index, in sections on "Audio-Visual Aids" and "Teaching Aids and Services," carries bibliographies of articles devoted to teaching aids in various periodicals.

A number of educational periodicals devote space monthly to keeping readers informed in the audio-visual field. For example, *Social Education* has a section titled "Sight and Sound in the Social Studies" which gives information concerning all types of teaching materials.

TYPICAL FILMS

These films are examples of material suitable and available for use in English classes. The list, which is based on entries in the *Educational Film Guide*, June, 1946 (H. W. Wilson Company, New York), is not in any sense complete.

American Spoken Here. 10min 16-sd[1]-apply TFC

This film gives the origin and history of several slang expressions and tells how they became part of American speech.

American Way. 10min 16-sd-$27; rent $1.50 1937 ITTCO

Emphasizes the rights guaranteed to Americans by the Constitution.

Auld Lang Syne. 67min 16-sd-$187.50 1940 Post

This depiction of the life of Robert Burns includes many of his poems.

David Copperfield, the Boy. 40min 16-sd-rent apply TFC

Scenes from David's life from his infancy to his departure for school.

Gray's Elegy. 17min 16-sd-$50; rent $2 B & H

Scenes of Stoke Poges and other places connected with Gray's life. Includes a reading of the poem.

Macbeth. 16min 16-sd-rent $2 1945 BIS

The murder and sleepwalking scenes.

Nature Speaks. 10min 16-sd-apply TFC

Readings of poetry against a background of mountain, lake, and seashore scenery.

[1] Sound

Parliamentary Procedures in Action. 12min 16-sd-$60 1941
Coronet

The meeting of a high school dramatic club demonstrates proper procedure in conducting a discussion.

Shakespeare and Stratford-on-Avon. 14 min 16-si[1]-$24; rent $1
1938 B & H

A tour of the town and a description of the chief events in the poet's life.

Subject, Verb, Object. 13min 16-si-color-$52 1941 Mitchell

This film emphasizes "big primary grammatical relations" and "thought blocks" in the sentence.

SOURCES OF FILMS

Only the sources referred to above are given here. For a complete list, see the *Educational Film Guide*.

B & H. Bell & Howell Company, 1801-1815 Larchmont Avenue, Chicago 13, Illinois; 30 Rockefeller Plaza, New York 20, N.Y.; 716 North LaBrea Avenue, Hollywood, California; 1221 G Street, N.W., Washington, D.C.

BIS. British Information Services, 30 Rockefeller Plaza, New York 20, N.Y.

Coronet. Coronet Productions, Glenview, Illinois.

ITTCO. International Theatrical and Television Corporation, 25 West Forty-fifth Street, New York 19, N.Y.

Mitchell. Stuart Mitchell, Chico High School, Chico, California.

Post. Post Pictures Corporation, 723 Seventh Avenue, New York 19, N.Y.

TFC. Teaching Films Custodian, Inc., 25 West Forty-third Street, New York 19, N.Y.

8. PLAY PRODUCTION

Perhaps the following bibliographies will give you a start in play production. I am listing only nonroyalty, budget, or percentage-royalty plays, for plays in these categories are not

---

[1] Silent

always easy to find. All these mentioned have been recommended by experienced teachers. Ask the firms whose names appear below to put your name on their mailing list so that you may receive information as it appears. Several companies offer helpful free material; for example, "Lagniappe" (meaning "a gratuity"), a leaflet giving information concerning plays, will be sent you five times a year by Row, Peterson and Company.

LONG PLAYS

All on Account of Luella (French — a budget play)
Just Like Cinderella (French — a budget play)
Let's Get Married (Baker)
Mamma's Baby Boy (French — a budget play)
Molly O'Shaughnessey (Row, Peterson and Company)
Murdered Alive (Baker)
New Fires: A Choric Pageant (Row, Peterson and Company)
Pulling the Curtain (French)
Spring Fever (Row, Peterson and Company)
Three Taps at Twelve (French)
Tommy's Wife (Baker)

ONE ACT PLAYS

All Through the Year (a collection of seasonal entertainments — French)
America in Action Series (Plays published separately — Dramatists Play Service)
Builder of Christmas Fires (Dramatists Play Service)
The Burglar (all women — French)
Just Women (French)
The Kleptomaniac (all women — French)
Kozlenko, William, *One Hundred Non-Royalty Radio Plays*, Greenberg, New York
Little Jack Horner (budget play — French)
The Love Pirate (French)
A Mad Breakfast (Baker)
Sauce for the Goslings (Better Speech play — French)

The Teeth of the Gift Horse (French)
The Terrible Meek (French)
Yearbook of Short Plays (published annually by Row, Peterson and Company)

BOOKS ON PLAY PRODUCTION

DOLMAN, JOHN, JR., *The Art of Play Production*, second revised edition, Harper and Brothers, 1944.
The author presents play production as a fine art, emphasizing design, harmony, balance, good taste, light, and color. Directions for acting and staging are also given.

NELMS, HENNING, *A Primer of Stage Craft*, Dramatists Play Service, 1941.
Here you will find specific suggestions for staging a play.

OMMANNEY, KATHARINE A., *The Stage and the School*, revised edition, Harper and Brothers, 1939.
This is a comprehensive textbook in play production and appreciation of drama, moving pictures, and radio.

SELDEN, SAMUEL, *Stage in Action*, F. S. Crofts and Company, 1941.
This gives directions for acting and producing a play.

SMITH, MILTON, *A Guide to Play Selection*, D. Appleton-Century Company, 1934.
In addition to listing plays, this English Council publication gives directions for staging them.

PUBLISHERS OF PLAYS

Walter H. Baker Company, 178 Tremont Street, Boston 11, Massachusetts.

Banner Play Bureau, 449 Powell Street, San Francisco 2, California.

Willis Bugbee Company, 428 South Warren Street, Syracuse 2, New York.

T. S. Denison and Company, 635 East Twenty-second Street, Minneapolis 4, Minnesota.

Dramatic Publishing Company, 59 East Van Buren Street, Chicago 5, Illinois.

Dramatists Play Service, Inc., 6 East Thirty-ninth Street, New York 16, New York.

Eldridge Entertainment House, Denver, Colorado.

Samuel French, 25 West Forty-fifth Street, New York 19, New York.

Frederick B. Ingram Productions, Rock Island, Illinois.

Longmans, Green and Company, 55 Fifth Avenue, New York 3, New York.

March Brothers Publishing Company, 208–212 Wright Avenue, Lebanon, Ohio.

Edna Means Dramatic Service, 525 Arlington Place, Chicago, Illinois.

The Northwestern Press, 2200 Park Avenue, Minneapolis 4, Minnesota.

Row, Peterson and Company, 131 East Twenty-third Street, New York 10, New York.

Publishers of Books Listed
in the Bibliographies

American Book Company, 88 Lexington Avenue, New York 16, New York.

American Library Association, 520 North Michigan Avenue, Chicago, Illinois.

D. Appleton-Century Company, 35 West Thirty-second Street, New York 1, New York.

Blakiston Company, 1012 Walnut Street, Philadelphia 5, Pennsylvania.

Thomas Y. Crowell Company, 432 Fourth Avenue, New York 16, New York.

Crown Publishers, 419 Fourth Avenue, New York 16, New York.

Doubleday and Company, Inc., Garden City, New York.

E. P. Dutton and Company, 300 Fourth Avenue, New York 10, New York.

Eyre and Spottiswoode, 14–16 Bedford Street, Strand, London, England; American distributor: William Collins' Sons and Company, 70 Bond Street, Toronto 2, Canada.

Ginn and Company, Statler Building, Boston 17, Massachusetts.

Harcourt, Brace and Company, 383 Madison Avenue, New York 17, New York.

Harper and Brothers, 49 East Thirty-third Street, New York 16, New York.

Hastings House, 67 West 44 Street, New York 18, New York.

D. C. Heath and Company, 285 Columbus Avenue, Boston 16, Massachusetts.

Henry Holt and Company, 257 Fourth Avenue, New York 10, New York.

Houghton Mifflin Company, 2 Park Street, Boston 7, Massachusetts.

Iroquois Publishing Company, 106 East Fayette Street, Syracuse 2, New York.

J. B. Lippincott Company, 227–231 South Sixth Street, Philadelphia 5, Pennsylvania.

Longmans, Green and Company, Inc., 55 Fifth Avenue, New York 3, New York.

Lyons and Carnahan, 2500 Prairie Avenue, Chicago 11, Illinois.

The Macmillan Company, 60 Fifth Avenue, New York 3, New York.

McCormick-Mathers Publishing Company, Wichita, Kansas.

McGraw-Hill Book Company, 330 West Forty-second Street, New York 18, New York.

G. and C. Merriam Company, Springfield, Massachusetts.

Thomas Nelson and Sons, 385 Madison Avenue, New York 17, New York.

Newson and Company, 72 Fifth Avenue, New York 11, New York.

Noble and Noble, 76 Fifth Avenue, New York 17, New York.

W. W. Norton and Company, Inc., 100 Fifth Avenue, New York 10, New York.

Odyssey Press, 386 Fourth Avenue, New York 16, New York.

Prentice-Hall, 70 Fifth Avenue, New York 11, New York.

Rand, McNally and Company, 536 South Clark Street, Chicago 5, Illinois.

Random House, 20 East Fifty-seventh Street, New York 22, New York.

Rinehart and Company, Inc., 232 Madison Avenue, New York 16, New York.

Benjamin H. Sanborn Company, 221 East Twentieth Street, Chicago 16, Illinois.

Science Press, Lancaster, Pennsylvania.

Scott, Foresman and Company, 623–633 South Wabash Avenue, Chicago 5, Illinois.

Charles Scribner's Sons, 597 Fifth Avenue, New York 17, New York.

Silver Burdett Company, 221 East Twentieth Street, Chicago, Illinois.

The H. W. Wilson Company, 950–972 University Avenue, New York 52, New York.

John C. Winston Company, Inc., 1006–1016 Arch Street, Philadelphia 7, Pennsylvania.

World Book Company, 333 Park Hill Avenue, Yonkers-on-Hudson, New York.

INDEX